Imperial Japan and Defeat in the Second World War

SOAS Studies in Modern and Contemporary Japan

SERIES EDITOR:
Christopher Gerteis (SOAS, University of London, UK)

EDITORIAL BOARD:
Stephen Dodd (SOAS, University of London, UK)
Andrew Gerstle (SOAS, University of London, UK)
Janet Hunter (London School of Economics, UK)
Barak Kushner (University of Cambridge, UK)
Helen Macnaughtan (SOAS, University of London, UK)
Aaron W. Moore (University of Edinburgh, UK)
Timon Screech (SOAS, University of London, UK)
Naoko Shimazu (NUS–Yale College, Singapore)

Published in association with the Japan Research Centre at the School of Oriental and African Studies, University of London, UK.

SOAS Studies in Modern and Contemporary Japan features scholarly books on modern and contemporary Japan, showcasing new research monographs as well as translations of scholarship not previously available in English. Its goal is to ensure that current, high-quality research on Japan, its history, politics, and culture, is made available to an English-speaking audience.

Published:
Women and Democracy in Cold War Japan, Jan Bardsley
Christianity and Imperialism in Modern Japan, Emily Anderson
The China Problem in Postwar Japan, Robert Hoppens
Media, Propaganda and Politics in 20th Century Japan, The Asahi Shimbun Company (translated by Barak Kushner)
Contemporary Sino-Japanese Relations on Screen, Griseldis Kirsch
Debating Otaku in Contemporary Japan, edited by Patrick W. Galbraith, Thiam Huat Kam, and Björn-Ole Kamm
Politics and Power in 20th-Century Japan, Mikuriya Takashi and Nakamura Takafusa (translated by Timothy S. George)
Japanese Taiwan, edited by Andrew Morris
Japan's Postwar Military and Civil Society, Tomoyuki Sasaki
The History of Japanese Psychology, Brian J. McVeigh

Postwar Emigration to South America from Japan and the Ryukyu Islands, Pedro Iacobelli
The Uses of Literature in Modern Japan, Sari Kawana
Post-Fascist Japan, Laura Hein
Mass Media, Consumerism and National Identity in Postwar Japan, Martyn David Smith
Japan's Occupation of Java in the Second World War, Ethan Mark
Gathering for Tea in Modern Japan, Taka Oshikiri
Engineering Asia, Hiromi Mizuno, Aaron S. Moore, and John DiMoia
Automobility and the City in Japan and Britain, c. 1955–1990, Simon Gunn and Susan Townsend
The Origins of Modern Japanese Bureaucracy, Yuichiro Shimizu (translated by Amin Ghadimi)
Kenkoku University and the Experience of Pan-Asianism, Yuka Hiruma Kishida
Overcoming Empire in Post-Imperial East Asia, Barak Kushner and Sherzod Muminov
Imperial Japan and Defeat in the Second World War, Peter Wetzler

Forthcoming:
Gender, Culture, and Disaster in Post-3.11 Japan, Mire Koikari

Imperial Japan and Defeat in the Second World War

The Collapse of an Empire

Peter Wetzler

BLOOMSBURY ACADEMIC
LONDON • NEW YORK • OXFORD • NEW DELHI • SYDNEY

BLOOMSBURY ACADEMIC
Bloomsbury Publishing Plc
50 Bedford Square, London, WC1B 3DP, UK
1385 Broadway, New York, NY 10018, USA
29 Earlsfort Terrace, Dublin 2, Ireland

BLOOMSBURY, BLOOMSBURY ACADEMIC and the Diana logo are
trademarks of Bloomsbury Publishing Plc

First published in Great Britain 2020
Paperback edition published 2021

Copyright © Peter Wetzler, 2020

Peter Wetzler has asserted his right under the Copyright, Designs and
Patents Act, 1988, to be identified as Author of this work.

Cover design: Tjaša Krivec
Cover image: Japanese Emperor Hirohito walks through the ruins of Tokyo following
US Air Force bombing in the later months of the Second World War. (© World History
Archive/Alamy Stock Photo)

All rights reserved. No part of this publication may be reproduced or
transmitted in any form or by any means, electronic or mechanical,
including photocopying, recording, or any information storage or
retrieval system, without prior permission in writing from the publishers.

Bloomsbury Publishing Plc does not have any control over, or responsibility for,
any third-party websites referred to or in this book. All internet addresses given
in this book were correct at the time of going to press. The author and publisher
regret any inconvenience caused if addresses have changed or sites have ceased
to exist, but can accept no responsibility for any such changes.

A catalogue record for this book is available from the British Library.

A catalog record for this book is available from the Library of Congress.

ISBN: HB: 978-1-3501-2081-5
PB: 978-1-3502-4679-9
ePDF: 978-1-3501-2082-2
eBook: 978-1-3501-2083-9

Series: SOAS Studies in Modern and Contemporary Japan

Typeset by Integra Software Services Pvt. Ltd.

To find out more about our authors and books visit www.bloomsbury.com
and sign up for our newsletters.

To Mika, Marc, and Jessica

Contents

Note on Text	x
Preface	xi
Introduction	1
1 Wartime Events, Historical Hindsights and Insights	9
2 Kamikaze Attacks, Planning before and after the Fall of Saipan	59
3 Tôjô Hideki, Man of his Times	89
4 Failing Strategy, Lack of War Materials, and Tôjô's Fall	123
5 Capitulation: Hubris and Unquestioning Belief in a Religious Ideology, some Conclusions	147
Notes	179
Bibliography	221
Index	236

Note on Text

The author is solely responsible for all of the material appearing in this work. No assistance was sought or accepted. Likewise, no financial support was sought or accepted for the purpose of researching and writing this book.

All translations are by the author except where otherwise indicated. All Japanese names are put in their normal Japanese order, family name before given name. In the endnotes and bibliography this means that no comma is placed between the family name and given name of Japanese authors of works in Japanese. Only where a work by a Japanese author is written in a Western language is a comma so placed, as with the authors of all works not in Japanese.

The following institutions have been especially helpful while I was researching and writing this book:

East Asia Department, German National Library, Berlin.
Military Archives, National Institute for Defense Studies, Tokyo.
Library, National Shôwa Memorial Museum, Tokyo.
Modern Japanese Political History Materials Room, National Diet Library, Tokyo.
East Asia Institute, Ludwigshafen.

I am grateful for the permission to access their facilities but they, of course, bear no responsibility for the contents of this book.

Preface

In 1934 H.D. von Doemming, Chief of the German Press Bureau (Deutsches Pressebüro) in New York, analyzed Japan as "the dilemma for the West":

> The three basic problems of the occidental state are: State, Church, and Race [...] This triptych appears self-evident to Europeans, because the occident's entire history is built upon this fundament; it is only natural that the European, as long as he attempted to press Japan into the schema used here and to judge Japan according to the criterion accepted here, had to founder (in his attempts to understand Japan) [...] We in the occident know the concepts State or Church or Race. The Japanese do not know the differences (between them) because for them they are one.[1]

Then Doemming analyzes Japan in terms of what he thought was the most important element in this triad: race. He says, for example, that a Japanese cannot become a Christian because he is racially bound to Shintô. Likewise a Catholic or Protestant cannot become a Japanese because his church does not draw any racial lines of distinction.[2]

Doemming's presentation was entirely based on a racist view of life. Not a polemic or an aggressive sort of racism, just matter of fact—so it is racism. The presentation, given this base, is very analytical and logical. It is a description of Japan's situation in the world not based on empirical values but on racist premises that, however, were not intended to denigrate or humiliate. Quite the contrary, Japan was celebrated because Japanese convictions about state, church, and race were held together by the latter, and it was right and good.

In 1936 Ernest H. Pickering wrote,

> The language of Japan is the same as ours. It tells of the right of each individual soul to life and happiness, and of each country to act as a true mother to her children. Nationalism dulls our ears to this human language, and thinking only of ourselves we end up in destroying one another.
>
> A cleavage on nationalistic or racial grounds between East and West would be disastrous beyond all foretelling.[3]

Pickering was a member of the British Parliament (1931–35) and previously had spent four years in Japan (1927–31), finally as Professor of English Literature at Tokyo Imperial University. At the beginning of Pickering's work he reported that during this visit to Japan (Autumn 1935–Spring 1936) a Japanese leader asserted, "we of the West have a double standard of morality—one which we apply to ourselves and other Western peoples, and one which we apply solely to Japan. What was right, or, at least, not wrong, if we did it, was quite wrong if Japan did it."[4]

This was no doubt true, but the Japanese often overlooked their own prejudices and misconceptions. In Imperial Japan the leader of the Japanese nation, the Shôwa Emperor, promoted state matters—constitutional monarchy, science, industry, and the military—for the sake of the imperial line, not to modernize and bring peace and prosperity to the Japanese people and other Asians. He favored peace and prosperity, but was above all responsible for the "national essence" (*kokutai*) including the Imperial House. This came to involve expansion in Asia. Consistent with his understanding of his obligations he, along with his political and military leaders, was responsible for starting wars in Asia and the Pacific. The trappings of modernity were fostered as expedients for promoting, not just preserving and protecting, traditional Japanese culture, especially the imperial line. As a consequence, for the alleged aim of preserving the Yamato race and civilization, Japanese military leaders belittled serious industrial and military deficits, and maintained that war with the United States and her allies could not be avoided, and the Shôwa Emperor reluctantly agreed.[5]

With a leading German journalist, Doemming, a former member of the British Parliament, Pickering, and Pickering's anonymous Japanese leader one sees differing ways of analyzing Japan's situation prior to the War in the Pacific, according to very different convictions—German racism, British liberalism, and Japanese Asia for the Asians, a sort of "asianism." German racism in the form of Nazism eventually co-opted the state.[6] Liberal politics in Great Britain was seldom more than grandiloquent posturing and realistically did not preclude nationalism at home and imperialism overseas.[7] Japanese asianism postulated that other Asian countries would be led, meaning dominated, by Japan. One less odious example of this during the Second World War was the Greater East Asia Co-Prosperity Sphere (*taitôa kyôeiken*).[8] Each -ism was useful, and dangerous, within its own ethnic box. Each was a key element in a sanctimonious sort of nationalism that stirred emotions, and promoted and legitimized pointless wars in Europe and Asia. The wars that ensued were destructive beyond all previous experience or even imagining. They finally ended in mid-1945.

For Japan the Second World War ended on August 15, 1945. On June 8, 1945 an Imperial Conference was held in the Imperial Palace. The purpose of the conference was to assess Imperial Japan's ability to continue the war. It was quickly established that there was an abundance of manpower and a lack of war materials. Improvement in the latter situation was not expected. By the end of the year there would be no serviceable ships and no prospects for building new ones. Raw materials could no longer be brought to Japan. The resulting shortage of aviation fuel was an especially grave matter. The navy would run out at the end of August, the army by the end of September. Also, modern warplanes could no longer be built. Domestic communication and rail transport systems were breaking down. The population was threatened with starvation. Japan's totally hopeless material situation was itemized. Moreover, it was feared that the masses might turn against the military and the government. The multitudes were there but their usefulness to the military was doubtful and mobilizing many would be detrimental to productivity. Then great emphasis was placed on mobilizing the people's martial spirit and loyalty to the imperial nation-state. This report to the throne originated in the Imperial Army General Staff.[9]

The Imperial Navy General Staff also prepared an assessment for the same conference, and the navy's evaluation of Imperial Japan's material situation was similar to that of the army. But the navy had a more optimistic view of the people as instruments of war. All were seen as men-and-women-at-arms. The Imperial Headquarters Navy Department report included the statement, "The entire military [meaning population] should be steeped in the spirit of suicide attack." When called upon each person should be ready to perish doing as much damage as possible to the invading enemy. The army and navy would pursue this tactic until US leaders and their people grew war weary.[10]

Things worked out differently. Nearing the end, the army vice-chief of staff, Lt. General Kawabe Torashirô (1890–1960), had the army air force cooperating with the navy and playing a key role in defending against the Allied Forces coming to invade the home islands. His plans included "improved" kamikaze tactics, without accounting for where the warplanes and fuel for them were to come from, not to mention the failing cooperation between the army and navy. Similarly, a number of overseas troop commanders telegraphed that they would continue fighting, presumably with scant resources.[11] Later, former Vice-Chief of Staff Kawabe remained unrepentant. Immediately after the war he repeated the claim often recited by high politicians and military men that Imperial Japan "was thrown into an unnecessarily miserable situation" by the Western powers as she sought to realize her destiny in an environment dictated by them.[12]

Kawabe justified past actions only a year after defeat without addressing the main reasons for Imperial Japan's downfall: hubris fostering trivialization of the Allied enemy, a lack of war materials, dissension between the army and navy, and—a factor not addressed in this study—ignominious barbarism in other Asian lands.[13] As seen in his postwar "Monologue," the Shôwa Emperor entertained doubts about Japan's military leaders. After the Imperial Conference he was discouraged and dismayed (*rakutan*) by the dismal lack of war materials.[14]

Clearly, in order to overcome actual material deficiencies military authorities called for additional sacrifices. They still proclaimed Imperial Japan's "inevitable victory" (*hisshô*), though by that time neither Emperor Hirohito nor his service leaders thought that Japan could win the war. The priorities were to save the Imperial House including the "national polity" deceit and as much of the military's honor as possible, with no regard for the number of lives that would be lost. These were the intended fruits of "two thousand years of benevolent Imperial Rule."[15]

The purpose of this book is to:

1. address a period critical to ending the War in the Pacific: mid-1942 to mid-1945 with an emphasis on the fall of Saipan and the ensuing fall of the Tôjô Cabinet, including the role of the Shôwa Emperor in these events;
2. introduce a distinctive framework of analysis: differentiating between the nation and state—the nation as justifying religious ideology and the state as an executive—and to look at the apparatus in wartime Japan, the imperial institution–military relationship–Emperor Hirohito (1901–89) vis-à-vis, for example, Tôjô Hideki (1884–1948);
3. introduce various Japanese sources important to understanding wartime events in Japan, with an emphasis on contrasting authorship and contents; and
4. address Imperial Japan's defeat, which was eventuated and exacerbated by self-assuring hubris including the belief in a "unique" religious ideology.

Introduction

The present work addresses events critical to the ending of the Asia-Pacific War. Here I do not seek to condemn the Emperor or Imperial Japanese military leaders for the wars in the Pacific and Asia. Instead, the focus is on the disastrous results of the belief by Japanese leaders in their own racial superiority, which was based on prefabricated myths as history and the emperor's concomitant command authority. In order to do this, a distinction is made between the institutions of the state and the nation: in Imperial Japan military leaders were the operational leaders of the state and the emperor was the head of the national cult, which sanctioned the former's activities. This helps one to better understand wartime events, including what the emperor did and did not do, intertwined with the activities of his advisors, especially those in the Imperial Army and Navy.

Nation and state

Presently, most historians readily acknowledge Emperor Hirohito's detailed knowledge of political events and military operations during the War in the Pacific. However, many assume his knowledge of specific policies indicates ipso facto that he mandated them. Some commentators assert that nearly all significant events during the war were subject to Hirohito's influence and direct orders—even when known historical records pertaining to particular events do not mention the Emperor. One reason for these sorts of assumptions is that many persons do not make a clear distinction between state and nation. Here I am not saying that the Shôwa Emperor and his advisors modeled themselves after some modern theoretical formulation, or one from Japan's past. Also, the emperor may not be seen as a god in the Judeo-Christian or Islamic sense of the term.[1]

These concepts may be important as such; however, they are not important themes in this work. Instead, the terms "nation" and "state" are adopted as key analytic concepts in this book.

Nation-states developed variously at different times in various locations. By the mid-nineteenth century both nation and state were "instituted and accepted the way princes or saints readily were earlier as preeminent guiding authorities," in the Western world. Confronted with this world, Imperial Japan's leaders unquestioningly set about building a nation-state and later their successors willfully purported to act as leaders of a modern nation-state. This is a study of the actions of the latter within their historical milieu at the end of the Imperial era. Therefore, though not usually concretely defined or distinguished, here the nation and state are delineated for purposes of analysis: a state is "a centralized differentiated set of institutions enjoying a monopoly of the means of legitimate violence over a territorially demarcated area." By contrast, "nations are natural, given, objectively existing human communities, each of which is assumed generally, in a vague and unreasoned way, not only to have its own common culture, myths, history, and destiny, but also to be a political community with a right to what is now called self-determination."[2] A state is an executive apparatus ruling and administering a defined geographical area. A nation is a commonly acknowledged set of beliefs, traditions, and spiritual orientations idolizing and legitimizing the actions of the rulers and administrators of a state. This conceptual demarcation is important to the interpretations presented in this book.

Friedrich Nietzsche in a different context described in a provocative way the distinction between nation and state:

> A folk, that is the body of God. A nation has earned this name only in so far as it has its own God, and obstinately rejects all other gods [...]
> The state, or organized immorality [...]
> Internally: as police, penal law, classes, commerce, family.
> Externally: as the will to power, to war, to conquest, to revenge.[3]

A nation needs a god of its own to sanctify organized immorality—the state. In Imperial Japan this type of god was not available. Meiji leaders thought that the emperor was the closest entity to this sort of god, and they made him into a quasi-replica of the Western European Christian God.

Modern Japanese emperors are the embodiment of Japanese culture and Japanese spiritual authority—the nation. Also while one might metaphorically say that an emperor was the nation, in Imperial Japan this did not mean—as in Europe and Russia—that he was the state and the sole executive authority. Many European kings, queens, and emperors and Russian tsars planned and implemented state policies and actions, but it was not necessarily so in Japan. In fact, the Meiji Constitution precluded this. Article 55 stated that the emperor's commands (Imperial Ordinances, Edicts, Rescripts, etc.) had no legal force without the signature of a "Minister of State." One should note, however, that this was meant to protect the supposed infallibility of the emperor, not to limit his powers. After all, according to the same Constitution the emperor "is sacred and inviolable" (Art. 3). The emperor, not the prime minister or the Diet, appointed and dismissed the ministers of state (Preamble, Art. 10).

Emperor Hirohito was the titular head of a modern state and the factual head of the nation. His position as head of the imperial family assured both. However, carrying out his duties as head of the nation—head of the "eternal imperial line" (*bansei ikkei no kôtô*)—did not necessarily include functioning as the actual head of state, who would, for example, plan and order the execution of military operations. These were the prerogatives of military leaders. The Japanese emperor as configured in Imperial Japan sanctified and was used to justify state policies and undertakings. Only the emperor was so envisioned. There were no terrestrial or celestial authorities above him. As shown in this book, the Japanese emperor was "the nation," but he was not in an absolute sense "the state."

My distinction between nation and state is conceived as a means of delineating historical roles, not as defining them. As they played out in Imperial Japan the role of the *state*'s leaders—the military as well as a few politicians and aristocrats—versus the role of the head of the *nation* and Imperial House—the emperor—had on occasion shifting nuances. They were not roles acted out according to a script chiseled in stone.

Kokutai, the "national essence"

One key Japanese term is central to the religious ideology underpinning the convictions and actions of the Shôwa Emperor and his military leaders, the imperial nation and state: *kokutai*. This is an often discussed, awkward to define concept. A standard Japanese language Shintô dictionary has two one-half densely printed pages on kokutai. In the beginning it says that kokutai encompasses "the customs and manners of a nation" (*kokufû*), "the state of affairs in a country" (*kokujô*), "the prestige and honor of a country" (*kuni no taimen*), "justice in and the moral obligations of a country" (*kuni no meibun*), "the foundations of a country" (*kuni no kiso*), and "the distinctive characteristics of a country" (*kuni no tokusei*), amongst others. Moreover, the concept applies to all countries, not just Japan. In Japan, over time, emphasis on particular aspects of the kokutai have changed. Japanese thinkers in the nineteenth and early twentieth centuries developed kokutai theory based on indigenous thought, especially in the Mito School, emphasizing the unique Japanese nation. Some chronicles trace the concept back to the late sixth and early seventh centuries and a revered legend in Japanese history, Crown Prince Shôtoku (who possibly never existed but a plethora of writings about him certainly do). Since my focus here is on historical developments in Imperial Japan toward the end of the Second World War and not theoretical discourses covering many times and places, I offer a "definition" suited to this age: "Kokutai" was an unquestionable dogma in Imperial Japan. It was not a clearly defined canon but a venerated sociopolitical order sanctified by the "eternal imperial line." According to Hozumi Yatsuka (1860–1912), an influential conservative jurist in Imperial Japan, "Kokutai" was the eternal inviolate, unbroken imperial line, ruling a sacrosanct everlasting family-land, Japan.[4] All Japanese were included in this folk-nation and all were loyal to the emperor—supposedly a descendant of Emperor Jimmu, the mythical founder of the nation. This belief was a given for Japanese leaders. It animated their wartime exploits including fighting on when all was lost. Who was the ultimate arbiter of the kokutai? Toward the end of the war this became a vexatious dilemma. The emperor saw himself as such; various military leaders on occasion saw themselves as such. They felt they knew how to preserve the kokutai better than the temporal head of the imperial line.

A single phrase translation of kokutai inevitably leaves out something. It is translated variously as "national polity," "national essence," or "body politic." In this book "national essence" is used because I believe this transmits more closely the meaning implied in Imperial Japan.

Overview

In this book one will see that the belief in the kokutai was crucial to wartime developments in Imperial Japan as five factors central to understanding Japanese problems with operations in Asia, the Pacific, and ending the war are explained: (1) the fall of Saipan and the Tôjô Cabinet, (2) kamikaze attacks, (3) Prime Minister Tôjô Hideki—the "war premier," (4) failing war materials, and (5) capitulation. An integral part of these explanations is an assessment of important primary and secondary Japanese sources covering these events.

This book is divided into five chapters to reflect the five factors:

1. **Wartime events, historical hindsights and insights:** Saipan's loss was strategically important for a number of reasons: it led to Tôjô Hideki's fall from power; it furthered the continuous undermining of the emperor's authority through false situation reports by various military leaders; it led to the beginning of kamikaze attacks; and it was the start of large-scale B-29 air raids on Japan by the United States, including use of the atomic bombs. Understanding these developments requires not only knowledge of the events but also familiarity with the historical sources used to describe and analyze them.

   Here an analysis of the wartime Shôwa Emperor and Prime Minister General Tôjô Hideki are offered, which focus on the fall of Saipan and the Tôjô Cabinet along with some of the important sources dealing with these disasters. These include, among others, the *Shôwa Tennô Jitsuroku* (Actual Record of the Shôwa Emperor)[5] and the *Senshi Sôsho* (War History Series).[6] Compiled under the auspices of the Imperial Household Agency and National Defense Agency respectively they provide differing perspectives for analyzing these events. My analysis extends beyond the fall of Saipan and the Tôjô Cabinet into 1945. Among other things these records testify to incessant infighting between army and navy leaders throughout the war. Moreover, despite the ostensible power wielded by the head of the nation, Emperor Hirohito, Imperial Army and Navy leaders often assumed that their (state) priorities were more important than national, imperial prerogatives.[7]

2. **Kamikaze attacks, planning before and after the fall of Saipan:** Following the shocking defeat of Saipan on July 8, 1944, Emperor Hirohito, the general public, and most army and navy leaders were greatly disturbed. Quite unusual at the time, the Navy General Staff as well as the Navy Ministry received many letters of encouragement. Among them, the navy claimed, there was a great increase in those advocating "certain-death certain-kill" (*hisshi hissatsu*) tactics, i.e., suicide attacks. Systematic kamikaze strikes were initiated three months later on October 25, 1944.

   Here too a state–nation division of roles is observable. The head of the nation—the Emperor—was not involved in planning nor did he sanction these tactics before their initiation. Also, they were not planned and carried out by the "maverick" Vice-Admiral Ônishi Takijirô (1891–1945) acting alone, as many still assume. Rather, after the tactic was authorized by specific state leaders, the Imperial Navy General Staff, Ônishi launched the first suicide attacks. Previously plans for various types of suicide missions, at sea and in the air, were put forward by various naval officers on an unsystematic basis at various times starting no later than 1932.

The suicide tradition in the army and the historical and cultural memory of the *tokkôtai* pilots have been treated extensively,[8] but most authors do not consider the long development of "kamikaze" tactics within the Imperial Navy. Three key figures who came to know each other in 1928 played important roles in these developments: the future admiral, Capt. Yamamoto Isoroku (1884–1943); future vice-admiral, Lt. Cdr. Ônishi Takijirô; and future imperial aide-de-camp and later Capt. of the light aircraft carrier *Chiyoda*, Lt. Jô Ei'ichirô (1899–1944). Here the pathos, covered by many, of those who "volunteered" for these missions is only dwelt on briefly. Instead, these attacks are examined from the point of view of sporadic military planning and putative imperial sanctions of these tactics.

3. **Tôjô Hideki, man of his times:** Many years ago Robert J.C. Butow wrote, "Tojo was a reflector, not a creator of national thought." He "was a militarist—misguided, naïve, and narrow in outlook; he regarded war as a legitimate instrument of national policy."[9] In this chapter a broader portrait of Tôjô and his milieu is presented in order to better understand wartime developments in Imperial Japan. Tôjô is examined as a state and war leader. This account serves as background for army and navy sometime use of the Emperor (head of the nation) to legitimize their activities. At this time state leaders throughout the world "regarded war as a legitimate instrument of national policy," but Japanese military leaders' disregard for materials and logistics, initiation of suicide attacks, and more generally provocation of social-economic devastation toward the end of the war verged on nefarious, criminal conduct.

4. **Lack of war materials, failing strategy, and Tôjô's fall:** From early 1943, Prime Minister Tôjô increasingly emphasized the value of the Japanese spirit in war. National spirit was supposed to make up for the failings of state leaders: the dearth of war materials was one impetus behind Tôjô's emphasis on Japan's unique spiritual qualities. Here the conflicting army and navy strategies surveyed in Chapter 1 are pursued further in some detail. Also Hirohito's knowledge of the situation is addressed. In particular, sea transport was vital to Japan's war efforts and during the war the transport of men and materials to and from distant areas in the empire became an acute problem. In February 1943, Tôjô had already asserted in parliament that

ships were not the only way to transport freight overseas. One could put 500 or even 1,000 tons in large rubber sacks (*fukuro*), which could be towed over the ocean. Also one should look into using large wooden rafts (*ikada*) for the same purpose. Inventiveness and fighting spirit would win out.[10]

It was a desperate situation. Increasingly raw materials could not be brought to Japan for producing essential resources such as fuel and steel; military outposts could not be replenished and reinforced. The battle for Saipan is one important example of these difficulties and their consequences: the loss of that strategically important island and the fall of the Tôjô Cabinet, both sorely regretted by the Emperor, were important in Japan's slither into defeat.

5. **Capitulation: Hubris and belief in a religious ideology, some conclusions:** In this chapter "The end" is addressed. Hubris, blind belief, and defeat: support for a hopeless war, atomic bombs, and Soviet entry into the war, the final days, a postmortem, and war guilt. Army Minister General Anami Korechika's ambiguous road to ending the war illustrates the confused war circumstances. Here too assessments of historical sources important to our understanding of these events are integrated into the analysis.

A concluding interpretation: Imperial Japanese leaders insisted on continuing the war long after all was obviously lost. Many ask why. It appears that the disastrous prolongation of the war was rooted in the collective Japanese fear of loss of face and the extinction of their empire—a desperation that galvanized self-assuring hubris based on unquestioning belief in their nationalistic religious ideology.

The founders of the imperial state envisioned the imperial line and kokutai as the spiritual basis of their empire. They infused the minds and hearts of the people to follow unquestioningly government authorities, much as these early leaders postulated the role of Christianity in most Western nations.[11] This made the national essence-inclusive emperor an "ultimate concern" for Japanese rulers and ruled alike. Many years ago Paul Tillich (1886-1965) addressed this phenomenon: "Our ultimate concern is that which determines our being or not-being." Of considerable importance is the relationship between preliminary and ultimate concerns—various concerns about our worldly existence versus God, being and non-being. Many people elevate a preliminary concern to ultimacy. This he unequivocally condemns as idolatry: "the best example [of the elevation of a preliminary concern to ultimacy] is the contemporary idolatry of religious nationalism."[12] One might say that when a state and the idolatry bolstering it are so elevated then the continued existence of this construct has ultimate meaning for its leaders and their followers. In Imperial Japan the gods (*kami*) and the imperial line, existence, being and non-being, were linked to the survival of their folk and state. This led them to risk and well-nigh lose all. Following defeat, the nation and its head, the emperor, were transformed but survived; the state with military executives, and the military itself, did not.

Finally, this is not a condemnation of the Japanese national ethos or an affirmation of the Western Judeo-Christian based-national ideologies sanctifying various states then and now. Rather, insofar as criticism might be implied, my skepticism is directed toward *nation*-centered religiopolitical ideologies "marketed" to bring people to unquestioning devotion to *state*-imposed political and martial adventures.

1

Wartime Events, Historical Hindsights and Insights

The following is an analysis of the fall of Saipan, the Tôjô Cabinet, and related wartime events. The accent is on the Shôwa Emperor and General Tôjô Hideki, prime minister 1941–44, and some of the important sources dealing with their activities as war leaders.[1] This chapter is divided into two parts. Part 1 emphasizes historical sources and part 2 focuses on the Emperor's authority. Herein the distinction "state" versus "nation" is clearly seen, as the Emperor's role in decision-making is depicted in various ways depending on the source. The Emperor could not be ignored, and he was not. He was one of the elites involved in the decision-making process, but his principal role was to sanction that which was decided, not to dictate policies or military operations. Also, the very existence of the Emperor allowed others to sanction policies in his name that he had not approved, which on occasion were contrary to his wishes. The decision not to try to retake Saipan immediately after its loss, seen below, is but one example. The events, the Emperor's participation in them, and the sources about them are intertwined. It is impossible to completely separate these factors and still have a realistic, if not always tidy, history. The emphasis in this chapter is on varying perspectives, of which there are many. The focus is on specific events crucial to ending the war.

The fall of Saipan in mid-1944 was a major step toward ending the war, and the battle itself greatly influenced how the war ended. The United States announced securing the island on July 9, but the successful US invasion on June 15 signaled to many Japanese leaders its loss, which stimulated a heated debate involving the Emperor about retaking the island. In the end, however, Imperial Headquarters announced on July 8, the "honorable deaths" (*gyokusai*) of the troops there one day earlier. A headline in a newspaper from that time states: "Our troops on Saipan, all die heroically in battle."[2]

Here, among others, the "Actual Record of the Shôwa Emperor" (*Shôwa Tennô Jitsuroku*, STJR) and the "War History Series" (*Senshi Sôsho*) are examined as historical records to help illustrate these events and problems with the available sources. The former chronicles Hirohito's life, including developments during the Shôwa era, 1926–89 and Japan's response to external political and military pressures. The latter is a series of narratives based on documents and commentaries treating various military actions by the Imperial Army and Navy during the Second World War.[3] Differences in information included and the usefulness of these works as historical sources are addressed as they are referenced along with other records and books covering these events. Where specific events are covered in more than one source, emphasis is on the source's content and consistency, not a strict chronological ordering of events. The story begins with the events leading up to the fall of Saipan. Both records show the Emperor's dependence on, as well as increasing wariness of, his military leaders. The leader of the nation came to harbor suspicions about the veracity of the information he was receiving from state military leaders.

Part 1. Sources

The *Shôwa Tennô Jitsuroku* (Actual Record of the Shôwa Emperor)

The completion of this record was announced with much fanfare on September 9, 2014. It was featured in the major Japanese newspapers including the *Asahi Shimbun*. The following information is taken from that publication. The STJR, with some 12,000 pages in 61 volumes, took 24 years and 5 months to complete and involved 112 people. In Japan and overseas 3,152 sources were examined.[4] It forms a chronological record of Emperor Hirohito's life (1901–89), compiled under the auspices of the Imperial Household Agency. It is a secondary source containing many references to secondary as well as primary sources—diaries and records of persons involved in these events. A number of copies of the original were available at the Imperial Household Agency Archives from September 9 to November 30, 2014. During this time I examined specific parts of the record that dealt with events well known to me. The publication of the record was completed in 2019.

After examining the Actual Record of the Shôwa Emperor focusing on the subject of this book and the beginning of the War in the Pacific, I met with one of the experts who reported on it in the *Asahi Shimbun*, Hosaka Masayasu. Hosaka is a nonfiction writer who has written many books on the war. I ventured, and he agreed, that there is very little new information in the record. Since then he has published a two-volume work on the record in which he is very critical of the manner of presentation, as is the historian Hara Takeshi.[5] Besides their works a number of other books have been published describing and analyzing the record. Several, but not all of them, will be referred to below.

The STJR is neither objective nor a swindle. Rather, the parts relating to topics covered in this book show that given the publication of many of the sources used, this record is an attempt to balance published "facts" with a positive image of the former emperor as the head of the nation: the image the Imperial Household Agency officials wish to transmit to the public now and to posterity. The priority is on serving the Imperial House as the pinnacle of the national cult, not the state.

New implications

Although the STJR contains little new information, one aspect of the Record's contents is very new. In this work the Emperor's knowledge of, and at least tacit sanction of, certain military campaigns, which up until his death Emperor Hirohito denied knowing the specifics about, is clearly documented. The implied acceptance of imperial imprimatur of controversial war operations by the Imperial Household Agency, a bastion of defense of Imperial House tradition, will change the landscape of discussion about specific actions and, more generally, the Emperor's participation in war planning and execution. Turning back the clock, one particular example is taken up since it is well known and universally condemned (at least in the United States): the attack on Pearl Harbor December 7, 1941.

The attack on Pearl Harbor was mentioned in an Imperial Conference November 5, 1941. This was a very long conference that began at 10:30 a.m. and extended into the late afternoon. The Emperor was not present the entire time. War with the United States was deemed "inevitable" (*yamu wo einai*). At 3:25 p.m. the army and navy chiefs of staff met alone with the Emperor. The army chief of staff presented plans for opening a war with the United States, Great Britain, and Holland. The navy chief of staff did not present the plan in detail, but he did tell the Emperor that among others an "air attack" (*kûshû*) on Hawai'i was planned:

> Also, the emperor received a report from the Navy Chief of Staff about deliberations on Imperial Navy operations plans for a war with the United States, Great Britain and Holland. Employing a mobile attack unit with six aircraft carriers as the main element, an air attack on the main enemy fleet stationed in Hawai'i is planned.[6]

Twenty-seven different sources are listed documenting this Imperial Conference. However, one of Hosaka's criticisms of the record is illustrated here: the citations are vague and unreliable. Only titles are listed, one after the other, with no hint of where the information in each might be found or which source refers to a specific event.[7]

On December 1, the attacks were sanctioned at an Imperial Conference. The Conference began according to the STJR at 11:38 a.m. and extended into the late afternoon. In the beginning Prime Minister Tôjô summarized previous cabinet discussions saying the (intractable) situation between the United States and Japan had not changed, and he requested that the Imperial Conference decide to open war with the United States, Great Britain, and Holland. At 2:00 p.m. after long discussions with the cabinet and Imperial Headquarters the president of the Privy Council, Hara Yoshimichi (1867–1944), summarized the proceedings and came to the conclusion that war was inevitable (*yamu wo einai*). The phrase is repeated several times. The Emperor entered at 3:45 p.m. He listened to further discussion and sometime after 4:30 p.m. he too came to the conclusion that war was inevitable. Hirohito sanctioned the decision and ordered the army and navy to cooperate closely, not without reason. Army and navy enmity went back many years in Imperial Japan.[8] Despite this order, and many more during the war, as related below, their hostility only ceased with the collapse of the empire.

On December 3, at 10:45 a.m. orders were sent to Commander of the Combined Fleet Admiral Yamamoto as an Imperial Decree (*chokugo*). Therein the Emperor says the fate of the nation hangs on success or failure. The Combined Fleet's responsibility is very heavy, and he expects them to annihilate (*shômetsu*) the enemy.[9] Here one vividly sees Emperor Hirohito's situation: he sanctioned starting a war beginning with attacks on Pearl Harbor and various other places in the Pacific and Southeast Asia. He knew full well what was going to happen. But he did not participate in planning these operations and formally ordered implementing them after being presented with a *fait accompli*: the general staffs and cabinet both had decided that war was inevitable and this was the best way to go about it.

Later on December 8, 1941, the results of the attacks opening the Pacific War were reported to the Emperor. Among them it was reported that the "surprise attack" (*kishû*) on Hawai'i was a success:

> The emperor received a report concerning the landing of our forces on the Malay Peninsula, the success of the surprise attack on Hawai'i, the bombardment of Singapore, the military situation after air attacks on Mindanao, Guam, and Wake.

Eight different sources document this report, with the same problems as noted above.[10] Although the attack on Pearl Harbor began before an official notice from Tokyo was delivered to officials in Washington, DC, (possibly) indicating that war was coming, this provocative blunder is not mentioned.

That the Emperor was informed of the plan to attack Pearl Harbor well before it took place is nothing new.[11] That a work sponsored by the Imperial Household Agency confirms he was informed in this manner, however, is new and significant. In the November 5, Imperial Conference the phrase "air attack" was used in the navy operations report to Emperor Hirohito concerning Hawai'i; in the December report to the Emperor this action was labeled a "surprise attack." As seen above, among the six operations cited only the Hawai'i attack was called a surprise attack. In another record of the Imperial Audience of November 3, from the Imperial Army General Staff the operation was termed a surprise attack.[12] Perhaps this difference in terminology—an air attack becoming a surprise attack—went unnoticed, or perhaps the compilers of the STJR would like the Emperor to be treated more favorably in future histories, i.e., he supposedly did not know a surprise attack was planned.

Similar discussions between the Emperor and Imperial Japan's military leaders, and reports on proposed as well as ongoing military operations can be found in the STJR. For example, as shown below, this record reports on establishing the "absolute national defense perimeter" in September 1943, the decisive defeat on Saipan, and the subsequent resignation of the Tôjô Cabinet in mid-1944. The affirmation by the Imperial Household Agency that the Shôwa Emperor was informed of specific military operations prior to their execution and that he subsequently received reports on their success or failure immediately after they were carried out is significant; however, this information does not show that the Emperor ordered the planning or execution of these actions. It does show that he was well aware of what was being planned, took part in discussions about military matters, and knowledgeably as well as formally sanctioned military operations including those that marked the beginning, continuation, and finally the end of the Pacific War.

The Senshi Sôsho (War History Series)

The source used in many accounts of Japanese wartime activities is a reliable work, the War History Series, 102 volumes put together at the Bôeichô Bôei Kenkyûsho Senshishitsu (Defense Agency, Institute for Defense Studies, War History Office), now the Japanese National Institute for Defence Studies, Center for Military History (Bôei Kenkyûjo Senshi Senta). Similar to the STJR it also is a secondary source in which many primary sources are cited. Different from the STJR, it was compiled by former military—read state—leaders. The work is arranged by themes. One of the first volumes is on the Pearl Harbor attack (*hawa'i sakusen*). Other themes have various volumes devoted to them, for example the Imperial Headquarters, Army Department (10 volumes) and the Imperial Headquarters Navy Department, Combined Fleet (7 volumes). The information is arranged within each theme in chronological order, but the various volumes were not published in sequence.[13] Since most of the volumes were compiled in the 1960s and 1970s some may be somewhat dated. However, they are based for the most part on primary sources from the Military Archives of the National Institute for Defense Studies (NIDS), Tokyo, many of which have not been published but may be seen there; therefore this series is still important. Primary sources cited by the authors indicate that Hirohito was extensively informed about military matters, including the importance of Saipan. This is also discussed in the STJR, but in places the two sources contain dissimilar commentaries on these events.

The War History Series has been examined extensively, likewise a number of unpublished sources cited therein. Two sources often quoted in various volumes of the series are the "Sanada Jôichirô Shôshô Nikki" (Major General Sanada Jôichirô Diary) and the "Nakazawa Gunreibu Daiichi Buchô Nôto" (Navy General Staff, 1st Department, Department Head Nakazawa Notes). Both are available in the NIDS Military Archives. In mid-1944 Major General Sanada was Head of the Imperial Army Operations Department (*Sanbôhonbu Daiichi Buchô*) and Rear Admiral Nakazawa was Head of the Imperial Navy Operations Department (*Gunreibu Daiichi Buchô*). Sanada (1897–1957) and Nakazawa (1894–1977) were active in rival services, and they both spent many years on their respective general staffs. The writings of each were compared with relevant volumes in the War History Series.[14] There are no practical differences between the primary source materials and the contents of the respective series volumes. These examples illustrate my experience generally when consulting this work: it is very reliable. Also, the staff in the Military Archives at the NIDS are very helpful in locating and explaining source materials stored there.

The Imperial Headquarters

Finally, a very interesting collation of primary source materials must be noted: the Imperial Headquarters Army Department Records Relating to

Imperial Audiences.[15] Here the various types of audiences with the Emperor involving the Imperial Headquarters are explained, and selected copies of the handwritten records are presented. The Imperial Headquarters was organized around the two chiefs of staff and existed to lend dual (army and navy) support to the Emperor in military matters. Decisions were reached at an Imperial Headquarters Conference. There were no civilian members. Not even the prime minister or foreign minister attended these conferences. The members from each service who formally attended included the chiefs and vice-chiefs of staff, the heads of the respective operations departments, and the army and navy ministers. If the Emperor was present he was accompanied by his chief aide-de-camp, and it was called an Imperial Headquarters Imperial Conference (*daihon'ei gozenkaigi*), which was not the same as the generally known Imperial Conference (*gozenkaigi*). Other lower-ranking members of the general staffs were called to attend when specific information was required. If the Emperor did not attend, decisions were later presented to him by the chiefs of staff for approval.

These documents are important due to the far-reaching influence of one special section in the general staffs. For example, practically speaking the Imperial Headquarters Army Department was the same as the Army General Staff. In the general staff those responsible for the planning and direction of military operations had the most influence, and they played a very important role in formulating political policy: the Imperial Army General Staff No. 1 (Operations) Department and therein the No. 2 (Operations) Section. This No. 2 Section was not only charged with planning strategy and operations, they also prepared the drafts of the reports made by the chief of staff to the throne. The reports to the Emperor were made by the chief of staff but were in fact drawn up by this section of the general staff. Therefore the decisions made by the Imperial Headquarters Army Department and sanctioned by the Emperor were quite often the decisions arrived at in this section. The section was made up of about twenty officers with a colonel as the section chief. There were three subsections: operations, communications and supply, and air forces—each led by a lieutenant colonel with a number of majors and captains serving under them. The operations subsection had the most personnel and influence. The unofficial elite career route in the Imperial Army went from communications and supply subsection chief (lt. col.) to operations subsection chief (lt. col.) to operations section chief (col.) to operations department chief (major general). Also to be included among the elites were those assigned to Section 20, War Operations Planning (*sensô shidô*) of the General Staff.

Accordingly, official policies and records were produced by a rather obscure group of middle-ranking officers in the general staff who had an inordinate impact on decisions about national military strategy. Since national military strategy involved many overseas operations, they also strongly colored Japan's foreign affairs. But at that time military operations overseas were not subject to review or amendment by any of the civilian cabinet ministers, including the prime minister and foreign minister. This meant these middle-ranking career army officers greatly influenced Imperial Japan's official foreign policy. Along with some like-minded staff officers posted overseas, these were the field grade officers who were, according to many postwar analyses, the "militarists" behind Imperial Japan's wars of aggression in Asia and the Pacific.[16] Key middle-ranking army officers, from captain to colonel, also had an impact on the nation's internal politics. For example, Col. Arisue Seizô, mentioned below, influenced the formation of the Abe Nobuyuki Cabinet in mid-1939. Col. Hattori Takushirô, treated extensively below, was another such officer.[17]

The navy general staff was organized similarly, but there was an additional authority, the Commander of the Combined Fleet (*rengô kantai shireichôkan*), with great influence on naval operations. Also, the navy when compared to the army, was much less inclined to get involved in politics.[18]

Various commentaries

Several other war accounts are worthy of note. The first history of the war in Japanese came not long after its end. Hattori Takushirô, formerly a colonel and member of the Imperial Army General Staff, published *Daitôa Sensô Zenshi* (A Complete History of the Great East Asia War) in 1953, and it has been reissued a number of times. Considered important, the US War History Office translated it into English. Later it was translated into Italian and French from the English version. Hattori also extensively covers the fall of Saipan. For those responsible for policy-making, Japan's defeat at Saipan meant that a way had to be found to end the war with a negotiated settlement. However, Hattori's notion of "those responsible for policy making" was different from that of many politicians and bureaucrats: with the previous debacles at Midway and Guadalcanal certain prominent persons such as former prime minister Konoe Fumimaro and Lord Keeper of the Privy Seal Kido Kôichi began to search for ways to achieve peace, but according to Hattori they were not important in the decision-making process. With the defeats in the Philippines, Mariana Seas, and on Saipan those really responsible—Imperial Headquarters and the general staffs in the army and navy—came to realize they could not recover, rearm, and continue fighting, as previously thought. A way to peace, which emphatically did not involve total capitulation, had to be found. And this was a dangerous undertaking because one false step could precipitate the unacceptable: unconditional surrender.

Hattori writes in a very colorful, controversial manner, and he obviously had access to records from the Imperial Army and Navy made available to the public many years later. There is a brief list appended in a later edition of the book enumerating some of these sources but, as was usual in Japan at the time even among professional historians, he does not include footnotes or a detailed bibliography. Since he was from the Imperial Army and most sources are from the army, his presentation is biased intermittently in favor of his branch of service and against the navy. Nevertheless, he is extremely critical of army preparations on Saipan as well as those by the navy units that were supposed to carry out operation "A-go," the naval action to defeat the US fleet in the area (known in many Western sources as the Battle of the Philippine Sea and also as the Great Marianas Turkey Shoot due to the large number of Japanese warplanes downed). Specifically Hattori says the defenses on Saipan were poorly organized and recently arrived troops were inadequately prepared and integrated with those long on station. Navy personnel included many who were new and insufficiently trained, and their facilities ashore were poorly organized and constructed. At one point he adds that of the available naval aircraft only about 20 percent actually took part in the fighting. The rest did not show up or were lost due to the Imperial Navy's own incompetence.[19]

Not surprisingly, former navy leaders viewed things differently. Admiral Toyoda Soemu (1885–1957), appointed Imperial Navy Combined Fleet Commander from May 3, 1944, and Chief of the Imperial Navy General Staff from May 29, 1945, published his memoirs five years after the war. They are more personal and less a "history" than Hattori's work. Toyoda noted in his memoirs that the initial briefings he received as Combined Fleet Commander about the general war situation and operations planning included Saipan. It was the best-fortified stronghold in the Pacific. It was impregnable. Later Toyoda realized, however, that what he had been told was totally wrong. The naval area commander was senior to the commanding army general on Saipan, but the army was responsible for defenses on the island. The navy did not even suspect that the enemy would attack Saipan, and Toyoda strongly criticized the army's lack of preparations.[20] Even after the war Hattori and Toyoda are another example of the dissension between the army and navy that earlier had contributed to Imperial Japan's military defeat.

In both narratives the Emperor plays no part in these events. He is not even mentioned. Hattori says that Imperial Headquarters along with others from outside of the military, who are not identified, recognized full well the strategic importance of Saipan. After Saipan was invaded by US forces they then advocated making plans to retake the island. Independently, Toyoda wrote that navy leaders were of the same opinion. Both the army and navy made explicit plans, but in the end it became clear that the Japanese army and navy did not have the wherewithal to retake the island, or even resupply the forces still fighting there, and the plans were abandoned. The Emperor's insistence in this matter as detailed below from other sources plays no role in these narratives. In an appendix to Hattori's work Inaba Masao, formerly a lt. col., member of the Imperial Headquarters Staff, and Army General Staff at the end of the war, says that after much wrangling between the army and navy ministries, as well as between the military services and the government, compromises were reached and army–navy coordination invented. Then the decisions were presented formally to "the Emperor who had no direct responsibility" for the policies he was to sanction. All believed this was the best way to do things. There was no strong single unified state political and military policy-deciding organ, and in fact sometimes it was impossible to arrive at a policy decision.[21] As for the nation, Hattori's history and Toyoda's memoirs reflect Inaba's description of the Emperor's lack of involvement in this chaotic decision-making process in that both never refer to him or his authority. Of course, this does not mean the Shôwa Emperor was not involved; rather, it reflects the interests and inclinations of many persons when these works were written as well as others who later wrote ancillary commentaries on them. For some years after the war, in the interest of maintaining the Imperial House and line, the reigning emperor was excluded from most accounts of prewar and wartime military planning, coordination, and operations. Consistent with his feelings during and after the war, with his history Hattori led the way in promoting this historical subterfuge.

Col. Hattori Takushirô

Col. Hattori (1901–60) had a remarkable career. Over 500 military officers committed suicide after the Mikado announced Japan's surrender, taking responsibility for the country's defeat.[22] But not all influential officers took their own lives after the surrender announcement. Hattori, along with the two staff officers mentioned above, was among those who did not.[23] At the end of the war he was a regimental commander near Chongqing in China and finally a divisional commander. Before assuming the first position at the beginning of March 1945 he was twice Chief of the War Operations Section (*sensô sakusenka*) on the General Staff. During his career he was a strong war advocate. He played key roles in directing operations, among others on Guadalcanal, in China, and earlier leading troops in the Nomohan Incident, all of which ended in defeat. Some say he was even instrumental in precipitating the incident at Nomohan. In fairness one author, a former member of the Imperial Army General Staff, says that Col. Hattori apparently was a brave, able, commanding officer in China who respected those under his command and was respected by them.[24] Earlier after the fall of Guadalcanal he "took responsibility" and resigned, but Tôjô still favored him and made him secretary to the army minister, a post concurrently held by Prime Minister Tôjô at that time. Less than a year later he was again appointed Chief of the War Operations Section. He survived surrender and was not indicted after the war. In the late 1940s and during the 1950s he was involved in right-wing activities including, according to the CIA, a plot to assassinate Prime Minister Yoshida Shigeru, which was never put into action.[25] He appears to have been, like Tôjô, one of those enthusiastic officers totally convinced of the supposed special quality of the Japanese folk and their unique "national essence." This enthusiasm seems to have been important to his military career and postwar undertakings. Yamamoto Tomoyuki, source for this information, has a sympathetic view of Hattori and like-minded persons, and does not refer to the assassination plot.[26]

In a recent publication Handô Kazutoshi and Hosaka Masayasu mince no words in criticizing Hattori and his activities during and after the war—including his "arbitrary" history. The two authors released a book in 2008 titled *Great Leaders and Foolhardy Leaders of the Shôwa Era*; therein they define the latter as "leaders (shô) in positions of responsibility who were absolutely irresponsible."[27] Hattori is one prime example. He is designated as such because he helped plan and carry out a number of operations that failed miserably, as seen above. But he always managed to evade any responsibility for his planning and decisions, during and even after the war.

Furthermore, Hosaka and Handô say that Hattori's history is seriously flawed. It is divided into two parts: the first from the US point of view and the second from the Japanese perspective. It was compiled by the "Hattori Kikan" (Hattori Organ) in the Fukuinchô (Agency for Returning Veterans) to mislead authorities connected with the Tokyo War Crimes Trial and also to promote Japan's rearmament. Hattori was to some degree successful in achieving these aims, but according to Hosaka, reading his history now shows what a "liar" (*usotsuki*) he was. Major General Charles Willoughby, MacArthur's intelligence specialist (of little repute), liked the work and had it translated into English. Later he recommended Hattori as chief of staff of the new Self Defense Forces, but Prime Minister Yoshida, who was well informed of Hattori's past, vetoed the selection.[28] Thus the first "complete history" of the Pacific War in Japanese contains some interesting information, but it was personally and politically motivated—intended to relieve the authors of prosecution as war criminals, and to promote conservative politics and rearmament in Japan. Poorly informed US Army authorities had the work translated and recommended it to others. One must keep these circumstances in mind when reading it.

Early critics

Over the years a number of historians and journalists became skeptical about conduct of the war and the whitewashed image of the Shôwa Emperor. Early on, Inoue Kiyoshi wrote a strong critique of the emperor system from a Marxist point of view, which was published in 1958.[29] In 1975 he published *Tennô no Sensô Sekinin* (The Emperor's War Responsibility), a succinct well-documented work cited below.[30] Shortly thereafter Fujiwara Akira, a former army officer who graduated from the Army Academy and in the postwar years was a prominent historian influenced by Inoue, published *Tennôsei to Guntai* (The Emperor System and the Military) in 1978. Therein he wrote that the Emperor did indeed actively influence events during the war, including the period extending from the beginning to the middle of 1944. For example in February 1944, with the loss of the Marshall Islands, a change of command was called for. At that time Tôjô, already prime minister and army minister, had himself appointed Chief of the Army General Staff. Sugiyama Hajime (1880–1945), chief of staff till then, and many general staff members opposed this concentration of power in one man. Sugiyama even appealed to the Emperor but Hirohito backed Tôjô and the matter was settled, according to Fujiwara. Later in June of the same year, with the defeats in the Marianas including Saipan, the Emperor finally "lost confidence" in Tôjô, which spelt the end of his government. The long-standing intrigues against Tôjô were successful and the cabinet was obliged to resign. Fujiwara writes, as for "the independence of the right of supreme command (*tôsuiken*), this was not the independence of the military. It was one aspect of the absoluteness of the emperor's power."[31] But things were not so simple. As shown in more detail later, Fujiwara disregards the fact that military leaders demurred when confronted with Hirohito's demand that Saipan be retaken: after due deliberations no attempt was made to retake it. This is only one of many similar incidents where imperial wishes, and even commands, were respectfully ignored. Hirohito as leader of the nation commanded respect; military leaders, however, often turned a blind eye to his role as leader of the state.

Early Western histories

In another account of Saipan, Delmer Brown, in one of the first postwar authoritative works in English on "nationalism in Japan" (1955), described the consequences of the Saipan defeat, citing contemporary Japanese sources.

> But in spite of concentrated and spirited fighting, Saipan fell in July. It was recognized as a disaster, and Tôjô found that he could not resist demands—primarily from the Navy—that he resign. A leading newspaper, the *Asahi*, concluded that with the enemy now in occupation of Saipan, it was quite clear that the next step would be to carry out air raids on Japan in order to destroy production and to break Japanese morale.[32]

As we now know, the demands came from court officials, imperial princes, and many "elder statesmen" (*jûshin*)—former prime ministers some of whom were retired admirals, and navy leaders. Brown does not mention the Emperor in connection with these events. Throughout his book his view is that right-wing nationalists and militarists acted in the Emperor's name without consulting him. Brown reflects the interpretation accepted in the United States for many years until shortly before the Shôwa Emperor's demise in 1989. A contemporary work by Robert J.C. Butow expressed this widely entertained opinion in the West as follows:

> For the Emperor successfully to have intervened in such a way as to direct state affairs along lines more in accord with his personal conscience would have required him to be a man of less retiring personality, with a very practical grasp of political affairs. [...]
>
> Although he did lack power, the Emperor was in a position to influence and to inspire those around him. The capacity for doing so effectively altered with circumstances beyond imperial control and depended on the line taken by his advisors, but the essence of this somewhat intangible factor was always the gravitational pull of the throne.[33]

It was generally assumed at the time that the Emperor was a man of good intentions, but he was unassertive and not well informed about practical political and military matters. We know now that this was not the case.

Nevertheless, leaving aside the fact that the Emperor's knowledge of and participation in military planning was unknown to most contemporary scholars, it is not surprising that the Emperor was aware of the coming consequences of the defeat on Saipan. As noted above, a national newspaper published an article on the imminent danger of air attack on the home islands.[34] Also he was well aware of Tôjô's declining popularity in the military and civil hierarchies. However, other commentaries weight this constellation of events somewhat differently.

According to Butow, shortly after the war former Imperial Navy leaders pointed to defeats at Midway and Guadalcanal as "*the* turning point" in the war. The loss of Saipan was also mentioned occasionally, but "this is generally considered to be several steps beyond the turning point stage. Those who continued to hope, after Midway, for a favorable change in fortune knew, after Saipan, that their hopes had lost all meaning."[35] This is a somewhat inconsistent statement. When one's hopes lose all meaning this is certainly of serious consequence. Suzuki Kantarô (1868–1948), a former admiral and prime minister at the end of the war, wrote in an autobiography that the fall of Saipan was the beginning of the end—the final defeat of Imperial Japan.[36] Also, later authors have reevaluated the importance of the Saipan defeat.

Japan's military defeats were having a cumulative effect. Finally in the naval battle in the Philippine Sea and the aerial rout in the Marianas shortly before the invasion of Saipan, Japan lost three large aircraft carriers, four smaller ones were damaged, and she lost 395 warplanes. Naval operations chief at the time, Rear Admiral Nakazawa Tasuku (later vice-admiral) recalled some years after the war that abandoning Saipan and the above-mentioned decimation of the fleet were decisive losses for the navy and ultimately the defense of Japan.[37] In the words of a later Japanese author, the Imperial Navy effectively had no more "striking power." At the end of June 1944 this opinion was shared by leading American as well as Japanese military men, for example, Admiral Ernest J. King (Commander US Fleet) and Yonai Mitsumasa (1880–1948)—a former prime minister, retired admiral, and elder statesman. Also, by this time Section 20 War Guidance in the Imperial Army General Staff had already begun to seriously study the best ways and under what circumstances the war could be favorably ended.[38]

Imperial Navy losses and reports about them

According to Hosaka Masayasu, moreover, the Chief of the Naval General Staff lied to the Emperor about Japan's inordinate losses in the Mariana and

Philippine Seas by significantly reducing their numbers. Much earlier Edward Drea commented briefly on the situation: in October 1944, "Once again wildly inflated battle claims misled Hirohito into thinking the series of air and sea battles stretching from Taiwan to Okinawa had ended in a great Japanese triumph."[39] In his later work Drea says much the same thing: service staffs and civilian ministries "offered the emperor selective, and sometimes contradictory, data in order to gain imperial support for their programs. Hirohito thus often operated on incomplete or biased information, and sometimes in near isolation."[40] Hosaka commented: at this time, mid-1944 and thereafter, the Emperor was purposely not told about the dire situation of the Imperial Navy, but he was becoming increasingly aware that there were discrepancies between reports from the general staffs and reality.[41] The problem of ascertaining what information was transmitted to the Emperor and why his military commanders, trained and indoctrinated above all to be loyal to the Emperor and "national essence," falsified operations results is an issue that complicates investigation into the events presented hereafter. It is addressed in more detail below.

The fall of Saipan, summed up briefly, brought Japan within range of US long-range B-29 bombers and this was strategically very important. As the authors of the biography of Field Marshal Sugiyama indicate, senior army officers recognized this danger.[42] The Emperor was acutely aware of this menace even before Saipan fell. Also, the defeat on Saipan precipitated the fall of the Tôjô Cabinet. Saipan was a major military disaster, and the fall of the cabinet moreover signaled the failure of Tôjô's and Hirohito's attempts to end the army–navy feuding long hindering Japan's war efforts. These developments together were clear signs of the deteriorating times, from the Japanese point of view.

Saipan, myth, and consequences

Saipan was the first island to be taken by the United States that was a Japanese territory prior to the beginning of the war. The ferocity of the fighting and "heroic suicide" of so many civilians as well as soldiers and sailors was played up in Japan to stimulate patriotic fervor.[43] The battle also had an important influence on how US authorities ended the war. Due to Japanese suicide tactics, including civilians as well as military personnel, a so-called "Saipan-ratio" became part of US planning. Authorities estimated killing seven Japanese soldiers on Saipan cost one American killed and several wounded. Extrapolated, this meant Japanese fanaticism would take a toll of around 500,000 US soldiers and sailors killed and many times that wounded with an invasion of Japan proper.[44] The alternative was the atomic bomb and entry of the Soviet Union into the war, which was intended to, and did, convince the Japanese to surrender unconditionally.[45]

The Saipan statistics, however, were more fiction than fact. A postwar evaluation says that the number of civilians who died helping defend Saipan was greatly inflated for propaganda purposes. Of the approximately 22,000 civilians on Saipan about 15,000 survived the battle, and most of those killed died during the pre-invasion naval bombardment.[46] Nevertheless, in Japan and among US military authorities the number who died and their manner of dying were believed to be much more, and more "heroic." In Japan this "myth" was used to stimulate patriotism among civilians; in the US military it was used as a basis for predicting the astronomical costs of invading Japan and later for justifying the use of two atom bombs.

The absolute national defense perimeter

The battles on Saipan and in the Philippine/Mariana Seas were eventuated about one year earlier when the Japanese established an "absolute national defense perimeter" (*zettai kokubôken*). Saipan and the Marianas in the South Pacific along with Truk Island were on the outer edges of this perimeter. According to a postwar account by Satô Kenryô (1895–1975), formerly lt. general and chief of the Military Affairs Bureau in the Imperial Army Ministry, this was done because Tôjô Hideki, prime minister and army minister at the time, was pressured by the Emperor to draw a clear line of defense after numerous losses in the South Pacific. Satô had a very long career in the army, graduating from the Army Academy in 1917 and serving on active duty until the end of the war in 1945. He was a strong advocate of military influence on the government and later the war. Also he was a trusted subordinate of Tôjô's. After the war he was convicted as a Class A war criminal of "the overall conspiracy" and of waging war against China, the United States, the British Commonwealth, and the Netherlands. He was acquitted of "ordering, authorizing or permitting atrocities" and "disregard of duty to secure observance of and prevent breaches of Laws of War." He was sentenced to life imprisonment.[47] After the San Francisco Peace Treaty in 1952, convicted Class A criminals were gradually released from prison. Satô was the last to be released, on March 30, 1956. The account below is from Satô's war memoirs published in 1966.[48]

After the battle for Guadalcanal, August 1942 to February 1943, the defeated Japanese withdrew but no new line of defense was defined. Some time in July 1943, Tôjô demanded that Satô consult the army general staff and that they should clearly establish a new line of defense. The book manuscript places this exchange on July 8, 1943.[49] In the book Satô tells Tôjô that due to the leapfrog tactics of the enemy this was impossible. No one knew where or when the next landing would come. "This one cannot exactly say. Even the Army General Staff, even the Navy General Staff they cannot say where the enemy can be checked; also they cannot make a plan for a counter offensive." Tôjô was not at all satisfied with this answer. He told Satô, "The emperor is extremely worried about this." Satô then asked, "Did the emperor even say something about it?" Tôjô answered,

> Actually the emperor said something to the effect, "Imperial Forces, Imperial Forces" [kôgun], while saying this, when the enemy makes a landing then inevitably we are defeated. An enemy landing has not been smashed even once. Can't we crush an enemy landing somewhere? I frequently ask Nagano [Navy General Staff Chief] and also Sugiyama [Army General Staff Chief] but it seems nothing at all can be done! Then what will become of the war!?[50]

In the manuscript Tôjô says further, "This is operations. Since it is a command matter, [the emperor] should address this to Imperial Headquarters. [The emperor] requested information a number of times but neither Nagano nor Sugiyama answered."[51]

Satô depicts Tôjô in his book as being quite disconcerted due to the Emperor's worries. He says that up to this time he had never heard Tôjô say that something must be done because the Emperor said so. "In so doing [Tôjô] was making the emperor responsible; [yet he said this] also because he thought he should take responsibility for giving advice [hohitsu]. However, he conveyed something in the above way this one time only. Of course [Tôjô] denied these were the exact words of the emperor."[52] Following this discussion the army and navy conducted studies in various departments about where this defense line should be established. Finally, on September 25, 1943, in a liaison conference the "absolute national defense perimeter" was defined. On September 30, an Imperial Conference was held in which this perimeter was officially decided.

The Emperor was indeed extensively informed about developments in the Pacific and elsewhere. Various sources (see below) include numerous statements showing that in mid-1943 he was already extremely anxious due to the many defeats in the Pacific area. However, in the STJR from June 26 to August 4, 1943, while there are many notations about the war situation in the Pacific and on one occasion Emperor Hirohito again urged the army and navy to closely cooperate and crush the next amphibious landing, there is no sign that the Emperor was alarmed.[53] Nor is there any indication that his urgings were heeded.

According to another authoritative work, on the day when Tôjô reportedly said the above to Satô, July 8, 1943, Hirohito had an audience with Army Chief of Staff Sugiyama about the "war situation." "In limited areas there is much fighting but isn't there somewhere we can go on the offensive? This is mainly a navy matter." Sugiyama answered, citing a draft prepared for the audience on the retaking of Rendova, one of the Solomon Islands in the Pacific: "However you look at it the army does not have the transport. If we had the transport, we could do as you say. This follows what the area commander has said. If previously we had prepared a great move etc. [...] In the end according to the area commander this cannot be done." The Emperor nodded his head and said, "The air force has been greatly weakened, including the army's, can't we quickly strengthen it?" Sugiyama answers that in the new situation the planes must be prepared and somehow shipped or flown out to where they are needed. The Emperor said that things must be done quickly and Sugiyama replied that the army was doing so but that the navy needed to expedite matters. Finally the last noted statement by the Emperor during this audience is a wish but not a command: "Can't we strike them somehow." It appears that the Emperor was reduced to pleading to the army chief of staff to somehow do something. Hardly a heavyweight "supreme commander." This exchange may be seen in a published source, the *Shôwa Tennô Hatsugen Kiroku Shûsei* (Collected Records of Remarks by the Shôwa Emperor), but the STJR only notes an audience with Sugiyama and provides no information about what was said.[54] In the STJR there are many similar notations—an audience with someone is recorded but not what transpired. This format is much the same as many notations in the *Kido Kôichi Diary*.

Army–Navy Combined Command

During this time, from the first ten days of August to the end of October 1943, apart from the above issue, an extensive plan for combining the army and navy commands was being considered by both. The proposal was drawn up by two middle-ranking officers from the army and navy, and presented to their superiors in their respective general staffs. It moved up the chain of command and was eventually presented independently to the respective chiefs of staff. Some in the Operations Department, Navy General Staff believed that without combining the command structures the war probably could not be won. Their thinking, however, was divided into two facets, revealing once again mistrust and unrealistic aspirations. It was important that the navy take over command of all air forces, but they were not so keen on a combined general staff. Navy leaders were convinced that the former was necessary to win the war in the Pacific. (But they knew that it was very unlikely the army would agree to such a move.) Moreover, an unwritten rule stipulated that they could not intimate that the war could be lost, and if lost there was no one among the navy leaders who was willing, as chief of a combined command, to shoulder the army's part of the blame for the defeat. Also the navy balked at forming a combined command because they feared the navy would be "swallowed up" by the egotistical army. Considering their relative political influence at the time, this was not an unrealistic fear. Finally, the plan was not enacted and Suzuki Tamon asserts that the respective services' strategies for winning the war were basically antagonistic. Navy strategy called for an "early decisive battle" (*sôki kessen*) but the army projected a "protracted war" (*jikyûsen*). Each insisted that their particular strategy was the only way to win and both refused to compromise.[55] Later in March 1944, Tôjô—who was then prime minister, army minister, and army chief of staff—proposed a combined army–navy command under something like a chairman of the army and navy staffs (*bakuryô sôchô*) with the respective chiefs of staff subordinate to this official. Mainly due to navy opposition this also came to naught[56] and army–navy discord continued up to the very end of the war.

Even planning for the defense of the home islands was marked by disagreements between the two services, despite the Emperor's attempts to break this gridlock. A memorandum made in the Imperial Headquarters Army Department on February 20, 1945 noted among other things that there was still disagreement about uniting the army and navy and that the navy feared it.[57] On March 1 and 2 the Emperor spoke with Kido Kôichi and some members of the imperial family about this problem. On March 3, there was again an army–navy conference on uniting their efforts, which came to nothing. Therein the army also called for changing the cabinet administrative system. That afternoon the Emperor once again addressed the army and navy ministers calling on them to (1) unite the army and navy; (2) unite the army and navy ministries; (3) establish an air force; and (4) unite the ship and weapons management headquarters. Imperial Navy Minister Yonai Mitsumasa replied that the army and navy might be placed at parity under a supreme commander (*daigensui*), but the other three points were not under consideration. Imperial Army Minister Sugiyama Hajime replied similarly: point one seems necessary, but the latter three points involved complicated matters in need of serious study. During March these issues were discussed for a number of days among army and navy leaders, but nothing was done. The leader of the *nation*, the Emperor, urged, even ordered, that the army and navy commands be united, but *state*, military, leaders ignored him. Later the war situation worsened further and on May 26, 1945 the Imperial Navy Ministry building was destroyed during an American bombing raid. Nevertheless, the navy refused a proposal by the army to unite their ministries in one building. One of the editors of a volume covering these events commented long after the war, "In this way, finally the army–navy integration problem meant that even the unification of the supreme command at one place of work was not realized, and the army and navy continued their fateful mutual opposition till their final extinction."[58]

As Yamada and Matsuno, Suzuki, and even the STJR show, the Emperor received a vast array of information about military operations and administration. The former two present reports to the throne in addition to the above, for example at the end of May 1942, reports about the newly occupied areas early in the Pacific War and detailed estimates of military forces in the United States, England, and other places were provided to the Emperor. Later Emperor Hirohito received detailed information on the varying opinions of military leaders in Tokyo concerning the battles for Guadalcanal, Saipan, and in the Marianas, among others. The Emperor was privy to the progress of the war, and the ongoing struggles not only between the army and navy but also within the respective services. Nevertheless, these records of imperial audiences do not show Hirohito ordering and achieving a modus vivendi between the army and navy, or defusing the factional infighting in the respective services. Likewise he did not unilaterally decide military policies and order operations.[59]

Thus the available sources show that the Emperor was well aware of army–navy disunity and the problems it was causing, but despite being the supreme commander of the army and navy according to the Meiji Constitution, he was unable to order his commanders to unite their services to better carry out the war. Here and in numerous other instances Imperial Navy leaders were the ones who blocked the integration of the command structures desired by the Emperor. Perhaps this was due to the fact that especially after defeats in the Philippine/Mariana Seas and the fall of Saipan the army was, relatively, even more strong and influential than the navy.

Yet, apparently within the navy itself communication was lacking at times. When Rear Admiral Nakazawa was appointed head of the First (Operations) Department of the Imperial Navy General Staff in June 1943 his predecessor only told him "Since you know well what the situation is, I have nothing special to relate. As for the future, do what you think best." Nakazawa was given no written materials, which greatly surprised him. Later he mentioned the situation to Admiral Shimada Shigetarô (1883–1976), and Shimada told him that when he was appointed navy minister in October 1941 he received no reports from his predecessor.[60] Here is a former member of the Imperial Navy General Staff lamenting the lack of communication in his own command. This was confirmed by the navy minister who became concomitantly chief of staff in 1944. Moreover, the authors of the volumes in the War History Series, the source for much of this information, were mainly one-time members of the Imperial Army and Navy. Usually former members of the respective services worked on the volumes concerning their erstwhile organizations. It is doubtful that they would have unfairly presented their earlier services in a negative light. Of course, two incidents of this sort among very many changes of command among high-ranking officers in the Imperial Navy do not make for a lost war, but they indicate together with other problems cited that they appear to have had homemade communication deficits.

More Imperial Army and Navy dissension

Disagreements between the army and navy ran deep, and they were not confined to policy matters in Tokyo. Lt. (at that time Major) General Miyazaki Shûichi wrote in March 1943, before the above events and after Japanese forces withdrew from Guadalcanal one month earlier, some "Summary Remarks Relating to Operations in General – South Pacific Area Operations Peculiarities and Lessons Learned."[61] He was especially concerned with the defeat on Guadalcanal, where he served as chief of staff of the 17th Army from October 1942 until withdrawal in February 1943. He emphasizes the lack of coordination between the army and navy, in particular their respective air corps. Cooperation, he says, is essential to regain control of the air, and control of the air is essential for winning the war. The Military History Society editors who prepared Miyazaki's Diary for publication conclude, "Finally, the problem of the unification of commands and subsequently control of the air, together, could not be improved up to the end of the war. This was a major reason why the Greater East Asia War ended in defeat."[62]

Not everyone was of the same opinion. After the war a long-time head of the Imperial Navy Operations Department, Vice-Admiral Nakazawa Tasuku, wrote that he never thought there was feuding between the army and navy. And one of the editors of his postwar recollections, former Rear Admiral Yamamoto Chikao (1896–1980), agreed, citing numerous occasions of cooperation between the two, including the battle for Saipan.[63] However, Nakazawa in the same memoirs then lists a number of points about which the army and navy disagreed. This includes the military strength of the navy and also basic orientations, especially the navy's policy of avoiding involvement in politics, while the army actively did the opposite. (Contrary to Nakazawa's assumptions, Teshima Yasunobu concludes in a recent work [2015] that during the 1930s in response to the army's increased meddling in politics the navy too became more active. Due to the navy's weakness in comparison to the army though, navy leaders were inclined to be more rigid [and less effective] than the army.[64])

Dissension between former members of the Imperial Army and Navy continued long after the war. In his book Satô says many times that a consensus was achieved between the army and navy as confirmed on September 25, 1943, in the liaison conference on the "absolute national defense perimeter" even though it was not. Also he criticizes the navy at the same time for its apparent lack of a clear definition about where this line of defense should be drawn and what it should be called.[65] However, the recollections of Vice-Admiral Nakazawa Tasuku say that this claim by Satô is based on incorrect suppositions about navy policies.

> That the navy was not enthusiastic about the establishment of the perimeter, as claimed by Mr. Satô Kenryô in his postwar recollections, is the speculation of a third party uninformed about the real intentions of those involved. The navy for a long time had planned offensive operations within this framework. However, at the time of the opening of the Greater East Asia War those concerned with such plans ignored years of preliminary research, plunged ahead, and excessively expanded the operations area. The chance of engaging in erroneous operations or falling into a situation that was impossible to control became acute.
>
> The opportune time was already lost. Our sea transport lines had been destroyed by the enemy, ship losses greatly increased, and transporting arms and materials was not easy. Moreover, since the enemy's counteroffensive came from the northern shore of New Guinea and proceeded in the direction of the Philippines our general staff insisted that the defense of this area should take priority. Therefore, the defense of the Marianas and West Caroline Islands had to be delayed.
>
> If the defense of the Mariana area had begun previously and sea transport had proceeded as desired, this area would have been strengthened about half a year earlier and we would have been able to counter the enemy offensive that came in June 1944. Then the miserable defeat probably would not have happened.[66]

While army (Satô) and navy (Nakazawa) interpretations about why and where the "absolute defense perimeter" was established, and the consequences of it, are not contrary they differ greatly. Also, as seen above, Sugiyama told the Emperor on July 8 that the problems in the South Pacific were due to problems within the navy. Nakazawa did not deny these problems but placed them on the doorstep of earlier planners in the army as well as the navy. Planning was strongly influenced by the army, and the navy was somehow supposed to overcome the problems enumerated by the army, for example Sugiyama above.[67]

Moreover, Nakazawa's recollection of the initiation of plans for an absolute defense perimeter differs somewhat from the above discussion. He says that when he was appointed head of the Operations Department of the Navy General Staff on June 15, 1943, the advance of enemy forces in the Pacific had reached a critical stage. He insisted then that the army and navy deliberate on:

> Establishing a sea sector where control of the sea and control of the air must absolutely be secured. As a result [...] at an Imperial Conference on 30 September 1943 a "greater area of war control that henceforth should be maintained" and a "policy concerning immediate urgent measures for the greater area of war control that henceforth should be maintained" was decided.[68]

Later he says, similar to the above statement, that it was decided at the end of September 1943 that Saipan should be the strong point of this perimeter. However, due to the intense counteroffensive of the enemy in the Solomon and Marshall Islands and a drastic decrease in sea transport possibilities, the rapid build up of fortifications on Saipan became impossible.[69]

Preludes to Saipan's fall

The above is a brief account of specific events in 1943 and 1944 pertinent to the fall of Saipan and several of the important sources currently used to evaluate them. Examining further the statements by the Emperor together with the notes made at Imperial Headquarters shows in detail the nature of the deliberations and Hirohito's influence on them. After the establishment of the "absolute national defense perimeter" and prior to the fighting in the Marianas, Emperor Hirohito commented on a number of ongoing military operations, for example in Burma and China. His comments show he was informed about military campaigns but not thoroughly so. According to the Collected Records of Remarks by the Shôwa Emperor,[70] he first mentioned the expected US assaults in the Marianas on June 13, 1944, two days before the American invasion of Saipan. However, in the Actual Record of the Shôwa Emperor an audience with the navy chief of staff is noted but not Saipan. Saipan is first mentioned in this record on June 15, during a discussion with Kido. Kido reported simply that the US forces had landed. If the Emperor said anything it is not noted.[71]

In the Collected Records of Remarks by the Shôwa Emperor, however, the Emperor's interest in operations in the Marianas is clearly indicated on June 13: "The resolve surrounding the A-go operation [see below] is indeed very good. Since this is a very important operation on which the fate of the nation hangs, I desire results like those of the Battle of the Sea of Japan. See to the encouragement of the operational forces."[72]

This he said to Admiral Shimada, chief of the Navy General Staff. Shimada replied he would convey this message immediately to the Combined Fleet. The Battle of the Sea of Japan is the famous engagement in May 1905 during the Russo-Japan War in which Admiral Tôgô Heihachirô (1848–1934) ambushed the Russian Baltic Fleet in the Straits of Tsushima and destroyed two-thirds of it. The meaning of Hirohito's remarks is unmistakable: a decisive victory was vital to Imperial Japan's future existence.

The Emperor mentioned the Mariana action again the next day, June 14, to Tôjô during an audience in the latter's capacity as chief of the Army General Staff. (He was also army minister, munitions minister, and prime minister at the time.) "In the first engagements our officers and men are putting up a good fight. However, in comparison to the enemy, are not our forces (*heiryoku*) insufficient? If somehow we lose Saipan, since we can then expect frequent air raids even on Tokyo, the island must be saved at all costs."

Tôjô replied, "[With the army] joining in the navy's operations, we believe we can thwart the Americans' invasion plans. Even now the Combined Fleet is positioning to prepare a decisive battle. The army and navy are cooperating very closely and we will smash the American forces. We expect to crush their planned assault."[73]

Despite Tôjô's reassurances the Emperor remained skeptical. On June 16, he again questioned Tôjô about the adequacy of Japan's forces. "Saipan: Does not the enemy have 2 D[ivisions] of forces? Are not our forces insufficient? Why are [our forces] so light?" If an answer was given it is not noted.[74] Hirohito's judgment was probably based on the size of a division in the Imperial Army, approximately 20,000 men. During the Second World War a US division, similar to those of the Japanese, varied according to the task but was about 15,000 men. In fact the US landed approximately 71,000 troops on Saipan. The Japanese had about 30,000 defenders on the island.

During this same time the amount of information found in the Secret War Journal of the Imperial Headquarters, Army Department War Leadership Group[75] is prodigious but references to the Emperor seem to have been avoided. It includes no notices about audiences with the Emperor concerning the battle for Saipan. There are numerous notations about the operation itself as well as in China and Burma, and the reports coming out of both Burma and China were better than those about the Marianas. Saipan was not initially of great concern. Events in Europe are also noted, for example the German use of a new weapon (the V-1). Whether it is an "unmanned aircraft" (*mujin hikôki*) or a "huge rocket catapult" (*dairoketto ishiyumi*) was unclear. Reportedly it caused a great tumult in England.[76] On June 8, 1944, there are comments about the Allied landings in northern France, southern France, and Norway (Normandy?). Germany is thought to be distorting Japan's relation with the Soviet Union. There is an optimistic assumption that proved to be incorrect: "For the time being, in the Pacific area it appears there will be a stagnation of aggressive war operations. But politically one should anticipate air raids on the home islands." Also, there are some interesting terse evaluations of US military leaders in the Pacific as well as the army chief of staff in Washington:

> MacArthur: astute (*eibin*)
> Nimitz: decisive action following careful deliberation (*jukuryo dankô*)
> Halsey: virile, tough (*seikan*)
> Marshall: thoughtful, meticulous; enjoys colleagues confidence (*shiryo shûmitsu; jinbô ari*)[77]

Saipan invaded

The situation on Saipan was already heating up and the following is a day-by-day account of this battle from a Japanese army perspective:

> June 11: large-scale air raids on Saipan are noted. The planes "appear to have come from the enemy mobile force. The extent of damage is unknown. Also, one can expect raids on Palau and Guam."[78]

> June 12, 13: air raids on Saipan. On the latter date 400 planes are reported, of which thirty were downed. Reinforcements, two battleships and a submarine unit are to be sent. On June 13, same source, Japan's losses at sea since the beginning of the war are estimated: 1942: 2,460; 1943: 9,939; to mid-1944: 17,775; total: 30,374 sailors and soldiers.

> June 14 (numerous notations): among others there is information about troop strength, and supplies and provisions for them in Burma, the mid Pacific, northern Australia, and northeast areas. Matsuwajima in the Kurile Island Chain was bombarded, etc. Also "some 20 or more ships are bombarding Saipan, and we strongly expect an invasion tonight or tomorrow morning.

The insolent maneuvers of the enemy will be countered by the Imperial Navy to be sure, and the army with eager enthusiasm fully expects to destroy (the enemy)."[79]

June 15: "04:50 the enemy began landing on Saipan. There are 40–50 transport ships, an estimated one division. Our (army) forces stationed on Saipan come to 12 battalions, and the navy one battalion. The 31st Army Command is there. Certainly this will be the Tennôzan (decisive battle) of the Pacific area. In this great decisive battle we pray for and fully expect the highest fighting spirit and bravery from the soldiers in the field."[80]

This army record clearly indicates that extensive information about ongoing operations was available. The extent to which the Emperor was privy to this information is, however, unclear.

In the Tôjô Cabinet Prime Minister's Secret Record there is a note saying Tôjô received a report about Saipan from Head of the 2nd Department Arisue (Col., later Major, posthumously Lt. General Arisue Yadoru), Imperial Headquarters, Army, but its content is not noted. In the STJR the Emperor stated on June 18 that Saipan must be saved. Tôjô later said to his secretaries, "An announcement should be made openly: Saipan etc. are not at risk."[81] This was noted by one of Tôjô's secretaries, Col. Akamatsu Sadao on June 19, together with the failure of operation A-go. Akamatsu commented that this defeat made the Saipan situation difficult, but the failure of operation A-go was announced the next day, as stipulated by Tôjô.[82] Operation A-go was the navy's plan for a large counter offensive in the mid Pacific, Philippines, and northern Australia. Reinforcing Saipan was dependent on its success. In the Tôjô Cabinet Prime Minister's Secret Record operation A-go is not mentioned and the impression is that Tôjô is saying, after Hirohito's admonition, Saipan has been invaded but there is no danger. This can be announced without reservation. However, in the Akamatsu Diary Tôjô's statement seems to have to do with both the failure of operation A-go, a great defeat for the navy, and the invasion of Saipan. Meaning: the former will not adversely affect Japan's defense of Saipan, and the failure of operation A-go should be announced. Rather different emphases.

Political maneuvering in Tokyo

At the same time another dimension to the machinations in Tokyo emerged. The discussions in Tokyo related in the diary of Rear Admiral Takagi Sôkichi (1893–1979) bring to light the discord in the navy general staff and Navy Ministry at the time of the actions in the Philippine/Mariana Seas and on

Saipan. The long-standing dissatisfaction with Tôjô and especially Admiral Shimada surfaced. Many officers in the navy general staff were exasperated because they felt Shimada did not properly represent the navy's interests. Some of these officers came to the conclusion that Shimada would never relinquish his position as navy minister of his own accord. Thus it may be necessary to employ violence (*bôryoku*) to remove him. Perhaps an auto accident involving a number of vehicles would injure him seriously enough so he would have to resign. But the extremity of the idea greatly surprised and displeased Prince Konoe, among others. Also the plan, even if a success, was unlikely to bring about any positive results due to factionalism within each service as well as the debilitating rivalry between them.[83]

Nevertheless, in Tokyo power intrigues continued unabated. Rear Admiral Takagi's diary relates that on June 16 Admiral Okada Keisuke (1868–1952) had a discussion with Chief of Staff and Navy Minister Shimada about the war situation and the possibility that Shimada should step down as navy minister. Shimada lamented the burden of the simultaneous appointments but eventually declined because there was no one appropriate to appoint as navy minister. Okada disagreed and made several suggestions, including Admirals Yonai Mitsumasa and Suetsugu Nobumasa (1880–1944), but Shimada disagreed saying it would be difficult to return them to active duty. Takagi notes this was not necessarily so. Moreover, Shimada asserted, resigning as navy minister might bring down the Tôjô Cabinet, which was undesirable.[84]

At the time the end results of the Philippine/Mariana Sea battle (Operation A-go) and the fighting on Saipan were not known in Tokyo. But if both turned out to be total defeats, Takagi feared this would cause a great tumult (*daikonran*) in the navy. As it turned out, opposition within the navy to Shimada as navy minister was an important factor in the fall of the Tôjô Cabinet. Wishing to reform from within, many ranking officers strove to remove Shimada as an obstacle to reform. Finally the elder statesmen withdrew their support for Tôjô, and this in addition to opposition by many naval leaders contributed to the fall of the cabinet, though this was not their primary objective.[85]

Different records, different information

During this time, and during most of the war, different records contain different information about the same events depending on their respective priorities. For example, up until the practical abandonment of Saipan on June 25, there is no mention in the Tôjô Cabinet Prime Minister's Secret Record or Col. Akamatsu's

Secret Diary of an audience with the Emperor. But we know from other sources, for instance the Collected Records of Remarks by the Shôwa Emperor, there were in fact a number of audiences in which this and other military matters were discussed. Also, the only notation in the Imperial Headquarters Army Record about an audience is on June 17. In the note Lord Keeper of the Privy Seal Kido Kôichi reported an air raid in Kyushu. While the above Imperial Headquarters Army Record reports telling the Emperor of the air raid, Kido's diary only notes an audience. He asked the chief aide-de-camp about the air raid in northern Kyushu on June 16, and apparently reported it to the Emperor the following day. (Kido had audiences with the Emperor almost every day at this time, including June 16 and 17. What was discussed during these particular audiences is not noted, as is often the case in Kido's diary.[86]) The Imperial Headquarters Army Record presents the Emperor in a positive light, reporting that he said air defenses in Kyushu should be thorough-going, the killed and wounded taken care of, as would be expected of any ruler. For information reported to the Emperor about Saipan one must look elsewhere.

The reasons why the Imperial Headquarters Army Record and the two above military sources did not note other audiences concerning certain war operations overseas, which we know from other sources took place, are to date unknown. One might speculate that this sort of information was intentionally omitted in order to protect the Emperor. Responsible military authorities appear to have purposely left out references to the Emperor in records about the worsening war situation, implying he could not be held responsible for what was unknown to him. More recently, as noted previously, several authors have come to think that the general staffs purposely lied to the Emperor concealing their great losses.[87] Whether or not the Emperor was appropriately informed, the Imperial Headquarters Army Record does show that in the Pacific things got worse, not better.

> June 16, Saipan: "We now estimate the enemy troop strength at two divisions."[88]
>
> June 18: "Today the Saipan garrison is severely beleaguered by the enemy, and we received a report that the division commander and his staff died in battle, unconfirmed. In line with the above, in order to save Saipan at all costs it will be strengthened with two divisions, and the immediate implementation of operation A-go will be ordered."[89]

Operation A-go, as noted above, was the navy's plan for a large counter-offensive in the mid Pacific that failed. The plan was fixed on June 15, but previously on June 13 the navy seemed to have misgivings about its possible success.[90]

Unrelated to these doubts, but clearly related to the failure of the Imperial Navy offensive, US Naval Intelligence with the help of some Filipino guerrillas acquired the plan before its implementation. It was translated and transmitted to the commander of the US 5th Fleet.[91] This led to the decimation of the Japanese forces, especially their aircraft carriers and air corps on June 19, as the Combined Fleet steamed toward Saipan.

Secret codes and the Imperial Navy and Army

The Imperial Navy was especially naïve and negligent with regard to the possibility that their secret codes had been compromised. More than one year earlier the commander of the Combined Fleet, Admiral Yamamoto Isoroku, had been ambushed and killed during a flight on an inspection tour to the forward areas. This was made possible by the irresponsible radio communication of his flight schedule to these areas that was intercepted by US forces. After the fact this possibility occurred to the Navy High Command. Officials in Tokyo as well as in the Southeast Pacific made investigations. Doubts and speculation remained: a chance happening, compromised secret codes, espionage, etc. But both authorities reached the conclusion that their codes were unbreakable and the air attack on Yamamoto's group must have been an unplanned coincidence.[92] This same sort of negligence contributed to the later debacle in the Philippine/Mariana Seas.

After the war, a report about the earlier American ambush of Yamamoto was published in the Japanese *Asahi Newspaper* on September 14, 1945.[93] Nevertheless, with respect to the battle for Saipan and the naval engagements in the Philippine/Mariana Seas, even in the 1960s former members of the Imperial Army appear not to have known how extensively their military communications were compromised.[94] Returning to that time, in the Actual Record of the Shôwa Emperor and the Collected Records of Remarks by the Shôwa Emperor, reports to Hirohito about possible leaks in secret military communications that might jeopardize operations are not noted. It is noteworthy that compromised codes are treated in the Secret War Journal of the Imperial Headquarters, Army Department War Leadership Group as seen above but not in the two records of statements made by the Emperor at this time compiled by persons not associated with the military.[95] Perhaps the Emperor was not informed of this problem, or if he was he had nothing to say. As the leader of the nation a critic was not to be expected, and there was nothing for him to sanction.

Saipan, the veiled end (day-by-day account continued)

June 19: the Secret War Journal notes regarding Operation A-go: "The Imperial Navy will engage in a great air battle on which hangs the fate of the Navy." The army commentator "prays that in the worst case, the result is a draw."

June 20: On the previous day the Japanese fleet suffered the loss of 300 planes. Though the situation is unclear in Tokyo, it appears that the fleet has withdrawn. A dark mood enveloped the Imperial Headquarters.[96]

However, according to the Actual Record of the Shôwa Emperor the situation was viewed somewhat more positively in Tokyo:

At the Ogakumonjo [the Emperor's secondary school as crown prince where he often held audiences during the war] from 4.30 to 5.05 in the afternoon the emperor received a report on the war situation from Shimada Shigetarô Chief of the Navy General Staff. In this report from 4.45 the navy chief of staff explained that according to Imperial Headquarters, on the afternoon of 15 June the enemy advancing on Saipan came ashore on one corner of the island. Thereafter follow-up forces are being strengthened but the defending troops are fiercely battling them and causing them great losses. At the same time, our air forces are attacking continually the large enemy force that appeared in the Mariana Seas area, and since the 12th until today [the 20th] we have sunk one battleship, two cruisers, one destroyer, and one submarine. Also more than four aircraft carriers, two battleships, four cruisers, six transport ships, one ship of unidentified type have been damaged and more than 300 aircraft brought down. However our ships and aircraft have also suffered considerable losses. (Citing the Chamberlain's diary, the Valet's [*toneribito*] diary, the Military Adjutant's diary, Okei Kenichi Taisa's [Col.] diary, and the *Yomiuri Hôchi* [newspaper].)[97]

This shows simultaneously the detailed information about military operations the Emperor was receiving and the way it is reported in STJR—supported with references lacking specifics like page or chapter numbers. It is not mentioned, but other sources show that this so-called war situation report is quite optimistic, if not an outright fabrication. Despite the "considerable losses" noted, it did not give the Emperor a realistic view of Japan's situation after these battles. Of course one must distinguish between what we know now, what the Emperor might have known, and what he probably knew, i.e., appears in reports to him.

Senshi Sôsho, War History Series, volume 75, *Daihon'ei Rikugunbu* (Imperial Headquarters, Army Department) volume 8, enumerates the same battle results as above, citing the *Asahi Newspaper*. By contrast the *US Navy Operations Yearly Journal* (*Beikoku Kaigun Sakusen Nenshi*) says the following:

Vis-à-vis Admiral R.A. Spruance's 5th Fleet, US ships damaged: 2 battleships, 2 aircraft carriers, 1 heavy cruiser. Japanese losses: over 300 aircraft, 2 aircraft carriers sunk. Against Vice-Admiral M.A. Mitscher's carrier task force in a battle lasting two days in the Philippine Sea the Japanese lost 395 carrier-based planes [92 percent], 31 seaplanes [72 percent], leaving 35 carrier-based planes and 12 seaplanes operational. Also an estimated 500 planes stationed on Guam were lost. US losses over the two days were 130 planes, 76 pilots and aircrew members.

The same work lists the total losses of the Imperial Navy Combined Fleet as follows:

> Most land based planes; of the 9 carriers in the engagements 3 large and medium carriers were sunk, 4 damaged with only 2 small carriers left undamaged. No battleships or cruisers were sunk and damage to them was light. But of the ca. 450 carrier-based planes about 400 were lost.

The American journal was obviously not available to the Japanese, but the source for this assessment appears to be the above-mentioned unpublished "Sanada Jôichirô Shôshô Nikki" (Major General Sanada Jôichirô Diary).[98] This meant relevant negative information was on hand but may not have been disseminated to all persons concerned. Also, as Vice-Admiral Nakazawa later noted the Combined Fleet had lost most of its fighting power. In a recent account Suzuki Tamon says that already in December 1943 at the battle of Bougainville the navy's task force carriers (*kidôbutai*) were temporarily incapacitated.[99] This appears then as a prelude to the Philippine/Mariana Seas losses, which sounded the death knell of the Imperial Navy. But this was not generally acknowledged then, and the extent of the Emperor's knowledge about the situation is open to question.

The Secret War Journal of the Imperial Headquarters, Army Department gives no exact figures but also says,

> June 21: During the previous night the Japanese fleet sustained considerable losses while withdrawing from the above engagement. "For the nation this is extremely regrettable [...] and we must study how to continue conducting the war."[100]

This is anything but optimistic and the commentary is not noted in STJR. Does this mean that the Emperor was left uninformed about these losses? Does no comment in STJR imply that the high command was withholding negative information? On the other hand, if indeed this evaluation was transmitted to the Emperor but not entered in this record, then this is an attempt now to paper over the Emperor's responsibility for continuing to support a hopeless war. The

Emperor probably did not have all of this information at hand, certainly not that from the *US Navy Operations Yearly Journal*, perhaps and perhaps not that in the Major General Sanada Jôichirô Diary, but the authors of STJR did. Unfortunately due to the sometimes slanted presentations in a number of sources it is often difficult to acquire reliable statistics and impossible to ascertain who knew what, when. Here one does see, however, that the Emperor was quite possibly ignored as state leader and commander-in-chief of the armed forces; or perhaps as leader of the nation since he had nothing to sanction nothing was reported to him.

The combat losses at sea meant that the navy could not offer assistance at Saipan. The navy could not harass the US landing fleet, and it could not support a convoy to reinforce the troops on Saipan. This was a disaster vis-à-vis maintaining the Japanese position on the island and others in the immediate area, especially Tinian and Guam.

> June 22: The army–navy conference, noted above, in which the army maintained the navy's plans to reinforce Saipan were unworkable, is not noted in the Secret War Journal Imperial Headquarters. However, in the Actual Record of the Shôwa Emperor the importance of Saipan is emphasized again, and there is a much more optimistic list of the Saipan battle results: Japanese losses were supposedly only one carrier, two supply ships, and 50 planes.[101]

> June 23: the Secret War Journal Imperial Headquarters, Army Department does record the new drastic situation:
>
> In view of the importance of Saipan, with the remaining aircraft carriers as the main force, mobilizing and gathering what ordinary aircraft there are, it appears [the navy] is determined to revive Plan A. Risking a waste of forces and tacitly ignoring the overwhelming power of the enemy fleet, within 10 days the cruel situation of Saipan could even engulf the main islands, the southwest and Taiwan. Even if the navy's resolve is not the best policy for the nation, now in the present situation it seems to be an inevitable course of action. The army has also grasped the essential nature of the mid Pacific for national defense, and not fallen into abstractions. [The army] will endeavor to lend adequate support.[102]

Saipan was lost, as at least members of the Imperial Army General Staff realized. In this record the above notation is followed by a long description of the situation in Imperial Headquarters as (state) leaders there deliberated on how best to deal with the new situation in the mid Pacific, and they created "a record for historians after we are dead and gone." For the nation's leader—the Emperor—more was at stake: he sought not just to remain well remembered in history, above all he had to preserve the "eternal imperial line" and this hallowed obligation guided his actions, and inaction.

Part 2. Imperial authority

Most mortals do not know exactly what role the Shôwa Emperor played in these and many other events during his reign. We have many details from primary sources and interpretations. The former are often disputed; most of the latter, up until quite recently, are heavily dependent on the ideological leanings of the interpreters.[103] Concerning the war years, some say the general staffs largely ignored the powerless Emperor, for example Reischauer and Hata.[104] Also, in the part of his autobiography on ending the war published in 1946, former Prime Minister Admiral Suzuki Kantarô explained how the Emperor was not involved in the political decision-making process. He sanctioned the government's decisions but this was a formality, part of a political process that he stood outside of and above.[105] Others take the opposite extreme: the Emperor unilaterally influenced and/or ordered most everything that happened, for example Yamada and Bix. (Note: Bix's book has been quoted often as an authority. Therefore it cannot be ignored and it is referenced where relevant throughout. At the same time, when referring to Bix's work his misinformation cannot be disregarded either. This is not a "Bix critique." Though not widely known, George Akita has already done this.[106]) Somewhere between these two poles some say the Emperor was informed of the transpiring events, but insofar as he influenced them it was only in the direction of achieving an early peace, for example, Large.[107] This seems to be the preconception too, which animated the compilers of the above Actual Record of the Shôwa Emperor.[108] More recently, Matsuda and Suzuki take a more discriminating stance saying that the Emperor participated in but did not dictate these political and military processes.[109]

As for Saipan and Hirohito's contributions to related military decisions, all of the above persons treat the fall of Saipan as a significant benchmark, denoting the impending defeat of Imperial Japan. Both army and navy losses in the battles in the Philippine/Mariana Seas and on Saipan were very high. And as noted above, therewith Japan was within range of US strategic bombers. Although the Emperor's participation in and influence on these events is presented in very different ways, in my opinion, evidence from personal diaries of persons near him during the war and internal commentaries by members of the army and navy general staffs indicate he at times actively participated in the decision-making processes surrounding these operations but did not dictate them. Much more often he was called on to sanction plans already made, or carried out. Neither of these undertakings made the Shôwa Emperor a war criminal who was never brought to justice.

Independence of supreme command

Underlying the relationship between the Emperor and his military leaders was an important principle, the "independence of supreme command" (*tôsuiken dokuritsu*). The army and navy general staffs bore sole responsibility for planning and carrying out war operations. The cabinet, including the prime minister, and the army and navy ministers could not meddle in this process. It was a jealously guarded preserve. (The respective army and navy ministries were responsible for political-administrative affairs; the general staff carried out actual war preparations and operations.) Also very important, the army and navy were separate equal parties vis-à-vis war activities and they were not obliged to consult or cooperate with one another in planning strategy and operations. More often than not this meant they competed with and opposed each other. Edward Drea shows clearly that from beginning to end the Imperial Army was riven with factional infighting and that cooperation between the army and navy was almost nonexistent.[110]

Thus there was a civilian government that could not directly control the "military government," and within the latter there were two opposing instances competing, especially during the war for strategic priorities and materials.[111] Finally state leaders, the chiefs of the army and navy general staffs, and the army and navy ministers reported directly to the nations's leader—the Emperor—not to civilian authorities, and Hirohito did on a few occasions exercise his right to influence their activities. State and nation in tension. Elaborate formalities at court clearly indicated the Emperor's authority over his military advisors. But they usually were older and had much more experience than him. Accordingly the Emperor, with few exceptions, functioned more as a mediator negotiating with his senior generals and admirals than as an all-powerful monarch giving them orders. This constellation—cabinet, army, navy, emperor each attempting to determine war policy—had a devastating effect on Imperial Japan's war efforts during the Second World War.[112]

Imperial questions = commands (?)

Military and civilian advisors recorded many of the Emperor's suggestions and urgings, such as those above, but how did they respond to them? Were the Shôwa Emperor's musings, questions, and criticisms regarded as imperial orders that were obeyed accordingly? I think not. But Herbert Bix postulates, "Hirohito alone, however, could display leadership by using the technique of the substantive question that carried the force of a command."[113] Though he does not provide any sources for his assumption, Bix may be referring to numerous comments by the Emperor made in the form of "imperial questions" (*gokamon*). These were questions by the Emperor directed at those serving him, including military leaders. Sometimes they were in fact questions. Often they were used by Hirohito to express his opinion about specific issues and operations. For example, concerning air force reinforcements for New Guinea and Guadalcanal in 1942, on August 7, the Emperor "asked" about the advisability of doing so. And the army chief of staff said they had no such intentions. The Emperor commented similarly again on September 15, and November 5. After the third time, army leaders apparently felt they could no longer discount these "queries" and on November 6, it was decided that some Army Air Force planes would be dispatched to New Guinea and Rabaul. Thus the army evaded the Emperor's "commands" for three months, and in all cases these imperial commands were made in the form of rhetorical questions. That is, few if any officers in the army general staff responded to them as simple questions and at the same time they were not dealt with as imperial commands to be carried out forthwith.[114] As this example shows, while the Emperor was informed and did on occasion influence military operations, claims that he was a supreme commander whose imperial orders were immediately obeyed are unfounded.

Finally in mid-1945, during the battle for Okinawa, Yamada Akira says that the Emperor did indeed influence the military's actions there on a number of occasions, among others by offering imperial questions. For example, at the beginning of April 1945 Emperor Hirohito noted in an imperial audience that the increased kamikaze attacks by the air forces had inflicted significant damage on the enemy's ships. But what was the surface fleet doing? Then, suddenly on April 5, the battleship *Yamato* and six other ships sortied out against the enemy fleet. All were sunk on April 7, with a loss of 3,721 men. Also, on several other occasions pointed questions led to actions that ended in disaster. Yet, Yamada remarks that the Emperor did not seem to fully realize what the consequences of his imperial questions might be.[115] Were they indeed seen as imperial commands to be immediately obeyed that would not have been the case.

On at least one occasion the Emperor's inquiries led not to decisive action but to additional deception. After the naval battle in the Coral Sea, May 4–8, 1942, a preliminary report was presented to the Emperor on May 8. He was not entirely satisfied and said so directly. The engagement had been broken off, but if the enemy fleet was not pursued and better results were not forthcoming an imperial rescript of praise could not be issued. On May 12, a comprehensive battle report was presented to the Emperor. In it far more enemy ships were listed as sunk or damaged. The Emperor was satisfied and an Imperial Rescript of Praise was sent to Fleet Commander Admiral Yamamoto. The fact was, however, the improved battle results were invented for imperial consumption. The sea battle was not further pursued as desired by Hirohito; enemy losses were simply inflated on paper. This is one example of numerous similar deceptive reports to the Emperor by military leaders during the war.[116] The topic is pursued below.

One of Bix's frequently cited historians, Yamada Akira, quotes the exchange between the Emperor and Sugiyama on July 8, 1943, above. The Emperor did indeed ask detailed questions about various war theaters, which the army chief of staff was expected to answer, and the Emperor appears on occasion to be dissatisfied with the answers he received. Also Yamada cites the September 30, Imperial Conference where the "absolute national defense perimeter" was officially established and he includes a map showing where it was. He does not relate the information from Satô above about how this came to pass,[117] and since behind-the-scenes strategy discussions between the Emperor and Tôjô are not mentioned in these sources Yamada does not refer to them. Bix, however, is not put off by this lack of data:

> The emperor and Tôjô were determined to get Japan back on track strategically. They had re-examined their guidance of the war and agreed to contract all Pacific fronts while at the same time launching a new offensive in the eastern part of New Guinea. The new absolute defense line would be established well behind the line of contact with the enemy; there, at strategically selected points in rear areas, the army and navy and their air forces would reorganize, rebuild, concentrate, and prepare to defend aggressively with immediate counterattacks.[118]

Nevertheless, counter to Bix's theory of cooperation between the Emperor and Tôjô, which resulted in a new absolute defense line, as shown above, there was mutual consternation, according to Lt. General Satô, who took part in these events. This was due to dissension between the army and navy, related by Satô in his book,[119] which became part of a "plan," which was finally approved by the Emperor. The Emperor took part in these discussions, but his active role in drawing up this plan seems to be a figment of Bix's imagination. No source is given for the above cooperation and none known to me relates such. However in other sources, including one used by Bix, further information about the awkward compromise sanctioned on September 30, is to be found.

Daihon'ei Rikugunbu (Imperial Headquarters, Army Department) volume 7, shows the Emperor discussing operations on Rabaul and Truk, and asking about the merits of striking the enemy at sea. No orders are given. Later the differences between the army and navy are delineated: the army proposed a line of defense approximately 2,000 kilometers behind the Marshall–Gilbert Islands line desired by the navy. This gap proved to be unbridgeable. September 23, a "present operations guidance course" was outlined in "research before the emperor" (*gozen kenkyû*).[120] This guidance course including the lack of consensus between the army and navy was then discussed in a Supreme Command Liaison Conference on September 25, and sanctioned on September 30. Thus Emperor Hirohito sanctioned an "absolute national defense perimeter" including army–navy disunity in the fall of 1943, which presaged the defeats on Saipan, Tinian, and in the battles of the Philippine/Mariana Seas in the summer of 1944. If the Emperor's "substantive question(s) [...] carried the force of a command," why did his numerous questions and imperial decrees about dissension between the army and navy not bring it to an end? It was a very serious problem. Were the "all-powerful emperor's commands" so easily ignored? Perhaps military leaders, as state leaders, did not always take the Emperor, as spiritual leader of the nation, seriously when it came to executing military (state) plans.

Before this decision, on September 15, 1943, the Emperor received an extensive assessment of the enemy's (mainly US) strength of forces, probable future offensives and increases in fighting ships and aircraft over the next year and a half. This was accompanied by an estimate of Japan's fighting power and disposition of army and navy units. It also includes numerous avowals of close cooperation between the army and navy, while the enumerated particulars demonstrate the opposite. It shows the Japanese were already in a desperate situation and they knew it. For example, they estimated the United States alone would have about twelve aircraft carriers operating in the Pacific by the end of 1943, increasing to eighteen by the end of 1944. Opposing the Americans the Japanese had in September 1943 three aircraft carriers and about 2,500 warplanes stationed on the islands in the area, not all of which were operational.[121] This is revealed in a copy of the original handwritten report from Imperial Army records. It clearly shows these great material differences and the disagreement between the army and navy on establishing the defense line.[122] The obvious unfavorable alignment of power did not discourage the general staffs from continuing their feuding or stimulate a realistic approach to war policy-making. The Emperor was a part of this chaotic decision-making. He sanctioned decisions and this made them imperial orders, but he only rarely initiated or contradicted policies drawn up in the army and navy general staffs. Moreover, as seen here, he did not control the bureaucratic processes by which army and navy policies were conceived and could not resolve the attendant deficiencies and dissension in the military.

Emperor as supreme commander

The information and explanations prepared by army and navy officers for the Emperor show that he was extensively informed about operational matters including: (1) receiving orders sent out from the Imperial Headquarters, which he sanctioned, (2) having operations plans explained to him, and (3) being present for war-game exercises and research. Also he received various reports on the war situation: (1) daily reports made by the Imperial Army and Navy Supreme Commands (*tôsuibu*), (2) reports made after overseas investigation tours by army and navy general staff members, and (3) reports about the war situation by army commanders (*gunshireikan*) and also commanding officers in the fleet.[123] To be sure, theoretically the Emperor could have vetoed or mandated revisions of the orders and plans he received. The materials I have seen to date indicate he did this only on very rare occasions. It is very important that Hirohito ordered the army and navy on numerous occasions to cooperate, such as in the Imperial Conference on December 1, 1941, when opening a war with the United States and her allies was decided upon, and in the Imperial Conference on September 30, 1943, establishing the absolute national defense perimeter, but as shown in this chapter military leaders usually accorded these directives due respect and then overlooked them. After all, the Emperor was head of the nation but not on many occasions the state.

Moreover, there is yet another aspect concerning the Emperor's role as supreme commander that has until very recently received little or no attention. After comparing the Actual Record of the Shôwa Emperor with various other sources, Handô Kazutoshi and Hosaka Masayasu concluded that only a few months after the beginning of the Pacific War the general staffs began to falsify the results of war operations in reports to the throne. Reported damage and destruction to US forces as well as Japanese losses were so far from the actual results that one cannot consider them simple mistakes or "exaggerations." For example, the Chiefs of Staff knowingly lied to their emperor (*kyogi no hôkoku*) immediately after the "Doolittle Raids" in April 1942, claiming nine bombers were downed in Japan, while actually none were shot down over the home islands.[124] After the battle at Midway June 3–5, 1942, results were similarly falsified. According to the STJR on June 10, Hirohito was told that one Imperial Navy aircraft carrier was sunk, and one carrier and one cruiser seriously damaged. In fact four carriers were lost, but on July 6, two of these sunk carriers, the *Akagi* and *Hiryû*, appeared in the Combined Fleet Reorganization Plan presented to the Emperor by Navy Chief of Staff Nagano Osami (1880–1947).[125] The Emperor had to approve such reorganization plans, and in this case he did so thinking the navy had more aircraft carriers than they actually did.

However, in documents published following the war long before the STJR and the work containing the assertions by Handô and Hosaka, Kido Kôichi wrote at the end of March 1943, almost one year after the defeat at Midway, that the Emperor was indeed informed properly of these losses. Likewise he was promptly informed of the situation on Guadalcanal including "the success of the advance in a different direction," i.e., retreat from the island. The Emperor, Kido says, "was well informed about the entire war situation," and this is one of the main reason for the Emperor's discouragement in March 1943.[126] Yamada Akira in his prize-winning book *Daigensui Shôwa Tennô* (The Supreme Commander Shôwa Emperor) citing Kido accepts that the Emperor was properly informed of both defeats.[127] Clearly there is a lack of agreement about the expeditiousness, extent, and accuracy of the information the Emperor received from his military leaders.

Hosaka in his book about the STJR pursues the emperor deception theme at some length. Addressing reports to the throne from mid to end of 1943, he terms them "hollowed-out war directives." After citing reports to the throne by Army Chief of Staff Sugiyama Hajime and Navy Chief of Staff Nagano Osami about the military situation in Rabaul and New Guinea, Hosaka says that, "before the emperor they engaged in none other than prevarication." Moreover, the general staffs even "fictionalized war results" and then requested an imperial edict praising the commanders who supposedly had produced these positive results. This amounted to stabbing the Emperor in the back twice.[128] Also in late November and early December 1943 the battle results from Gilbert Island and Bougainville were similarly falsified.[129]

Later, the same can be seen in the initial reports in October 1944 about the success of the first "kamikaze attacks." Then the Emperor reportedly said, "So did it really have to come to this? But well done!" Handô's interpretation is that the first sentence is from "the Emperor" while the second is from the "Supreme Commander." Nation as distinct from State leader, though Handô does not use this terminology. Later, on November 13, after a report to the Emperor about the first kamikaze attack by an army unit, the Bandatai, the Emperor's words were especially fateful. The October 26 report about the first attack by the navy on October 25, showed one plane sinking one aircraft carrier. A report to the throne on October 28 lists even more enemy warships sunk and severely damaged. The army, wanting to improve on this, reported the sinking of a battleship and a supply ship and the Emperor issued "words of praise" (*gokashô*), which were transmitted to the front. On December 7 the Emperor issued more words of praise for army suicide attacks by another unit previously on Saipan. In fact, in the attack by the Bandatai no ships were sunk, but imperial praise constituted imperial approval and the attacks were increased and continued. This information comes from various sources, but during this time the notations in STJR have no specific content. They only say the Emperor granted audiences to the army and navy chiefs of staff. Or, for example, the new Navy Chief of Staff Oikawa Koshirô "reported on the attack by the Shinpû Tokubetsu Kôgekitai (Kamikaze Special Attack Unit) Shikishima etc." Specific results are not listed.[130] The Emperor's response to beginning suicide attacks is addressed in more detail in Chapter 2 on kamikaze tactics.

False reports to the Emperor continued throughout the war and obviously affected any efforts to influence decision-making about how or whether to carry on the conflict. They at least make the situation very complicated. In a conversation with Hosaka (February 12, 2016), he said military leaders lied to the Emperor but he had other unofficial sources of information and was not necessarily deceived. Therefore it is difficult now to ascertain what exactly Hirohito knew, assumed, and did not know.

Perceived and unperceived record discrepancies

Yet, another interpretation may be relevant. Many years earlier, even before the war in China or the attack on Pearl Harbor, there were discrepancies between what the Army General Staff reported outside army circles and actual events. For example, an army account of the famous Imperial Conference of September 6, 1941, when national policy vis-à-vis war with the United States and Great Britain was discussed extensively, may be seen in the Record of Imperial Conference Proceedings. This is found in the "Record of Answers to the Throne to Questions by the Emperor During Imperial Conferences." According to Tamura Yasuoki, if one looks at the original (*genbun*) one clearly sees additions to the handwritten record made by the Imperial Army General Staff. But if one looks at a printed version of the same record one cannot discern between what is true and what is false.[131] Col. Arisue Yadoru added notes in various places. He made these additions to the shorthand record after the conference. This edited version was later conveyed as historical fact.

Statements by the Emperor during this Imperial Conference found in Kido Kôichi's diary,[132] cited by many historians, were formulated in this way. After the Imperial Conference of September 16, Kido met with the Emperor's chief aide-de-camp and asked him about the conference on September 6. And Kido recorded after the fact "the emperor's remarks" the chief aide-de-camp gave him. They were "the emperor's remarks," including those added by Col. Arisue, transmitted by the Supreme Command through the chief aide-de-camp to Privy Seal Kido. Tamura calls this entire account "nothing more than a record of answers to questions by the emperor subsequently trumped up by the Supreme Command." And he demonstrates that the famous poem, "The Seas of the Four Directions" (*yomo no umi*), the Emperor reportedly recited in the September 6, Imperial Conference (showing him to favor peace) is not cited in extensive notes about this Imperial Conference left by Lt. General Tanaka Shinichi nor in the notes by Privy Council President Hara Yoshimichi and other high officials. But the poem is in the "historical record" produced by the Supreme Command, and noted ten days after the event with the date September 6, by Kido in his diary. Moreover, the Emperor did not remain silent during the conference but asked questions on eleven different occasions.[133]

This is Tamura's interpretation, one I have not seen anywhere else. One must ask, given that the Imperial Army was in favor of war, why would the Army General Staff add something indicating the Emperor was against it to the record? Perhaps to protect the Emperor if worse came to worse since even then many military leaders doubted that Japan could win such a war.[134]

Section 20 of the Imperial Army General Staff (War Operations Planning) produced Tamura's source of information, the Record of Answers to the Throne to Questions by the Emperor During Imperial Conferences.[135] It contains records of audiences with the Emperor, which Tamura asserts probably are in a similar record made by Imperial House officials of questions by the Shôwa Emperor and answers in Imperial Conferences but which has not been published. One might assume that in the army general staff record, here and later in the war, some high-ranking army officers willfully interpreted events on occasion to make themselves and the Emperor appear in a better light. But this was not something that was done systematically. Here, for example, it appears that Col. Arisue made such additions on only two occasions—after the Imperial Conference on September 6, and again after the Elder Statesmen Conference on November 29. The notes from the audience with the Emperor on November 3, 1941, concerning a possible war with the United States and England were not touched up in this manner. (But, Tamura does not note the report to the Emperor during this audience by the Navy Chief of Staff Nagano on the plan to attack Pearl Harbor found in the handwritten record of the Army General Staff.[136])

False reports to the Emperor and willful editing of records of imperial conferences and audiences undermined Hirohito's position as supreme commander and head of state, leader of the organization that plans and executes war activities. When he voiced periodically his opinions about concrete military plans or operations, he did so based at times on faulty information. Moreover, in the context of the Imperial era these falsifications constituted lèse-majesté vis-à-vis the emperor, the head of the imperial line = the nation, the entity legitimizing among other things war operations. Given the training and indoctrination these officers received, how did they justify, to themselves at least, this deceit? (Addressed below.) Finally, the occasional surreptitious doctoring of official reports and records greatly complicates the task of later historians dealing with these events. Of course it would be naïve to assume that "official records" are always written without prejudice but this factor needs to be taken into account more than it has in the past. These problems will be taken up again later.

More on the Emperor's authority

Disparate views abound. Yet when treating the events in 1944, which came about after the desultory establishment of the absolute defense perimeter in September 1943, the confusion that reigned in the military is not to be found in the works of many historians, including highly respected Japanese scholars such as Fujiwara Akira and Yamada Akira. Both pass over this real problem and maintain that the Emperor led Japan's war efforts in a decisive manner. Leaving aside for the moment army–navy disunity, both Fujiwara and Yamada report instances where the Emperor appears to have actively intervened in military planning and execution. Much later Suzuki describes and analyzes in great detail specific occurrences between 1943 and 1945, during which the Emperor was actively involved in discussing military planning. On occasion I agree with these historians, especially Suzuki. I do not maintain the Shôwa Emperor was simply a passive kibitzer sitting on the sidelines during the war. As Fujiwara points out, legally and traditionally the right of command was vested in the Emperor. One must remember, however, the legal situation was unimportant to many, and this "tradition" was partly a revival of an imagined ancient past and partly a modern invention, not a continuous historical convention. This was of course unknown to most Japanese and their allied enemies at the time.

The Emperor made his opinions known during the course of the war but, in addition to those noted above, other authoritative interpretations of the events and the Emperor's role in them vary. For example, Fujiwara Akira says the replacement of Sugiyama by Tôjô as army chief of staff in February 1944 and Tôjô's downfall in July of the same year demonstrate the absolute power of the Emperor,[137] but Stephen Large depicts their relation at this time as one of mutual dependency, with Tôjô wielding much power. Citing Otto Tolischus's opinion published in 1944 he even seems to excuse the Emperor since Tôjô "had become a virtual dictator [...] who had shorn the Emperor of the vast vestiges of power and had left him only in the role of a god who was in Tôjô's keeping."[138] Tolischus was sent to Japan by *The New York Times* in January 1941. Shortly after the attack on Pearl Harbor he was arrested and whilst in prison he was tortured. In 1942 he was sent back to the United States as part of a prisoner exchange. The source of his information about the relationship between Emperor Hirohito and Prime Minister Tôjô is unknown. Yet having once postulated and published Tolischus's speculations, they still hang in the air in discussions about the Emperor's real power and authority.

Later, Large steps back from this position saying, "The bonds between the Emperor and Tôjô were in fact unusually strong. Although the emperor very much wanted to end the war, he depended on Tôjô to manage the war effort until such time as peace became a realistic possibility. Similarly, Tôjô depended on the Emperor to support him against his critics."[139] This is a long way, on the one hand, from Tolischus's conjectures and, on the other, still further from the interpretations of Fujiwara and Yamada who place "managing the war effort" squarely on Hirohito's shoulders. In his work on the Emperor's War Responsibility, Inoue Kiyoshi calls Tôjô a dictator, who enjoyed the "absolute protection" of both the Emperor and Privy Seal Kido. Unlike Large but like Fujiwara and Yamada, he does not see the authority of the Emperor being thereby diluted. Rather it demonstrates the strength of imperial power and this support allowed Tôjô to become a dictator. Inoue cites records from both Kido and Sugiyama in support of his opinion.[140]

Which is to say, Large and Inoue, differing from Fujiwara, interpret similarly the relationship of the Emperor and Tôjô in February 1944, when Tôjô became, along with his offices of prime minister and army minister, chief of staff: both see mutual strong bonds between them. Likewise in July 1944, when Tôjô was obliged to resign. But with respect to the latter event they come to opposite conclusions about the power and authority of the Emperor. Large sees an extensive coterie of persons—for example, Privy Seal Kido, former Prime Minister Konoe, the Princes Takamatsu, Higashikuni, and Asaka—putting pressure on the Emperor to abandon Tôjô. The Emperor finally acted in accord with this advice. Inoue sees the influence flowing in the opposite direction: the Emperor enforces his all-powerful will through these people, especially the former two. Of course, Inoue did not have access to Large's thinking on the matter because his book was published some seventeen years after Inoue's. Large, however, did know of Inoue's work—it is noted in his bibliography, but apparently he thought it unimportant or irrelevant to his thesis about the Emperor.

Many years later the Actual Record of the Shôwa Emperor depicts Tôjô's appointment as army chief of staff less dramatically. On February 19, 1944 Tôjô proposed this change to Privy Seal Kido and later to the Emperor. Two days later Chief of Staff Sugiyama presented one of his usual reports to the throne and at the end of the audience he requested to be relieved of his office and duties. At the same time he voiced his misgivings about Tôjô taking this post in addition to his other ones. The Emperor replied that he too had his doubts but Tôjô quieted them saying he would exercise due caution. The next day Army Chief of Staff Sugiyama and Navy Chief of Staff Nagano were both relieved with an Imperial Letter thanking them for their services.[141] Tôjô then became prime minister, army minister, and army chief of staff. His trusted colleague Navy Minister Shimada Shigetarô was simultaneously appointed navy chief of staff, as requested by Tôjô. Perhaps the unembellished "objectivity" of the Actual Record here is intended to avert well-known assertions about the Emperor's willful influence on political and military affairs: according to this record the Emperor acted based on Tôjô's advice.

Suzuki has a rather different analysis of the situation. He asserts that the Emperor above all wanted to keep the ongoing disputes between the army and navy from bringing down the cabinet. (If one or both military ministers resigned from the cabinet and the respective service declined to provide someone as a new minister this would force substantial policy changes or resignation of the entire cabinet.) The Emperor thought a cabinet fall would have serious consequences for Japan's military and diplomatic adventures overseas. To prevent this he was inclined to accept Tôjô's proposal of combining the service ministers and chiefs of staff in a single person from each respective service.[142]

Hirohito's authority

In fact, in a display of imperial authority ten days prior to Tôjô's proposal, Hirohito demanded that the two chiefs of staff reach a compromise vis-à-vis the burning issue of the day—the allocation of warplanes. On February 9, he issued an imperial edict (*okotoba*) to the navy chief of staff telling him to settle the issue "in the spirit of mutual give-and-take" and avoid a breakdown of the cabinet, which would have adverse effects overseas.[143] Nevertheless, not everyone took this edict at face value. Capt. Fujii Shigeru in the Operations Department of the Navy General Staff attributed these sentiments to the Emperor's advisor Privy Seal Kido Kôichi. Those involved in these events, like later historians, interpreted imperial authority in various ways. Which is to say, the Emperor's authority, his position as head of the nation, was not questioned but his prerogatives as head of state, for example this imperial edict, were. This was a state matter. Obfuscating, might not the edict be glossed over because it originated from the Emperor's advisor, not the Emperor?

Eventually the warplanes issue was settled in a summit conference with the army and navy chiefs of staff and their respective ministers attending. There, Army Minister Tôjô cleverly said allocating more aluminum to the navy for aircraft would contravene the decision of the Imperial Conference in September 1943, which established the absolute national defense perimeter. Imperial conference decisions could not be changed and the issue was settled. Aluminum was allotted on a parity basis with the army relinquishing a small amount more to the navy. During these negotiations the sacrosanct authority of imperial conference decisions was important, but no one referred to the recent imperial edict.

Shortly later, not only Army Chief of Staff Sugiyama opposed breaking the long-standing tradition of a division of power in the army and navy—meaning one officer could not be simultaneously army/navy minister and chief of staff—but also Army Inspector General of Education Yamada Otozô and many other high-ranking army and naval officers also opposed this move. But Tôjô had convinced the Emperor of the necessity of combining the offices of army minister and army chief of staff in one person, himself. And he proposed the same for the navy in the person of Navy Minister Shimada. In this way the war could be better prosecuted. The Emperor decided accordingly, despite strong opposition.

From the Emperor's point of view this was desirable because in addition to avoiding the danger of a cabinet breakup, Tôjô and Shimada were known to cooperate well with one another. However, this change did not bring the army and navy to cooperate better. The navy continued to plan for an "early decisive battle," while the army planned a "protracted war." According to Suzuki Tamon these opposing strategies go back as far as the beginning of the Pacific War and even before.[144] Hirohito's reasons for supporting the break with tradition were well known but independent; obstinate army and navy planning were more important than the Emperor's intentions. Suzuki's presentation is worthy of note because, contrary to many of his predecessors, he analyzes the situation in terms of contemporary political and military issues independent of a moral frame of reference pointing to subsequent questions about war responsibility.

Moral history

This sort of moral substratum animates studies by Inoue, Yamada, Bix, and many others. They attempt to show that in the sense of postwar allegations of starting and pursuing an illegal war Emperor Hirohito was never brought to justice. He was never called to account for actively planning and directing Imperial Japan's War in the Pacific and Asia. Hirohito denied doing so until he died, and these authors seek to demonstrate the opposite. For example, in accord with Inoue's premise of an all-powerful emperor, with the establishment of Japan's "absolute national defense perimeter," Yamada Akira says the Emperor demanded that the navy not move "with all caution" into northeast New Guinea, but "aggressively": "Moving in with all caution is wrong, you must attack!" Clearly an order was intended. And two days later the apprehensive navy fliers in the area began their attacks.[145] Here in late 1943, as later in 1944 and 1945, the Emperor appears to have directly influenced matters. However while this order was obeyed, this was not always the case, and most "imperial orders" were the result of planning by the general staffs. State officials planned; the nation's leader sanctioned. Moralizing Hirohito's actions is uncalled for. As noted elsewhere, the Shôwa Emperor was part of a power-wielding elite which included top bureaucrats, military men, and sometimes politicians. The Emperor inevitably made his thoughts and concerns known to military and political leaders, but they were not always regarded as imperial orders then, and his actions are not always appropriately interpreted now given the sources presently at hand and the practical division of responsibilities.

As noted above, primary sources cited in the War History Series show Hirohito was given much information about military matters, and they clearly indicate his role, and lack thereof, in operational planning. These sources are important for understanding the distinction between imperial knowledge of versus influence on events. As emperor and head of the nation Hirohito was informed of military affairs. But since his position as head of state was restricted by politicians and military officers acting in his name, he did not consistently order the planning and execution of military actions. For example, at the beginning of volume 6 of the Imperial Headquarters, Navy Department, Combined Fleet compilation, the authors summarize the relation between the emperor, Imperial Headquarters, and commander of the Combined Fleet: The Meiji Constitution stipulates that the emperor is the supreme commander of all military forces, and the Commander of the Combined Fleet suitably advises him. However, in fact, since entering wartime conditions the responsibility and authority for planning and executing naval operations lay predominantly with the commander. Moreover, according to naval tradition the views of the commander of the Combined Fleet were considered to be of overbearing importance.[146] Seen in this way, the contradictory assertions by Large and Fujiwara outlined above are both *partly* correct. The Emperor was the supreme commander, but in a time of war he did not invariably command. Records available now show he was extensively informed about military matters, and he did voice his opinions on these matters. Yet these records also show that the Shôwa Emperor did not systematically plan and initiate military operations during the war. Establishment of the absolute defense perimeter in the fall of 1943 and the battle for Saipan in June–July 1944 exemplify this situation.

The Emperor: Retaking Saipan and imperial authority

As for Saipan, in Tokyo on June 16, Tôjô reported the successful landing of US troops there the previous day. For many military men this signaled the island's loss. Hirohito said it must be retaken and his urging received due attention. A detailed investigation of the feasibility of retaking the island was conducted by both services, and on June 19, the Emperor sanctioned the retake plans. (Yamada says the plan was completed provisionally on June 21.[147]) In any case, the navy had shortly before lost the resources necessary to carry out these plans in the battles of the Philippine/Mariana Seas. Discussions continued and on June 22, at a joint army–navy staff conference the army asserted that the navy's plans were unworkable. Finally on June 24, the army reached the conclusion that Saipan was lost and at the beginning of the next month the defending garrison there should die honorably (*gyokusai*).[148] Tôjô as army chief of staff and Shimada Shigetarô as navy chief of staff reported this conclusion to the Emperor. The Emperor was not pleased and called for a meeting of the Supreme Military Council (*gensuifu*), the field marshals, and the fleet admirals. They affirmed this conclusion on June 25, and Hirohito accepted it, reluctantly, or even under protest.[149] Here we have an informed emperor consulting with his senior military commanders and accepting their advice, however disinclined, not a leader exercising dictatorial powers.

In fact, similar to many other issues, it is still difficult to ascertain exactly what the Emperor's stance was. For example, the Supreme Military Council meeting of June 25, is also described in some detail in STJR. The conclusion that Saipan would be abandoned is clearly noted, but there is no indication that the Emperor opposed this decision and was unhappy with it. Also, after this date up to July 10, including July 8, when it was announced in Japan that the imperial forces collectively had met honorable deaths, there is no mention of Saipan in the STJR.[150] This is, however, typical. Throughout, the lack of specifics in the various notations in the Actual Record of the Shôwa Emperor leave much room for speculation about many events. Moreover, due to obfuscation by the prime minister and general staffs, and the unprofessional conduct of the latter, for example specious reports to the Emperor, one must often speculate about what Emperor Hirohito knew and advocated as well as to what extent he was (willfully) misled, or simply left uninformed.

Therefore, the extent of the Shôwa Emperor's authority as head of state and commander-in-chief of the armed forces in Imperial Japan is difficult to ascertain. It appears to have varied with the circumstances. At the present time there is no discernable pattern to the essential features of his authority or his manner of exercising it. One might speculate that Emperor Hirohito acted consistently only in that his first priority was always the promotion and preservation of the imperial line—core of the nation. This led to contradictory actions from political and/or military points of view. His role in starting and ending the war, for example, is often criticized for being inconsistent from both viewpoints. "If the emperor could end the war and was against it anyway, why did he approve going to war?"

The answer is simple: these were two very different situations. Just prior to beginning the war with the United States and her Allies, state civil and military authorities presented Hirohito with a *fait accompli* favoring war, and as head of the nation he sanctioned this decision. At the end of that war his civil and military advisors could not reach a consensus decision, and the Emperor decided to terminate it. The situations were different: a consensus decision was reached to begin the war, but no consensus could be reached to end it.[151] Therefore the Emperor's actions were not contradictory. Both of these imperial decisions, along with many others, are best understood not just in terms of politics and military strategy, but also with reference to their influence on safeguarding imperial prerogatives. Unilaterally asserting regal rights as commander-in-chief could be counterproductive. As seen in this study, the

Emperor was not a dictatorial monarch. Assuming positions he knew were contrary to those of Imperial Japan's military leaders would in the long run undermine his aura and authority. He was able to exercise sometimes more sometimes less influence on wartime events based on his authority as head of the nation but was hobbled by military leaders as head of state. Hirohito's status as emperor of the nation insured that he was regarded with awe by his military leaders, but this did not guarantee unconditional acquiescence to his executive authority as head of the state.

Finally, one must remember, as explained above, that two of the major sources covering these events are not entirely unbiased. Both have problems as sources for the Second World War in Asia. The STJR is a secondary source compiled at the behest of the Imperial Household Agency interested in transmitting an auspicious view of the Emperor. The War History Series was compiled mainly by former members of the Imperial Army and Navy, often inclined to rectifying postwar charges of militarism. The former like the latter is based on many primary sources, but while many sources cited in the War History Series may be seen at the NIDS military archive, the STJR sources are stored in archives not easily accessed and misinterpretations are difficult to ascertain. As noted throughout, the STJR is often incomplete: many imperial audiences are noted without saying what transpired; and information appearing in other sources about wartime activities reported to the Emperor is simply left out. The War History Series is more complete vis-à-vis command decisions and war operations. Politics is less well covered. I personally value the War History Series as a reliable reference far more than the STJR. However, this evaluation is based on my use of each while researching the materials found in this book. Mine is not a review of these works in their entirety. That would be a mammoth study in and of itself.

Also, one of the foremost Japanese historians dealing with Shôwa history, Itô Takashi, views the STJR from a different perspective. The chronicle is a beginning, not an end. It will be the starting point for much future research about the Shôwa era. This means that historical sources not used or extensively exploited should become the focus of future investigations.[152] Itô seems to be saying that the many individuals in STJR who had audiences with the Emperor, where little or nothing about what transpired is noted, should be investigated. Likewise sources only listed but not thoroughly documented must now be explored as hints at possible new information. This approach certainly does leave much room for future work.

In this study, however, the focus is on how the war was brought to an end in Japan and the factors influencing these events. Besides the various developments above, one very important factor shaping this process needs to be considered: the suicide attacks initiated after the fall of Saipan and the Tôjô Cabinet. Especially the loss of Saipan, many ships, warplanes, and seasoned men underlined the precarious position of Imperial Japan at this time. As will be demonstrated next, stimulated by these cataclysmic losses, kamikaze tactics were called up to reverse the increasingly dismal trend of the war.

2

Kamikaze Attacks, Planning before and after the Fall of Saipan

The fall of Saipan at the end of June to the beginning of July 1944 shocked not only the Shôwa Emperor, Prime Minister Tôjô, and the commanding officers of the Imperial Army and Navy. The general public in Japan was greatly disturbed, and the Navy General Staff as well as the Navy Ministry received many letters of encouragement. Among them, the navy claimed, there was a great increase in those advocating "certain-death certain-kill" (*hisshi hissatsu*) tactics, a locution for suicide attacks, in order to protect Imperial Japan.[1] In fact this calamity stimulated the implementation of these "new attacks," but contrary to what has been generally accepted until recently Vice-Admiral Ônishi Takijirô did not originate their planning or act alone in authorizing them. The Emperor sanctioned the first attacks on October 25, 1944, in the Philippines after the fact, but he had nothing to do with their planning or inception. However, long after the tactic demonstrably had failed to diminish US war resolve or slow the progress of the US Fleet toward Japan, military (state) leaders, and to some extent the Emperor (nation), advocated using suicide attacks to the bitter end.[2]

In the following the tragedy, covered by many, of those sent on these missions is only treated briefly. Instead, these attacks are examined from the point of view of sporadic military planning and putative imperial sanctions of these tactics. Also, the effectiveness of this tactic and the Shôwa Emperor's apparent support of military leaders who continued the use of kamikaze tactics late in the war are addressed.

Culture of war

Japan has a long "war culture" history that Imperial Japanese leaders could draw upon to justify and romanticize suicide tactics. Going back to the thirteenth century a tradition of sacrifice for one's lord and fighting to the death were idealized and celebrated in popular sagas that were recited at the residences of preeminent warriors (*bushi* or *samurai*). As we now know, these stories were often embellished in the direction of loyalty and self-sacrifice in order to please the leading samurai paying the entertainers. Be that as it may, these war tales (*gunki*) had a strong appeal and authority as exemplifications of martial spirit earlier in history and later in Imperial Japan. One of the first and most well known is the *Tale of Heike*. The text was composed during the thirteenth and fourteenth centuries. This is the story of the fall of the powerful Taira clan (1131–99), culminating in the Gempei War (1180–85). The downfall of the Taira and ascendancy of the victors, the Minimoto, marks the rise of warrior culture as the primary culture carrier in Japan. It was the beginning of some 670 years of samurai rule. The first few lines of this story are familiar to many and set the tone of that culture, which in Imperial Japan, and for some even today, epitomize the warrior spirit and sacrificing oneself for one's liege lord:

> The sound of the Gion Shôja bells echoes the impermanence of all things; the color of the *śāla* flowers reveals the truth that the prosperous must decline. The proud do not endure, they are like a dream on a spring night; the mighty fall at last, they are as dust before the wind.[3]

Taira no Kiyomori was the head of the clan who were defeated. In this tale he was depicted as a proud, selfish, contumacious man. As interpreted in Imperial Japan, loyal soldiers and sailors should not be self-obsessed and arrogant. The self-important fall; they are but "dust before the wind." Instead they should become part of something larger than themselves—the imperial tradition. This was to be achieved as self-sacrificing subjects—soldiers of the emperor.

During the Imperial era many publications, official and unofficial, cultivated long-idealized martial virtues.[4] A spirit of selfless commitment to a group, a military unit, was propagated, often coerced, as soldiers and sailors became "human bullets" (*nikudan*), fought on till all were annihilated on remote Pacific islands (*gyokusai*), and others who trained for and carried out kamikaze attacks in planes, boats, and mini-submarines. Later, in the chapter on Tôjô Hideki, one sees how Tôjô emulated this tradition as exemplified by a popular hero of his day, Kusunoki Masashige, who fought and died for Emperor Godaigo in the fourteenth century. First, however, in this chapter "the nuts and bolts" of kamikaze tactics are examined.

Introduction

As seen below, certain individual navy officers began developing substantive plans for suicide attacks in mid-1943. The initial focus was more on seagoing attacks: motorboats loaded with explosives, mini-submarines, human torpedoes, etc. Attack planes came slightly later. The plans were not coordinated or widely circulated, and they were often but not always labeled "special attack" (*tokkô*) tactics. Sometimes they were also called "surprise attack weapons" (*kishû heiki*) without saying exactly what was meant. The Emperor, for example, was informed by Navy Chief of Staff Shimada Shigetarô on July 8, 1944, that the navy was going to establish a new "No.1 Special Unit Base" for developing, testing, and training personnel in the use of "various types of surprise attack weapons." The presentation to the throne did not explain what sorts of weapons were intended. The plan was set in motion two days later. At this time the Navy Ministry also began to recruit "certain death volunteers." The focus was on officers under the rank of navy lieutenant and non-commissioned officers.[5] Whether or not Emperor Hirohito was informally informed of the details of these plans is unknown presently.

Also, the Imperial Army began working on several special attack plans shortly before the fall of Saipan. One of them involved suicide tactics. The plan called for constructing small light boats that were to be loaded with explosives and rammed into the hull of an enemy warship. After the initial tests were successful, high army officials directed that 1,000 be built and they began recruiting "volunteers" to pilot them. As will be elaborated on below the Emperor seems to have been informed of these plans at the beginning of August 1944. Before formal plans were initiated, according to General Kawabe Masakazu (1886–1965), a few army pilots employed kamikaze tactics on their own initiative during several operations at the end of May 1944.

Kawabe was for some time responsible for and devoted to developing fighting spirit in the Office of the Army Inspector General of Education. His descriptions accord with his avid interest in promoting the Japanese spirit, even after the war. Worthy of note, Kawabe wrote a manuscript following the war with the intention of transmitting "military spirit" to the Japanese people: "the emperor, that is, the state" and "the state, that is, the emperor"; also: "loyalty, that is, patriotism" and "patriotism, that is, loyalty." Emperor, state, loyalty, patriotism all are one—an inspiration for the people. At the end of this work Kawabe wrote a parable about dying honorably, "The Soldier's View of Life and Death." Therein dutiful devotion to one's country is said to transcend concerns about life and death. As a soldier, however, Kawabe never achieved this enlightened state. Instead, as is often so with those who "preach" nationalistic convictions, he prescribed them for others not himself, and he met a natural death in 1965 at the age of seventy-nine. The concluding line of his parable, written three to four years after defeat, reads, "Alas! The spirit of suicide attack, this should not perish together with our nation's (vanquished) armed forces." The text was reprinted many years later (1959, 1980) with the same intention as earlier, to inspire (long-forgotten) military spirit among the people.[6]

Kamikaze, early paper plans

Previous to the desperate times of 1944 to 1945, various navy officers had seriously considered suicide tactics. Navy Capt. Jô Ei'ichirô was especially interested in aviation possibilities. He made preliminary plans that included the types of planes that might be used, how they should be outfitted, and how they should attack different types of ships.[7] With detailed plans he approached specialists in air warfare, for example in the Office of the Chief of Administrative Affairs, Aviation Bureau of the Naval Ministry on June 29 and 30, 1943. He also spoke with Vice-Admiral Ônishi Takijirô, office chief at that time and again on July 2. Ônishi's response, as recorded in Jô's diary, is an interesting indication of how difficult topics were approached at high levels in the Imperial Navy. On Jô's first visit Ônishi said "I understand (ryôkai) your views," but he did not say he agreed, approved, or disapproved. After the second visit Jô came away with a more positive, if self-serving, interpretation of Ônishi's position:

> The opportune time for this has yet to come, and complete approval could not be given. Of course as a junior officer one does not receive an order from his superiors whereby this is put into action. Even a superior officer would find it necessary to think very carefully about deliberately putting this into practice. Still, as a junior officer receiving silent assent, if one obtained materials and pilots one could put this plan into practice. As a junior officer with resolution unchanged, one waits for an opportunity when transferred to another post.[8]

In fact, Jô had been interested in desperation attack tactics for a long time. It can be document back to his time as a superior student at the Naval War College (kaigun daigakkô) from December 1930 to December 1932. When he graduated he raised the topic in his "operational graduation examination paper." Therein he termed the tactic "human-bullet body-ramming" (nikudan *tai'atari*) attacks. He sent a copy to then Chief of the Naval Air Command Headquarters Yamamoto Isoroku.[9] Which is to say, the idea of planned suicide attacks was circulated to some superior officers in the mid-1930s. It seems not to have been flatly rejected. However, none of these superior officers openly approved of Jô's proposal. Later when he presented his plan to Ônishi he had been an aide-de-camp for over two and a half years; he could expect to be transferred in the near future and he hoped to pursue the tactic later. He was in fact transferred to sea duty on February 15, 1944; appointed captain of the light aircraft carrier *Chiyoda*. He was killed in action when his ship was sunk. Ironically it appears that Ônishi enacted the idea Jô brought to him mid-1943 on the same day Jô was killed, October 25, 1944.[10]

Some time earlier another officer in the Navy General Staff was making concrete plans along these lines, and other members of the general staff were accordingly informed. Capt. Kuroshima Kameto (later Rear Admiral), who became Chief of the 2nd Department, Weapons and Mobilization (*senbikôsabu*) Imperial Navy General Staff, originated the idea on July 19, 1943. Little is known about Kuroshima. He was very brilliant and likewise eccentric. From October 1939 to June 1943 he was a Combined Fleet staff officer, and under Yamamoto Isoroku he was the senior staff officer instrumental in formulating the Combined Fleet's plan for the attack on Pearl Harbor.[11] Later as Chief of the 2nd Department he mentioned preliminary investigations of suicide tactics on August 6, 1943, in a meeting of the department. He termed it "collision attack by combat fighter planes." He mentioned the same tactic in a meeting of the same department on August 11, attended by Navy Chief of Staff Nagano Osami, Vice-Chief of Staff Itô Sei'ichi, and Navy Minister Shimada Shigetarô, among others. At this time Kuroshima also developed a plan for using motorboats loaded with explosives to ram enemy warships. It appears that the leaders of the Imperial Navy General Staff were informed of advanced planning for suicide attacks and if they categorically rejected the concept, this is not noted.[12] Tôjô Hideki was prime minister and army minister in 1943, but due to the independence of the respective services he may not have been informed about this preliminary planning inside the Navy General Staff. Nevertheless, as seen below, Tôjô too advocated similar tactics and the army also planned and engaged in suicide attacks. It appears that the Emperor was not informed of these in-staff developments.

The authors of this War History Series volume say that mid-1943 Jô submitted his idea to Ônishi only, and it took a year and many months before it was officially submitted to the Navy General Staff. There is no doubt, however, that Capt.

Kuroshima's motorboat proposal as well as Jô's kamikaze plan, made at about the same time, were the bases of the suicide boats "Shinyô" and the Kamikaze Special Attack Corps "Shinpû Tokubetsu Kôgekitai" initiated mid to late 1944.[13]

Vice-Admiral Ônishi Takijirô

Vice-Admiral Ônishi (1891–1945) was a highly respected naval aviator. In mid-1944 he was attached to the Munitions Ministry as general manager of the General Office for Aviation Armaments. He was designated the commanding officer of the 1st Naval Air Fleet on October 5, 1944, and transferred to the Headquarters, Southwest Expeditionary Fleet. He was well aware of the capabilities, training level, and productivity of air units. They suffered from a lack of materials, good planes, and well-trained, experienced pilots. Most of the latter had already been killed in action. He acknowledged that the pilots at hand had little chance of inflicting any significant damage on enemy war ships before being simply shot down and "dying a dog's death." His answer to this disastrous situation was kamikaze tactics. In this way young inexperienced fliers might at least harm the enemy and die an honorable warrior's death.[14] Previous to the above designation Ônishi may well have conveyed his opinion secretly to the Navy General Staff while still in the Munitions Ministry. In any case, at that time the navy was already secretly preparing "special attack weapons."

After the failure of the A-go Offensive in June 1944 (Battle of the Philippine Sea and the Great Marianas Turkey Shoot, see Chapter 1), the Imperial Navy suddenly was confronted with a very critical war situation. Ônishi was then called upon to improve the navy's performance in the Southwest Theater. The authors of this volume of the War History Series speculate that members of the Navy General Staff assumed this last-ditch effort—the "divine wind special attack force" (*shinpû tokubetsu tokkôtai*)—had become necessary and that Ônishi was the only ranking officer in naval air who could carry this off.[15] However, Mori Shirô says that in mid-July Ônishi was already scheduled to be sent to the Philippines due to his opposition to the appointments of Tôjô Hideki and Shimada Shigetarô as both chiefs of staff and ministers of their respective services. This may well be true as Ônishi was unorthodox and not reticent about voicing controversial opinions. He was very unpopular in the Navy Ministry, but after the fall of the Tôjô Cabinet and official relief of both Tôjô and Shimada his transfer was put on ice.[16]

Ônishi embarked on a career in naval aviation early on, in 1915. He came to be highly regarded and was a robust, taciturn person who was self-confident but not self-obsessed. His career was endangered while a junior officer when he slapped a geisha at a geisha-house and was expelled from the Imperial Navy Staff College for conduct unbecoming of an officer. (His name was stricken from the list of officers in that class.) Through a combination of hard work and tactical planning genius he overcame what would have been for many a career-ending episode. Later, Admiral Yamamoto secretly entrusted him with researching the surprise attack on Pearl Harbor, clear evidence of the high esteem in which he was held. But after the attack he maintained it was a failure. He criticized Yamamoto's surprise attack tactics (correctly) because they united the American people behind the war effort.

In September 1944, Ônishi was again slated to take up command of the 1st Naval Air Fleet in the Philippines, and he subsequently initiated kamikaze tactics there. But he did not act alone. Before he left for the Philippines, Ônishi asked for and received approval (*ryôshô*) from the general staff to initiate this emergency tactic should it became unavoidable. Genda Minoru of the general staff noted this in a draft for a telegraph message written on October 13. This message was then sent from the chief of the Imperial Navy Operations Department (Rear Admiral Nakazawa Tasuku) to the commander 1st Naval Air Fleet (Ônishi) on October 26, 1944, the day after the first such attack. Thus there can be no doubt that Ônishi conferred with appropriate navy officials in Tokyo in advance about initiating suicide "body ramming attacks" (*tai'atari kôgeki*), using this specific term. And Genda subsequently placed 150 "zero fighter planes" at his disposal for this purpose.[17]

On the way to the Philippines, Ônishi met Admiral Toyoda Soemu, commander of the Combined Fleet, who was returning to Tokyo from there. They witnessed several battles in the skies over Shinchiku (Xinzhu, the northwest part of Taiwan) on October 12–14. The American Gruman fighters were clearly superior to the Zeros and their pilots. This supposedly convinced both that suicide tactics were unavoidable.[18] Finally, on October 20, at the Mabalacat Air Base, Philippines, this special unit was officially constituted— the "*Shinpû Tokubetsu Kôgekitai*" (Divine Wind Special Attack Corp). It was divided into four units, *Shikishima, Yamato, Asahi,* and *Yamazakura*. Later that night Ônishi officially assumed command of the 1st Naval Aviation Fleet and announced this the next day. He officially ordered the 201st Air Command to be formed up as a special attack unit and informed Admiral

Toyoda in Tokyo accordingly (telegraph transmission 2347, October 20). Also as commander 1st Naval Aviation Fleet he informed the following authorities of his orders: Contact (*chakushin*): the Combined Fleet, the Commanders of the Southwest Expeditionary Fleet; Report (*tsûhô*): Commanders of the 2nd, 3rd and 5th Fleets, Commander of the 2nd Naval Air Fleet, Imperial Headquarters, Navy Dept. (telegraph transmission 2359, October 20). Both telegraph texts are reproduced in this source. They say in clear terms that these suicide units have been organized to attack enemy aircraft carriers in the area.[19]

Other naval initiatives; imperial foreknowledge

Previously, in mid-1944, at least two other naval officers in the South Seas evaluated the war situation similarly, apparently without contact or collaboration with Ônishi. Commander Matsu'ura Gorô, who had served in the 1st Air Fleet General Staff since the time of Vice-Admiral Kakuda Kakuji (July 1, 1943–August 2, 1944, when he was killed on Tinian), had come to the same opinion. In August 1944, Matsu'ura was hospitalized when he again contracted dysentery. During the time it took to recover he became convinced that the United States, after decimating the Japanese fleet in the Philippine Sea and capturing Saipan and Tinian, would try to take the Philippines. Through his experience in this area he was also convinced of the military superiority of the US fleet and only drastic measures could succeed. This could only mean "body ramming" attack, but one could not issue such an order. Instead he decided to look into skip bombing, an extremely dangerous low-level bombing tactic.[20]

Also, prior to Ônishi's arrival in the Philippines one officer on his own initiative had already flown a body ramming attack on October 15. Rear Admiral Arima Masafumi, commandant of the 26th Naval Air Command killed himself, attempting to crash his plane into an enemy aircraft carrier in the Straits of Taiwan. Prior to taking off he emphasized to Rear Admiral Nakazawa Tasuku, head of operations in the Navy General Staff, and Rear Admiral Takagi Sôkichi that his pilots were insufficiently trained and the aircraft in poor mechanical condition. He came to the same conclusion as Ônishi, as far as one now knows independent of him, that suicide tactics were the only effective way to achieve the desired battle results. He set out wanting, in accord with navy tradition, to set a good example, as a "certain death leader spearheading the way."[21]

Arima and Nakazawa attended the Naval Academy (graduation 1915) and later the Imperial Navy Staff College (graduation 1928) at the same time. In the latter, during a war games exercise "certain death one-way attack tactics" were brought up and the subject of heated discussions. In the end it was concluded that these types of attacks were excluded from military tactics. In about 1941 Arima mentioned to Nakazawa that in a discussion with another officer about air tactics he opposed certain death air attacks. Later Nakazawa explained Arima's actions as a reflection of his fighting spirit, but this was something he did of his own volition and it could not be ordered.

However, as shown below, contrary to the assertions of Nakazawa and Matsu'ura, suicide missions were indeed ordered. Also the evaluations by Ōnishi and Arima contrast starkly with romanticized postwar popular notions of Japanese pilots in general and kamikaze pilots in particular late in the war. For example, one reads on the cover of a book first published in 1973, *I was a Kamikaze* that "kamikaze pilots had to be highly trained to crash exactly on target and to evade dense anti-aircraft fire."[22] Theoretically this was of course true, but by mid-1944 Japan had neither well-equipped and maintained planes with sufficient aviation fuel nor time to train and season pilots as this description assumes. The content of the book belies this cover-blurb intended to attract rather than correctly inform readers. Also a number of Imperial Navy officers spent considerable time and energy hyping the patriotism and heroism of the kamikaze fliers during and after the war. As Ohnuki-Tierney shows, many of these works are only reliable as examples of Imperial Japanese propaganda not as factual historical accounts.[23]

Shortly after Arima's certain death attack, Ōnishi initiated the special attacks previously authorized. (I do not know if he was informed of Arima's sortie.) Beforehand he properly informed high authorities in the Imperial Navy of his intentions. Ōnishi's first "special attack" took place on October 25, 1944. Since the Imperial Headquarters was among those informed in advance, one might assume that the Emperor was also accordingly informed. However, as shown in Chapter 1, the Emperor, despite being commander-in-chief of the armed forces, was not always informed of individual operations nor was he always given accurate, reliable information in the reports he received about them. I have yet to see any documents affirming or denying advance reports to the Emperor about these attacks. As seen below, he was informed immediately after the first such attack by the naval aviation fleet under Ōnishi's command. Given the nebulous nation-state relationship in Imperial Japan, military leaders often did not request in advance imperial sanction for individual war operations.

Imperial Army kamikaze attack official orders and the Emperor

The situation in the army was also problematic but in a different way. Should one request imperial sanction (*jôsô saika*) for this tactic, or should the army minister on his own authority officially attach the volunteers to commanders on the front lines? The general staff maintained that the special attack tactic was a responsibility to be borne by central authorities. Only in this way could planning, training, and execution of these tactics be placed within the authority of the involved commanding officers. Army Ministry officials, especially those in the army air force headquarters, thought differently. Sacrificing pilots who lacked training and had only poorly manufactured and equipped aircraft was a positive contribution to the war effort. But it was improper to order this in the name of the emperor. Attaching these men and materials to front line units was to be done on the basis of principle. This tactic was not to be officially ordered but announced as an army secret. Finally after much discussion the latter, Army Ministry course of action was adopted. On November 1, 1944, Imperial Order (*chokurei*) 649 was issued manifesting that participants in special attacks would be advanced two ranks.[24]

This description does not explicitly say so, but the implication is that the Army Ministry issued Imperial Order 649 without the knowledge or approval of the Emperor. Thereafter, according to this source, for officers in charge of forming these units selecting members was a great problem. Selection was supposed to be based on acquiring individual volunteers, but the sentiments of those involved differed greatly depending on the individual, the atmosphere in his unit, the war situation, etc. Research on volunteers was conducted already before the publication of this War History Series volume in 1970. In summary, there were very many pilots involved and no doubt among those who formally volunteered there were a number of persons who were not entirely convinced of the value of what was being demanded of them.[25]

Lt. General Sugawara Michiô (1888–1983), commander of the 6th Army Air Force from December 26, 1944, to the end of the war, was immediately involved in carrying out kamikaze tactics. He left a large number of recollections about these events that remain unpublished.[26] In his memoirs he stated that in the beginning there were more than enough volunteers, but after a short time their numbers dwindled, as at the same time army authorities in Tokyo called for an increase in kamikaze attacks. This put commanding officers in the field in a bind when they tried to meet these demands with real volunteers. No doubt the actual situations varied with time and place, but undeniably pressure was put on the undecided to volunteer. Many finally did, according to Sugawara, in the spirit of the folk hero Kusunoki Masashige (see below), sacrificing themselves for their emperor. After the war he became known for advocating kamikaze tactics and more—Sugawara condoned, at least, putting pressure on future "patriotic volunteers" and appears to have physically forced some unconvinced fliers to depart on these one-way missions. For these reasons he was labeled "foolhardy" by Handô and Hosaka in their book *Great Commanders and Foolhardy Commanders of the Shôwa Era*.[27] Also, he repeatedly told those leaving that in the end he too would carry out a suicide mission. He never fulfilled this promise. He became a chicken farmer after the war and lived to the age of ninety-five. In recollections written in 1969, long after the war, he reaffirmed his previous viewpoint and actions.[28]

Kamikaze, blurring the beginnings

Returning to the navy, Hosaka Masayasu has examined in detail the beginnings of the kamikaze corps. He too showed that the reputed originator of these attacks, Vice-Admiral Ônishi Takijirô, did not act alone in formulating this policy. He was the first to employ these tactics while stationed in the Philippines but, according to Hosaka, in all probability it was decided upon by the Imperial Navy General Staff previously.[29] As seen above, it was definitely so decided. Using his work, one can see how and why muddy waters have clouded this issue for many years.

In his postwar Recollections Vice-Admiral Nakazawa (then Rear Admiral and Operations Department chief) reported a meeting between Navy Chief of Staff Oikawa, Vice-Chief of Staff Itô, himself, and the designated Commander of the 1st Naval Air Fleet Vice-Admiral Ônishi on October 5, 1944. In it, as seen above, the latter listed the deficiencies of the Imperial Navy Air Corps and said there was only one way to overcome these problems—through "certain-death body ramming tactics." After a long silence only the chief of staff spoke: the request was approved but no one was to be ordered to take part in such a mission.[30] The last part of Oikawa's order seems to have been ignored.

Yet, Rear Admiral Nakazawa is one of the main sources for attributing responsibility for this tactic to Vice-Admiral Ônishi. Hosaka points out that in other postwar statements Nakazawa may well have been intent on exonerating the Imperial Navy General Staff and himself from the onus of authorizing so-called "kamikaze attacks." As shown above, this meeting took place before

Ônishi left for the Philippines where the attacks were begun on October 25. It is doubtful that Ônishi would have followed this course had the general staff not approved his request, but in an interview in July 1977, Nakazawa contradicted what appears in his recollections saying that prior to the first suicide missions in the Philippines there was "absolutely no movement for something like this in the Navy General Staff." Also when asked if on October 1, an assembled "human bomb" group, Unit 721, had not already been trained, Nakazawa said he did not know.[31]

After the war Genda Minoru also denied knowing anything about this conference and the telegram text cited above. In an interview for a Japanese newspaper (*Chûgoku Shinbun*) in 1987, he said he had no recollection of such a telegram. Considering the parlous military situation and gravity of what was being authorized this seems unlikely. Hosaka comments that Genda in an elegant manner sought to evade responsibility for his role in the beginnings of the kamikaze tactics. And in general, although it is clear that the leaders of the Navy General Staff were involved in and bore responsibility for initiating these tactics they were never called to account. A maverick officer, not the state, was responsible. Perhaps another reason for this was that after October 25, Ônishi actively advocated these attacks in the Philippines, and in his testament he seems to have been reconciled to accepting this responsibility.[32]

Prince Fushimi Hiroyasu

After the loss of Saipan the "special attacks" received new emphases. Prince Fushimi Hiroyasu (1875–1946), Emperor Hirohito's uncle and navy chief of staff from February 1932 to April 1941, mentioned the necessity of resorting to "special weapons" against the Americans, without saying what exactly he meant. He said this after the June 25, 1944, meeting of the Supreme Military Council. This was the meeting where it was decided, against Emperor Hirohito's urgings, that it was impossible to retake Saipan (see Chapter 1). He said this to the chiefs of staff and service ministers (General Tôjô and Admiral Shimada). The compilers of this source speculate that the Prince was "calling for a new weapon that would surprise the enemy." Tôjô mentioned proposed "balloon bombs," but Shimada, who was informed of the new suicide weapons being developed in the navy, only said the navy had two or three ideas without mentioning anything specifically. The army's plan involved large balloons with bombs attached launched high into the stratosphere such that they would be blown to the United States, where they would eventually come down and the bombs explode. The navy, unmentioned, had already gone further. Trial production of four types of seagoing "certain-death certain-kill" special weapons had been ordered in mid-1944. One weapon, a proposal of Kuroshima's from a year earlier, a motorboat loaded with explosives whose driver would ram a warship, had gone into mass production.[33]

Army plans

In mid-1944, even before the final decision was reached on June 25, that Saipan could not be retaken, the army seriously began developing suicide motorboats. The project was begun on June 15, the day when US troops first came ashore there. It was surrounded in secrecy and pushed forward with great haste. The boats were given the cover-name "contact craft" (*renrakutei*) and the designation "re" (from *renraku*). In the beginning research was done on ways for pilots to leave the craft just before it rammed the enemy ship. This was determined to be extremely difficult and these sorties were conceived of as missions in which the boat pilots would not return alive.[34]

Plans were completed on June 25, and the next day the army began trial production. On July 8, the first boat was completed, and trial runs begun the following day. Each craft weighed one ton, was powered by a 70 horsepower automobile engine, and had a top speed of around 20 knots. It could remain underway five hours and carried two 100-kilogram (220 lb) bombs. The pilot was supposed to ram an enemy warship at the waterline and sink it. There were various problems to be solved including spiritual leadership, because these were certain death missions; selecting targets and ways of approaching them; maintaining the boats' secret cover, etc. However, the army command expected successful completion of the trial runs and called for producing 1,000 boats by August and 3,000 by October. Perhaps they saw themselves in competition with the navy, which already had a similar boat with a top speed of 27 knots. During this time volunteers were recruited. Unfortunately this source does not tell us how many boats were actually constructed, how many missions attempted, and what their rate of success was.

Another project involved the above-mentioned bomb-balloons that were to be launched into the stratosphere. The balloons were to be made of Japanese-style paper (*washi*) pasted together with plant-based glue (*nori*). This was especially attractive because it did not rely on normal military materials, which were in short supply and greatly contested between the army and navy. Also the balloons were unmanned. Both projects, particularly the latter, show how desperate Imperial Japan's military situation had become.

Irrational attack plans

Some thoughts on the irrationality of the kamikaze tactics:

1. They were based on the long-cherished assumption that by making the war too expensive for the Allies in men and materials, the United States would agree to better peace terms. During the Pacific War, however, the Japanese had ever-increasing losses and at no point was there any indication of US war weariness.
2. From mid-1943 increased antagonism between the Imperial Army and Navy was due to two major factors: differing war strategies and competition between them for war materials. The latter became ever more acute as losses increased and available materials decreased.
3. As seen below (Chapter 4) already from early 1943 and even more so in 1944 a lack of sufficient ships was hampering the war effort and material shortages precluded building enough ships to relieve the situation.

Kamikaze tactics were initiated even though they could only worsen the predicament, further depleting men and materials. In his autobiography published after the war, Suzuki Kantarô, prime minister at the end of the War in China and the Pacific and a former admiral, wrote the same thing: "from the point of view of war strategy, smashed-jewel-ism (*gyokusaishugi*) is clearly war-defeatism (*haisenshugi*)."[35] Notwithstanding, a July 9, 1944, plan ordered that materials were to be requisitioned "special capacity" for building seagoing "special attack weapons."[36] The following projects were planned:

Shinyô: a small motorboat loaded with explosives, a crew of one. Plans called for building 300 in July, 500 in August, 600 in September, and 800 in October. Six meters long, 1.6 meters wide, 1.35 tons, top speed 23 knots, range approximately 250 nautical miles, 12 centimeter cannon, loaded with 300 kilos of explosives.[37]

Shinkai: a mini-submarine about 20 meters long. It was to be piggy-backed on a normal submarine near to Allied warships. Then the crew would attach an explosive to the hull of an enemy ship, which exploded after the mini-sub had escaped. The plan calls for twenty in July, eighty in August, and sixty in September. But due to production difficulties none were completed.[38]

Kaiten: "human torpedoes" in trial manufacture. Trial runs were planned, and in August and September fifty were to be produced each month, twenty in October. One crew member, designed to ram an enemy warship underwater. Adopted for use May 28, 1945. First intended to attack enemy warships at anchor, but later used for defense of harbors from attacking warships.[39]

SS *Kanamono*, also *Kairyû*: small mini-submarines, two crew members. Plans called for fifty to be built in September and October and 150 in November. But in July it was only in trial production and mass production proved to be difficult. Eventually twelve were put into operation on May 28, 1945.[40]

These numbers and all of the plans were not realized, but obviously, with one exception, all of the resulting operations were one-way—neither men nor weapons returned for future use. As seen above the army had similar plans in the works. Moreover, the problem of the lack of warplanes hampering Japan's war efforts would hardly be improved by adopting these tactics in the respective army and navy air corps.

The Emperor and kamikaze

The Emperor's well-known response when he was first told of these attacks on October 26, 1944, has been cited by many, including Yamada Akira: "So did it really have to come to this? But well done!"[41] He said this to the reporting authority, Admiral Oikawa Koshirô (1883–1958), navy chief of staff. The Emperor was shocked and demanded an explanation, which the Navy Department drew up and presented to the throne on October 28. The Kamikaze Special Attack Unit Explanation to the Throne Document (*Shinpû Tokkôtai Osetsumei Shiryô*) is a detailed record of attacks made shortly before on October 25–27, and the (supposed) results. Time, place, number, and types of warships attacked and the numbers damaged and sunk are presented. Also there is a clear explanation of the difference between these attacks and previous suicide attacks: "This special attack unit [*tokkôtai*] differs from the special assault units [*tokubetsu kôgekitai*] or death squads [*kesshitai*] of the navy up to now in that by plunging according to plan into an enemy warship there is no chance of returning safely."[42] The meaning is clear: soldiers and sailors stranded on an island with no chance of resupply, who then engaged in suicide attacks, had not been sent there for that purpose. But these fliers were sent out with the express purpose of crashing into an enemy warship and no one planned on them returning safely. According to Yamada, repeating perhaps Ônishi's explanation above, this was an act of desperation by navy leaders based on two factors: (1) the pilots' lack of skills meant that normal attacks with bombs and torpedoes could not bring the hoped for result, and (2) with a battle death young men would be given an efficacious way to die.

The Emperor was briefed on this tactic immediately after the first attacks, and his "Well done!" was transmitted to the fleet, which became an important factor in pressing on with these types of attacks.[43] Different from Handô Kazutoshi's interpretation (see Chapter 1), as intended by Yamada, this document shows definitively that the Emperor was informed of these tactics and, at least, did not disapprove of them. Hosaka Masayasu maintains, however, that the Emperor displayed even more remorse on two occasions. On October 30, Imperial Navy Minister Yonai Mitsumasa reported to the Emperor on the war situation. Afterwards the Emperor reportedly said, "So did it really have to come to this? That is indeed regrettable. But well done!" Also he said to Imperial Navy Chief of Staff Oikawa, "To the unit members, my regret about these deaths is unbearable."[44]

None of the explanations the Emperor received contain information about who in fact planned and approved the implementation of the attacks. Earlier the Emperor was informed on February 24 and 26, 1942, about the use of "special attack mini-submarines" in the attack on Pearl Harbor.[45] This information also came after the fact. The use of these "special weapons" involved extremely high risks for their crews and only one man survived, disgraced because he was captured by the Americans. These mini-submarines differed from later special weapons: provisions, admittedly sketchy, were made for picking up surviving crew members after the operations were completed. Hirohito was shown pictures of the men and statements they left behind upon departure. Thus the Emperor was informed about the extreme risks involved and did not object, but these were not intended officially as suicide attacks. Later two more attacks were carried out: Diego Suarez Bay, Madagascar, a Vichy-controlled French colony on May 29, 1942; and Sydney Harbor, Australia on May 31, 1942. There were no survivors. From mid-March 1942, the "war gods" who attacked Pearl Harbor were eulogized in the press repeatedly, as were those who took part in the later attacks. Thus the Emperor certainly knew about these sorts of tactics, along with everyone else in Japan. These "heroic actions" were widely celebrated and apparently no one at that time criticized these virtual suicide tactics.[46] State and nation appear to have agreed positively about the use of this tactic.

Mini-submarines for the Pearl Harbor attack

A brief note on the development of these early mini-submarines since they were precursors of what came later: Navy Capt. Iwamoto Kaneji in the Imperial Navy Fleet Administration, 1st Department, 2nd Section (chief of torpedo weapons), came up with the idea at the beginning of 1932. He called it a large-scale manned torpedo. In the summer of the same year he completed a concrete plan and presented it directly to Prince Fushimi, chief of the Imperial Navy General Staff. The Prince responded, "Will this not ram (the enemy ship)?" Capt. Iwamoto answered, "It is rather like certain death but I am thinking about retrieval. It in no way involves certain death." Thereupon the Prince decided the weapon should be developed, and stipulated that the Navy Ministry do it.[47] It required years of planning, tests, trial runs, and revisions before the mini-sub was ready for use. The project was surrounded by extreme secrecy. The Imperial Navy formally put it into service in September 1940. It was seen as an offensive weapon not for use in local waters or for defense purposes. Initially construction of ten and then twenty-four were ordered. By August 1941, twelve mother vessels, submarines for transporting the mini-submarines, were also completed.

At the beginning of September 1941, leading members of the "Special Mini-Submarine Unit" approached Admiral Yamamoto, commander of the Combined Fleet, and requested that he adopt their plan to enter Pearl Harbor and attack warships there. Yamamoto refused because there was no possibility of recovering the crews after the attack. At the time the special unit leaders did not know that an attack on Pearl Harbor was being planned. They studied ways to recover the crew, including sending a radio signal that a pick-up sub could home-in on and attempt a recovery. But Yamamoto refused again for the same reason. At the beginning of October, however, he relented and gave "silent approval" after the running time of the sub had been extended. Many on the Combined Fleet Staff doubted the plan would work, but due to the enthusiasm of the Mini-Sub Unit members the plan was approved. The Mini-Sub Unit then practiced at a harbor in Japan where the entrance was similar to that of Pearl Harbor. Also, they received charts for the harbors at San Francisco, Hong Kong, Singapore, and Sydney.

Finally, five of these mini-submarines approached Pearl Harbor at the time of the attack, and two, maybe, three entered the harbor. Each submarine had a two-member crew, a pilot and an enlisted man who managed the mechanical controls. The pilots were all officers: Navy Lt. Iwasa Naoji (26 years old), Lt. (jg) Yokoyama Masaharu (22), Lt. (jg) Furuno Shigemi (23), Ens. Hiro'o Akira (22), and Ens.

Sakamaki Kazuo (23). The other crew members were all non-commissioned officers: 1st Class Petty Officer Sasaki Naokichi (30), 2nd Class Petty Officer Ueda Sadamu (25), 1st Class Petty Officer Yokoyama Shigenori (24), 2nd Class Petty Officer Katayama Yoshio (23), and 2nd Class Petty Officer Inagaki Kiyoshi (26). None of the crews were recovered. One pilot, Ens. Sakamaki Kazuo, was captured. After PO Inagaki's gyro-compass malfunctioned, he beached the craft, became unconscious, and drowned.[48] The other nine "special attack mini-submarine" crew members were zealously celebrated as war heroes (*kyûgunshin*, "nine war gods") during the war and posthumously promoted by two ranks. Sakamaki was stricken from the Imperial Navy roles because he became a prisoner of war. (The ranks given above are their active duty ranks, not those after posthumous promotions.) Each submarine was armed with two torpedoes to be fired at enemy ships. They were not supposed to ram the opposing warships and none did. These were the special attack mini-submarines reported to the emperor late February 1942.

Capt. Jô Ei'ichirô's plans, the Emperor, and two important officers

Capt. Jô was an aide-de camp to Emperor Hirohito when he presented his ideas personally to Vice-Admiral Ônishi in mid-1943, but it seems doubtful that under the circumstances—a controversial plan with no approval from his superiors—that Jô would take this up with the Emperor. However, since Herbert Bix in his well-known book engages in some vague speculation about Jô, he is again briefly addressed, in particular the implied relation between the two and kamikaze tactics. Among other things Bix says that Jô was a "skilled pilot." My research shows that Lt. (as of December 1924) Jô Ei'ichirô (1899–1944) was stationed at Kasumigaura Naval Air Base from February 1923 to November 1927, four years and nine months. Beginning in May 1923, he was a flying student for about one year. The future Admiral, Capt. Yamamoto Isoroku (1884–1943) was there September 1924 to December 1925, and during this time Jô instructed him in flying techniques. Also the future vice-admiral commanding the kamikaze corps, Lt. Cdr. Ônishi Takijirô (1891–1945), was there from January 1925 until February 1926. Which is to say, all three officers were at Kasumigaura together for almost a full year in 1925. For Yamamoto it was his first experience with flying, and much later after Yamamoto's death Jô commented in his diary that he had a very good "gut feeling" for flying, and Jô felt earlier that he would surely become a great man. Until Yamamoto's death they had a special relationship according to the editor of Jô's diary, Nomura Minoru.[49] One must remember though, Yamamoto was a charismatic figure fifteen years older and far senior to Jô. Their relationship may have been "special" but it was also distant. If either had anything to do with Ônishi then it is not noted here. But one might assume a relationship between the three was formed in 1925 at Kasumigaura. Later, as seen above, Jô sent Yamamoto his early ideas on suicide collision air attacks (c. 1933); Yamamoto secretly entrusted Ônishi with doing research for the attack on Pearl Harbor (c. early 1941); and much later Jô showed Ônishi personally his detailed plans for suicide air attacks (mid-1943), which may have influenced the latter's thinking.

Another connection going back to this time is with Yamamoto Sakae. Jô was junior to Yamamoto as a pilot at Kasumigaura, and he was also one year junior to him at the Naval War College. While at the air base, he came to know Yamamoto Sakae and his wife, and in August 1926 married the wife's younger sister. Later, in the Philippines, Yamamoto Sakae was under Ônishi as the commanding officer, 201st Naval Air Command and responsible for executing the first kamikaze attacks.[50] Thus, it appears that several key persons involved in the preliminary planning and later execution of kamikaze air attacks as well as the future commander of the combined fleet came to know one another in the mid-1920s at Kasumigaura Naval Air Base. Unfortunately, one cannot know if this topic was a part of their discussions at that time. However, throughout this time and later (1943 to 1944), nothing is mentioned or implied about the Emperor having anything to do with any of these events.

After leaving the air base Jô was attached to and commanded several air units. In 1928 to 1929 he served as a unit commander on the aircraft carrier *Hôshô* where Ônishi was flight commander and on another (*Akagi*) where Yamamoto was the captain of the ship. One can see that in 1943 Vice-Admiral Ônishi knew Jô but was quite superior to him, and if he was his "friend," as Bix asserts, it is not noted. Also, if the Emperor regarded Jô as a "friend" it is not mentioned in the source Bix cites. For example, the Emperor did not spend "nearly two hours relaxing in the aide-de-camp's duty office" on February 20, 1942, as Bix claims. The Emperor (unnamed, inferred from the word *shutsugyo*) came after 8:00 p.m. and remained one-and-a-half hours. There is no mention in Bix's source of Jô and his visitor "relaxing" during this time. Assuming it was the Emperor, he may have been there to obtain clarification about the detailed action reports to the throne that afternoon from the navy chief of staff, or to clarify diverse issues that arose during reports earlier the same day from several admirals and an army general. As shown in Chapter 1 and briefly in Chapter 5, many of the reports from the general staffs to the throne were piecemeal, contained exaggerations, and were none too clear. Also, Jô was a commander (not lt. commander) and advanced to navy captain during his time as aide-de-camp.[51] Emperor Hirohito was very conscientious about understanding fully and correctly the reports made to him, including those by his military leaders. Perhaps that is why he visited the aide-de camp's office. It seems very unlikely that the Emperor and a promising but untested middle-ranking naval officer were friends.

Finally it should be noted that on August 2 and 4, 1944, it appears that the Emperor was informed of the army's plans to build small boats loaded with explosives for ramming into the hull of enemy warships. On August 2, the army minister reported to the throne on capabilities, production, and recruiting of personnel; on August 4, the chief of staff reported on unit organization, deployment, etc. Also on August 12, a film about these suicide boats was presented to Hirohito. If he raised objections to the tactic itself and the building of craft suitable for executing it, this source and various others known to me do not mention it.[52] If Hirohito did not object, the army may have taken this as "silent approval," but this too is speculation. However inconclusive and unsatisfying it may seem, records show that the Emperor as head of the nation was provided with specific kamikaze war plans made by army (state) leaders. These records do not show that he was actively involved in the planning or that he sanctioned it.

Tôjô and suicide attacks

Apart from the speedboat tactics described above, the Imperial Army also engaged in aerial kamikaze attacks. General Ushiroku Jun (1884–1973) became inspector general of army aviation in March 1944, and thereafter he was a staunch advocate of these tactics. Tôjô as prime minister, chief of staff of the army, and army minister in the first half of 1944 appears to have been involved in enacting this policy in the army. But his role in taking this decision is disputed. Around June 20, 1944, shortly after the US invasion of Saipan, Tôjô reportedly visited the training schools for army pilots and artillerymen. At that time bombing raids by B-29s were anticipated in Japan, and he asked the students, "When enemy planes come, how will you meet and attack them? How do you intend to attack them and bring them down?" The students replied, "With high firing cannons." Tôjô, typically showing his short temper, replied impatiently,

"To attack and down the enemy planes one employs first of all, and second of all, fighting spirit [*seishinryoku*]." The students were reportedly very perplexed by Tôjô's exhortation.[53] This was not an isolated incident. He said something similar at another pilot training center on March 12, of the same year.[54] Much later on February 26, 1945, elder statesman Tôjô had an audience with Emperor Hirohito. The Emperor had called upon each elder statesman to give him his assessment of the very critical war situation. During his audience with the Emperor, Tôjô expressed his admiration for the kamikaze fliers, citing a twenty-year-old who was in kamikaze training. If the Emperor said anything it is not related in this source.[55]

Tôjô and a number of his colleagues advocated this new tactic, but many in the army high command opposed it, especially those in the aviation corp. Nevertheless, Tôjô and his supporters were not to be denied. It was generally conceded that the aviators' poor showing was the main reason for the war turning against Japan. Snide remarks by members of the Army Ministry and general staff were directed at the air command. "Why are things going so poorly in the air?" And, "Aren't they lacking in fighting spirit?" etc.[56] Especially in April and May 1944, pressure increased greatly as General Ushiroku transmitted this discontent to the air corps command. Previously, the commander of the air corps, Yasuda Takeo, who was known to be against this tactic had been replaced by Ushiroku, who was a protégé of Tôjô's. At that time an officer in the air command, Naitô Susumu, recorded the contents of a meeting chaired by Ushiroku:

> The commanding officer (Ushiroku) spoke first: "In order to make a breakthrough in the present war situation, a certain-death 'body-ramming' unit is to be formed." This was expressed as a type of question about the possibility of forming such a unit. But none of our superiors had anything to say. Thinking this is really a terrible thing I, probably shaking with emotion, raised my hand and in a rather emotional way expressed an opposing opinion. The commander of the air corps thinks that the lack of success in the war is due to the slovenly performance of the air corps, but I would like to emphasize that there are problems with the equipment and the way it is used. Then because Major Ishikawa rose and said, "I agree completely with Major Naitô's opinion," in accord with an order of the commanding officer it was declared that this conference had not taken place and the meeting was called off.[57]

Also in April and May 1944, Tôjô reportedly said the following during meetings of the department heads in the army general staff: "We estimate that from June B-29s will begin bombing Japan. In order to dampen the enemy's spirits, it will be necessary to hurl our bodies one on one against the enemy aircraft."⁵⁸ This was an obvious call for using kamikaze tactics, but it is not entirely clear if Tôjô directly ordered that these tactics be employed. Yet, Tôjô mandated suicide before surrender in the *Field Service Code* (*Senjinkun*) of January 1941, well into the war in China and some eleven months before the attack on Pearl Harbor.⁵⁹

The *Field Service Code*

The *Field Service Code* (*Senjinkun*) is an official army advisory disseminated in Tôjô's name, which was later published as a book for public use. The philosophers Inoue Tetsujirô and Watsuji Tetsurô as well as the Japanese language and literature scholar Yamada Yoshio reviewed it for correctness, and the renowned writer Shimazaki Tôson and the poet Satô Sônosuke also made contributions. The work did not just appear "out of the blue." It is a military code with two of the basic texts in Imperial Japan on loyalty to the emperor and the nation-state in the background, the Imperial Rescript on Education (*Kyôiku Chokugo*) of 1890, and the Fundamental Principles of Our National Polity (*Kokutai no Hongi*) of 1937. In the latter one reads for example, "offering our lives for the sake of the emperor does not mean so-called self-sacrifice, but the casting aside of our little selves to live under his august grace and the enhancing of the genuine life of the people of a State."⁶⁰

Following up, Tôjô's work is filled with the usual platitudes about Japan's superiority based on her unequalled spirituality and mythology presented as history. The samurai tradition is elaborated on as a role model for officers and men alike. The title of the first chapter is "Land Ruled by the Emperor" and the first sentence reads: "Great Japan is the Land ruled by the Emperor." Later the first chapter of the second section, Honoring the Gods, begins: "Japan is the land of the gods [...] We Japanese people from birth always defend that which is right and true; we are a people who can believe in the blessings of the gods."⁶¹ Meaning, the Japanese are blessed by the gods. Throughout the volume the unity, spiritual strength, and thereby the martial vigor of the Japanese folk are explained and proclaimed. Concomitantly soldiers in the field should never surrender:

> Esteem one's Name: Those who know a sense of shame are strong. Care for the honor of those back in your hometown and your family; at all times strive to live up to their expectations. Live without the humiliation of being taken prisoner, and [in so doing] die without leaving a blemish on your name!

Transcending life and death one should strive to accomplish one's unique mission.

Happily carrying out an order, one throws himself onto a deadly [battle] field.[62]

Convictions about the superiority of the Japanese race and accepted social byways in Japan dovetailed with the injunction to never surrender. Surrender was tantamount to betraying family, friends, superiors, even the emperor. It was a breach in military discipline, and it meant breaking faith with being Japanese. Army Minister Lt. General Tôjô Hideki codified this as an injunction, and it also came to be obligatory for those in the navy. Thus respect for military orders and fear of loss of respect and identity as a Japanese—as a special human being—were important impetuses for being a good Japanese fighting man and the willingness to fight to the death. In this way, common soldiers and sailors came into contact with the imperial state and nation. Also, these expectations were transmitted to normal civilians. There was the media mentioned below, and quite a number of books based on Tôjô's tract were published. They were directed at inspiring the people to similar devotion, for example the *Citizens Field Service Code (Kokumin Senjinkun)* by Maj. Gen. (res.) Nakashiba Suezumi. Moreover, as seen above, after the war was lost, former General Kawabe Masakazu applauded this code and the military spirit, among other martial virtues, in an essay written to inspire Japanese in postwar times.[63]

Before and during the war, holding out and dying for honor and a lost cause, "the nobility of failure," was a respected part of Japanese tradition. Tôjô was well aware of this tradition and appears to have identified with it: he idolized Kusunoki Masashige (1294[?]–1336). In Imperial Japan the tale of this well-known folk hero was used to demonstrate the unity of two key concepts in prewar ideology: loyalty (*chû*) and filial piety (*kô*). Kusunoki died supporting Emperor Godaigo (1288–1339) in his futile attempt to defeat Ashikaga Takauji (1305–58) and restore political power to the imperial house in the Kemmu Restoration (1333–36). In a like manner Tôjô saw himself as a military man in service of the emperor come what may,[64] and he expected the same sort of devotion from all soldiers and sailors.

Self-sacrifice for emperor and nation

Sacrificing one's self for emperor and nation had many far-reaching implications. Most modern accounts focus on navy and army suicide tactics late in the war.

Yet, beyond general societal indoctrination, concrete schemes of this sort were put forward in the navy and later in the army sporadically from the beginning of the 1930s. They, as well as later military planning leading up to their initiation, receive little attention. Rather, the heroism or tragedy of those sent off to die and their motivation for participating in these operations is portrayed. Dying for the emperor came to be romanticized. The departing poem of a kamikaze pilot reads:

> My good old village; my good old friends
> Now I will discard everything and
> Looking to the safety and peril of the nation
> I go out
> Living for eternal justice
> Here my great sortie begins
> I return to the land of the spirits
> My body scatters like the cherry blossoms
> Transformed into a spirit which guards our land eternally
> When it comes to this
> I become a splendid mountain cherry tree in bloom
> I return to my mother's honored place, rustling in the wind. (Written by Ogata Jô (23), who died in the Battle of Okinawa, April–June 23, 1945)[65]

This poem reflects, and is a part of, the purported tradition of devoted sacrifice to emperor and nation by the kamikaze fliers. Tôjô promoted this tradition for himself and others. He said more than once that he too was prepared to sacrifice himself, but not everyone was happy to be sent off to the front or to "volunteer" to become a suicide pilot. Many years ago I knew a man who expressed his misgivings very clearly. From 1973 to 1976 he was a fish wholesaler living near Sendai. During the war he had been a cook, and at the end of the war he was volunteered to a "special attack unit." He always maintained that he had no real choice in the matter. He was taught how to take off and steer a plane using primitive implements on the ground. There were no landing exercises. Finally, the unit he was in ran out of gasoline. He never took off, and at least after the war he was very happy that things had worked out this way.[66] A German journalist confirmed this point of view in a book published in 2001. The work contains interviews with former kamikaze pilots, who for one reason or another lived through this experience, and with people who knew ones who died. None of the eleven persons interviewed considered it an honor to be chosen to fly and die in this way. And they all said many years after the war that they and their compatriots who perished were not volunteers in any sense of the word.[67]

[Interviewer:] It is often said that the kamikaze missions were voluntary and that there were no orders. Was it really so?

Hamazono Shigeyoshi: That is an absolute lie. This I say in all clarity. The "schemers" in headquarters, I assume the emperor also was a part of it, they decided that it should appear to be free of coercion. We had to appear to be willing volunteers […] It was said we are now a kamikaze corps. Those who do not agree should hold up their hands. Who could do that? In the atmosphere prevailing at that time, as a pilot who defends the skies, no one could dare to raise his hand [in protest]. No way.[68]

Another interviewee remembered that he and his fellow pilots were surprised and shocked by this new tactic. One man in his unit did refuse this "honor," but finally he was forced to volunteer in writing for a kamikaze unit.[69] When Hamazono's final mission neared he visited his family for what all assumed was the last time. But they did not talk openly about it. The interviewer found this difficult to understand, and Hamazono explained,

At that time one probably thought it was a great honor when a son died for the fatherland. The family and the sons themselves thought this way. We were educated to do this. In the schools there were only stories about wars, emperors, and the like. There was nothing else. We were poured into this mold. I don't think it bothered me then.

There were people in our village who after receiving a death notice, called out from the village office steps, "My son died an honorable death. Long live the emperor!" When one hears this today one thinks, "my God were they stupid!" But that was how we were educated in those days. I was born into that sort of age.[70]

One should remember that these are testimonies from persons many years after the war. Other testimonies show that during the war not just Tôjô and a few fanatics were convinced of the rightness of Japan's cause and the meaning of their personal sacrifice. Nevertheless, toward the end of the war apprehensions about defeat became an object of military and public concern, as did firm conviction and devotion to the emperor.

Reality changes. In 1942 and 1943 self-doubt did not mean doubt about Japan's cause or her ability to prevail. Indeed, few persons were plagued with misgivings about a possible defeat at that time. But the kamikaze pilots at the end of the war were in an entirely different situation. The few remaining testimonies we have show that some were understandably horrified by what was demanded of them. Like Tôjô, they knew the war was lost, but few thought of their own lives as being "light as a feather." Rather, social pressures, moral and spiritual factors, nationalistic deceptions, and orders from state (military) authorities interceded in their thoughts, feelings, and decisions. Tôjô was a strong advocate of this spirituality, morality, and nationalism. But nationalistic sentiments were not confined to the militarists and right-wing politicians. Emiko Ohnuki-Tierney has shown how a few highly educated, idealistic young men drafted out of places such as Tokyo and Kyoto Imperial Universities were also dedicated to imperial ideology.[71] No doubt the author of the above poem, Ogata Jô, was not the only kamikaze pilot, whether by air or sea, who shared noble visions of these convictions.

Serving the national essence

Participation in a kamikaze mission was an order that could not be refused, and this was generally known, not just in the military. As the sister of one of the pilots recalled, "Refuse to join a kamikaze unit? No. That was not possible [...] When one received this order one could not refuse. That's the way we also [she and her school comrades] understood it."[72] Some regarded it as a duty and honor, others did not. The training of officers and men in the Imperial Army and Navy reinforces this impression. Moral injunctions were accompanied by physical abuse and threats. All were an integral part of military training. Group pressure and physical beatings were regularly employed in the training of ordinary recruits; moreover these measures also were condoned at some of the schools where future officers were educated.[73]

Like Tôjô many Japanese were taught from childhood to be devoted to the national essence, to the empire headed by the direct descendant of the (mythical) first emperor of Japan Jimmu Tennô. Education, culture, moral convictions, and military training combined to make the Japanese fighting man the highly feared opponent that he was. Soldiers and sailors feared moral condemnation and social ostracism more than death, not to mention the physical consequences of not carrying out orders. So animated, not all but certainly too many met their end—ultimately charging, flying a plane, or steering a boat loaded with explosives into the enemy. This they did as obedient disciplined servicemen following the directives of military, state leaders, to preserve the embodiment of Japanese national culture and tradition—the emperor. In so doing many also sought to avoid bringing disgrace upon themselves, their families, and their hometowns.

Suicide attacks as official policy

Suicide attackers, in particular the pilots, have been romanticized, portrayed as self-sacrificing heroes and sacrificial lambs. Their organizers are mentioned in a number of works, especially Vice-Admiral Ônishi, and Navy Captains Kuroshima and Jô. Moreover, as seen above, in the hype lauding the heroism of the mini-submarine personnel involved in the attack on Pearl Harbor, these tactics were not a military secret hidden from the public. Much later, without going into exact details about how "special attacks" were to be made, the topic was the subject of a radio broadcast prepared by the Imperial Navy General Staff.[74]

Few, however, draw what seems to be the obvious conclusion: special "certain-death, certain-kill" attacks were considered ad hoc by a number of high officers in the Imperial Navy (at least) for a number of years and were made a part of official policy in an acute context in October 1944. They were not simply bizarre ideas initiated and pursued out of the blue by a few fanatics. They were not a spin-off of so-called "honorable death" practices—a foredoomed fight to the death when obviously defeated, "smashed jewels," seen first on Attu Island in May 1943 and later on Saipan, Iwo Jima, etc. in mid-1944 and thereafter. Finally, Yamada Akira says that during the battle for Okinawa the importance of the island and extent of the fighting led to dropping the pretense that the fliers involved were "volunteers."[75] The special attack tactics proposed in the mid-1930s by several navy officers (Iwamoto and Jô), in mid-1943 (Kuroshima, Jô's proposal to Ônishi), and in mid-1944 by high army officials, reflect the disregard for human life typical of some officers in the Imperial Army and Navy. The plans and proposals were consistent with the directive of no surrender seen in the *Field Service Code* issued in Tôjô's name in 1941. Against this backdrop preplanned, systematic suicide tactics finally came to be enacted due to the desperate situation of the navy following the defeats in the Philippine/Mariana Seas and the fall of Saipan.

The unquestionable orders to selected special attack volunteers were supported and justified by the indubitable "national essence," with the Emperor at its core. Emperor Hirohito was informed of this tactic immediately after its initiation. As seen above, he may have been informed about advanced planning but, if so, the extent of his information is as yet unknown. There is no known record of him ordering or participating in such advance planning. He did criticize army and navy leaders because their lack of proper planning led to "honorable death" practices earlier.⁷⁶ Much earlier, if aware of the contents of the *Field Service Code*, there is no record of him raising objections. Later, as seen above, there is no record of him objecting to kamikaze tactics after their actual initiation. And as plans were made to defend the home islands, the Shôwa Emperor did not object to the use of special attack tactics.⁷⁷ One might conclude that at first promoting the fortunes of the Imperial House and later saving it were more important to him than the lives of his subjects.⁷⁸

Results

We know now certainly better than high Japanese military officials did then, but not unknown to them, that these suicide tactics were costly and ineffective. There are no definitive figures on which all agree, but Nishiyama Takashi says that in 1944 to 1945, "the army deployed 1,185 airplanes and the navy, 1,295, for the one-way suicide missions. Among the total, only 244 aviators reportedly accomplished their missions, damaging 358 Allies' ships to various degrees [...] only 16.5 percent." (How 244 successful one-way attacks damaged 358 ships is a mystery to me. Perhaps the statistics are not correlated.) Another source says some 3,913 kamikaze pilots died during the war. These included 2,525 from the navy, mainly ages eighteen to twenty, and 1,388 from the army, mostly ages eighteen to twenty-four.⁷⁹ Tsuneo Watanabe and the editors of the Yomiuri Shimbun volume on the war, *Who Was Responsible*, have much higher sums: in the Philippines before fighting ceased in January 1945 some 700 kamikaze pilots died; in the battle for Okinawa the army engaged extensively in these suicide tactics, and more than 9,500 soldiers came to a similar end.⁸⁰ No source is given and perhaps the Okinawa figures include suicide attacks to land and sea as well as in the air. Ohnuki-Tierney has again different statistics: of 3,300 kamikaze planes 11.6 percent hit their targets, 5.7 percent near miss, 5.3 percent shot down, 49.9 percent no information, 72.5 percent no return, and 27.5 percent returned.⁸¹ In any case, these tactics were especially costly in terms of materials and profligate in terms of the lives of the young men who volunteered to die for emperor and nation.

It should be noted, however, that at the time the kamikaze attacks did have one desired effect: Allied soldiers, sailors, and their commanding officers were shocked by the tactic and worried about the increased damage inflicted by the suicide fliers. This had, on the other hand, undesired consequences for Japan. Allied military commanders became more, not less, determined to defeat this ferocious enemy. Also, the tactic convinced military *and* political leaders that the costs of invading the home islands and subduing Imperial Japan would be extremely high. They knew that massive kamikaze tactics were planned for the home island last-ditch defense. They did not know, however, about the desolate condition of most aircraft, the pilots' lack of training, or that the Japanese air forces were "running on empty." Spotty intelligence may well have contributed to the decision by President Truman to use the atomic bombs when they became available.[82]

Finally, a point of history: the original "divine winds" serving to inspire the Imperial Japanese nation and individual pilots, which thwarted the Mongol invasions in the late thirteenth century, quite possibly never came. Recent research shows that records from that time contain nothing about kamikaze. According to Hattori Hideo, director of the Kumamoto Literature and History Institute and specialist in Japanese medieval history, the first invasion attempt (November 1274) probably ended when the Mongols withdrew to avoid the oncoming winter weather, which normally does not include typhoons. In the second it appears they suffered heavy losses and ran out of food. This attempt came in August (1281), but while there may have been typhoons in the summer and early autumn, they are not noted in contemporary records. Rather, in both cases, the fierce resistance of the Japanese bushi and prayers at various Buddhist temples and Shintô shrines were said to be significant in driving off the Mongols.[83]

Moreover, "the land of the gods" was revived as an appellation in Japan then but not as was usually assumed in the late nineteenth and early twentieth centuries in Imperial Japan. During the thirteenth century some postulated anew Japan as the "land of the gods" as a reaction to Buddhist thought. Buddhist cyclical chronology put Japan at this time on the far edge of creation in the "days of the latter law" (*mappô*), a region shrouded in darkness. Instead some Japanese thinkers depicted Japan as the land in the middle of the universe where the buddhas took the form of Japanese gods due to the superiority of these gods (*honji suijaku setsu*). This was an inner directed theory emphasizing the uniqueness of Japan. It came to be transformed after the Mongol invasion attempts as an emphasis on Japan's superiority over other lands.[84] Much later, since there is no mention of divine winds in medieval documents, the typhoons appear to be embellishments added to past events in Imperial Japan: kamikaze as divine winds were part of the folklore invented in the latter half of the nineteenth century when Imperial Japan was threatened by European and North American powers. In the mid-twentieth century they were again called upon to help preserve the "eternal divine land" Japan during the Second World War.[85] In the end though, the modern divine winds contributed mainly to Imperial Japan's self-destruction.

Furthermore, when considering the relation between the secular and divine in Japan, one might remember that religious convictions for the Japanese historically have a different role in society than in the West. "Looking back at history, in Japan religion generally does not impinge on the interests of the state or national society. At all times secular authority dominates spiritual authority."[86] Imperial Japan was an outstanding example of this situation. The nation (emperor) was honored and respected but often dominated by state (military) leaders. Here "dominate" does not mean "absolute control." Kamikaze missions were ordered by military leaders. The Emperor for whom these soldiers and sailors died, sanctioned the tactics after their initiation and did little, if anything, to hinder these operations. Perhaps he was influenced by his military leaders, in particular Prime Minister General Tôjô Hideki. Tôjô did not set these attacks in motion, but he pursued policies that provided a favorable atmosphere for them, and he will be considered in some detail next.

3

Tôjô Hideki, Man of his Times

Any consideration of the Second World War in Asia, the Pacific, and its termination in Japan must include Tôjô Hideki. His cabinet fell, he was relegated to the reserves as an army general, and became an "elder statesman" one year prior to "the end." Nevertheless, before and after his fall from power he greatly influenced these events.

Many years ago Robert J.C. Butow wrote, "Tojo was a reflector, not a creator of national thought." He "was a militarist—misguided, naïve, and narrow in outlook; he regarded war as a legitimate instrument of national policy."[1] Put another way, Tôjô was in every respect a professional military man. For him arriving at and executing definitive decisions were of utmost importance. His famous chiding of the vacillating Prime Minister Konoe Fumimaro reflects this: "Sometimes a man has to close his eyes and leap from the terrace of Kiyomizu Temple." On occasion politicians too must make resolute decisions. Tôjô within his coercion-colored milieu was persevering and inventive, but his "narrow minded" decisiveness precluded bringing a broader worldview or new social perspectives into his decision-making.[2]

In the following I do not attempt to add details to or refute Butow's work. Rather, a broader portrait of Tôjô and his milieu are presented in order to better understand wartime developments in Imperial Japan. Tôjô is examined as a state and war leader. As the leader of the state for some two years and nine months he was the top executive of the land and a trusted advisor of the leader of the nation—the Shôwa Emperor. Before this time he was a high-ranking army officer and after it a former prime minister, one of the elder statesmen (*jûshin*). In the former capacity he was to a lesser extent a state executive and in the latter he was still an advisor to the emperor. This account addresses Tôjô and Hirohito, secular power vis-à-vis "national essence" leverage in Imperial Japan, with an emphasis on the former. It serves as background to army and navy sometime use of the emperor to legitimize their activities.

Introduction

Many regard Tôjô Hideki as the ultimate "militarist" behind Japan's war of aggression. But at least one person, his wife, saw him differently. Many years after the war ended Tôjô Katsuko asserted that on the night before the attack on Pearl Harbor she saw him in his study at home sitting erect facing the imperial palace weeping. He knew what was about to happen; knew of the general atmosphere at the imperial court as well as the Emperor's apprehensions; and knew he could never adequately explain the opening of the war. According to this commentary, Tôjô was indeed overwhelmed by the weight of his responsibility for these actions, and he turned toward the imperial residence and asked for support from heaven. Still, on the same evening Tôjô met with Vice-Minister of the Interior Yuzawa Michio and Army Vice-Minister Kimura Heitarô. (Prime Minister Tôjô was at the time also interior minister and army minister.) Afterwards Yuzawa wrote in a newly revealed memo describing Tôjô's mood: Before these offensives Tôjô was "greatly relieved" even "tipsy" because Japan's highest spiritual authority, the Emperor, had approved his war plans and he was sure Japan would win.[3] But one should be wary of both descriptions: Tôjô's wife was well known during and after the war for championing his cause, as well as her own, and the memo seems to be somewhat scurrilous.

After the war Tôjô was purposefully forgotten, and now even in Japan many do not recognize his name. But all know of a much publicized group to which he belongs: Tôjô is the most prominent of the fourteen convicted and seven executed Second World War Japanese war criminals who are enshrined at Yasukuni Jinja in Tokyo. Millions of others who died in the service of the Japanese nation-state are honored there also, but the presence of these convicted war criminals combined with visits to the shrine by various prime ministers, especially those of Koizumi Junichirô (prime minister 2001–2006), have kept numerous controversies alive. Were Tôjô and his convicted colleagues really war criminals? Or were they victims of "victors' justice"? Immediately after the war many persons in Japan held Tôjô responsible for starting it, for his dictatorial rule from 1941 to 1944,[4] and for losing the war. Many assume he and other high military officers were guilty as charged. But one might assert that they were simply loyally doing their duty as professional soldiers in accord with what they learned in state sponsored schools—military prep schools, at the Army Academy, at the Army War College—in line with the Constitution of Imperial Japan and the expectations of their superior officers. Conceivably they absorbed the lessons about the destiny of their fatherland too unquestioningly and as state leaders became unconscionable aggressors in the name of the nation—the emperor.

Briefly illustrated, Tôjô's personal secretary Col. Akamatsu Sadao related that on the evening of December 8, 1941, Tôjô celebrated the successful attack on Pearl Harbor and places in Southeast Asia in an ebullient manner with a few trusted colleagues at the prime minister's official residence. The seating at the banquet table illustrates the protocol of that day, and Tôjô's personal priorities. Directly opposite him sat Navy Minister Admiral Shimada Shigetarô; on Tôjô's left was army chief of staff General Sugiyama Hajime and on his right Navy Chief of Staff Admiral Nagano Osami. Leaving out the secretaries (six), eleven prominent persons were present, most in or from the military. Tôjô thanked the gods for their divine assistance and called on the Japanese people to "win the holy war at all costs.[5]" His statements prior to and at that time are indicative of what sort of person Tôjô was. According to Akamatsu, previously the Emperor had asked his prime minister what the prospects were in the event of war. Tôjô told the Emperor, and he repeated at this celebration, "our country over time becomes superior through the combined power of material [*mono*], training [*kunren*], and inner spiritual strength [*seishinryoku*] [...] and this battle result is surely a godsend which exemplifies the power of the combination of material, training, and inner spiritual strength." The prominent nonfiction author Hosaka Masayasu also cites this statement and comments that Tôjô repeated this favorite phrase of his "seishinryoku" a number of times.[6]

Also, the gods and inner spiritual strength veiled cruelty: Tôjô's reputation as an unscrupulous militarist was not without grounds. Later during the war, as prime minister and army minister, he encouraged the use of prisoners of war (POWs) as forced labor contrary to international laws known to him. Though he knew they often fared badly, dying due to the harsh conditions, he once told POW camp commanders, "you must place the prisoners under strict discipline and not allow them to lie idle doing nothing but eating freely for even a single day."[7] Nevertheless, Butow's evaluation written many years ago quoted above is well to be remembered: "Tojo was a reflector, not a creator of national thought."[8]

Since Butow wrote his superb study, of course, a number of source materials have been published that were not available to him. Four of the most extensive collections are: the Army General Staff War Command Group War Logbook, the Secret War Records; the Tôjô Cabinet, the Prime Minister's Secret Records, A Record of the Words and Deeds of General Tôjô Hideki; a Collection of the Recorded Remarks by the Shôwa Emperor; and the War History Series.[9] Also most recently there is the work cited extensively in Chapter 1, the Actual Record of the Shôwa Emperor.[10] These sources overlap in places, which is not just tedium but an opportunity to compare events during the war in works by different compilers and editors. Reading through these records reveals a consistent picture of Tôjô. He was a very correct uncompromising narrow-minded government official. Under the circumstances as he saw them then he did his best to observe protocol, regulations, and laws, but he opened a war and was oblivious to humane considerations at home and abroad. He never denied opening the war, but few statesmen of that day, and even now, did/do not regard war as a legitimate instrument of national policy. Tôjô did what he thought necessary in the given situation, and the imperial state did not allow critical consideration of the doctrines buttressing the nation that Tôjô and many other military officers had learned earlier. This led to the calamity of the Asia-Pacific War and atrocities such as the undeniable rape of Nanking. Moreover, paradoxically, the training and indoctrination future officers received—in particular, obsessive devotion to the imperial line and national essence—also was instrumental in Imperial Japan's eventual defeat.

Tôjô popularized

Previously I have characterized Tôjô Hideki as a callous bureaucrat in uniform, but several wartime volumes I recently discovered suggest he may have been more. This supposition is based in part on the following three works: the *Field Service Code, Explanation to the People*, issued in Tôjô's name in January 1941 when he was army minister; a *Biography of Tôjô Hideki: Sincere, Man of Steel*, published shortly after Japan's successful attacks on Hawai'i, the Philippines, and the Malay Peninsula, etc., which is of course a very laudatory description; and, finally, *The Road to Certain Victory*, a collection of his speeches and rejoinders to questions in parliament during the first months of 1943.[11]

In these books one sees the development of a Japanese-style personality cult gilding the "leader" Tôjô. However, their publication was not orchestrated. The 1941 *Field Service Code, Explanation to the People* is an edited book based on an original service manual manuscript by Tôjô. The manual is filled with the usual platitudes about Japan's superiority based on her supreme spirituality and mythic origins presented as history. Soldiers probably had to read it. Whether or not it was widely read by civilians is difficult to tell. The 1942 biography and 1943 collection of statements made by Tôjô in parliament seem to have been well read. The 1942 work was reissued sixteen days after it was first published, and for the initial publication of the 1943 work 20,000 copies were printed. In all of the works an emphasis on Japan as the land of the gods and the superiority of the Japanese spirit is clearly expressed.

These works are examples of the popular dissemination of jingoistic ideas during the war beyond military circles. The idea that the Japanese folk, by demonstrating the proclaimed unity and strength of spirit, are superior to others, especially the English and Americans, is propagated; that folk and their leaders become bigger than life. Tôjô himself is not apotheosized, but as author of one of the works and subject of the other two he is projected to the people as something more than a bureaucrat in uniform. He is not an object of worship or adulation, but he does merit great respect as the person promoting and embodying Imperial Japanese articles of faith. As seen in the commentary on Tôjô below and throughout this book, the spiritual foundations presented in these works were basic to Tôjô's convictions about how to run the Japanese state and prosecute a war. Accordingly in the 1941 *Field Service Code* one also reads, "Thought war is one important aspect of modern warfare. We must not only destroy the enemy's steadfast beliefs about the Imperial State [*kôkoku*] and their propagated falsehoods, freely we must engage in disseminating the Imperial Way [*kôdô*]." On the same pages there is the basic principle that the army should show love and compassion for the people.[12] Unfortunately for many the army did not always honor this principle.

The 1942 biography begins with the Japanese Declaration of War of December 8, 1941, and a "Supplication to the Great Imperial Rescript Declaring War" by Prime Minister and General Tôjô Hideki.[13] The work ends with "man-on-the-street" like praise for starting the war and Tôjô:

Finally we did it!
I've been waiting for this!
After all without Tôjô, we'd be going nowhere!
"There's nothing to be said. With this I'm relieved."[14]

The account of Tôjô's life in this work begins with his family background, his childhood and aspirations to join the army, his training and career up to the above point in time. Naturally the record includes much praise for Tôjô, large and small. For example, when he was assigned to the Konoe Division, he was known for his strictness during training more than any other 1st lieutenant. But he was devoted to the men under him and when making his rounds at night he put on straw sandals in order to not wake the light sleepers.[15] Eleven pages are devoted to the *Field Service Code* including excerpts from injunctions therein. The injunctions are without title and divided into various topics such as "Imperial State," "Imperial Forces," "honoring the gods," "filial piety," etc.[16] These exhortations are followed by a section on "Certain Victory"—the topic of a radio broadcast by Tôjô following the Declaration of War. Here the theme is elaborated on and at the end there is a paragraph warning that if the war goes on for a long time there will be hardships, the people must be devoted to the imperial state and ready to make sacrifices for it.[17]

After the war Tôjô faced the consequences of losing it in the Tokyo War Crimes Trial. There one must say his training and education were further in evidence as he testified in a manner designed to relieve the Emperor of any war responsibility.[18] However, Tôjô was not simply a fanatic, and he will be looked at below as a man of his time, an embodiment of the imperial Japanese nation, state, and what went wrong.

The Tôjô family

Tôjô Hideki was the son of an army officer who upon retirement was promoted to lieutenant general (Tôjô Hidenori, 1855–1913). The family was traditionally one branch of the Hôshô Line of Nô masters in Edo. In 1832 they were forced to move from Edo to Morioka in order to retain their status as Nô masters. There the family received a stipend of 160 *koku* rice from the local lord. This was quite a good stipend for a middle-ranking samurai at the time, but the head of the house Jônosuke received it as a Nô master, not a samurai. Jônosuke and his successors made respectable livings teaching Nô to local notables and their children. Due to a peasant uprising in 1853 the incumbent Daimyô was replaced and Nô fell out of favor. The new lord apparently "ordered" the head of the Hôshô house to change his name to Tôjô and pursue neo-Confucian learning. In 1856 Hidetoshi complied, desiring to retain his stipend. (It is unclear if this change was ordered or due to personal proclivities.) After the Restoration (1868) the family lost their stipend, and Hidetoshi scraped out a living teaching Nô and neo-Confucian philosophy. Hidetoshi's situation was very similar to that of many middle-ranking samurai at the beginning of the Meiji era, but as noted above his was not a family with a samurai background.[19]

The first real warrior in the family was Hidetoshi's son Hidenori. In search of something more promising he went to Tokyo in 1873 and enlisted in a school for training non-commissioned officers for the new Imperial Army. After completing this training he was made a sergeant in the infantry and sent to Kyushu. There he fought with the newly formed Imperial Army against the samurai-led Satsuma uprising in 1877—the last challenge to the power and authority of the new regime in Tokyo. He distinguished himself in this conflict, was made a sub-lieutenant, and later in 1883 he entered the first class of the newly established Army Staff College (Rikugun Daigakkô). There he was taught, among others, by the German advisor to the Meiji government for military affairs, Major Jacob Meckel (1842–1906). Meckel's organization of the Japanese army and the tactics he taught were preserved as basic principles in the Imperial Army until the end of the Second World War. Hidenori graduated first in his class (1885) and subsequently had a brilliant career, despite the fact that he did not come from Chôshû (roughly present-day Yamaguchi) or Satsuma (roughly present-day Kagoshima). Officers from these areas, especially from Chôshû— the so-called Chôshû-clique (*Chôshû gunbatsu*)—dominated the army well into the 1930s, and later Tôjô Hideki attributed this discrimination to his father's "only" reaching the rank of lieutenant general upon retirement.[20]

Hideki was the eldest of six children, with the resultant privileges and bearing the attendant family expectations. This does not seem to have bothered him, but we know very little about his early years. One of the few sources dealing with his father, mother, and upbringing is the above biography. It contains, however, only a mix of platitudes about his upright, stern parents and resulting family life. He is said to have greatly feared confronting his father after getting into mischief, for example, and he was known from a very early age for being quick, decisive, and quarrelsome—qualities which characterized his entire life and career.

Early on Tôjô supposedly wanted to pursue a career in the army. During his first years of formal schooling he was not the best student and was something of a troublemaker. His mother was called to the school for this reason several times. He was remembered for having an extremely unyielding spirit and would not be deterred from doing well enough to achieve entry into the army academy (and before, an army prep school). At times he got into fights with "big kids" and was trounced. But when pinned down and caught around the throat, Tôjô would never concede defeat. He held out and eventually his opponent gave in. And he was quite conscious of his indebtedness to those above him, as with his school principal the source of the above story.[21]

Which is to say our knowledge of Tôjô's early life is rather romanticized— consisting of anecdotes about how he was, based on what he became: a persevering general and prime minister intent on getting his way, unswervingly loyal to the imperial line and national essence. One must remember that when this biography was written Tôjô had just stood up to the "bullying" Western powers and he was for most Japanese a hero. Thus, most Japanese then probably accepted this semi-fictional biography as fact. This makes the descriptions interesting, and this sort of handling of a hero is not unique to Japan or Tôjô.

Ethics teachings and Tôjô

Tôjô entered the Tokyo Regional Army Preparatory School in 1899 at the age of fifteen. Apparently his marks were still not particularly noteworthy but his quick temper was, and here he received the nickname "fighting Tôjô." However, he experienced a transformation during his second year at the school, according to this telling. Suddenly he began to study seriously, and he came to be known for his academic diligence. One contemporary later reported that in a fight involving seven or eight students Tôjô came out on the losing side, and he realized that, "No matter how strong, one can only deal with a single enemy. And in order to win, even when one brings considerable power to bear against an adversary, without learning, after all, one is done for."[22] Later he was also reputed to exhaustively examine as many aspects of a problem as possible before reaching a decision.

Tôjô entered the Central Army Prep School in 1902 at age eighteen. In reporting the episodes thereafter, developments in China dominate the biography. Emphasis is on military training and the strenuous accelerated course. There is little about Tôjô himself, but laudatory narratives about training and later the Russo-Japanese War and the cadets' burning desire to be commissioned and get into the fray before it was over. The narrative emphasizes the success of Japan's policies at home and ventures abroad. Finally Tôjô entered the Army Academy as an advanced student in 1904, 17th Class, and he was commissioned a 2nd lieutenant, infantry, in 1905 shortly before the end of the Russo-Japanese War. He was sent to the mainland immediately after being commissioned but saw no action.

Here, in order to look briefly at ethics teachings then, I depart from this "biography" and turn to information about the army prep schools revealed in recent research. The Meiji government officially established special preparatory schools for training future military officers through an imperial ordinance (*chokurei*) of 1896. Therein the purpose and policies of the military schools were delineated. In all of Japan there were six regional centers, one each in Sendai, Tokyo, Nagoya, Osaka, Hiroshima, and Kumamoto, and a Central Preparatory School in Tokyo. They provided general education and specialized military exercises intended as preparation for a military career. Also these schools put great emphasis on spiritual training. It was explicitly stated that whether or not a student was suitable material for becoming an officer was not something limited to academic achievement. Developing appropriate spiritual qualities was indispensable.[23] As for the Tôjô all later came to know, of particular note is the general definition of the purpose of the Regional Army Preparatory Schools, which includes a phrase about the importance of "the cultivation of military spirit."[24] The second article of the 1898 "General Education Plan for the Army Regional Preparatory Schools," issued one year before Tôjô entered the school in Tokyo, stated: "Cultivate feelings of reverence for the emperor and love of country." This article was elaborated upon as follows:

> After all, the independence and prosperity of a country is based on the people's sincere loyalty and devotion. If the people fail, even to the slightest degree, to overflow with this feeling, do not combine their efforts and follow obediently their leaders, the national destiny will never be preserved. For the sake of being able to light up the national glory eternally the education at the Army Preparatory Schools adopts, in particular, this idea. The students are enlightened and guided, and this feeling [of sincere loyalty to the throne] should be developed and cultivated.[25]

One can see that the inviolability of the emperor and the very survival of the nation were said to be at stake. In line with this trend, at the Sendai Regional Army Preparatory School between 1899 and 1901, the Student Supervisor ordered that during the night watch each student was to be tested on the content and interpretation of the Precepts to Soldiers and Sailors. Most cadets memorized them. Not to be outdone by a school in the provinces, at the Regional Army Preparatory School in Tokyo every morning students worshipped the imperial palace and their parents, and in their rooms they respectfully read the *Imperial Precepts to Soldiers and Sailors*. This was not done at all army preparatory schools at this time, but one can see here that authorities placed special importance on moral-spiritual training at the school Tôjô attended.[26] We do not know how he felt about this training at that time, but we certainly do know about his extraordinary loyalty to the Emperor when he was an army general and prime minister. Also, the future emperor was similarly indoctrinated at the school he attended. Emperor Hirohito and his military leaders shared similar convictions about Imperial Japanese history and culture.

Here one must remember that in Imperial Japan mythology was taught and accepted by most as history. For example, in 1933 incoming Japanese History students at Tokyo Imperial University were explicitly told to differentiate between "applied history" (*ôyô shigaku*) as taught in the schools and "genuine history" (*junsei shigaku*) as learned and researched at a university. This meant, a highly respected retired history professor announced, that though the imperial dynasty actually only extends over 600 years, since up to now (1933) everyone has been taught that the dynasty is 2,600 years old this is what should be taught. The inviolable *Nihon Shoki* (AD 720), base of the ideology supporting the imperial nation, is the source of this information and these sorts of truths were not to be criticized or called into question.[27]

Other records show that shortly before Tôjô entered this system moral instruction was increasingly emphasized at all army preparatory schools. In an ordinance from 1897 entitled "Moral Instruction Specifications" topics are listed for teaching at the regional schools. The *Imperial Precepts to Soldiers and Sailors* and the *Imperial Rescript on Education* were the basis of this education. The list begins with the "essence of morality." And this is defined as follows:

> The imperial ancestor [Emperor Jimmu] is the founder of our empire. He is the lord and father of our ancestors. The emperor is the legitimate [heir] of the founder of the imperial family and imperial ancestors. The subjects of our emperor are also descendants of this branch [of the imperial family]. Rendering up the mind and body of the people and exhausting sincere loyalty, this is to requite the grace [*on*] of the blessings of successive emperors, and at the same time this is the rationale informing the way that serves our ancestors.[28]

One can see even in this short excerpt the classical mix of Shintô mythology as found in the earliest histories of Japan, the *Kojiki* (AD 712) and *Nihon Shoki* (AD 720), and Confucian devotion to one's ancestors as propagated for many centuries. In Imperial Japan this meant devotion not only to the ancestors of one's own family but much more devotion to the ancestors of the imperial line. The purpose of this instruction obviously was to instill in officer cadets the unique Japanese moral values that were centered on the nation Japan—founded and legitimized by the imperial line. The imperial line and its heavenly progenitor the Sun Goddess were by definition unique to Japan. An omniscient deity and humanitarian values transcending Amaterasu Omikami, the Japanese emperor, the empire, and Japanese morals were not only incompatible with this doctrine, they were inconceivable for most. Moreover, such was contrary to the Meiji Constitution. Therein the state pronounced the emperor an inviolable supreme being. Of course not everyone who attended one of these prep schools and later the Army Academy believed unquestioningly the imperial ethics taught in them. Tôjô, however, unquestioningly accepted this doctrine and later ardently espoused it.

As for success in school and later in life, Tôjô denied that he or anyone else was endowed with special talents. Success was solely a matter of how hard one worked, and he worked hard long hours. However, for some very talented/successful persons, doing well is not enough. They need norms and guidelines that prescribe proper conduct and how activities are to be carried out. Also, some yearn for something meaningful to which they can devote themselves and put their talents to use. They want something to believe in. Tôjô Hideki appears to have been that sort of person: the Imperial Army provided the former; the imperial line and national essence satisfied the latter need. And when worst came to worst he did not abandon his convictions. They were worth more to him than life itself.

However, one should be aware that some of Tôjô's contemporaries thought that he went to extremes with his articles of faith. Toward the end of the war, former Admiral, Grand Chamberlain, and Prime Minister at the end of the war Suzuki Kantarô (1867–1948) said Tôjô was inordinately obsessed with his own convictions. "One cannot win a war only with convictions." And when Tôjô sought to obstruct efforts to end the war based on his beliefs, Suzuki let slip to confidents near him that he thought Tôjô a "mad-dog" sort of a person.[29]

Supreme values

Tôjô along with many of his contemporary future officers imbibed what they were taught—that the highest value in life was serving unconditionally and without reservation the imperial line, and by extension state officials who spoke in the name of the emperor. No higher authority or set of values was entertained. This can be seen clearly in the topics on the "essence of morality." Besides the normal education topics included in cadet education, as noted above, reverence for the emperor, love of country, and reverence for the gods were emphasized.[30] In the Imperial Army normal planning and risk assessment were affected by these "higher" Japanese values.

In particular, the aforementioned moral values legitimized national policies. For example, self-defense may not be a moral principle, but it is the unquestioned right of any nation. In Imperial Japan it was a duty legitimized in the name of unconditional commitment (obligation) to the imperial line: a generally accepted conviction was given particularistic roots. Commitment to the imperial line and national essence were the basis of the politics of "self-preservation and self-defense." The term, *jison-ji'ei* in Japanese, appears in the last paragraph of the Japanese war declaration of December 8, 1941, summing up her reasons for going to war. *Ergo*, war was unavoidable as Japan sought to honor the imperial ancestors, defend the imperial state, and assure everlasting peace in Asia.[31] Self-preservation and self-defense are still accepted by many as legitimate justifications for going to war.

Japanese claims of freeing Asia from Occidental colonialism were not just a postwar afterthought. During the war a number of Asians agreed with and applauded these efforts. Even Thailand, neutral before the beginning of hostilities, praised this offensive. For example, a Thai delegation to Japan at the end of April 1942 explicitly called for the "thorough expulsion of the British and Americans from all heaven and earth in Asia."[32] One could also say, of course, that the Thai delegation was only doing, sensibly, what was expected of them at the time.

Later self-preservation and self-defense became a conspicuous leitmotif at the Yûshûkan, the war museum at Yasukuni Shrine. However, immediately after the war, during the debate among the Allies on whether the Emperor was to be made responsible for it, this important issue was forgotten. After it was decided (provisionally) that Emperor Hirohito was not to be charged, Tôjô the war premier assumed center-stage. Consistent with the moral values learned at the Army Preparatory School and Army Academy he assumed responsibility for opening the war—a war of self-preservation and self-defense. But this line of reasoning was rejected during the Tokyo War Crimes Trial as a vindication for initiating the war.[33] Regardless, Tôjô's justification for going to war at the War Crimes Trials was consistent with his earlier convictions.

Long before this finale these extreme proto-religious convictions adversely affected rational decision-making in Imperial Japan. Prior to the war many high-ranking Japanese officers knew that US military-industrial might far exceeded that of Japan. Nevertheless, Japan went to war. But some maintain, "war with the United States was not chosen. The decision for war was rather forced by the desire to avoid the more terrible alternative of losing status or abandoning national objectives."[34] Japan felt threatened with humiliation and ruin, and therefore had to fight against the United States and her allies. This Japanese understanding of self-preservation and self-defense and the Japanese moral values informing these concepts were important before and during the war. Tôjô Hideki was a leading proponent of these beliefs and attendant policies. Loyalty to emperor and nation overshadowed at times the formulation of rational military, state policies and at other times this loyalty became a masquerade cloaking the ambitions of state leaders. Nonetheless, there were well-known fabled precedents for Tôjô's approach to politics and war.

Historical models

In 1899, the year in which Tôjô entered the Regional Army Preparatory School in Tokyo, significant changes were made in the plan for teaching Japanese morals. After introducing students to the "characteristic knowledge and attitudes of the cadets at the school," morality was taught as history without overwhelming students with abstract concepts. Instead during their first two years at the school they were given concrete examples of persons from the past who embodied correct morality. This sort of "history" was a standard approach in all schools at this time.[35] A prime example that Tôjô and his contemporary cadets especially heard about is Kusunoki Masashige (1294[?]–1336), a famous folk hero in Imperial Japan. He was used to demonstrate the unity of two key concepts in prewar ideology, loyalty (*chû*) and filial piety (*kô*). Kusunoki supported Emperor Godaigo (1288–1339) in his futile attempt to defeat Ashikaga Takauji (1305–58) and restore political power to the Imperial House during the Kemmu Restoration (1333–36). Finally, after initial successes, following the Emperor's command he went into a hopeless battle at the Minato River (near present-day Osaka) and was defeated. He committed suicide, and this battle spelled the end of Godaigo's cause. Due to his selfless devotion to the Emperor, Kusunoki was especially honored in Imperial Japan as a perfect example of loyalty to the Imperial House.[36] And Tôjô Hideki admired greatly this paragon of imperial virtue.

In accord with the above imperial command when Kusunoki advanced into the Hyôgo area, he stopped off on the way to his confrontation with the Ashikaga to visit his ten-year-old son Masatsura. He tells his son that they are meeting for the last time, and "You [Masatsura] should unflinchingly follow your father's wishes and be completely loyal to the sovereign. This is the highest order of filial piety."[37] After his father's departure Masatsura continually sought out news about him. Upon hearing of his demise he was on the verge of committing suicide, but his mother restrained him reminding him of his father's last wishes. Would he be un-filial and ignore them? Of course not. After he grew up he remained unwaveringly loyal to Emperor Gomurakami (1328–68) (of the southern court—successor to Godaigo). He was regarded as a threat by the Ashikaga and after many engagements finally was defeated by them. Before this final clash he visited the Emperor, informed him of his intentions, and bid him farewell. The Emperor praised him for his loyalty. He went into the conflict with a small force against a large army at Shijônawate (in the eastern part of present-day Osaka). He was defeated, killed, and his brothers, legend has it, committed suicide by stabbing one another, all dying on the same pillow. The story ends with a proverb: "The loyal subject comes from a house of filial piety!"[38]

The man was the means to an important message: Kusunoki Masashige was a devoted supporter of the Imperial House, and as such he embodied the two Confucian virtues deemed most important in prewar Japan—loyalty and filial piety. The seeming contradiction between the two was resolved by his actions and admonitions. Because of its importance in Imperial Japan, this highly praised characteristic, the unity of loyalty and filial piety, needs elaboration. Herein is a potential conflict that is not readily discernible today. Might not one's obligation to one's own parents and ancestors (filial piety) be incompatible with one's obligations to the state (loyalty)? What if an only son is ordered to the front when his only living parent is sick and in need of care? Here is a latent contradiction and purposefully amalgamating these two ideals was important. It was a potential no-win situation at that time since many recruits came from the countryside where their contribution to meeting their family's workload and other responsibilities was essential to the survival of their kinsfolk. Going into the army was a "great honor" and vital to the Empire's independence and self-defense, but the absence of a working member of the family might endanger the existence of the core element of the Confucian ethical system—the family. Appropriately this possible ethical conflict was the theme of many moral stories.

The dilemma was solved in a manner not really unique to Japan. Briefly, since a person's house ancestors are ultimately related back to the Imperial House, loyalty to the emperor and state is the same as filial piety with respect to the imperial ancestors *and* one's own ancestors. One's personal house ancestors are the objects of lesser veneration; Imperial House ancestors are the objects of greater veneration. The obligations to one's own ancestors one calls "filial piety"; obligations to the Imperial House one calls "loyalty." In the end though they are the same. But these ethical duties, like everything else in Imperial Japan, have a hierarchical relationship—the Imperial House and the nation stand above a common person's house, and if a person is called upon to sacrifice himself for the nation this takes priority over his own house. The Meiji government put this in terms more readily acceptable to most people: "loyalty to the emperor equals loyalty to one's parents."[39]

This threatening inconsistency was not a recent development. The last line from the Kusunoki tale quoted above is a proverb that comes from ancient Chinese history. Consulting the source of this proverb—the "Wei Biao Zhuan" (Biography of Wei Biao) in the *Hou Han Shu* (History of the Latter Han Dynasty, compilation completed *c.* AD 432) and other Chinese texts dealing with this topic shows two things: (1) prewar Japanese while prosecuting a war in what they regarded as a backward area, China, nevertheless respected Chinese tradition; and (2) that the possible contradiction between loyalty to one's ruler and filial conduct with respect to one's familial authorities and ancestors was also the subject of considerable debate in premodern China.[40] Thus the topic, provoked by the contradiction between the necessities imposed by pursuing modern state designs and revered national customs from the golden past, was not something new. Rather, after being confronted with this problem, modern Japanese adopted ancient Chinese wisdom, which they in turn adapted to their needs, here to interpret and employ Japanese history to reinforce the underpinnings of the emperor and his empire of the rising sun.

Other objects of educational focus were selected and interpreted similarly— as models for emulation in Imperial Japanese society, not as objects of historical interest. Intuitive loyalty to the emperor and filial piety, perseverance, xenophobia, respect for rural origins, the heritage of many young officers, were propagated through paradigms. Teaching about these figures Japanese morality was transmitted using well-known highly respected persons from the past. Mass indoctrination began at an early age.

Moral and spiritual fortitude

From 1899 moral instruction was more strongly focused on the emperor, and after the above introduction moral teachings took a more uncompromising form in the third year at the regional army preparatory schools. The topics were more rigorous. A brief review of the school curriculum shows that a number of themes encouraged values for which Tôjô later became well known:

> The national essence and the military system.
> Loyalty, patriotism, personal moral duty (*honbun*), integrity, honor.
> Propriety, obedience, dignity, benevolence, conformity/cooperation.
> Valor, courage, discretion, temperateness.
> Fidelity, obedience-disobedience, and that which conforms to the right way to live and that which does not.
> Simplicity/modesty/frugality, uprightness/honesty/integrity.
> Sincerity, morality.[41]

Also, a brief comparison shows that these topics are nearly identical with the ones in the third year of moral instruction in the plan formulated in 1922. Clearly the guidelines for moral instruction, meaning also the desired moral inclinations of army officers, were conceived and promulgated when Tôjô was in a preparatory school for future army leaders, and this basic orientation was preserved and enhanced throughout the prewar years.

Later while he was at the Army Academy the "Information for Army Academy Students" newly emphasized the importance of moral factors:

> Officers are the mainstay of the army, the home of military esprit de corps. The ebb and flow of this spirit relates immediately to the strength of the entire army. What indeed is military spirit? It is self-sacrificing loyalty, courage and fidelity which one devotes to the emperor. It is to properly observe the proprieties and submit to military discipline emphasizing modesty and simplicity. That is, the students at our school should thoroughly cultivate this spirit. They should take care to earnestly cultivate strength and eschew effeminacy. They should follow the way of learning, should study diligently and should perfect completely the self-discipline [necessary] to becoming one day a new officer.[42]

Like the other officer candidates, Tôjô was instructed from an early age about the importance of moral and spiritual fortitude. Later he was noted for his uncompromising discipline and unswerving loyalty to the Emperor. He acquired this reputation well before the Tokyo War Crimes Trial, where he consciously assumed all blame for starting the war—shielding Emperor Hirohito from war crimes charges.

General Tôjô, belief over rationality

Tôjô Hideki is an illustration of the "believers" in prewar Japan. He was an exceptionally successful Imperial Army officer, but he was not an anomaly. He was an ideal product of imperial Japanese education—an example of the amalgamation of rational thinking (state) and irrational spiritual nationalism. During his time as prime minister he approached his managerial responsibilities in a pragmatic way. This refers not only to military matters. He was also a politician. For example, in February 1942 importing and distributing rice, which was insufficient, was discussed in a cabinet meeting. There is no record of this being made public, but when rice was distributed at a number of places in Tokyo, like any politico, Tôjô visited them on those occasions. Shortages of other foodstuffs were an ongoing concern. Tôjô noted this in his reports and where possible initiated measures to alleviate the problems.[43]

Later, as can be seen in his sworn affidavit prepared for the Tokyo War Crimes Tribunal, he was extremely well versed in official procedures and prided himself on following them precisely. For example, in explaining the process by which Japan came to an alliance with Germany and Italy, he cites very clearly and logically the official decisions made before he became prime minister. It was government policy before he assumed office.[44] He was not an initiator; in supporting the alliance he was only doing his duty to carry out government policy previously decided. (One could argue of course that he sought to lighten his culpability, but a verdict against him and the death sentence were foregone conclusions early on in the proceedings.) This extreme bureaucratic rationality was combined with a similarly extreme sense of loyalty to the emperor and national polity, which sometimes overshadowed his perception of the realities of modern warfare. For example, confronted with diminishing war potential and failing productive capacity, on June 20, 1944, Tôjô told his subordinates enthusiastically, "The strong point of the Japanese is that everyone risks all; we are daring, not afraid of death. Against one enemy aircraft carrier we send in one plane and with it can defeat the carrier. This is the strength of Japan."[45]

Before the beginning of the Pacific War Tôjô was well known as a war advocate. Therefore even among other highly placed persons also known for their favorable disposition toward the military, for example Prince Higashikuni, his appointment as prime minister was difficult to understand. How could the Emperor, with the counsel of his political advisor Kido Kôichi, appoint Tôjô prime minister if they were against war with the United States and her allies?[46] Nonetheless, Tôjô was appointed the leader of the government, ostensibly to control the volatile army, and a war ensued. To be sure, Tôjô was not a member of the Imperial Way Faction and was not one of those known as an advocate of fighting with "human bullets."[47] However, as seen above, even before the war with the United States and her allies began, Tôjô promulgated a *Field Service Code* mandating a no-surrender policy for the Imperial Army. Later as the war approached a conclusion he knew would be disastrous, he too grasped at spiritual straws hoping to achieve what was by all rational accounts impossible—victory over an enemy obviously superior in material and manpower. Or at least the war should be made less costly to lose in terms of preserving national honor and the national essence, by making it more costly for the enemy to win. This was the logic behind the obligatory spirit and rationale that informed the refusal of Japanese troops to surrender—the so-called "honorable death": a desperate fight to the death when obviously defeated and the infamous kamikaze tactics.[48] Tôjô also espoused these beliefs and policies, but as with most government leaders, the chance that he personally would be called upon "to embrace a bomb" was very small. Mass indoctrination included deceiving oneself.

Approach to command

Tôjô received his commission during the Russo-Japanese War and was an ambitious field grade officer in the mid-1920s, when military funding was cut and internal problems were troubling the army. But he was not the type of person who doubted himself or his calling. His moral and spiritual convictions underpinned a very determined, if not always realistic approach to actual issues. This one can see clearly in the first-hand description of him by Col. Akamatsu. Akamatsu was dependent on Tôjô for his career and was an unabashed admirer, but his descriptions are from postwar personal memoirs and were not intended to promote himself or relieve his mentor of responsibility. He wanted to show how Tôjô conceived of and carried out his responsibilities.

Tôjô was accepted, respected, admired, and feared by many. Even after the war he was described as an unrepentant, loyal soldier. Tôjô was an extreme believer in sedulous preparation—in school (finally), military, and political matters. As noted above, he implacably maintained that there are no superior persons and that failure or success depends on the effort one makes when developing and executing plans. Military genius and charisma played no role in his thought. This can be seen in his personal statements to others.[49] Rather than genius, Tôjô emphasized something important to him all through his career: unrelenting endeavor and assuming responsibility for what one does and does not do.

> The strength and weakness of a soldier rests entirely on the question of his sense of responsibility. People are not superior or inferior. In the end it is a matter of whether a person has an uncompromising sense of responsibility. When effort is channeled such that one strives unceasingly, authority accrues. Which is to say, if a soldier has a resolute sense of responsibility, he is strong.[50]

These convictions strongly informed his policies as prime minister. In March 1944, when Japan obviously was on the brink of losing the war, Tôjô's remedy was increased self-sacrifice and increased effort. This was not simply a call for kamikaze pilots. The entire society was to be transformed. Students, workers, companies, all were to work for the state in a symbiotic manner and contribute to doing the impossible—winning the war.[51] At this juncture, unquestioning loyalty to the emperor, the imperial state, and a resolute belief in the spiritual superiority of the Japanese folk informed his actions. And this combination of devotion to the head of the nation, emperor, and diligent hard work as an army, state, official characterized his life and career.

Earlier, as an army commander, Tôjô made exhaustive preparations. This can be seen in the way he led a campaign in Mongolia while Kwantung (*Guandong*) Army chief of staff.⁵² In the planning stage he consulted with experts in various fields. After a plan was decided upon, it was carried out with great attention to detail. Later as prime minister, he conducted himself in the same way. Before the opening of the war with the United States, Great Britain, and their allies the people had to be united. Tôjô consulted with important cabinet members, the Privy Council, army and navy general staffs, and the elder statesmen (as ordered by the Emperor). Finally the decision for war was reached. It was, according to Akamatsu, not based on coercion or the like, but thorough preparation, honesty and fidelity, and trust in the sincerity and loyalty of the people and their love of country.⁵³

This appears like adulation, yet these priorities and convictions are consistent with Tôjô's articles of faith and those taught in the army prep schools and the Military Academy. Notably missing in Akamatsu's memory of this rationale is practical evaluation of the relative industrial and military strengths of the opposing powers. These sorts of evaluations were available, but in the interest of "national interests" they were neglected.⁵⁴ Also missing was that Tôjô never led a division in combat but directed an army (for fifteen months). In the mid to late 1930s he became known for his administrative proficiency and prowess as a contender in the unending factional disputes within the Imperial Army. These skills paved the way for his rise to power. Later, in mid-1941, members of a "Tôjô clique," who like Tôjô were strong war advocates, were maneuvered into key positions in both the army general staff and ministry.⁵⁵

Tôjô as a political leader

More generally, consistent with learned spiritual and moral beliefs, diligence and power politics, Tôjô sought to rule in an autocratic "Japanese" way. "The true way of Japanese politics is manifested by uniting the people and emperor as one, i.e. [bringing together] the ruler and the entire nation."⁵⁶ The following is a statement by Tôjô recorded by his private secretary on the occasion of domestic political reforms at the end of September 1943. It is a good un-dramatic description of his approach to politics:

> First of all, politics is something that is in accord with reality; secondly it is important that it should be appropriate to the times. As for the policy of strengthening the country's internal situation, if one does this in half a year or even a year from now this is surely of little use. In the "Yokuseikai"

[*Yokusanseijikai*: a "one-country-one-party" political association formed by Tôjô in May 1942] what is proposed reflects what supposedly is the atmosphere among the people. Herewith one understands the general tendency, the atmosphere surrounding what the people want. Then in the Cabinet at the last cabinet meeting [September 17, 1943] I presented a tentative plan. A variety of opinions were obtained, and should the emperor have an opinion on this matter I asked to receive it in a day or two. As in the cabinet meeting yesterday, one cannot say there were surprises and this sort of preparation is important.

Which is to say, the Cabinet remarks include various [opinions] which are in that plan. Which is to say, if one looks at the times and does not act, this is not politics. Moreover, rather than doing something which is more or less in accord with what the people are thinking, one must do something which is about one step ahead of them. Doing something two or even three steps ahead, this is not the politics of a country in which the people are led. One proposes something one step ahead, and the people feel a little bit of pressure. One must do something thought to be somewhat shrewd. One must engage in a sort of politics in which pulling together sufficiently the country's power, including both young and old among the people, the slow moving people, nearly all of them, can be drawn along. The people move along in a lax way. In response to this it is important to lead the people from a position about one step ahead of them.

There are persons who are called idealists. The ideas of people like Ishiwara [Kanji, 1889–1949] are good, but they are not put into practice. Ideas that are not put into practice, because a person's feet do not touch the ground, they do not constitute politics that lead the people. The concepts of idealists have many points that engage me as concepts, but as for politics that is put into practice I do not utilize them as they are.

I myself am not a politician. I am merely someone in the army who for many years simply only put strategy as it is into practice.

What is more, in deciding something, the above preparations only are insufficient. If there are persons in the Cabinet at this time who oppose these measures, what should one do on this occasion? Should one steam-roller on or not, etc. Last Sunday I considered these various points at length.

In case opposition emerges in the Cabinet, immediately without going into detail I bring up matters that should be anticipated one after the other. I present them as proposals. If one makes preparations to this extent one can rest assured that one is able to make progress with matters.

Now, there is talk about the prime minister's careful preparations when Foreign Minister Tôgô [Shigenori, 1882–1950] opposed the establishment of the

Greater East Asia Ministry and a possible change in cabinet officers emerged. Also there is the question of the bad atmosphere in part of the Peers Council and attendant preparations for suspending it on the day it went out of session.

(Note [in the original text]: The Prime Minister made careful preparations, and therefore afterwards matters were dealt with promptly point by point.)

The vast majority of the people are grey in color. A very small number of them dabble in various words of criticism. Therefore, as one who would lead the people, it is important to grasp firmly the vast majority of grey colored people and quickly pull them along. The grey vast majority will come along accordingly if the leader says something is to be white or go to the right [or whatever]. As for something which becomes white naturally, if one simply lets it happen one will wait for 100 years for it to come about.[57]

Tôjô saw himself as a very practical, disciplined, devoted servant of the emperor and state, not as a particularly talented or patriotic man. If records like the one referred to here and others elsewhere may be believed, with caution, this seems to be a reasonable evaluation.

Contemporaries have maintained that Tôjô became an autocrat and brooked no opposition to his interpretation of what was in the best interests of emperor and empire.[58] No doubt his reputation for being decisive, strict, and even personally ruthless is not without grounds. Already at the end of 1941, two weeks after the attack on Pearl Harbor, he instructed in a cabinet meeting that high officials and the press should be properly informed of government policy on specific issues and that they should conduct themselves accordingly.[59] Also, he was not above manipulating political processes. At the end of April 1942 he told the minister of the interior that steps should be taken to insure that the upcoming election came out in the government's favor. One of these steps was the formation of the above-mentioned Yokuseikai to promote Tôjô's political agenda. Included therein were many leading politicians and businessmen. After the election turned out as planned, he then focused on concentrating political power such that he could control national affairs better.[60] This included oppression of dissenters using the Tokyo Military Police (*kempeitai*). For example, Tôjô was apparently behind the military police arrest of Nakano Seigô, a journalist, right-wing politician and Tôjô detractor, in late 1943. Under duress, Nakano committed suicide while Kempeitai officials considered his fate.[61] Violence and threats were an integral part of his world, and applying them to achieve what he identified as the Emperor's ends was for Tôjô simple common sense.

However, many government leaders equate their personal programs with those of the nation-state and Tôjô was in this sense far from being unusual.

This willful identification of a leader's personal values as those of his country is one of the basic, largely unaddressed problems of the modern nation-state as an unchallengeable authority. Indoctrination by nation-state authorities and self-deception compliment one another. Together they may stifle opposition, furthermore, state indoctrination of the populace in a national ethos can also blind leaders as well as followers to impending realities. They come to believe their own fables. Ultimately in Imperial Japan this was important to her loss of the War in the Pacific.

A new vision of society

According to records by his secretaries, in March 1944, responding to insufficient production of war materials, Tôjô proposed a radical reform of the Japanese school system and business world. The plan appears almost socialistic in content but that was not his intent. It was born out of the necessities deriving from a war Japan was losing, not some political philosophy or set of religious teachings. A section head from the Munitions Ministry appealed on March 12, 1944, for the mobilization of students from the second year of middle school up to increase industrial production. Three days later Tôjô made the presentation summarized below to the department heads of that ministry. Devotion to the emperor is certainly to be seen therein, however, not as a preamble to but a basis for and legitimization of, the new order and new sacrifices. The plan is an interesting mix of social industrial facts and wishful thinking.[62]

Tôjô began with statistics about the number of workers it takes to keep a soldier in the field in Japan, Germany, and America: 12:1, 4:1, 8:1 respectively, whereby in Japan the base figure is for the total number of workers, in Germany only male workers, and in the United States female workers. Then Tôjô notes briefly the numbers of students that might be mobilized in Japanese industry. He quotes the memoirs of former British Prime Minister David Lloyd George (prime minister 1916–22) to the effect that a strong folk will not necessarily win a war, rather the one that best knows how to employ appropriately its labor resources. This is followed by a sermon on the reform of labor in Japan, the mobilization of Japanese students without harming their pride and self-respect, and Tôjô presented an outline of his thoughts on how the state should be reorganized:

Changes in the essential qualities of a company (after the war):

1. Company = capital, labor, materials
   a. Rights and interests — [superseded by] state compensation
   b. Capital and materials — state enforcement
   c. Labor — conscription

2. Calling forth Japan's special characteristics
   a. Loyalty of the military centered on the imperial house
   b. Solidarity of the people centered on the imperial house
   c. Mutual assistance and security of the family system centered on the imperial house

3. Up till now our social structure was Occidental in form (a method whereby people were gathered centered around the firm). The Japanese way is that a company must emerge in a collective relationship with a region.
   a. The school system remains in its present form and engages with companies, or the school is industrialized. (Brigade of the Dedicated)
   b. Utilization of redundant labor forces in the local neighborhood associations [*tonarigumi*]—through links with factories in production or through blood relationships this is possible. (Worker care …)

4. Obstacles
   a. The heads of [business] executive groups [must be] changed
   b. Subcontractors involving undesirable but unavoidable relations: taking commissions, false accusations, pretext of military secrets.
   c. Poorly trained skilled workers

1. Dislike of being used by a company. Can't all be done under state supervision?
2. What office shall take charge of mobilizing the students?

   - Regard for Japan's National Essence
   - Leaders can turn gray into white or into black.

This is followed by statistics on the numbers of students at the middle school and high school level, boys and girls, who might be mobilized.

This plan reflects two things: the desperate state of Japan's war industries already in early 1944, and Tôjô's conviction that trying harder will bring success regardless of fact-based odds to the contrary. The Imperial House and national essence were both the foundation for overcoming the impossible and the reason for doing so—true belief will in the end triumph and the essence of Japan must be saved at all costs. In fact though, true belief led only to more destruction and defeat.

Law

Equally important to his manner of making and executing decisions was Tôjô's understanding of law. It was quite different from what in the West was accepted (if not always practiced as evidenced in part at the Tokyo War Crimes Trials).[63] He believed that modern law is not something originally Japanese, therefore rational Western legal standards were not beyond question.

> One must not forget that present-day law has a history [only] going back to the Meiji Era. As everyone knows, it is a legal system learned in the occident and set up accordingly under the circumstances of the time when Japan strove to conclude equal treaties with many countries. At the imperial universities etc. this Western style law was taught. However, Japanese law of old had three legal statutes and this sufficed. [*Sanpôjô* refers to the *Fa San Zhang* of Emperor Gao-zu (256–195 BC) founder of the Han Dynasty. It alludes to a simplification of the law for the benefit of the people reducing it to three crimes: murder, wounding another, and theft.[64]] Japan's special quality is the premise that people are [basically] good [*zennin*]. By contrast occidental laws are formulated from the standpoint that people are wicked [*akunin*], and these bad people must be eliminated. Therefore, in Japanese law through skillful handling by the judge one must bring into being good persons. [Then a well-known concept seen in the history of the Song Dynasty, *Song-shi*, compilation completed in 1345.] I think one may call the Ôoka Court a Japanese-style court. [This refers to the adjudication of Ôoka Tadasuke (1677–1751).[65]] But nowadays how are things? According to actual law a thief active during a bombing raid cannot be sentenced to death. The faults in actual law are self-evident.[66]

Tôjô believed in adapting the law to the times, here wartime. Based on his belief in acting in a Japanese way to bring out the good in people and the necessity of adapting to wartime conditions, he thought it necessary and right to apply the law liberally as he saw fit. That this sort of action abrogated the predictability of the law and the equality of all before the law did not occur to him. Or if it did, it was not mentioned here. One reason he made suppositions like those above was that he projected similar assumptions onto the Emperor. "The emperor in observing his myriad people regards them benevolently as all having the same virtue. Even a bad child is precious. In any case it is still a child, and this is the Japanese way. If there is a bad person, the Japanese way is to somehow mend this person and make him good."[67] Since the people are his children, the Emperor could not admonish or even cajole them in those difficult times. Tôjô acted therefore as a sort of representative of the Emperor when such was necessary. He said this to one of his secretaries on the day he was appointed prime minister.[68] The Emperor, as Tôjô saw him to be, legitimized his actions, some of which included persuasive practices decidedly less than benevolent.

On a totally different occasion at a different time he again denigrated Occidental law in favor of that found in Japan. "As for Japanese law, first comes the spirit [seishin] as the basis." For "Japanese law" one should study the basic law code from 1232 of the Kamakura Shogunate (Goseibai Shikimoku, also known as the Jôei Shikimoku) and the 17 Article Constitution of Crown Prince Shôtoku from the year 604 (Jûshichijô Kempô). The 1232 code was informed by the important Buddhist concept of dôri, the way and/or precepts followed by all beings. Hôjô Yasutoki (1183–1242), one of the founders of the shogunate as a system of rule, "made frequent use of the term [...] as a designation for the spirit of, and practical byways in warrior society." Others have called this a simple basis for settling disputes based on practical reason and the common sense of that day.[69]

As for the 17 Article Constitution, some experts now deny that Crown Prince Shôtoku authored it, or that he ever existed. This hypothesis was of course unknown until very recently. In Imperial Japan (and for many years later) the "Constitution" was an extremely well-known and highly revered document strongly colored by early Japanese interpretations of Chinese Confucianism, Buddhism, and Taoism. Of special interest, "this Constitution exhorts the people to lay aside partisan differences and accept imperial rule in order to achieve social harmony."[70] Social harmony is a classical Chinese Confucian priority. Emphasizing it together with hereditary Imperial House rule is an Imperial Japanese construal of these ethics. Promoting Confucian social harmony in the name of, and for the sake of, the Imperial House and the kokutai—meaning Japan's rulers, the national essence, and the dependent social order—were basic to the Imperial Japanese way of life. And this was basic to Tôjô's thinking. He insisted that, "All people must march along in step toward winning the war, and laws should be interpreted to this end. It is of no use if the law is preserved and the state is destroyed. The Ministry of the Interior and Ministry of Justice must act firmly."[71]

Proximity to power

For Tôjô the sacrosanct position of the emperor in Japan played a central role in his thinking about the law and government. Tôjô was devoted to these ideals, and because of his efficiency and unswerving devotion to the emperor he came to be called the "razor adjutant" (*kamisori jikan*) as he climbed up through the officer ranks. When he was appointed army minister he left his post in Manchuria and flew directly to Tokyo despite a violent storm; he then became known as the "blitz minister" (*dengeki daijin*),[72] a combination of blind ambition and blind loyalty. It appears Tôjô sought to embody, quite successfully, the ideal officer devoted solely to the emperor and his nation. Thus, for example, since the war in China was imperial policy it was a given. Did the Emperor *personally* sanction this policy? No one asked the question. Government policy was imperial policy. As for foreign objections, Japanese policy was not imperialistic any more than the enclave of Western nations in China, American rule of the Philippine Islands, the French in Indochina, the Dutch in Indonesia, the British in Hong Kong and India, etc. Thereafter a chain reaction set in. Moves in China, Southeast Asia, and later the surprise attacks on Pearl Harbor and other places in Southeast Asia were made to support the Imperial Japanese given.

Also one must remember that while Tôjô was an extreme, he was an eminent man in his own milieu. In this sense only was he an exception. His devotion to the emperor was not unique to him personally. Maruyama Masao, perhaps the most highly respected political scientist in postwar Japan, wrote that devotion defined as proximity to the Emperor was an integral part of the leadership mechanism in prewar Japan.[73] The Imperial House was the center of the Japanese polity, and a person's relative closeness to it in large part defined his influence and authority in society. In particular, military officers were imbued with the idea that they were something special due to their nearness to the throne. Leading military leaders had audiences with the Emperor a number of times each week. Also, the Emperor was expected to have a close benign influence on the military. This became for some a very physical phenomenon, even as experienced by officer candidates. They felt highly honored, as select persons, because on certain occasions they paraded before the Emperor himself. He saw them and they saw him—an awe-inspiring experience.

> Mane waving [in the breeze] the clear sound of the horse's hoof beats in the cloudless spring sky, his royal highness passed by us in an elegant smart manner. Our parade swords glittered in the sunlight. What a wonderful manly feeling! We young men presented to the Regent, what a great honor![74]

Thus these young men, like Tôjô, became part of something larger than themselves—the imperial tradition. They became a living part of Japan's eternal history.

Nationalistic history and Tôjô

As indicated above, during the Imperial era the national history of Japan (*kokushi*) was an important support for national ideology.[75] Some still maintain that history was taught objectively and free of Japanese moral dictums during this time, but others inside as well as outside of Japan entertain serious doubts about this assertion. One of the historians well known then and often vilified now was Hiraizumi Kiyoshi (1895–1984). He in particular fascinated Tôjô Hideki long before he became a minister and politician. Hiraizumi was a professor of Japanese medieval history at Tokyo Imperial University. According to Ienaga Saburô, who was obliged to study and suffer under him, he was "famous for being the most extreme Japanist." But as Hasegawa Ryôichi shows, Hiraizumi was far from being the only historian in Imperial Japan associated with the "emperor-centered view of history" (*kôkoku shikan*).[76]

Hiraizumi's influence extended far beyond the lecture halls of the university. Tachibana Takashi says that although no one today recalls who he was, in prewar and mid-war times "Hiraizumi was in general society the most influential Tokyo Imperial University Professor in Japan." Later, as shown in Chapter 5, Hiraizumi was not forgotten by influential members of the Ministry of Education for many years after the war, though ironically he did not have much influence there during the war. He was, however, not just a history professor. Hiraizumi was a very prominent ideologue, and his influence in military circles extended to high- and middle-ranking officers, into the palace, and to pivotal leaders such as Konoe Fumimaro and Tôjô Hideki.[77] In the palace however, Emperor Hirohito seems not to have thought well of his "emperor-centered view of history."[78] Hiraizumi's nationalistic teachings sat especially well with the mid-level field grade officers often cited as the principal advocates of defending the *kokutai* at all costs. For example, at the very end of the war die-hard officers such as Lt. Colonel Takeshita Masahiko and Major Hatanaka Kenji, who advocated a coup d'état to thwart the Emperor's decision to accept the Potsdam Proclamation (meaning Japan's unconditional surrender), were said to be disciples of this "right-wing scholar."[79]

Hiraizumi's thinking and teaching about Japanese history was suffused by his interpretation of the *Jinnô Shôtôki* (Succession of the Divine Sovereigns) by Kitabatake Chikafusa (1293–1354). According to him, the Jinnô Shôtôki was the text in which the hallowed character of the Imperial House was historically substantiated; therefore it was the primary history text in Japan superseding even the *Nihon Shoki* from the eighth century. As is well known now, the imperial dynasty foundation myth is not in the main text of the *Nihon Shoki* and is only referred to briefly if at all in a supplementary section. But this passage was expanded upon and reconstrued over many years till in the thirteenth and fourteenth centuries it was central to Ise (Watarai) Shintô, which in turn influenced Kitabatake's thinking.[80] Perhaps this is why Hiraizumi and many other Japanese chauvinists before and after him were attracted to the *Jinnô Shôtôki* where the myth is amplified.

The Succession of the Divine Sovereigns begins with the famous statement, "Great Japan is the divine land. The heavenly progenitor founded it, and the sun goddess bequeathed it to her descendants to rule eternally. Only in our country is this true; there are no similar examples in other countries. This is why our country is called the divine land."[81] The *Dainihonshi* (History of Great Japan), written 1657–1906, transmitted this spirit to later times and it came to flower during the Meiji Restoration. At that time, the *Jinnô Shôtôki* was said to illuminate the nature of the divine imperial dynasty underlying the rationale of the modern Japanese nation-state.[82] This belief was reflected in Hiraizumi's writings on the past, said to be "history," which supported the imperial state and its expansion. One of his well-read works was a book published in September 1943, *Tempei ni Teki nashi* (Imperial Soldiers have no Rivals). In it one finds numerous statements, such as the following, that have more literary than historical merit: "Our country's history extending over several thousand years is permeated by sincere loyalty. Imperial Japan standing majestically, shining splendidly, is it not truly something of unequalled beauty throughout the world?"[83] These sorts of fanciful notions, propagated as historical facts, were appealing to nationalists, including Tôjô.

Beginning in 1932 Hiraizumi lectured four times a year at the Army Academy, and Tôjô was instrumental in engaging him. Two years later he began lecturing at the Naval Academy five times a year. At the army school several hundred persons attended each lecture, teachers as well as students. Tôjô and Hiraizumi met while the former was superintendent of the Army Academy. On April 16, 1934, Major General Tôjô attended the lecture. He had been appointed superintendent shortly before, on March 5. On April 16, Hiraizumi brought a long sword (*daitô*) with him. He drew the sword and lectured as follows:

> The Army! What is wanted are the elite; be like this sword! This sword—shortly before the Meiji Restoration, in February 1862 Awahara Nobuhide prayed to the gods and made it. It is 76 cm. long. In one breath, wielding it, no matter how strong the enemy he will inevitably be cut down. The Army! What is wanted in the elite is splendor; be like this sword! After the Russo-Japanese War the world has been peaceful up to the present, 30 years. An air of feeble evasiveness pervades above and below. The spirit of uprightness, bravery, service [to the country] has vanished and all is in vain. One morning if something comes up, the country is imperiled and something must be done—the Army! What is wanted is manly courage. No matter how great the enemies threatening us, amass and strengthen military power in order to advance and destroy them.
>
> However, only being an elite with valor, this is not enough. Look again at this sword. On one side we see engraved,
> Massifs may rend asunder, and seas dry up, even if the world comes to this
> And on the other,
> A treacherous heart vis-à-vis my lord, I will never have!
> As everyone knows this is a poem by the third shogun of the Kamakura Era Minamoto Sanetomo [1192–1219]. In it he pledges to retired emperor Gotoba [1180–1239] absolute submission in all sincerity, and whatever changes in heaven and on earth may take place, heaven forbid that this will change! That's what it's all about! Exalt the elite and valorous imbued with the spirit of undivided loyalty coming from the heart, only then is it something worthwhile. Military force is important it goes without saying, but if you wield force willfully as you wish, the world will only fall into confusion and the country be destroyed. The power of the Imperial Army can only be employed with an imperial order, and is something that should be exercised [solely in this way]. It should never be willfully misused.
>
> I repeat, the Army! What is wanted are the elite beyond comparison! Moreover, strong military power, guided by a spirit of loyalty, should only be used when sanctioned by an imperial command.[84]

The modern commentator Tachibaba laments the theatrics and the "narcissistic" attitude of Hiraizumi, but Tôjô found this lecture inspiring. Tachibana did not mention the final paragraph of the presentation above on the emperor's right of supreme command. It certainly drew attention then, two years after radical army and navy officers assassinated Prime Minister Inukai Tsuyoshi, May 15, 1932. He does note that in an interview with Hiraizumi many years later, in 1980, that the latter related (in a self-adulatory way) Tôjô's interest in his line of thought. Two days after the lecture in 1934, Tôjô telephoned Hiraizumi and addressed him in an extremely respectful manner. He was very impressed with the professor's speech and said that instruction at the Army Academy should be reformed accordingly. He was aware that Hiraizumi was an important busy man and could not lecture regularly at the Academy. But he would be very grateful if Hiraizumi would send one of his favorite students (*deshi*) to become an instructor there. One should be sent each year so that gradually the tenor of instruction would be changed. This Hiraizumi did for a number of years, and finally eight or nine of his former students were employed there.[85]

The young history scholar Ienaga Saburô was not one of these favored students. His dislike of Hiraizumi and his methods was well known. And Ienaga was not alone in his estimation, though there certainly was a dearth of dissenters at that time. Tachibana described a similar adverse reaction to Hiraizumi by Irokawa Daikichi. He too came to be known in postwar Japan as a liberal historian. Ienaga and Irokawa had serious misgivings about their calling in prewar times, but after the war they became highly respected historians, while Hiraizumi and his ideas fell from favor and were forgotten. Times changed, what is clear, however, are the grounds for Tôjô's admiration of Hiraizumi. He was no doubt impressed by the nationalistic tones and the admonition that military officers should only act when so ordered by the emperor. Tôjô was a stickler for following rules and regulations precisely and he was later known while prime minister for his devotion to the Emperor and attention to his directives. He was the head of the Military Police in Manchuria when a coup was attempted in 1936, and he had possible sympathizers rounded up immediately. This may have been due to factional infighting (*habatsu*) in the army as much as loyalty to the throne.[86] But one might conclude that two years earlier not only Hiraizumi's theatrical nationalism appealed to him but also the call for strict obedience to the emperor. In any case, his introduction of Hiraizumi's interpretation of Japanese history at the Army Academy certainly attests to his personal acceptance of this ideology and his promotion of its acceptance among army officers. Tôjô was not just in tune with the times, he helped popularize the lyrics being sung.

National consciousness

Naturally, there was in such a group-oriented society much peer pressure. Yet, those who resisted, even among intellectuals and others who later in public deeply regretted Japan's imperialism, are noteworthy in the prewar years only for their extremely small numbers. The combination of domestic education and propaganda disseminated since mid-Meiji times, along with collective intimidation, was oriented toward building a national consciousness and responding to external menaces. Of special note were the colonial practices of European nations and the United States as bases for their industrial-military power. Perhaps this led many Japanese to accept nationalism, militarism, and racism as the appropriate, inevitable accouterments of power. Japanese leaders prescribed this sort of education for all, and most unquestioningly imbibed the indoctrination offered and the policies their government pursued. Certainly, this can be said about Tôjô.

Tôjô Hideki appears to have been a very intelligent, brave man. Perhaps he was simply unreflective and used his intelligence to serve the state, not to question its foundations, the gods, or goals of the nation. For Tôjô, the strict self-discipline for which he was known, which he demanded from others, and his devotion to the national essence with the Imperial House at its apex, appear to have been personal proclivities that were reinforced by the years he spent at the army preparatory schools, the Army Academy, and as a young junior officer. The nation became the axis of his personal, social and professional priorities. But this background information is not meant to imply that he was not responsible for what he did and did not do. In fact, he was active in oppressing those who did express doubts about state policies and military strategies. These included at least one prominent politician, Nakano Seigô, as seen above, and the members of a small "early peace faction" in the army.[87] Perhaps he was extreme in this sense, but significantly within the environment of Imperial Japan, he was extremely successful.

After the war Tôjô was very unpopular in Japan, not because he started it but because of losing the war. And he was all but forgotten. Satô Eisaku (1901–75) who was a government official during the wars in China and the Pacific, a prominent politician after these wars, founding member of the Liberal Democratic Party (*jimintô*), and prime minister from 1964 to 1972 included no memories of him in his six volume diary.[88] Yet, Tôjô presented himself well during the Tokyo War Crimes Trials and now, after many decades of obscurity, he is regarded by a few as a patriotic hero.[89]

Tôjô, serving the national essence

Toward the end of the war, though he was no longer prime minister nor on active military duty, Tôjô Hideki was still influential. As a former prime minister he was an elder statesman who when called upon advised the throne on critical matters. Also, policies enacted while he was prime minister, army minister, army chief of staff, etc. were still followed after Tôjô left office. One of these was the so-called "special attack" tactic. As described above this scheme was encouraged by certain army and navy officers while Tôjô was in office. It was initiated after his downfall, not to win the war but to make the war "expensive" for the enemy in terms of human life and material such that it could be ended on terms less odious for Japan. This meant for many Japanese dying for the emperor and empire—part and parcel of wartime life. Tôjô was a strong advocate of these tactics and the spirituality, morality, and nationalism sanctifying them.

Tôjô Hideki may have ordered the preparation of these attacks. This is unclear, but even if he did not order them, he condoned the tactic at least and was no different from those directly involved. Tôjô was a military officer, a man of his times in Japan. He was not a dictator like Stalin. He was not a charismatic leader like Hitler or Mao Zedong. He was a well-trained, devoted military administrator. He played according to the (Imperial Japanese) rules, for the most part, long established before he came to power. This he emphasized at the War Crimes Trial following the war, but he did not thereby attempt to avoid responsibility for actions taken during his term as prime minister. He explicitly acknowledged his responsibility. His logic for so doing may be traced to his concept of *hohitsu*, advising the emperor. Advising the emperor meant taking responsibility for policies, especially when they did not succeed. "For me [Tôjô] the responsibility of advising the emperor means that if something is good, this in its entirety goes back to august imperial virtue; if bad this in its entirety is due to a minister's advice to the emperor."[90]

This dogma did not come out at the War Crimes Trial, but his acknowledgement of having a key role in advising and guiding the Emperor was gladly accepted by most in and outside of the courtroom. Other statements that did not fit well with Allied preconceptions were disregarded. For example, Tôjô's assertion that the war was one of "self-preservation and self-defense" was not taken seriously.[91] His denial of the existence of a military clique (*gunbatsu*) that pursued the war aggressively against the will of most civilian authorities received little attention. Both ideas ran contrary to the US policy of finding and punishing the "militarists" responsible for the war. Also, an inadvertent statement by Tôjô throwing doubt on the Emperor's lack of war responsibility was quickly corrected as deemed appropriate by Allied authorities. Prime Minister Tôjô, not Emperor Hirohito, was responsible for the decision to go to war.[92] The exigencies of the American nation-state overrode the assumptions of those serving the defeated nation-state, as the victors pursued preconceived truths. For this reason, many underlying problems, which led to the conflict, remained unexamined and now are mostly forgotten. Men such as Tôjô likewise.

However, one should remember Tôjô Hideki was a very successful (in)famous man. From 1941 to 1944 he was an army general, army minister, briefly army chief of staff, and the prime minister—one of the most well-known and feared men in Imperial Japan, perhaps the world. For nearly three years he was a trusted advisor to the Shôwa Emperor as he carried out his various official state duties. It appears that the Emperor had confidence in him, and in mid-1944 when it became evident to most highly placed persons that the Japanese were clearly losing the War in the Pacific, the Emperor only reluctantly parted with him.

As a high-ranking professional army officer Tôjô was a state leader and mass destruction was his trade; as a politician implementing Imperial Japanese ideology he also engaged in mass deception. Throughout the war he contributed mightily to both—destruction abroad and ideological indoctrination at home. As the war headed toward final disaster for Imperial Japan Tôjô did what he could as an elder statesman and retired army general to prolong it. Saving somehow a deception, i.e., the national essence together with the eternal imperial line, justified continuing the massive loss of life and devastation in Asia, including Japan. The emperor was an integral element of this constellation.

Tôjô respected the emperor and held him in awe as the embodiment of Japanese culture, the leader of the nation and Imperial House, but this did not mean that Tôjô invariably yielded to Emperor Hirohito vis-à-vis military and state affairs. As an army leader he saw himself as a defender of his state, the imperial tradition, and the emperor. However he interpreted this role in his own way. When judging Tôjô and the actions of many contemporary military officers, one might remember an aphorism from another time and culture: "*protectio trahit subjectionem*—protection drags subjection in its wake."[93] But this does not mean Hirohito was "a god in Tôjô's keeping." It explains in part the forced interdependencies state–nation, military–emperor. It recasts somewhat the relationship between Prime Minister General Tôjô and Emperor Hirohito together, as war leaders and losers.

4

Failing Strategy, Lack of War Materials, and Tôjô's Fall

Part 1: Intrigues

Intrigue and the Fall of the Tôjô Cabinet

In Chapter 1 while emphasizing the nature of the sources available and imperial authority, the fall of Saipan and subsequently Tôjô were examined. In so doing the intrigues surrounding these events were touched upon. Here conspiracies within the military as well as among politicians, bureaucrats and aristocrats will be surveyed. Then two other important factors that seriously affected the fates of those on Saipan, the Tôjô Cabinet, and the course of the war will be taken up—strategic and material deficiencies.

The last two years of the war was a confusing time marked with complex events, and the various descriptions of what happened reflect this confusion. As has been known for many years, intrigues designed to bring about the fall of the Tôjô Cabinet did not begin with the crises in the Marianas and the loss of Saipan. For example, Butow documents a meeting on March 7, 1944, between ex-premier Retired Admiral Okada Keisuke and Imperial Prince Fushimi onetime navy chief of staff in which the former told the latter, "'key personnel' in the army and navy had apparently 'lost confidence in their leaders' and that 'a wide gulf' was developing 'between the front lines and central headquarters.'"[1] Later, on June 27, Okada visited Prime Minister Tôjô and told him bluntly that Admiral Shimada Shigetarô was malapropos as navy minister. They had a very straightforward discussion in which Okada reiterated this charge and Tôjô countered by saying Okada's recent intrigues in this respect were deplorable. Replacing Shimada would mean the fall of his cabinet and this was not good for the nation or the war effort. Okada asked him to reconsider and Tôjô abruptly refused, terminating the meeting. Finally Okada, along with former prime minister Konoe Fumimaro, appears to have led a group that was instrumental in Tôjô's fall.²

The situation, however, was not as simple as it first appears. Long-standing army–navy quarrelling over money and materials was the key issue. This led many within the navy to resent Navy Minister and briefly Chief of Staff Shimada's cooperation with Tôjô. Many middle-ranking naval officers felt he had sold out to Tôjô, meaning the army. These and other similar altercations brought on Tôjô's political demise, but this was not something which came overnight. Within the *state* apparatus its leader, Tôjô became increasingly unviable. The extent to which the Emperor as leader of the *nation* was involved in these machinations has been addressed in Chapter 1 and will be taken up again below. Also in considering these events one must keep in mind that many of our sources are from avowed opponents of Tôjô and his government, as here former Rear Admiral Takagi Sôkichi.

Tôjô's autocratic manner of dealing with associates, politicians, and even some of the elder statesmen did not help matters. There was growing dissatisfaction with the prime minister and those who worked closely with him. At the same time, some of those against Tôjô were not totally sure that his departure as prime minister was desirable. Prince Higashikuni, for example, told Konoe on June 20 and 23, 1944, that despite the ongoing losses Tôjô should remain on so that at the end of the war he would have to take responsibility for it, relieving the Imperial House of this onus.³ The leader of the state, and if need be the state, might have to be sacrificed to save emperor and nation.

The Shôwa Emperor

As for the Emperor, Butow says that later in mid-July when the cabinet fell, "The Emperor was kept fully informed of developments, but—despite some statements to the contrary—he did not play any part in the fall of Tôjô. The three conditions [for continuing the cabinet which Tôjô could not fulfill, see below] posed by Kido on 13 July originated with the Lord Privy Seal."⁴ In his earlier book Butow treats the fall of Tôjô's cabinet similarly noting only that Kido informed the Emperor of what was going on. He does not imply the Emperor had any active influence on Tôjô's departure from power.⁵ The nation's leader stood aloof above state affairs.

Bix says the opposite. He maintains that those opposed to Tôjô knew, "Tôjô's power flowed from the supporting and far greater power of the emperor [...] they regarded the emperor as the main obstacle in their path to peace."⁶ Here

Hosokawa Morisada's diary is cited. Bix gives us no clue as to what this diary says. He does not enumerate the extensive deliberations in both the army and navy leading up to the decision not to try to retake Saipan. Also he does not include the statements made at the audience with the Supreme Military Council included in another text he cites, the Imperial Headquarters, Navy Department, Combined Fleet vol. 6 narrative. Both are examples of the limitations imposed by others on the "greater power" of the Emperor. Moreover, we must believe with him that, "Personally disappointed with the state of the war, Hirohito finally decided to withdraw his support of Tôjô, opening the way for Tôjô's enemies to precipitate the collapse of the entire Tôjô-cabinet on July 18, 1944."[7] No doubt the Emperor, along with many others, was not happy about how the war was going. As he interprets this situation, as usual, Bix makes the nation's leader an active participant, a schemer, meddling in state affairs. However, as demonstrated again below Hirohito's willful manipulation of events is Bix's assumption which, according to the records now available, distorts seriously the situation of the Emperor at that time.

The Actual Record of the Shôwa Emperor presents, of course, another picture:[8]

July 13: the Emperor and his political advisor Kido consulted about the war situation after the loss of Saipan—still regarded as a serious defeat. Shortly thereafter Tôjô visited Kido in his office and presented his plan to better pursue the war. Among other things, cooperation between the army and navy will be improved; Imperial Headquarters should be strengthened, and the cabinet reformed. Kido countered with his three conditions: (1) strengthen the supreme command; (2) the chief of the navy general staff and navy minister, Tôjô's trusted colleague Shimada, must go; and (3) some of the elder statesmen and members of the ruling class must be included in the cabinet. Later on the same day the Emperor told Tôjô that if conditions 1 and 2 were met number 3 should not be a problem. Hirohito in effect sanctioned Kido's plan.

July 17: the Emperor again regrets the loss of Saipan saying, "the failure to strengthen the Saipan defenses was a strategic mistake."[9] (If candid and correct this entry shows the Emperor's memory was faulty or he was engaging in wishful thinking: As pointed out above, the army and navy were in no position to "strengthen Saipan." The Emperor was informed accordingly and on June 25, he reluctantly acknowledged that reinforcing the island was unfeasible.)

July 18: it was reported to the throne that two days earlier all remaining members of the garrison on Saipan died in battle, and the Japanese civilians living there experienced the same fate. (Remember here, the number of civilians who actually died was greatly inflated for propaganda purposes.[10]) Also discussions about Tôjô and his cabinet culminated on this day, and the cabinet resigned en masse. Nevertheless, while the elder statesmen and Kido seem to have "lost confidence" in Tôjô, the deposed prime minister was among those the Emperor consulted about who should be his successor.[11]

Herbert Bix saw things differently: he depicts a petulant emperor "digging in his heals" in order to get his way as commander-in-chief. Also Hirohito connived to keep Tôjô but later was behind the downfall of the Tôjô Cabinet. Yet, long available records show something else (see Chapter 1). The Emperor was concerned about the very real prospect of the home islands, including Tokyo where he lived, coming within reach of US long-range bombers. He accordingly emphasized to the leaders of both services the importance of the Marianas and Saipan. This led members of the army and navy general staffs to carefully consider their options given their resources. But the Imperial Army balked. They said not without reason that the navy's plans and resources were lacking. The field marshals and fleet admirals were consulted, and agreed with the army. Also the army was more concerned about operations in China and Burma, which they defined as of ultimate importance to Imperial Japan. The navy was in a mess. They were accountable for the Pacific Area but they had neither the material means and modern technology such as state-of-the-art radar[12] or military intelligence nor the political clout to effectively carry out this responsibility. The Emperor could not change this situation.

Summarizing, after the fall of Saipan was acknowledged, leading members of the government and military as well as the elder statesmen, aristocrats, and advisors to the throne engaged in lengthy discussions about whether the Tôjô Cabinet should resign, or at least be reshuffled. Tôjô and Shimada both had aroused, for different reasons, considerable animosity and opposition among military and civilian leaders. The army and navy were not cooperating well as had been promised in February when breaking precedent each became chief of staff as well as minister of his respective service. Two major engagements ended in decisive defeats, with the loss of many men and much irreplaceable war materiel. These were important issues once again heatedly debated in the army and navy even involving retired admirals and imperial princes.

During this time, in addition to the plan to injure Admiral Shimada and cause him to relinquish the post of navy minister mentioned above, there were several plots to assassinate the increasingly unpopular Prime Minister Tôjô. Despite calls for his resignation from various elder statesmen such as Okada and Yonai, members of the imperial family such as Prince Takamatsu Nobuhito, and officers in the army and navy, Tôjô obstinately held on to his positions and power. Therefore it seemed that bringing him down personally was the only way to bring the Tôjô Cabinet down. Rear Admiral Takagi Sôkichi was a key member in one plot, and he left notes describing it. Another group, in the army, was led by Major Tsunoda Tomoshige who was under the influence of Ishihara Kanji. Tôjô resigned before any of the conspiracies were carried out.[13] Suzuki Tamon presents a detailed account of the discussions and maneuverings by the Privy Seal, Tôjô, the Emperor, various elder statesmen, and imperial princes but he does not mention these assassination plans.[14] As seen below, all of the above persons, including the Emperor, were involved in Tôjô's fall from power. But the Emperor did not manipulate these events, nor did he dictate their outcome. In fact he wanted Tôjô to remain in office.

Privy Seal Kido and other skeptics

The role of Privy Seal in these events is controversial. One historian, Noriko Kawamura believes he condoned, at least, violence if Tôjô remained obstinate. I do not agree with her interpretation. The text she cites, but does not translate, is a discussion on July 8, 1944, between Kido and Yabe Teiji, professor at Tokyo Imperial University. The discussion translated:

> [Kido:] If the domestic situation "brews" [unjô]; if one could say Tôjô has lost his bearings, if something [like this] does not happen, changing the political situation is impossible. If the situation is not heated up and beforehand I approached the throne and proposed a change, this becomes a palace "coup d'état." There is fear that responsibility would be shifted to the new cabinet and palace as accomplices.
>
> [Yabe:] The position of the Privy Seal, is it not the sole position for changing the political situation?
>
> [Kido:] The Privy Seal's position is not one of change. First, there is no such job entitlement. In the constitution there is nothing about advising the throne [hohitsu] at all times. If the situation starts to brew one grasps the rudder. By brewing situation, this means "a tumult." An act of "terror," worsening of the war situation.
>
> A minister of state's advice to the throne is different from advising the throne at all times.
>
> Providing for a successor in advance, because this is the same as perpetrating an act of "terror" for the sake of the successor, this is condemned. Yet even if literal "terror" with no plan or objective takes place, that cannot be helped. [Meaning, nothing can be undertaken even in the case of literal terror.]

I think an Imperial Conference with the elder statesmen would have the opposite effect. There is no one who could say before the emperor that this cabinet is not viable. That is something best said at tea-time. Also, the Privy Seal could have an individual audience with the emperor. There is no one [else] who can speak explicitly.

Also, as for the cooperation of Admiral Okada, one can do little more than that.[15]

As Kawamura notes, it appears that Kido had "apparent knowledge" about Admiral Takagi's involvement in an assassination plot, but I do not think he intimated here passive support of removing Tôjô by force. Quite the contrary, he said that even in the event of a real act of terror, he could not intervene. Here grasping the rudder to steady the "ship of state" is different from active intervention. This does not rule out the assumption that by this time Kido had withdrawn his support of Tôjô and he, among others, was keeping the Emperor informed of the current adverse course of political developments. Suzuki says that Kido's clever maneuvering behind the scenes was an important factor in the fall of the Tôjô Cabinet.[16] In any case, Hirohito must have known that Tôjô had become very unpopular and was the source of much tension in the military and ruling circles.

Some persons including the Emperor were concerned about the effect a cabinet resignation would have on civilian morale at home and the support of Asian allies abroad. At the same time, while then only covertly communicated, a few well-placed leaders, even the Emperor, began to doubt seriously that the war could be won (see, for example, the Admirals Nakazawa and Yonai in Chapter 1). However, in spite of numerous defeats optimistic hopes were entertained by many up to mid-1944, but from this time on leaders in Tokyo increasingly focused on how to best lose the war. This was not something that could be approached lightly. It was not only an unpopular topic, it was virtually forbidden to even hint openly that the war might be lost.

An Imperial Headquarters chief of staff

Much wrangling was going on behind the partitions[17] and the Emperor knew this. He was not digging in his heals and ignoring the advice of the chiefs of staff. He was consulting intensively with his military experts, civilian officials, and on occasion, contrary to his own wishes, with other members of the Imperial House trying to bring the government and military to formulate the best policy in the given situation. But he was not a puppet master pulling strings behind the scenes manipulating political developments. This can be clearly seen in the discussions about still another plan to unite the army and navy to more effectively pursue the war. Tôjô along with Imperial Prince Higashikuni proposed establishing an "imperial headquarters chief of staff system" (*daihon'ei bakuryôchôsei*). In the Imperial Headquarters, in addition to the two chiefs of staff an Imperial Headquarters chief of staff was to be placed over them, overseeing and coordinating their efforts. The Emperor said that in theory this was a fine idea, but unfortunately there was no one suitable to fill the new position. For this reason, finally, such a system was not established. But the Emperor did not simply veto the plan. He took it under consideration and carefully explained to Higashikuni why the system at present could not be set up. Suzuki says the Emperor did this to preserve his own influence in military matters. If such a position were created, the person filling it could greatly influence the Emperor's power. A "suitable person" meant for Hirohito someone he could trust enough to invest him with this amount of power.[18] Even if this is true, he did not act as a dictator or generalissimo, but as emperor consulting with members of the military. (Prince Higashikuni was an army general.) Similarly, he did not single-handedly engineer the fall of the Tôjô Cabinet.

Changing expectations

Long before Tôjô's fall, a number of the elder statesmen, several imperial princes and at least one member of the cabinet, Minister Without Portfolio Kishi Nobusuke, were actively conspiring against Tôjô,[19] and ostensibly in favor of opening peace negotiations. However, as seen a year later in an even worse situation peace at any cost, meaning total unconditional surrender, was not a tolerable option up to immediately before the precipitous disastrous end of the war. Painting the Emperor as a conniving intriguer and "the main obstacle" to peace is not supported by the documents now known to us. Kawamura shows that the Emperor was never against war but consistently advocated early on that Japan seek an early peace while still in a strong position.

> Although the Emperor continued to support the military's argument that Japan needed a decisive victory before entering into peace negotiations, all the sources quoted above, including the Emperor's own "Monologue," suggest that September 1943 was an important turning point in Hirohito's thinking and that he was rapidly giving up hope for Japanese victory through a decisive battle.[20]

In fact, the Emperor and Kido were already troubled by such doubts in March 1943. Despite these misgivings, much later, before the fall of Okinawa, the Emperor still subscribed to the idea that Japan must somehow attain a significant military victory in order to make negotiating for peace with, not victory over, the United States more propitious. But he was not the originator or sole advocate of this strategy. He was following the advice of his military leaders.[21] As seen above however, the fall of Saipan and subsequent fall of the Tôjô Cabinet effectively, fatally altered the war expectations and plans of army and navy leaders. It intensified their desire for one big strike to improve Japan's negotiation position. Desperation strategies were called up—the special attack tactics detailed in Chapter 2 of this book. These were military, state initiatives sanctioned, not planned, by the nation's head, the Emperor. Similarly, a differentiation of roles can be seen in the lack of adequate planning vis-à-vis war logistics and materials.

Part 2: Materials and Strategy

Failing materials and the strategy behind the fall of Saipan and Tôjô

Japanese leaders before and during the Second World War often neglected that which was real, especially Japan's lack of resources. For example, when war with the United States began in 1941, Japan was producing approximately 5 million tons of steel per year, tendency declining, the United States approximately 80 million tons, tendency rising. In 1943 to 1944 Japan produced approximately 3 million tons, the United States approximately 86 million tons. In 1945 at the end of the war Japan's steel production was sliding toward zero, the United States sliding down to approximately 75 million tons. Japan's yearly production was equivalent to production in the United States over two and a half days.[22] No doubt some of this information was not available to the Japanese before and during the war. However many future Japanese staff officers, including Fleet Admiral Yamamoto Isoroku, Lt. General Mutô Akira, and Vice-Admiral Nakazawa Tasuku, author of one of the sources frequently cited in this work, were in and toured the United States long before the war. They were suitably impressed by US modernity and industrial production.

For example, Lt. Com. Nakazawa (promoted to commander shortly before his return to Japan) was in the United States from March 1932 to February 1934. During this time he toured the United States and spent over a year at Stanford University. There he attended lectures on the US Constitution, Modern US Economics, and Modern US History. According to his memoirs, published two years after his death in 1979, he made the following evaluations of the American people (summarized):

1. Americans are a conglomerate of various different peoples. I had assumed they would lack solidarity, but this was not the case. The American people are united and defend vigorously their nation.
2. They are not much interested in past events but orient their decisions on future eventualities. They react very quickly, different from the Japanese who respond to situations conservatively and rather slowly.
3. With the motto, "number one in all things," they are pervaded with a spirit of supremacy.

Nakazawa went on with comparisons of the landmass, national resources, military preparedness, and more. He concluded that Japan should not go to war with the United States because she could never win.[23] After the war the prime minister at war's end, former Fleet Admiral Suzuki Kantarô remarked similarly in his autobiography that prior to the beginning of hostilities it was clear that Japan could not win a war with the United States. Her fleet was too small and her resources too few. Already in 1918 during a visit to San Francisco with two Japanese cruisers he said in a speech that war between the two countries would be of no use to either and that in the end Japan would lose such a war. Also, the future Fleet Admiral Yamamoto Isoroku said the same thing to Suzuki while serving as a staff officer under him.[24] The extent to which Emperor Hirohito was informed of these material circumstances is unclear.

Much later in March 1941 both Imperial Army and Navy leaders, and members of the respective general staffs and ministries, were made aware that, in the words of Army Ministry War Plans Section Chief Okada Kikusaburô, "it is not certain that our national material strength is adequate to carry out a long war against the United States and Britain." He wrote this in a revision of a national strength assessment. In particular shipping was vital to supporting Japan's overseas imperium and her domestic economy, both necessary for her to pursue war at all. Maintaining sufficient bottoms would be difficult at best. But as with many other hard material factors, military leaders "shuffled numbers" in order to make the impossible seem possible—a successful war with the United States.[25]

Moreover, the governor of the Planning Board (*kikakuin sôsai*), Suzuki Tei'ichi (1888–1989), presented advice based on Planning Board estimates that was confusing. In the last Konoe Cabinet and the following Tôjô Cabinet, Suzuki came to be known for ambiguity and turn-about policies. For example, during Konoe's last term he said that since materials were lacking war with the United States is coming, but if materials can be acquired a compromise might be possible. In the Tôjô Cabinet, however, Suzuki became a hardliner pushing for war with the United States. Which is to say, the board responsible for assessing Japan's material situation provided vague contradictory information and advice while its head advocated war. Many think that Suzuki was personally responsible for this lack of definitive counsel about Japan's materials and resources shortly before the imperial government decided on opening a war with the United States and her allies. He was a retired lt. general who was involved in army factional disputes during his career. Associated with the "imperial way faction," after the quashed uprising of February 1936, he and many other imperial way adherents not directly involved in the revolt were sent to inconsequential posts far from Tokyo for some years.[26] Perhaps this prompted his nebulous positioning later on the important issue of resources. However, some staff officers saw this problem as a vital issue, for example Lt. General Mutô Akira.

Lt. Gen. Mutô Akira (1892-1948), Military Affairs Bureau chief in the Army Ministry from July 1939 to 1942, as described by Lt. Col. Ishii Akiho in contemporary notes, was a complex man. Mutô advocated Japan's march into the southern part of French Indochina (begun, July 1941). If war with the United States and Great Britain came military strongholds and the resources there were absolutely necessary. He and many staff officers did not think this action would provoke the US reaction that resulted—freezing Japanese assets in the United States and an oil embargo. The "four demands" by America, in the fall of 1941, which included the stipulation that Japan totally withdraw from China, made war with the United States for army leaders inevitable and, for Mutô at least, defeat equally inevitable. He realized that war was impending but thought a conflict with the United States was perilous and was greatly distressed by this prospect. He was acutely aware of US material superiority and worked to avoid the conflict, but under the circumstances army leaders saw few options beyond caving in to US demands. Finally Mutô advocated war because he was convinced that a nation that gives up without a fight will never rise again. War even given defeat was vital to resurrection. In the end, on August 15, 1945, when Mutô was chief of staff, 14th Area Army in the Philippines, he heard a broadcast from Tokyo announcing the war's termination. In his memoirs he wrote simply, "Japan lost."[27] During the war he was active in China, Sumatra, the Philippines, and Tokyo. After the war he was convicted of various war crimes and sentenced to death by hanging. Prior to the beginning of the war with the United States and her allies it is doubtful that a strong stance by Mutô based on material considerations, contrary to Tôjô's pro-war inclinations, would have made a difference.

As seen above, General and Prime Minister Tôjô Hideki along with many military leaders emphasized the value of the Japanese spirit and willing self-sacrifice for emperor and the national essence over mere material strength. With the worsening war situation from 1943 onward the Yamato ethos became even more important. This can be clearly seen in the diary of Col. Akamatsu. On June 19, 1944, after the defeat of the Imperial Navy in the Mariana Seas and the US invasion of Saipan, Tôjô said the following to his secretaries.

> The strong point of the Japanese is that everyone risks all; we are daring, not afraid of death. Against one enemy aircraft carrier we send in one plane and with it can defeat the carrier. This is the strength of Japan. Therefore if one thinks that when the enemy builds an aircraft carrier we also should build a carrier, if we simply resist using raw materials only, this probably would mean the defeat of our country that is lacking in productive power. In the end we make use of our strong point—with one plane we defeat one of the enemy's carriers. Using special boats, suicide units that defeat one enemy ship, the enemy can be beaten. If the time comes when I too must embrace a bomb and jump into the fray, of course I will do it. Making use of this Japanese strength, we must somehow win out. Our young people offer up their lives for the nation. Through sacrifice one gladly lays the foundation for successfully completing the East Asia War. It's really great![28]

Shortly thereafter on June 27, he said something similar to Heinrich Georg Stahmer the German ambassador to Japan.

> If one does not sufficiently recognize the special character of the Japanese, judgments [about us] will be far wrong. Due to the war situation in Saipan etc. even some Japanese run about uselessly willy-nilly. But the true value of a true Japanese is displayed when at the ultimate hour he develops a surprising amount of power [...] I believe sufficient recognition of this [trait] in the true Japanese is vital.[29]

Ambassador Stahmer's reaction to the statement is not recorded. This is another indication of Tôjô's extreme belief in the special nature of the Japanese folk and its leader the Emperor. Here as in the discussions in Imperial Headquarters it appears that not a few high-ranking military officers had lost touch with reality. Discussions about why losses were suffered were hardly noted. Not only was the importance of the proverbial Japanese spirit exaggerated, in addition plans often lacked concrete underpinnings. Where were all the men and material for saving Saipan to come from? There are formidable lists of navy and army units often including commanding officers' names. But the numbers are so great it appears that many of these units existed for the most part on paper only. In mid-1944 plans for transporting men and materials were spotty. The 5th Fleet in the northeast was to come to Yokosuka (near Tokyo) and escort the vessels, but the available transport vessels themselves were sparse at best.[30] Okabe Nagaakira, one of Hirohito's chamberlains from 1936 to 1946, was similarly skeptical about military planning:

> I had the feeling that the few war preparations and materials on hand were being expended little by little and things were going bad. But even with the situation worsening, among the higher-ups no one was about to take responsibility. In the Imperial Headquarters-Government Liaison Conference wonderful things were said but it was not a conference in which policies were formulated addressing how one should actually deal with the situation.[31]

Of course one must remember that Chamberlain Okabe was a Tokyo Imperial University Faculty of Literature graduate who never had anything to do with military service. Such persons in "pin-stripes" were notoriously lacking in "fighting spirit" and critical of those in uniform. More investigation needs to be done on the existing records by high military authorities in Imperial Japan. Perhaps we can establish to some degree what part of military planning late in the war was fact and what was wishful thinking. One such source follows.

Japanese outnumbered in men and material

Nakahara Shigetoshi shows that at the time of the battles in the Mariana Seas and on Saipan, the Japanese were hopelessly outnumbered both in terms of men and materials. The figures are somewhat unclear depending on whether one counts the firepower and manpower of the entire US force at Saipan or the men and materials landed. But the United States had, for example, on Saipan at least 1.3 times the manpower, 3 times the small arms, 2 times the number of machine guns, 5 times the artillery pieces, 6 times the tanks, and many more times the ammunition for the various weapons. Moreover, the United States could freely replenish used up and destroyed supplies, while the Japanese could not be resupplied. Japanese troops had to make do with what they had and when this ran out they were expected to die honorably—sacrifice themselves by resisting the enemy with few or no weapons (*gyokusai*).[32] This does not directly address the above issue of paper versus actual units, but it does show, surely more clearly now than at that time, the hopeless situation of Japan's military forces and unrealistic expectations of her military leaders, including possibly the Emperor, more than a year before the end of the war. The author of the above study, Col. Nakahara, termed the navy "idiotic" for saying an invasion was impossible. Moreover, he added, though the navy's great self-confidence was idiotic, the Emperor urged that Saipan be retaken. It appears that Hirohito was well aware of the strategic importance of Saipan but not well informed about Japan's material shortfalls vis-à-vis the US invaders.

Considering after the war the material and manpower differences, Nakahara knew retaking Saipan was impossible, as finally asserted by members of the army general staff and confirmed by the Supreme Military Council at that time. Whether or not he thought this during the war is not known, and as seen above the extent to which the Emperor was appropriately informed is unclear. However, not long afterward in a report to the Supreme War Guidance Council (*saikô sensô shidô kaigi*) on September 11, 1944, the Munitions Minister Fujiwara Ginjirô said, "With the changing situation in national resources I have no confidence in pursuing the war from now on. Ship losses, increasing coal and steel shortages, reduced aircraft production etc., all national resources are rapidly being drained."[33] Nakahara's position was corroborated and his explanations deserve our attention.

Nakahara was a graduate of the Army Academy and career officer, but he was basically an engineer. He was an artillery officer, also took a degree in electrical engineering at Tokyo Imperial University, and was given to statistical analyses leading perhaps to his use of the above epithet after the war. Nakahara's treatment of Japan's defeats from Guadalcanal to Okinawa is succinct, laden with figures on Japan's losses, and very critical of the Emperor and senior military officials. After the war he was in a position to know. His sources obviously include materials selected from those underpinning the oft-mentioned War History Series. Moreover, when these events took place he was a lt. col. in the Military Service Bureau, War Affairs Section, as Materials Group leader with six-years service there. The losses enumerated in his book closely accord with those in the above Imperial Headquarters, Army Department volume 8 and in volumes 5 and 6 of the Imperial Headquarters, Navy Department, Combined Fleet texts. No doubt earlier in the Materials Group he was plagued with the problem of failing war materials and resulting combat defeats.

Failing materials lead to more reverses

The lack of men and materials and the lack of reliable information about them also influenced a well-known infamous operation—the beginnings of the "Divine Wind Special Attack Corps." When Vice-Admiral Ônishi Takijirô arrived in the Philippines mid-October 1944 to assume command of the 1st Naval Air Fleet and initiate these tactics (see Chapter 2), Imperial Headquarters records showed he had 350 planes at his disposal. In fact there were only 230 planes there and of them only 149 were actually serviceable. That is, Ônishi only had approximately 40 percent of the planes available that Imperial Headquarters reckoned with.[34] This was good news for the to be requisitioned "volunteer" suicide fliers. However, the results hypothesized in central planning were once again based on highly inflated assessments of the materials on station.

Lt. Gen. Kawabe Torashirô, the last vice-chief of staff of the Imperial Army, was also confronted similarly with Japan's dire material situation. He was appointed vice-chief of staff in the Army Air Force Headquarters one year before surrender. (He lamented the appointment due to his own lack of experience in this area.) At that time he succinctly stated the predicament: "one drop of oil one drop of blood." Already in August 1944 he knew the supply of oil was literally drying up. Alcohol was being used as a substitute fuel, pilots were dying unrelentingly, and even if there were sufficient volunteers to replace them, there was only limited fuel for training. (Alcohol was mixed with the gasoline to extend supplies. It was extremely volatile and led to a number of accidents.[35]) Kawabe elaborated further on the crisis in August 1944:

> Throughout the country there was a movement to increase production of Satsuma sweet potatoes and to utilize pine tree oil [a base for turpentine]. The situation was so critical that there was increased talk about "special attack units" and "specialized special attack planes" but people were driven to this by the dire situation. Planes near junk status could not be sent on "special attacks" because their pilots required training for which fuel was lacking. They too needed flying skills and knowledge of military tactics.[36]

War materials were critical. In the battle for Leyte, October to December 1944, both the army and navy were soundly defeated. During the first few days, reports came in indicating that the Japanese air forces were oppressing the enemy, but Allied replenishments were endless and when the Japanese army and navy quickly ran out of materials and food they could not be resupplied. The Allies' relative strength quickly increased and the situation reversed itself. It was too late to send in an elite flying unit and the battle ended in defeat. In these reports, those sacrificed were mentioned only as war materials.

These are not the only instances where presupposed war materials were more fantasy than fact. As Suzuki points out, toward the end of the war the army and navy were again at loggerheads about who should receive what portion of the warplanes produced in one year. While actual production was approximately 26,000 planes, the army "settled on" 27,120 and the navy 25,130 planes for a total of 52,250 planes. These were obviously "theoretical" figures but they were nevertheless used in planning military operations.[37] Previously on September 30, 1943, a similar subterfuge took place at an imperial conference. As noted earlier, this is when the "absolute defense perimeter" was established. In order to ascertain the possibility of actually defending this perimeter the President of the Privy Council Hara Yoshimichi asked about warplane production. Was the projected number (40,000) attainable even though Prime Minister Tôjô estimated present production at about 17,000 to 18,000 planes? Both the Governor of the Planning Board Suzuki Tei'ichi and Minister of Commerce and Industry Kishi Nobusuke answered that they were determined to meet or surpass this goal. Asked if the navy could maintain the above perimeter if indeed 40,000 warplanes were produced, Navy Chief of Staff Nagano Osami gave a vague less than reassuring answer. There is no record of what the Emperor said at this conference but afterwards he expressed in clear terms his dissatisfaction with the disagreements between the army and navy.[38] Here again the leader of the nation received unreliable information and stated misgivings about failing army–navy cooperation, to no avail.

Ships and shipping

Another example of wanting materials and planning was the lack of attention to sea transport until it was too late. For example, the navy and army were very late in planning to reinforce Saipan.[39] Both in terms of ships and supplies and also simple logistics, shipping anything to Saipan took at least seven days, and previous experience should have told the planners that not everything would arrive intact promptly. In April, May, and June US submarines often attacked convoys going and coming from Japan's many island outposts including Saipan. One source indicates that sometimes they came through without suffering great losses. But on many occasions the losses were severe as on May 25, 1944. Two freighters going from Saipan to Palau were torpedoed and besides the ships themselves 2,956 tons of foodstuffs, 5,300 cans of aviation gas, 2,500 cubic meters of ammunition, 500 tons of cement, and 109 persons were lost. The danger was always present and coming ever closer to the home islands. For example, on April 23, 1944, a small convoy of six ships going from Kobe to Nagoya was attacked not far off the coast of Wakayama and one ship was torpedoed and sunk. Again near the Wakayama coast two freighters going from Kobe to Yokosuka were attacked and one sunk. The lost ship belonged to Japan Post, was 2,825 gross tons and had 700 men from the Imperial Navy their equipment and ordnance, supposedly about 3,000 tons on board. The cargo, 439 naval personnel, 25 crew members, and 4 others were lost.[40] The cumulative losses were not to be belittled. But while the above discussions continued about whether to try to reinforce Saipan as the Emperor desired, these material "facts of life" were disregarded.

Shipping crisis

Previously in November 1941 the shipping problem had been addressed without being able to formulate a viable plan. In an imperial conference on November 5, the Emperor learned that Japan was able to produce approximately 600,000 gross tons of bottoms per year, and the navy with slight misgivings agreed with this. In November 1942 shipping aroused a confrontation between the Army Ministry and the general staff but nothing concrete or realistic was undertaken.[41] Later at the beginning of 1943 the shipping crisis was discussed in parliament. This discussion on February 1, 1943, in the Diet was bizarre and shows how desperate Japan's situation was even at this date, more than two years before the end of the war. Ogawa Kyôtarô raised the question of shipping at a plenary budget meeting. Tôjô acknowledged that there were freight transport problems and that efforts were being made to increase ship production. He elaborated in the following manner (summarized):

> Perhaps however this measure will not suffice. Actually the navy is responsible for setting shipbuilding priorities. [As seen below, this was not entirely true. The cabinet was involved in setting goals for merchant shipbuilding.] In any case, ships are not the only way to transport freight overseas. One can put 500 or even 1000 tons in large sacks, made of rubber or anything, which can be towed over the ocean. Also one should look at using large wooden rafts for the same purpose. And we could requisition Chinese Junks to use as freighters. They have the advantage of not needing any sort of fuel, since they are sailing ships. If one thinks about it there are many possibilities. "Nothing is impossible for us humans." The government is looking into various ways of increasing our shipping capacity. But one cannot say that without ships sea transport of freight is impossible. There are many other ways, as suggested above. This spirit should guide us. [Ogawa responded by agreeing.] With or without ships if we give our

all, various geniuses will come forward and new transport possibilities will be found. This should become Japan's national policy.[42]

The Emperor may have been informed of this discussion, but it is not noted in the STJR.

Much later, according to the STJR, it appears the problem was reported at least one time in detail to the Emperor. On March 3, 1944, in an audience with Tôjô, as prime minister and army chief of staff, and Navy Chief of Staff Shimada Shigetarô he was told of measures to requisition ships from civilians and about possible compensation for them. This shortage of ships and its significance for war operations and national strength were explained. If Hirohito had any thoughts on this problem they are not related.[43] On March 17, he attended an army–navy Imperial Headquarters conference on the problem of securing sea transport. The reports were presented by the above-mentioned protagonists Major General Sanada Jôichirô and Rear Admiral Nakazawa Tasuku. Naval Vice-Chief of Staff Itô Sei'ichi (who became commanding officer of the 2nd Fleet at the end of 1944 and went down with the battleship Yamato on April 7, 1945) also participated in the discussion. At the conclusion the Emperor said, "I think today's serious research is satisfactory. I desire that we quickly move forward based on the research results. The Army should also fully cooperate in this endeavor!" It was a thorough-going conference lasting from 1:35 p.m. to 4:00 p.m.[44]

On March 30, 1944, the Emperor was told of the bombing of eleven freight ships and subsequent loss of life. He had condolence money sent to the Ministry of Transport and Communication. Later on June 12, he was told of several other freighters that were sunk and again condolence money was sent.[45] Also, on March 31, Prime Minister Tôjô reported the cabinet decision about how many ships were to be built in 1944 to the Emperor.[46] Thus one can see that some months before the Saipan disaster the Emperor was informed about the critical shipping problem: protection, loss, and construction of vessels. Also this problem was nothing new. Previously the army was forced to withdraw from Guadalcanal because a lack of ships prevented it from being reinforced and resupplied. On this occasion Hirohito also questioned this decision. Nevertheless, on January 4, 1943, Imperial General Headquarters (IGHQ) ordered the evacuation, "but in deference to field service regulations announced that it was advancing in a different direction!"[47]

Here one should note that according to the standard Japanese dictionary *Kôjien*, *tenshin*, "advance in a different direction" was the term for retreat (*taikyaku*) used "in deference to the field service regulations" by the Imperial

Army throughout the war, not just at Guadalcanal. This is but another example of how the military with euphemisms sought to make their losses appear less inauspicious. In the long run, however, it appears that they not only fooled others. They were taken in by the cumulative effect of their own deceptions.

The reports to the Emperor about the shipping problem were sporadic and, as seen in the above commentary, if the STJR is an accurate indication, he was only informed of a small fraction of those actually lost. Also, if he took decisive action vis-à-vis transport and freight shipping prior to the US invasion of Saipan on June 15, it is not noted in the STJR. His statement at the end of the conference on March 17, was but another of many admonishing the army and navy to cooperate closely, paid little heed by both. In the end Saipan could not be reinforced, it fell and as the war continued on shipping became ever more problematic. As reported in the Supreme War Guidance Council on August 11, 1944, there was a lack of material, fuel, and trained workers, and war losses could not be adequately replaced. Transport at sea and on land was becoming extremely difficult due to dramatic net losses of ships and trucks since the beginning of the war. This source does not say if the Emperor was accordingly informed.[48]

Toward the end of 1944 transport shipping losses were increasingly reported during imperial conferences. Yamada Akira provides evidence showing that from October to December 1944 Hirohito was extensively informed about naval matters including detailed reports on commercial shipping losses. However, the sources Yamada uses do not cover the time before and during the fight for Saipan, and they do not say how the Emperor reacted to this information.[49] Moreover, Komamiya Shinshichirô says that the records are incomplete. Convoy formation: navigation, speed, position each day at noon, combat situation, and other difficulties were supposed to be recorded but often were not. Much is hearsay evidence from those who lived through the voyages. The navy ships accompanying the freighters were small, not heavily armed and captained by reserve officers called up from the merchant marines. Regular officers were mostly used on destroyers and larger ships employed in fleet operations.[50]

Transporting oil and aviation gas was especially critical. By the end of 1944 petroleum stocks in Japan had dwindled such that in the near future planes and warships no longer would be able to operate. It was then decided that "special attack transport convoys" (*tokkô yusô*) must be formed. One had to expect that only a certain percentage of the ships would come through. These were called the "southern operations convoys" and initiated on January 20, 1945. Prior to this there were special tanker convoys for large tankers with a speed of over 13 knots. But these brought little improvement in the situation.[51] In effect so-called "special attack," meaning suicide tactics, were extended to freight transport missions. A lack of foresight brought on disaster.

Navy ill-prepared

During the war the Japanese navy was totally unprepared for the losses of commercial vessels being incurred. Sinkings in the first year of the war were in accord with prewar estimates, but losses increased dramatically from the second year onward. The navy made studies about the causes and found that by far (69 percent) enemy submarines were responsible. Enemy warplanes accounted for 23 percent of the losses and surface ships 8 percent. More graphically, the Munitions Ministry calculated that up to the end of July 1944, 4.5 million tons of bottoms were sunk. After the war investigation showed that in fact around 4.8 million tons were lost. In either case, prewar estimates based on the First World War proved to be wrong, mainly due to vastly underestimating US submarine effectiveness in the next war.[52]

Prior to the war the problem was well known but its importance discounted. For example, future Vice-Admiral Nakazawa Tasuku worked up war games on total war with the United States while he was chief of the 1st Section, Operations Department in the Imperial Navy General Staff from 1936 to 1939. He concluded that if the war lasted longer than two to three years war materials and logistics would become a problem. Transport to and from the home islands would become especially problematic due to attacks by US submarines. Then, the author of this commentary says, with insufficient national resources and war materials Japan plunged into an unwinnable war.[53] The report was "filed," forgotten.

Later on January 30, 1941, Vice-Admiral Inoue Shigeyoshi chief of the Imperial Navy Air Force Headquarters presented a report to Navy Minister Oikawa Koshirô, *Shingunbi Keikakuron* (A Plan for New Armaments) in which he emphasized the importance of strengthening the navy's capacity to defend the sea lanes against attack by US submarines and warplanes. However, the general staff had other priorities: preparing for a decisive sea engagement that would make such defense measures superfluous. And Inoue's report found only a minority of support in the Navy Ministry. During the war destroyer class ships and airplanes suitable for attacking submarines were seriously lacking and plans for rectifying these deficits never really were carried through. Also the navy failed to lay mines on the high seas as an anti-submarine measure.[54]

According to the US economist Jerome B. Cohen, during the war, "For every ton of shipping the Japanese were able to build, three were sunk; and given the inadequate merchant tonnage with which Japan began the war, her merchant fleet was being whittled down to nothing."[55] Despite later claims to the contrary by Vice-Admiral Nakazawa Tasuku, the Imperial Navy, "was indifferent to the problem of protecting the nation's shipping lanes [...] Thus, on a theoretical level, the Japanese navy acknowledged the problems of protecting Japan's merchant shipping, but it failed to undertake any concrete measures that would make such protection effective."[56] But of course the navy was not alone in neglecting the materials and logistics necessary for winning a war. The United States superior industrial capacity and access to important raw materials contributed greatly to Japan's defeat. But equally important, Japanese military policy, for example "smashed jewels" on numerous Pacific islands, kamikaze tactics, and "all hands go down with the ship," forced an irresponsible squander of men and materials leading to a lack of experienced army and navy personnel as well as a lack of war materials toward the end of the war.[57]

Tôjô and material deficits

Like many Japanese, Tôjô was well informed about the mismatch between Japan and the United States. The first edition of the *Heibonsha Encyclopedia* published in 1931, the same year as the invasion of Manchuria, presented this vividly for all to read.[58] Later, as indicated above, in 1941 a number of studies of Japan's material resources were made. One by a senior officer involved in gathering and evaluating intelligence about the United States went so far as to state, "If the ratio of industrial strengths of both countries could be kept at the current level, war damage to the United States must be 100 percent while damage to Japan must be limited to 5 percent for the duration of the war."[59] But reports such as this that came to negative conclusions were either optimistically revised or overlooked. Deception in the imperial state included self-deception.

During the war Tôjô said on at least one occasion, noted above, that productivity in Japan was lacking in comparison with Germany and the United States. To put one man in the field the Japanese needed twelve in industry, the Germans only two, and America eight. The problem is brought up, but if anything other than an unrealistic paper proposal for a state-planned economy was undertaken, it is not noted.[60] Tôjô acted within this framework, sometimes ignoring and/or denying concrete problems that did not fit into his worldview. It does not appear that he was a diabolical maniac. Nor was he possessed of criminal instincts. He did what he was trained to do: prosecute a war as a state leader in the name of his emperor and nation. For this he was responsible, and after the war he willingly acknowledged this responsibility knowing full well what the consequences would be.

Finally, this combination of poor strategic planning and underrating the importance of materials and associated logistics was an extremely important factor in Japan's defeat. Tôjô Hideki in his various official capacities was a significant part of this problem. If he had paid more attention over the years to this issue, the war materials situation, resupplying Saipan and other outposts elsewhere in the Pacific may not have reached crisis proportions in mid-1944, and his government may not have become an object of intense criticism and intrigue, at least not at this time. A little success sometimes goes a long way. Instead, as seen in his speech to parliament in February 1943, in his statement to German Ambassador Stahmer in June 1944, and elsewhere, the problem was not approached realistically. It was redefined as one of Japanese mind over matter. He was not the only advocate of these fantasies, but he abetted support of sacred folklore and slighted the profane material realities of war at great cost to his country and countrymen. This contributed to fighting on in a lost war for the sake of honor and emperor adopting, among other stratagems, the ill-fated kamikaze tactics initiated during the battle for the Philippines in October 1944, continued and expanded to the end of the war (see Chapter 2).

Imperial Navy's inept strategy

Indifference to material deficiencies and overseas logistics contributed to strategic shortcomings, despite warnings to the contrary. Moreover, Vice-Admiral Nakazawa maintains that at the time of the battles in the Marianas and on Saipan, the strategy employed by the Japanese Imperial Navy was quite inappropriate. In his postwar analysis he lists four strategic failures that contributed to the naval defeat in the Mariana/Philippine Seas and the fall of Saipan:

1. Insufficient war materials and preparations for the coming engagements.
2. Wavering on the part of the commanders of the Combined Fleet vis-à-vis "all-out war," and unnecessary waste incurred by transferring air power and war materials from one locale to another.
3. Difficulties in constructing defense fortifications on Saipan.
4. Inappropriate planning by Vice-Admiral Ozawa Jisaburô, commander of the fleet in the Marianas, and a simple lack of luck.

Of course Nakazawa's analysis profits from hindsight and some authorities dispute his last point, but unlike Col Hattori above he was a navy planning expert and his assertions are worth considering briefly.[61]

1. Nakazawa maintained that when he was Operations Section chief in the Imperial Navy General Staff in 1940 extensive preparations were made in the mid Pacific, but in June 1943 when he returned to the general staff as Operations Department chief this had all been undone. His predecessors, "hunting a deer failed to see the surrounding mountains." They were intent only on attack in order to extend the front lines and did not consider defense problems. In late 1943 when it was decided to strengthen the forces on Saipan and in the Caroline Islands the navy's transport possibilities were greatly reduced and there was a lack of materials. A rapid reassembly of forces was impossible.

2. On May 26–29, 1944, the army and navy were undecided about where to concentrate their forces: the Marianas, the Caroline Islands, or New Guinea. Then on May 29 "all-out war" was ordered; shortly thereafter the order was rescinded and then again repeated. The fleet wavered. On June 13 when preparations for Operation A-go, the naval offensive in the mid Pacific, were initiated, the "all-out war" orders were again suspended and efforts focused on the Marianas. With these changes in war emphases air forces were moved about resulting in unnecessary losses. Also, quite a number of pilots caught malaria and collapsed. These losses and the waste of resources contributed to the later defeats.

3. Construction of defense fortifications was hindered by the lack of experience of the construction battalion sent from Manchuria to Saipan. The soft earth in Manchuria was quite different from the coral sand of Saipan and the latter slowed and impeded construction considerably.

4. Nakazawa deemed Admiral Ozawa's strategy inappropriate because the latter planned and sought out a large decisive battle in the face of the enemy's superior forces. Considering Japan's resources at the time, he should have pursued an "out of range" tactic of seeking out enemy forces beyond their immediate striking range and attacking individual units hit-and-run. After weakening the enemy forces and achieving a balance of power, then a major attack could have been ventured. Moreover, the fortunes of war were not on their side. After traversing the San Bernardino Straits and while moving toward the Mariana area the Japanese forces were discovered and attacked by submarines. They lost two aircraft carriers including the flagship *Taihô*. Later Ozawa's fleet was decimated; the enemy landing on Saipan could not be repulsed and Japanese troops there could not be resupplied. However, in fairness to Ozawa one should note that several postwar accounts say that it is unclear if the strategy outlined by Nakazawa could have been successful in the Philippine-Mariana Seas engagement. Fuchida Mitsuo, among others, who led the air strike on Pearl Harbor and also participated in these battles stated as much after the war.[62]

Nakazawa did not mention another crucial problem: the transition from a battleship navy to one focused on air war and aircraft carriers. Many senior Japanese naval officers were trained in the former strategy but the War in the Pacific was dominated by the latter. This became especially clear in mid-1944. The engagements on Saipan and in the Philippines involved many thousands of amphibious troops, but Japanese forces, including transport ships, were attacked from above by US air forces and from below by her submarines. Many naval leaders were ill-prepared for these developments, and as a result the Japanese lacked appropriate materials and the means to bring them where needed.[63]

Following the above defeats Nakazawa tendered his resignation as chief of operations to the Vice-Chief of the Navy General Staff Vice-Admiral Itô Sei'ichi saying he no longer believed Japan could win the war. Therefore it was inappropriate for him to continue on in his present position. He asked to be transferred to the front lines. However, after short silent deliberation Itô said he was "entirely of the same opinion" and asked Nakazawa to stay on, which he did. The war must be carried on. Here one sees the importance of the loss of Saipan and navy fighting power at that time. Also this confirms the questionable motives of high Imperial Japanese military officers mentioned by the postwar diplomat Iguchi Takeo. Not only before the attack on Pearl Harbor but also as the war slowly came to an end, military leaders were "more concerned with defending the honor of the nation than the lives and fortunes of its citizens."[64] This priority, entertained by many radical and not so radical officers, extended the twisted, tortuous road to unconditional surrender.

5

Capitulation: Hubris and Unquestioning Belief in a Religious Ideology, some Conclusions

Unconditional surrender—the Allied demand versus the Imperial Japanese proviso that the national essence and imperial line must be preserved—roughs out the final difficulty in ending the war. In the background loomed the battle for Saipan (June–July 1944). It was meaningful for war expectations and planning on both sides. As noted earlier, the battle of Saipan had an important influence on how US authorities ended the war. Due to Japanese fanaticism military leaders expected around 500,000 soldiers and sailors to be killed and many times that wounded with an invasion of Japan proper.[1] Perhaps this seems unrealistic now but it was pertinent then. Similarly, Japanese leaders had ominous expectations about the anticipated Allied invasion of the home islands. Those planning the defense of the country expected the worst if Japan were defeated and occupied. They feared that the land would be devastated, the Emperor taken prisoner, and that the people might under the circumstance become estranged from the military.[2] Imperial Japan as military authorities envisioned it would be destroyed. Therewith, they feared above all that the national essence and imperial line would be abolished.

The Imperial House was not unaffected by these fears. And, all things considered, the Emperor only resolved to terminate hostilities after all was lost. As the tragedy played out, however, he was not a sole edict-issuing autocrat. Up until mid-August 1945 in the desperate situation evident to all, according to Suzuki Tamon, the Emperor, Imperial Army, and Imperial Navy pursued mutually opposing policies: the Emperor sought above all preservation of the national essence. The Imperial Army advocated the drastic policy of continuing the war *sine die* even if it meant Japan's ultimate demise. The Imperial Navy sought a most favorable way of losing the war.[3] This debilitating state of affairs had existed since the fall of Saipan and the Tôjô Cabinet mid-1944, but nothing was done to end the conflict, even though many including the Emperor regarded these losses as cataclysmic events revealing once and for all that Japan had no chance of winning the war.

Support for continuing a hopeless war

Did Emperor Hirohito obstruct the search for an early peace? I think not. He had much to lose but remembered well his priorities and sided with the large majority of Japan's leaders in favor of continuing the war. As Kawamura says, he supported "the military's argument that Japan needed a decisive victory before entering into peace negotiations."[4] This meant he favored peace but held out for an improved negotiating position vis-à-vis the future of the Imperial House up to the end. Though they had no meaningful contact with one another, Hitler also followed the same policy on his way to defeat. At the end of July 1944 with the Allied Forces well situated in northwestern France Hitler advocated that, "Inflicting a defeat on the western Allies and halting their presumed march to victory would force them into armistice negotiations."[5] Both leaders stubbornly adhered to this strategy until defeated. Why did these very different war leaders in very different nations have the same delusions and follow this same fatal policy? The records point to each being self-obsessed with beliefs in their unique importance, their respective callings and the ideologies buttressing them, the Nazi "master race" in Germany and a unique "national essence" with an "unbroken line of emperors" in Japan. Promoting and preserving these fantasies justified aggression and atrocities abroad, sacrificing their own populations at home.

David C. Earhart summed up well the situation in Japan near war's end:

> By 1 August 1945, over sixty of Japan's cities had been devastated by incendiary bombing and the nation's war machine was all but destroyed. According to the media, however, the people's will to fight was anything but diminished by the prospect of an Allied invasion. "Certain Victory" (*hisshô*) was now praised in terms of a "Decisive War" (*kessen*) for the homeland that would end with the invaders repelled from Japan's shores. Presumably, the Allies would then desist in demanding unconditional surrender, which was unacceptable to the Imperial High Command. The Japanese government was prepared to let more blood flow to protect the national polity and the imperial institution. The covenant between god-emperor and his people was to be kept at any cost.[6]

Later, on August 12, 1945, after two atomic bombs and the USSR's attack on Japan—in an utterly desperate situation—Prince Asaka asked at a meeting of the Emperor's family, if the national essence could not be protected would the war continue? And Hirohito said it would.[7] He equated the nation with the imperial line even if it meant sacrificing as a matter of course thousands of lives.

This mutual identity was a given for him. Quite probably his support for the war lasted much longer than now seems reasonable because of the Emperor's imperial-line centered convictions and, in no small part, due to the profuse but unreliable and wildly optimistic reports about the war situation he received from his military leaders, beginning already in mid-1942. Due to the copious nature of the reports the Emperor received it appears he was well informed, but due to the false information many accounts included this abundance is deceiving. State leaders effectively misled the nation's leader. But that was not the whole story. It appears that Hirohito could not conceive of emperor, national essence, and folk otherwise.

At the end of the war, some say, Prime Minister Suzuki Kantarô and General Umezu Yoshijirô (1882–1949) chief of the Imperial Army General Staff, among others, followed the Shôwa Emperor's lead. They and other state leaders did not have the courage to live up to their responsibilities and lead the nation toward ending the war.[8] But the "state of play" was not so simple. Suzuki Kantarô wrote that as prime minister at war's end he attempted to bridge the gap between die-hard military leaders and the Emperor, in my terms between state and nation: The Potsdam Proclamation should be accepted and the impending destruction of Japan avoided.[9] Suzuki Tamon asserts that finally Emperor Hirohito felt, based on replies received from the Allies to Japanese inquiries about the conditions of unconditional surrender, that in the event of an occupation they probably would not destroy the national essence and Imperial House. And based on past experience, he felt he could not rely on the statements made by his military leaders about the advisability of fighting a decisive battle on the home islands. This situation contributed greatly to his "sacred decision" to end the war.[10] As indicated in this book, it appears that the main issue was how best to preserve the national essence, Imperial House, and military's honor, not the lives and livelihood of the Japanese populace, not to mention other Asian peoples. However, very often two other factors are said to have greatly influenced the Emperor's decision. One was entirely new and the other feared, but hardly prepared for.

Atom bombs and Soviet war entry

After the debacles of mid-1944, Imperial Japan's war-making capacity steadily declined, as did the aptness of her leadership. The Emperor and his civil and military advisors needed still another precipitous development to push them over the brink into surrender. Then came the two US atom bombs and the Soviet entry into the war one year later. The two US atomic bombs and the Soviet Union's declaration of war, all of which took place in the space of three days, August 6–9, finally forced the hands of all three—the Emperor and the military and civilian leaders into precipitating unconditional surrender. Which was more important to the imperial government's decision to surrender?

Hiroshima A-bomb: August 6; Soviet declaration of war on Japan: August 9 shortly after midnight; Nagasaki A-bomb: August 9 at about 11:00 a.m. Wilson D. Miscamble in *The Most Controversial Decision. Truman, the Atomic Bombs, and the Defeat of Japan* maintains that on August 8 Emperor Hirohito decided to end the war, "before any news of a Soviet declaration of war reached him." (This is certainly true; the Soviets declared war slightly later.) Hirohito told Foreign Minister Tôgô Shigenori, "now that such a new weapon has appeared, it has become less and less possible to continue war […] So my wish is to make such arrangements as will end the war as soon as possible." Miscamble argues that the atomic bombing of Hiroshima was the deciding event for the Emperor. But as Miscamble also says this was an imperial wish, not yet formal policy (or a command). An earlier work edited by Tsuyoshi Hasegawa is devoted to the relative importance of the A-bomb attacks versus Soviet entry into the conflict vis-à-vis ending the Pacific War. Hasegawa and four other historians agree to disagree on this issue. Their "disagreements stem from different emphases on certain sources and different interpretations."[11] The detailed accounts of the conferences in Imperial Japanese governing circles included in the essays are very useful, but as seen below this seems like a fruitless debate.

Several months before the Emperor's decisions the war situation had already taken another turn for the worse. The Soviet Union announced it would not renew the Neutrality Pact on April 5, 1945, and despite the one-year grace period stipulated in the Pact, some military and civilian leaders expected that the Soviet Union would declare war on Japan in the near future. This caused grave concern among army leaders as they were confronted with both a US assault on the home islands and war with the Soviets at the same time. In July and at the beginning of August these apprehensions continued unabated while concurrently, out of desperation, the army and navy hoped the Soviets would mediate an acceptable surrender.[12]

Suzuki Tamon shows that the Emperor mentioned his wish to end the war to Kido Kôichi on August 9 shortly before 10:00 a.m. in connection with the Soviet attack on Japan: the war situation must be quickly brought under control. Later during a cabinet meeting that began at 2:30 p.m., while Soviet entry into the war was being discussed, news of the Nagasaki atom bomb reached authorities in Tokyo. Finally, similar to Richard Frank in an earlier essay, Suzuki argues that Emperor Hirohito thought something else entirely was more important than the atom bombs or the Soviet offensive: preparations for thwarting the Allied invasion were far behind schedule and a final battle for the home islands was therefore impossible. In addition the Emperor thought the new weapon made continuing the war impossible after the United States invaded Japan. In any case, assuming that Japan would eventually capitulate, this final battle had no political purpose.[13]

Somewhat differently, Hatano Sumio documents extensively the disarray in the government and especially the military. He is very critical of Prime Minister Suzuki's disregard of his responsibility to advise the throne. Suzuki sought to unite the country behind the war while quietly working to end it. However, as prime minister, Suzuki and his cabinet should have decided to end the war and "advised" the Emperor accordingly. Instead, at the last minute, due to disunity between the high commands of the army and navy, he imposed an imperial decision on the Emperor. This "amounted to trampling on the throne advisory system and a collapse of the Meiji Constitution's de facto structure," ignoring the responsibility to advise the throne.[14]

Bringing these lines of reasoning together, it appears that it was not an either-or situation. The two atomic bombings and Soviet declaration of war all occurred at about the same time, within three days, and all weighed in on the decision-making process. They tipped the scales in the context of inadequate home island defense preparations, discord within the military, and Japan's dwindling war-making capabilities along with the impending societal collapse reported already in the Imperial Conference on June 8 (noted at the beginning of this book).[15] The domestic situation could not be totally discounted. All of these factors made the military defense of the home islands impossible, a final battle of annihilation even more senseless.

However, Emperor Hirohito could not decide these things alone. On August 8 and 9 he expressed his desire that the war be terminated as soon as possible to the foreign minister and Privy Seal individually. Independently a cabinet meeting on the afternoon and evening of August 9 was held in order to decide what to do under these new circumstances. During this meeting Minister of Justice Matsuzaka Hiromasa asked Army Minister Anami Korechika if they had countermeasures for dealing with the atom bombs. Anami answered that the atom bombs were "no big deal" (*taishita koto nashi*), and there were no doubt countermeasures. Then he cited a statement by a US war prisoner, a 1st lt. in the air corps to substantiate his claims. It is quite unlikely that a lowly 1st lt. would be privy to important information about these new weapons, and probably the officer invented the story when threatened during interrogation.[16] Even so, Anami recounted what he had heard in this meeting. This appears to be but another demonstration of the arrogance of army leaders. Or it may have been a purposeful distraction. Anami knew that with Soviet entry into the war, the situation in Manchuria and on the home islands was hopeless. The home islands defense was predicated on the Soviets not entering the war, but of course he was unwilling to admit this.

Army Minister Anami Korechika (1887-1945) and war's end

The atomic bombs may have been a surprise, but Soviet entry into the war was not. In Japan, faced with many setbacks and finally this dire situation, saving the army's honor and especially the national essence, including the Imperial House, were *the* important factors stimulating many activities toward the end of the war. State and nation both had to be preserved. Anami Korechika was a living example of these priorities.

The following is an account of the events leading up to surrender as experienced by Army Minister Anami Korechika. The convoluted, chaotic circumstances in Imperial Japan just prior to her capitulation are difficult to ferret out and understand. The actors appear to have been unsure of themselves, do not seem to have been fully aware of what their counterparts were doing, and real-time as well as postwar accounts reflect this confusion. At the Imperial Conference on August 10, in which the Emperor decided to accept the Potsdam Declaration (*seidan*) it was a question of Japan's chances in the war. Anami argued vigorously against this decision. But the Emperor said that preparations for the defense of the home islands were inadequate and that there had long been great gaps between planning and execution of the military's plans. Afterwards some officers, for example Army Vice-Chief of Staff Kawabe Torashirô, were totally demoralized because they recognized that Emperor Hirohito had lost faith in them, and the Emperor's doubts about the home island defense measures were important to eventually abandoning these army plans.[17] Then at the Imperial Conference on August 14, where the decision was reaffirmed, emphasis shifted to defending as much as possible the Imperial Army's honor and preserving the national essence. Various authors conjecture that some or all of these events contributed to Anami's thinking. Accordingly there was then and still is now significant disagreement about Minister Anami's motives: the "one-big-strike" doctrine (against the enemy to achieve a better negotiating position); the "haragei" theory (conveying one's intentions wordlessly to associates); "irresolution" theory (Anami was undecided about what to do); and the "total resistance" doctrine (fighting on to utter defeat). No doubt many other military men shared viscerally some of these thoughts. But Anami's most important motivation was that he had realized some days earlier that unconditional surrender was in the offing.

Complicating the situation domestically, the threat of a coup d'état involving the army minister loomed up. Gerhard Krebs believes that possibly Prince Mikasa Takahito (1915–2016, Hirohito's youngest brother) influenced Anami not to support a putsch by young officers bent on continuing the war. He wrote that Anami approached the Prince on August 12 and sought to convince him that he should join the "hawks" in favor of continuing the war. Moreover, he should persuade the Emperor to change his decision to end the war. Prince Mikasa answered Anami with a lecture about how the army had obstructed the imperial will going back to the Manchurian Incident in 1931 to 1932. The Prince had long promoted Anami's career. Nevertheless, according to Anami's secretary at that time Col. Hayashi Saburô, Mikasa's scolding incensed Anami such that he gave the Prince an impertinent reply. Yet, one interpretation of the poem Anami left for posterity when he committed suicide (see below) says he was atoning for "great transgressions" by the army over the years.[18] In any case, later when several officers asked Anami to participate in a coup planned for August 13, he expressed sympathy for their cause but refused to go along with them. The principal conspirators were disciples of History Professor Hiraizumi Kiyoshi, and among others Lt. Col. Takeshita Masahiko, Anami's brother-in-law. They assumed they knew better how to preserve the kokutai than the Emperor. Some of the conspirators, not including Takeshita, continued their efforts and tried to prevent a radio broadcast to the Japanese people by the Emperor at noon on August 15 indicating Japan would surrender: the Kyûjô Incident, finally thwarted during the morning hours of the same day in a skirmish around and in the imperial palace.

Anami did not become part of these plots but early in the morning on August 14 he seemingly contradicted his previous stance. Col. Arao Okikatsu of the Military Affairs Bureau, leader of the officers who visited him the night before, approached Anami again and together they concocted a slipshod plan to isolate the Emperor and prevent him from accepting the Potsdam Proclamation stipulating unconditional surrender. The Allies first had to confirm that they would not destroy Imperial Japan's national essence. However, Army Chief of Staff Umezu Yoshijirô refused to go along and the intrigue came to nothing. He told Anami that an imperial decision had been made and the army should surrender "in an open forthright manner."[19]

Shortly thereafter an imperial conference was convened. General Anami is famous because reportedly he spoke in tears during the Imperial Conference on August 14 and implored the Emperor not to surrender. Moreover, Col. Hayashi wrote that the general was central to those urging a final battle on the home islands. He maintained that his chief, Army Minister Anami, adamantly opposed surrender without a US guarantee to respect and preserve the national essence and imperial line. Anami, according to this description, was less devoted to the Emperor and more interested in asserting army priorities—in changing Hirohito's mind about acceding to US authorities and accepting unconditional surrender. But Hayashi's memoir is self-adulatory: among other laudable actions on his part from his postwar perspective, disregarding Umezu's considerable influence, he claims that he urged Anami not to contravene the imperial will,[20] and his chief acted accordingly.

Anami expressed concern about preserving the Imperial House and advocated one big strike to achieve a better negotiating position. He seems to have been disconcerted, believed it was possible to bring the United States to accept the continued existence of the Imperial House, and/or he sought to forestall the army coup-conspirators by appearing to agree with them. One key to the varying interpretations about Anami is what his secretary wrote after the war about his meeting with the conspirators led by Col. Arao. Hayashi says that Anami was not decisive about repudiating Arao's scheme, leaving room for the conspirators to think he really was sympathetic to their plans. Also, he and a number of other interviewees after the war maintained that Anami was totally convinced that the United States could be brought to friendlier terms through a big strike. However, Chief Cabinet Secretary Sakomizu Hisatsune later maintained that if Anami had openly opposed continuing the war some junior officers might have assassinated him. Also, Foreign Minister Tôgô Shigenori wrote later that despite Anami's vigorous posturing in cabinet meetings, he seemed worried about an uprising among army leaders, making negotiations then for a more favorable surrender impossible.[21]

Two other very different narratives show Anami stalling: checking the would-be rebels may well have been his intention. Both Robert J.C. Butow (1954) and the Gunjishi Gakkai (Military History Society, 1998) have detailed descriptions of the events in Tokyo between c. August 9 and 15, 1945, including Anami's role in them and his "final statement"—seppuku, suicide by self-disembowelment. Both show the army minister as a knowledgeable, dignified officer. Both have him forcefully but courteously representing the position of the army in cabinet meetings and imperial conferences, while at the same time he stalled precipitous action by the army officers planning a revolt.[22]

Another participant in these events, Cabinet Minister and Lt. Gen. (ret.) Yasui Tôji said many years later that Army Minister Anami had three priorities: (1) the war must be ended, (2) the national essence with sacrosanct Imperial House must be preserved, and (3) there were an estimated 2.7 million troops overseas and approximately 2.2 million in Japan, they must be controlled and prevented from staging a revolt. Two out of three of these priorities were achieved. Number two is the obvious exception. The national essence was discredited as nationalistic propaganda. The Imperial House was preserved but as an historic, symbolic entity, not contingent on an eternal imperial line. The last problem, revolt, was especially acute, at least as threatening as the aborted Kyûjô plot. An army uprising was perceived by various authorities in Tokyo as a real danger.[23]

Going back to the first Manchurian Incident in 1928 (the assassination of the Chinese warlord Zhang Zuolin) and the second Manchurian Incident in 1931 to 1932 (when the army without assent from Tokyo overran Manchuria), censured by Prince Mikasa, the army was known for its unauthorized activities. Abetting these apprehensions, in 1945 new Army Minister Anami received a report on April 12 from the Military Police saying, among other things, that army officers increasingly deserted, were engaged in taking bribes, and were insubordinate. Also, experienced non-commissioned officers in the navy distrusted their newly appointed (inexperienced) officers. Anami may have imparted this information to other officials. More ominous, according to Hatano Sumio a telegram about controlling the troops was sent in the names of Army Minister Anami and Chief of Staff Umezu on August 11 to overseas troop commanders. Also Yamada Akira shows, they sent telegrams again to various commands on August 14 indicating what was about to come. Above all, the army was to adhere to the Emperor's wishes and independent, insubordinate action was proscribed.[24] The August 11 telegram was sent in response to telegrams from army leaders in the Southern Areas, Bangkok, Singapore, and China who had intercepted telegrams from Foreign Minister Tôgô on August 10 to Switzerland and Sweden for transmission to the Allies saying Japan would surrender subject only to retaining the national essence and emperor. The overseas generals vowed to fight on. Moreover responses to the August 14 telegram from Anami and Umezu augmented these fears. Field commanders in Myanmar (Burma), China, and various other areas sent telegrams directly to the Emperor, very unusual, stressing their resolve to fight on. Direct appeals to the Emperor. Fear of unwanted, unauthorized army actions was not limited to the generals Anami and Umezu. Admiral Yonai mentioned it briefly to Rear Admiral Takagi Sôkichi on August 14. As a consequence in part, on August 16, one day after Emperor Hirohito accepted the Potsdam Proclamation meaning surrender, three members of the imperial family were sent overseas to transmit directly to expedition forces leaders the imperial will and enforce the surrender mandate. One each was sent to China, Manchuria, and the southern areas, and subsequent events demonstrate that these emissaries may have alleviated the situation. The war was terminated and there were no large-scale revolts in the armed forces.[25]

During the above intrigues and before the Imperial Conference on August 14, Anami visited Suzuki and presented him with a box of cigars. He would not be able to smoke them and he would be pleased if his colleagues would do so. Following the conference and the Emperor's reaffirmation of the decision to end the war, Anami supported the decision within the Army Ministry: he ordered that all officers had no choice but to obey the Emperor's wishes. Later he requested that the Emperor's announcement to the people be delayed until midday on August 15 and the Cabinet affirmed this. Still later he visited Prime Minister Suzuki at night and told him, "I represent the will of the army and presented extremely strong-worded opinions. I intended to support the Prime Minister, but instead only provoked all manner of conflicting opinions. As a cabinet minister I apologize deeply for that which should not have come about." Several hours afterwards he committed suicide. He left behind the following poem: "Laying down my life I offer up apologies [to the Emperor] for my great transgressions." Suzuki was deeply impressed. He greatly respected Anami for his military bearing and loyal but not destructive opposition. Anami's secretary Col. Hayashi was not so generous. He thought that Anami should stay on and see to the demobilization of the army. Thereafter there would be time enough for suicide.[26]

Here the mechanics of the cabinet system in Imperial Japan is important. One must remember that if a minister resigned and no one could be found to take the post, the entire cabinet had to resign. Both services, but especially the army, used this rule to blackmail the other ministers including the prime minister in order to prevail. On occasion the army minister or navy minister when in disagreement with a particular policy would threaten to resign while indicating that their respective service would not make another officer available to take the post—meaning the cabinet would fall. In this case if Army Minister

Anami had been adamantly opposed to surrender a coup was unnecessary. Had he resigned no replacement would have been provided by the army; the Suzuki Cabinet would have fallen and the war continued indefinitely. Suzuki and the Emperor were well aware of this situation.

General Anami was of course also mindful of it, but with positive consequences confirmed by oft-ignored contemporary sources: Foreign Minister Tōgō wrote later that Anami's refusal to participate in the coup d'état planned in mid-August was consistent with talks he had had with him beginning at the end of April. Also, on the evening of August 1, Anami told Cabinet Minister Yasui that under no circumstances would he resign and bring down the Suzuki Cabinet. "The Suzuki Cabinet is there to somehow save the state [*kokka*]. For this reason I will see the matter through together with Prime Minister Suzuki to the very end." And two other knowledgeable persons, Lt. General Wakamatsu Tadakazu (army vice-minister July 18–November 1, 1945) and Shimomura Hiroshi (minister and director of the Information Bureau in the Suzuki Cabinet) credited Anami with convincing Navy Minister Yonai Mitsumasa not to resign from the cabinet.[27] As it turned out, all cabinet members signed the surrender proclamation and the plotting came to naught.

As seen above, much has been written about Army Minister Anami Korechika and his sometimes-inconsistent activities. They seem to reflect the changing circumstances and his fluctuating state of mind. He believed Japan's national essence and the imperial line were sacrosanct, and that the enemy was disinclined to respect these values and allow them to be preserved. Some days before capitulation he knew that the war situation was hopeless but remained unreconciled. He wrote in his Memo on August 9, if the situation of the Imperial House was not properly resolved the Yamato Folk had no choice but "for the sake of justice [*seigi*] to fight to the end, dying in the name of an eternal cause [loyalty to the nation, *kuni*]."[28] On the same day, "Accept the three country [Potsdam] proclamation? Go as far as an 'honorable death' [*gyokusai*]?" On August 10, he wrote in the same Memo that the conditions of the Three Power Proclamation of July 26, "included nothing about the demand that the emperor's supreme authority to rule the state would not be changed and that with this understanding the Japanese government accepted it."[29] The dreaded unconditional surrender he continued to oppose but did not block. Humiliating surrender or honorable death, this summed up for Anami the options at hand five to six days before capitulation. In the end Anami did both: he signed the surrender resolution and arranged his own honorable death.

Values change over time and, different from the beginning of the twenty-first century, in Anami's day and age his notes do not show that he personally was a rabid war advocate. He advocated personal sacrifice for the nation, imperial line, and state meaning primarily the military's honor. But many persons called on others to die for the sake of loyalty to some eternal nation-state during the Second World War.

Of course the above accounts do not all agree. People write diaries, memoirs, and histories for different reasons. Often they are personally motivated and the results are not simply a record of what happened. Taken all together my impression is that Anami did not intend to sabotage Hirohito's decision. Rather, he attempted to bridge the chasm between acting as a loyal army officer (state official) and being loyal to the emperor (leader of the nation), with some success. In this respect, despite its self-interested bias, the record by Army Minister Secretary Col. Hayashi contains a thought-provoking insight. He sums up well Anami's practical situation: Anami was torn between loyalty to the emperor and supporting the officers in his ministry. Moreover, there was the gulf between army–navy presumptions of supreme command and decisions made by political leaders, conjointly at times with the emperor.[30] As depicted by Hayashi, Anami appears to personify nation versus state tension in Imperial Japan.

The end

Emperor Hirohito, leader of the *nation*, finally wanted to end the war, but he could not simply issue an imperial edict and bring the conflict to an end. He had to stifle army and navy, *state*, opposition first. On June 22, in a meeting with the "big six"—Prime Minister Suzuki, Army Minister Anami, Navy Minister Yonai, Army Chief of Staff Umezu, Navy Chief of Staff Toyoda, and Foreign Minister Tôgô—Emperor Hirohito told them, "This is not an order, however while I wish that preparations for the defense of the home islands be very well carried out, at the same time I want you to consider how to implement ending the war as soon as possible." After the meeting Suzuki told his secretary Sakomizu he was pleased that the Emperor had stated very clearly what he had been reticent about saying directly up to this time. Nevertheless, dissent continued.[31]

At the Imperial Conference on August 10, with the support of Navy Minister Yonai, Foreign Minister Tôgô, and President of the Privy Council Hiranuma, surrender was agreed upon despite opposition from the army (especially Anami) and certain elements of the navy, which continued. On

August 12, the army and navy chiefs of staff met with the Emperor and vigorously advocated rejecting the Potsdam Proclamation. It would mean the destruction of the national essence including the imperial line, and the country. Two days later Fleet Admiral Nagano Osami and Field Marshal Sugiyama Hajime met with the Emperor and urged continuing the war. During this meeting Field Marshal Hata Shunroku, who had just returned from an inspection tour of Hiroshima, expressed doubts about being able to repulse the enemy. But military opposition to surrender persisted; so the decision was reaffirmed on August 14. During this time, Hirohito also had to take into account certain fanatical middle-ranking officers, the "total resistance faction," and men such as former Prime Minister Tôjô, who advocated continued "resistance of the spirit"[32] in the face of failing war potential. It was a complex situation.[33]

Finally, using his authority as leader of the nation Emperor Hirohito cajoled and pressured military leaders to follow his lead and agree to end the war. A radio broadcast at noon on August 15, 1945, announced this decision. Hirohito's statement included,

> The war situation has developed not necessarily to Japan's advantage, while the general trends of the world have all turned against her interest. Moreover, the enemy has begun to employ a new and most cruel bomb [...] Should We continue to fight, it would not only result in an ultimate collapse and obliteration of the Japanese nation, but also it would lead to the total extinction of human civilization [...] it is according to the dictate of time and fate that We have resolved to pave the way for a grand peace for all the generations to come by enduring the unendurable and suffering what is insufferable.[34]

This meant unconditional surrender, though the Emperor never uttered this phrase. Indeed, the Japanese were told that the war and world had turned against Japan, the enemy had a barbaric new bomb, and the Emperor terminated the war for the sake of the "Japanese nation" and "human civilization." Japan did not surrender or capitulate. The words *kôfuku* and *kôsan* meaning surrender, and *haisen* meaning defeat were not used. Rather, the war was terminated, *shûsen*. However, on September 2, the "Instrument of Surrender," that stipulated "unconditional surrender," was signed by Foreign Minister Shigemitsu Mamoru on behalf of the Emperor of Japan and the Japanese government; and General Umezu Yoshijirô signed on behalf of the Japanese Imperial General Headquarters. Nonetheless, some Japanese later maintained, and many still believe, this was a mitigated unconditional surrender, meaning there was a "tacit understanding about preserving the monarchy."[35]

The unending war's end

After the war the extent of the destruction in Japan surprised the victors. According to John Dower, the Special Presidential Envoy Edwin Locke, Jr. reported to President Truman,

> "the American officers now in Tokyo [mid-October 1945] are amazed by the fact that resistance continued as long as it did." [...] he added, that in the opinion of some Americans the atomic bombs, "while seized upon by the Japanese as an excuse for getting out of the war, actually speeded surrender by only a few days." [...] the prestigious US Strategic Bombing Survey, similarly concluded that the presurrender estimates of Japan's capacity for continuing the war had been greatly exaggerated. This was ex post facto conjecture, but it reflected a common observation that Japan at war's end was vastly weaker than anyone outside the country had imagined—or anyone inside it had acknowledged.[36]

The last phrase, "or anyone inside it had acknowledged," is especially fateful but only half-correct. High-ranking Japanese military officers especially[37] and some politicians were well aware of their desperate situation, as the plans for the defense of the home islands demonstrate. Overseas "presurrender estimates of Japan's capacity for continuing the war had been greatly exaggerated," but these immediate postwar estimates greatly underestimated the willingness of Imperial Japanese leaders to sacrifice their own people for their professed ideals—the national essence and emperor.

Considerably before the spring of 1945, and before the "Great Strategic Plan for the Decisive Battle on the Home Islands" of January 1945, plans were being made to extend kamikaze tactics to the entire population of Japan. For example, on September 25, 1944, the Military Affairs Section of the Army Ministry drew up an opinion paper outlining what army policy should be in the event that the Philippines were lost: "General Research on Worst Case National Defense." Therein it was postulated that if defeated the home islands would be occupied, the military disarmed, the emperor system abolished, and the Japanese people enslaved. Promises by the enemy to do otherwise, army planners inferred, would not be honored after the Japanese agreed to end the war. Therefore the entire population should be mobilized, trained to use the weapons available, and the Japanese Folk (*yamato minzoku*) should fight to the last man (including women and children).[38]

> Even if the Japanese counteroffensives in the Philippines, Okinawa and Taiwan end disadvantageously, there is still considerable time until the [Allied] landings

on the home islands. Also, opposing the enemy landings on the home islands and their occupation, the army and people without doubt, women and children without doubt will engage in regular and guerrilla counterattacks at one and the same time. If this does not stop them, even if we are unsuccessful it will take some years until the enemy home island occupation system takes hold. What's more even after that our 70 million people will attack, kill and wound enemy occupation troops and their important leaders everywhere. Communication and transport networks will be destroyed. The Yamato Folk will resist to the last man and thereby we will be able to endure for several years.[39]

The authors of this study returned to their long-held conviction that the Japanese were willing to sacrifice almost everything and everyone, including themselves, for their national essence but the Americans were not so steadfast. They maintained that the costs of supporting over a million American occupation troops in Japan under these circumstances would become unacceptable in the United States. In this way Japan cannot win, but the national essence and emperor can be preserved. Suzuki calls this the "Army Dept's internal long-term continuing war theory [leading to] the voluntary withdrawal of American troops."[40] Some, such as former Prime Minister Count Konoe Fumimaro, were against the guerrilla tactics, but military leaders paid them little heed.

The two-times Chief of the War Operations Section in the Army General Staff, Col. Hattori Takushirô recalled shortly after the war that in January 1945 army planners were continuing on this track: the Allies intended to segment completely the main islands and decimate Japan's production facilities. Despite the great losses expected in the battle for the Philippines Japan's answer would be to increase sea and air attacks. But the US would bring the home islands under their military control. Then the army would establish bases on islands near the home islands and fight on from there. Hattori makes no mention of how arms and munitions were to be provided for this, nor is there any reference to the slightest chance of somehow winning out.[41]

Six months later as seen in the Imperial Conference on June 8, 1945, the army was still intent on pursuing this policy. And the navy not to be outdone was hastily preparing a variety of suicide craft for destroying enemy ships before troops could be landed on the home islands. Among them were those listed above, for example the *Shinyô*: a small motorboat loaded with explosives; the *Kaiten*: "human torpedoes"; *Kairyû*: small mini-submarines with two-man crews; also the *Ôka*: a human rocket bomb; *Kôryû*: a mini-submarine, and others.[42] Of course we do not know if the Japanese people and new military recruits could have been convinced and/or coerced into following such a policy, or if so for how long. In terms of Allied costs and casualties the atomic bombs may not have been as unnecessary as some have assumed after the war. Americans then were unaware of the above opinion paper, the transactions of the Imperial Conference on June 8, other similar policy initiatives, concrete army and navy defense preparations, not to mention conspiracies by some field grade army officers to stage a coup and continue the war. Nationalistic like humanitarian "what ifs" in history are quite unverifiable. Finally, the A-bombs were used, the Soviets entered the war and the fighting was terminated. However, the pretenses of not a few former Imperial Japanese soldiers were not.

Postwar pretenses

Postwar pretenses rationalizing Imperial Japan's downfall reflect long-held convictions and self-deception, not something new brought on by defeat. In Japan long before war's end the ethereal position of the emperor as well as the mundane actual war situation were tainted by surreal beliefs, lies, and deceptions regarding what was real, aggravated by sloppy procedures, and simple mistakes. This included not only the myths presented as history embellishing the imperial tradition but also as seen above the hyperbolic reports presented to the throne about the war situation, battle results, and the available war materials. One Japanese author, a former diplomat in the postwar era, argues that even before the attack on Pearl Harbor Japanese military leaders were engaged in deceptive stratagems: well aware of the huge material discrepancies between Japan and the US, Japan nevertheless went to war.

> This happens when the leaders are more concerned with defending the honor of the nation than the lives and fortunes of its citizens […] and the Army in particular was moved by the idea that defense of its honor and pursuit of its ideals was important enough to risk leading the nation to destruction—about as irrational a policy decision as one might imagine.[43]

The bureaucrats in uniform were responsible for starting a war they knew they could not win with the United States and her allies, according to a bureaucrat in pinstripes. This does not absolve the latter, but my focus has been on the former, and after the war many former military officers continued their self-deception.

Following surrender, former Imperial Army Vice-Chief of Staff Kawabe Torashirô, like his older brother General Kawabe Masakazu mentioned above, remained unrepentant. Immediately after the war he felt that Japan should look for the reasons for her defeat but the state and people had no need to feel ashamed and become embittered. Japan sought to survive and maintain its independence without discarding its own beliefs. Thus for Japan,

> Accompanying the in substance natural development to the full of our state and people, international problems naturally occurred. Regarding the facts behind the events which led to the outbreak of the war, certainly it is not necessary for us to reflect on this as a sin or crime. There is simply this problem: as we resolutely secured our position, were somehow thoughtful judgments made in order not to be defeated? Here deep reflection is required.[44]

And he repeated the claim oft recited by high politicians and military men that internationally Imperial Japan "was thrown into an unnecessarily miserable situation" by the Western powers as she sought to realize her destiny in an environment dictated by them. Since these nations had a suffocating hold on most of the world, when another folk sought to build a state of its own, inevitably it encroached on their spheres of power and influence. "Then if these intensely suffocating influences are not subdued, it must be self-evident that the desired results can in no way be attained." Of course overcoming this suffocating influence may come according to various physical principles, but if the situation is complex it may take quite some time. A synthesis of various material and immaterial powers should be brought to bear and one must persevere. Flexible political techniques are also necessary.

Thus former Vice-Chief of the Army General Staff Kawabe advocated searching for the reasons for Japan's defeat. But he was more interested in vindicating past actions only a year after defeat than addressing the main reasons for it: hubris, trivialization of the Allied enemy, self-deception, a lack of war materials, dissension between the army and navy, not to mention a factor not addressed in this study—ignominious barbarism in other Asian lands.[45]

Transition to the new order

Many persons, including a few of the military leaders mentioned above, were little affected by immediate past events and made a successful transition from positions of influence in the old Imperial order to ones of "responsibility" in the new democratic state. Two prominent examples are the brothers and co-founders of the ruling Liberal Democratic Party, Kishi Nobusuke (1896–1987; prime minister 1957–60) and Satô Eisaku (1901–75; prime minister 1964–72).

During the war, the former was a minister in the Tôjô Cabinet beginning to end; the latter, a bureaucrat in the Railway Ministry, became chief of its Control Bureau in 1941 and held various high positions in the ministry up to and beyond the end of the war. Both were members of the *Manshû Jinmyaku* (Manchurian Network), a right-wing group set up in the Japanese puppet state Manchukuo. The members of this group were politically influential there and in Japan after the war. Another interesting figure is Lt. Col. Takeshita Masahiko, mentioned earlier. In August 1945 he planned with a number of other field grade officers a military coup to forestall surrender. The plot was never carried out and some years after the war, much to the consternation of his former spiritual mentor the right-wing historian Hiraizumi Kiyoshi portrayed in some detail above, he came to terms with Japan's new democracy and refurbished emperor: he joined the Self Defense Forces and eventually became an army general.[46]

Worthy of mention also are three other wartime disciples of Hiraizumi's: Murao Jirô, Torisu Michiaki, and Yamaguchi Kôsuke. In the 1950s all became reactionary officials dealing with the accreditation of school textbooks in the conservative Ministry of Education. Murao at least was involved in the controversy in the 1960s surrounding the influence of "emperor-centered history" on postwar education. Hiraizumi may have been forgotten by most, but for many years after the war, through his former disciples and colleagues, his "Japanist" views influenced Ministry of Education policies. During and shortly after the war Hiraizumi was not considered an advocate of emperor-centered history. Rather, in the 1950s and 1960s former thought-control bureaucrats such as Murao used Hiraizumi's works to promote this sort of history among their colleagues and in the schools. School history textbook accreditation was especially problematic—it is still a thorny issue—and when Ienaga Saburô sued the government, i.e., Ministry of Education, in June 1965 to abrogate their censorship of school history textbooks, Murao testified as a ministry witness against Ienaga. (Ienaga lost this and several other long processes up until the last two in 1993 and 1997.)

These efforts to control texts used in school education were nothing new. Already in 1903 official school texts in history, Japanese language, ethics, and geography were issued. In the late 1920s and throughout the 1930s and 1940s a succession of bureaus were established in the Ministry of Education to insure the "judicious guidance of thought" in the schools.[47] Later, following this tradition, during the postwar years Murao, like Yamaguchi Kôsuke, Shida Nobuyoshi, who drafted the *Fundamental Principles of Our National Polity* (*Kokutai no Hongi*, see Chapter 2), and others, sought to enforce the teaching of conservative thought in the schools. They also wrote a number of books and essays on various Japanese cultural history themes and held posts in several universities after leaving the Education Ministry. It appears that there was much more continuity between the Imperial Japanese nation and state and postwar "democratic" Japan than has been depicted up to now. One of the major lacunae in our knowledge of these events is the lack of exact information (in Western language sources) about what persons active in the government and military in Imperial Japan did before and after "unconditional surrender"—an interesting topic for a future study: the influence of Imperial Japanese priorities on postwar Japanese politics.

A postmortem

Many have addressed the reasons for Imperial Japan's defeat in the Second World War. Several of these have been reviewed above. Below is the analysis of Vice-Admiral Nakazawa Tasuku, former chief of the Naval Operations Department. At the end of his memoirs he listed ten crucial issues (paraphrased below), a combination of information about Imperial Navy strategy and hindsight.[48]

1. "The Meiji Constitution Was Ill-Suited for Modern War (Total War)." According to the Meiji Constitution the emperor was supreme commander of the armed forces (Article 11). The chiefs of staff and service ministers rendered advice and assistance [*hohitsu*]. Generally this meant that in peace time military preparations were made which entailed only limited military power, mobilization of men and materials. Both the army and navy planned for a single decisive battle in which the enemy's basic military strength would be destroyed. This worked for Japan through the Russo-Japan War. But after World War I the situation changed completely. Material and spiritual resources had to be totally mobilized together. A country's assets were then expended. If these resources were not completely exhausted the war did not come to an end. And a country entering war sought to acquire supporting allies.

    However in Japan under the Meiji Constitution the responsibility for prosecuting a war was dispersed; government and military policies were not united. Instead military policy came to influence politics, but preparations for total war could not be made. War and defense are political matters but they could not be dealt with as such. [Lt. General Sawada Shigeru, vice-chief of staff 1939–40, was of a similar opinion vis-à-vis the

Meiji Constitution. Of note, Sawada even alluded to high-handed army arrogation of the imperial will. Also, in analyzing the emperor's role as commander-in-chief of the armed forces, as in the Meiji Constitution, he says this is based on history and tradition, commonly held beliefs in Japan not supported by historical facts.[49]]

During the latter half of 1943 when I, Nakazawa, was Chief of Naval Operations the war situation was disadvantageous. In order to turn things around the navy required more aircraft. I recommended that the majority of the available supplies of aluminum be allocated to the navy. My recommendation was not followed. In the end the navy only received ca. 7,000 tons of aluminum and the chance to revive the war situation was lost. In deciding the allocation of materials, if the discussions about shares for the army, navy and even civilian use became heated, then the previous years plan was used as a standard. In this way, one could not respond to the war situation.

Finally, in my opinion, the root of the problem was the Meiji Constitution.

2. "Political and Diplomatic Blunders." After the war there were great discussions about the merits of the Japan, Germany, Italy military alliance [Tripartite Pact]. Polemics aside, there were two basic problems: if Japan concludes a pact with Germany, could US intervention be prevented? And, with such a pact would there be sufficient power to resist the US and Great Britain? I am convinced that the Japan, Germany, Italy pact and our advance into the southern part of Indochina were aggressive threats to the US and Britain and a direct reason for plunging into the Greater East Asia War. Also the following war demonstrated well that an alliance with Germany and Italy in far away Europe was ineffectual.

After the war, the attack by our fleet on Pearl Harbor beginning the war has been extensively discussed. However, I count this attack as one reason for our defeat, or at least it hastened our capitulation.

I think that if the attack had been made with the intention of occupying Hawai'i for a long time that would be a different matter. But as it was, only intending to strike a blow at the enemy, it would have been better not to attack at all. If the enemy carrier group had been sunk, then there would be some room for discussion. Under the banner "remember Pearl Harbor" the United States prepared for total war. It was proclaimed to the world that Japan was the war advocate and ringleader. Japan was isolated internationally and pushed into a corner.

3. "Neglect of Our National Defense Policy and Our Strategic Program."
In 1907 immediately after the Russo-Japan War, Field Marshal Yamagata Aritomo presented to the emperor in an imperial audience our national defense policy and our strategic program. The United States, Russia and China were the assumed enemies. Later toward the end of World War I in 1918 and in 1924 after the Washington Naval Conference 1921–2 these were revised.

1931 came the Manchurian Incident; later in order to deal with the lack of treaties after 1934, in June 1936 defense policies and programs were revised adding Great Britain to the list of possible enemies.

In our strategic program, from among the United States, Soviet Union, China, and England a war with one was thought possible, not with two countries. However, shortly before the outbreak of the Greater East Asia War important persons in the government and military completely forgot this basic principle, or ignored it, and regrettably opened a reckless war.

Japan's war materials in a conflict with one country—for the navy the United States, for the army the Soviet Union—were sufficient to fight on for some time. But from the present [postwar] perspective we should have strictly warned against conducting a war with two countries.

The army and navy, based on our national defense policy and our strategic program, presented operations plans to the emperor every year for his approval. Afterwards various preparations were made accordingly. But in fact this was merely a convention followed every year. In the event of a war, we had no war plans. Around 1935 and '36 when Ishiwara Kanji was Operations Chief in the Army General Staff and Fukudome Shigeru Operations Chief in the Navy General Staff, the necessity of having a war plan was discussed, but the deliberations ended without enacting one.

The point is that national defense is not just an army-navy matter. It also should involve politics. In our country with responsibility dispersed and no experience in total war, it was impossible to unite various opinions and arrive at a definitive plan.

Beyond beginning a war, one must have the means to vanquish the opponent. Everyone knows well the history of Napoleon's expedition that extended as far as Moscow to be defeated by the winter snow. More recently, in the China Incident though our troops advanced to Nanjing and Hankow, the Chiang Kai-shek government fled to Chongqing and was not defeated. Then Japan fought against the United States, England and Soviet

Union but had no means to defeat them. Moreover, no one expected or was prepared for a protracted war in China.

Japan did not have sufficient stocks of war materials for a long-lasting war. Even if one seeks out raw materials in the southern occupied areas, transporting them to Japan requires ships and protection for them. This was a problem. As for the production of bottoms, warships and aircraft, as well as the supply of production personnel, we could never overtake the United States.

The national defense policies prepared by the general staffs and sanctioned by the emperor for many years dismissed strategic problems. We plunged into war without concrete estimates about how to end the war.

4. "Strategy vis-à-vis the United States, Tactical Mistakes." Our navy's strategy against the US involved engaging the enemy fleet in our area of the South Pacific. There the combined fleet and island based fighter planes would destroy the enemy in a decisive battle. Our type of naval forces, their capabilities, fleet training and tactics were all oriented toward such a battle. The enemy, alternatively, would sortie from a main base (for example Hawai'i) and using submarines and [carrier based] aircraft conduct hit-and-run raids and night attacks—a war of attrition. But perhaps due to our attack on Pearl Harbor the enemy did not come out and fight. Our fleet had to maneuver all over the seas subject to increasing attacks. Patrols using large aircraft were made to locate the distant enemy, or using radio-wave equipment locate and engage the enemy near us. The tactics we had developed and trained in for years were almost useless.

5. "Deciphering Secret Codes." In times past it was said, "One must keep one's plans secret" [Tale of Heike]. Even if one's plans are extremely good, if known to the enemy they will be very difficult to carry out. During the war the enemy's [decoding] activities were very proficient—the Battle of Midway, the death of Commander of the Combined Fleet Yamamoto, etc. The operations dept. proposed a number of times that the communications dept. examine whether our secret codes were being read by the enemy. They said this was entirely impossible and took no appropriate actions. They only were cautious about the method of transmitting important messages, various operational orders were sent at the lowest level etc. Counterespionage measures were only given occasional attention. After the war it became clear that the enemy acquired our codes and that the combined fleets operations plans in part came into enemy hands.

6. "Insufficient Attention to Control of the Sea and Air." For the navy, which exists to conduct sea operations the importance of control over the sea and air should be self-evident. But in our navy this awareness was lacking.

    Conducting operations among the various islands in the Pacific Ocean, if once control of the sea and air are lost, replenishments will be cut off and eventually self-destruction results. This is a tragedy beyond words. When I was Commander of the 5th Fleet we were part of the northern area forces. Two of the Aleutian Islands were invaded. I requested to Combined Fleet Headquarters that a base for land-based aircraft be setup. They said this was unnecessary. If enemy air attacks came the troops should dig holes and crawl into them. That will do.

    Invading islands without control of the sea and air is not only meaningless, it means leaving valuable troops in a lurch to die.

7. "Exaggeration of Kamikaze (Spiritual Power)." Our people since the opening of the country [1868] knew no defeat. They were taught that if we go to war we surely will win. Since the time of the Mongol invasions [1274 and 1281], and more recently in the Japan-Qing War [1894–5], the Russo-Japan War [1904–5], the Manchurian Incident [1931–2], and the China Incident [1937] we experienced successive wars and successive victories. Without knowing it we became conceited and disparaged the enemy.

    Thus we over-estimated ourselves and under-estimated the enemy, inviting disaster. Sun Tzu said, "Know the enemy and know yourself; in a hundred battles you will never be in peril."[50] However in our case, did we not go to war "not knowing ourselves and not knowing the enemy"?

    By contrast Americans are a collection of various peoples. We assumed they cannot endure hardship and deprivation. Also since they view conflict as a sort of sport, at the opening of a war if they are dealt a painful blow they will lose their will to fight. It was judged that their weakness as a folk had been disclosed. When it comes to a fight, our whole nation, officers and men together valiantly battling in the air, on the ground, and even submarine warfare will bring about brilliant military achievements. Even the Japanese military seemed to be convinced that the soul of Yamato is incomparable throughout world.

8. "The Great Difference in War (Materials, Weapons Technology) and Resupply Potentials." At the beginning of the war with the attack on Pearl Harbor, the battle in the Straits of Malaya, and the occupation of southern areas with natural resources we achieved remarkable war results. For this reason the army, navy and people in general became arrogant. In the

meantime the United States came to be united behind the war effort. War materials (especially new types of weaponry, war aircraft, radar, sonar, variable time fuses, bulldozers etc.) were quickly developed and produced. The counteroffensive came, and from the time when the Japanese fleet was destroyed at Midway, its speed increased. Because we extended the war theater beyond our military capacities, resupply could not be sustained, aircraft, commercial and warship losses increased, retreat followed retreat and finally the war ended in defeat.

9. In 1941 our country was confronted with unprecedented circumstances. If there had been even one politician or illustrious commander like Iwakura Tomomi [1825–83] and Kido Takayoshi [1833–77] of the Meiji Era, or Ôyama Iwao [1842–1916], Yamamoto Gonnohyôe [1852–1933], Kodama Gentarô [1852–1906], and Komura Jutarô [1855–1911] as at the time of the Russo-Japan War, Japan would not have become enveloped in this tragic war.

10. As an independent country, national defense is a politician's most important duty. National defense is something that politicians and each citizen should research and study. Everyone should engage in serious research about how the country should unerringly proceed and progress.

Nakazawa's insights are very interesting. Of course historians have even more hindsight now than he had then. Military experts point out that nations often fight wars as the last one should have been fought. Here, Nakazawa shows us that the Imperial Navy planned to fight the next war just as they had fought the last one. This was a grievous miscalculation considering that Japanese tactics in the Russo-Japan War were well known. Not to mention that subsequent significant developments in technology and armaments made previous war strategies obsolete. He writes eloquently about the foibles of kamikaze and the Japanese spirit but avoids mentioning the initiation of kamikaze air attacks, perhaps because as shown above he was involved in their official approval as chief of naval operations. In his exposition Japanese self-overestimation along with underestimation of the enemy are correctly faulted. But in topic ten he fails to mention the fact that before and during the wars in China and the Pacific top army and navy officials did not encourage politicians, normal citizens, or even the emperor to mix in military affairs. National defense was an exclusive army–navy domain, jealously guarded by each.

Moreover, unmentioned by Nakazawa, a lack of coordination between the army and navy and their mutual antagonism mentioned variously above seriously hampered Japan's war efforts. Nakazawa knew this, as did of course leading army officers. For example, former Army Vice-Chief of Staff Sawada Shigeru wrote after the war: before the outbreak of hostilities with the Allies in late 1941 but after the conflict in China was expanded in 1937, already in 1940 crucial disagreements between the army and navy seriously hindered strategic planning. Sawada also analyzed the army's role in Japan's defeat, and noted that their plans too were dated and unsuited for fighting the next war, i.e., the wars in the Pacific and Asia.[51]

One might say that while Nakazawa enumerated some of the reasons for defeat, no personal responsibility is acknowledged or conclusions drawn. He was not alone in this respect. His ten reasons for Imperial Japan's defeat are a combination of professional observations and self-serving recollections. Finally, like the Shôwa Emperor and many other responsible persons in Imperial Japan, after the war he also sought to avoid retribution for his wartime actions. At long last some of the leaders of the defunct imperial state were at one with their nation's leader. Like the latter, one of the former, Nakazawa, had regrets about how the war came out but if he reflected on the suffering and death caused by prosecuting one he does not mention it. Instead, after three-and-a-half years in Sugamo Prison as a war-crimes suspect he wrote following his release (not guilty),

> At war's end facing a new life I am without rank, office, or possessions. I am reminded of an old lyric,
> Degraded,
> Tears on my sleeve,
> One knows
> The depths of a person's heart.[52]

In the context of Japanese history, an echo of another aspect of the "soul of Japan" (*yamato damashii*), from medieval Heian Court society: Lineage, rank, office, and one's possessions frame a person's soul and sentiments.[53] Like the nobility of old, military leaders in Imperial Japan considered themselves nonpareil and others were left unconsidered.

Other views of the war's end

Japanese war leaders including Emperor Hirohito were little concerned with or even slightly remorseful about the carnage and suffering they caused in Asia and even at home in Japan. Slaughter abroad and sacrifices at home were taken for granted. Former Prime Minister Suzuki Kantarô was perhaps an exception. One year after the war in his autobiography he strongly criticized Imperial Japan, her political and military policies. He maintained that Japan must adhere to the stipulations of the Potsdam Proclamation, reform and revise the country.[54] During the war Suzuki, according to one historian, was ambivalent as to the justifiability of it. There was the question of the liberation and independence of Asia, and in general he looked on passively. After the war, in the last part of his autobiography, Suzuki appears to have become more critical. But he was dissatisfied with his "Circumstances at War's End," though he did not say why. The entire last section suggests a possibility, "One Year of a Defeated Japan" (*haisen nihon no ichinen*) reads like an American plan for Japan's postwar future—especially a section near the end: "Unified in Sincerity, a New Start."[55] It is not so indicated of course, but the slant and content lead one to speculate that US censors may well have heavily edited it. One wonders how many other postwar "documents" were warped in this manner.

In the conclusion of his book, Suzuki Tamon (no relation) analyzes succinctly the various factors that he believes weighed in on surrender deliberations among Japanese leaders: provisos of the unconditional surrender ultimatum, Japan's dwindling war materials, fanaticism in the Imperial Army and a possible coup, the atom bomb attacks, entry of the Soviet Union into the war, the possible outcome of a last-ditch home island defense, Soviet mediation between the United States and Japan, even a communist-style revolution—all were heatedly discussed. The costs of continuing an indefinite war (retaining their convictions about their inconsequent American adversaries) were seen as a negative factor for both sides. But the bottom line was the preservation of the national essence and imperial line.[56] No one, including needless to say the Emperor, was ready to forswear the Imperial House, the religious-ideological basis of the Imperial Japanese nation-state.

Yet, despite their many misgivings Japanese leaders stalked a capitulation that eventually involved relatively little bloodletting. Four main actors contributed to this outcome: Emperor Hirohito mandated acceptance of the Potsdam Proclamation and did not waver after making this decision; Prime Minister Suzuki held his cabinet together and administered the Japanese side of the process; and Army Minister Anami and Chief of Staff Umezu maintained discipline in the army. This enabled the suppression of die-hard insurrectionists and assuaging the apprehensions of many other officers still in favor of fighting to the end.[57]

Postwar destinies

The generals and admirals who finally agreed to end the war were portrayed afterward as archetypal military leaders. For example, General Umezu was the last Imperial Army chief of staff. He was the leading military officer who signed the surrender documents aboard the USS *Missouri*; he signed the order dissolving the Imperial Army; and he was charged with war crimes at the Tokyo War Crimes Tribunal. But according to the only extensive study of him, during the war he was not known as a jingoistic officer. He strived to succeed as an army officer but was disinclined to participate in factional disputes. In the mid-1930s he was involved in cabinet-building squabbles but sought neither political position nor financial aggrandizement. During the War Crimes Trial he became sick and was hospitalized. He was sentenced to life imprisonment but died suddenly in 1949 in the hospital. However, even as a general he never purchased a private residence and always lived in the official accommodation accorded him as an army officer. His last remains were therefore transported to the burned-out residence of the army chief of staff and placed in one room of an earthen warehouse there that was still standing.[58]

Following the war, the Tokyo GHQ Military Tribunal found Admiral Toyoda, the last navy chief of staff not guilty of all criminal charges and indictments brought against him. After his release from Sugamo Prison Toyoda presented in his memoirs a realistic if self-approving picture of Imperial Japan's military capabilities at the end of the war. But one must remember that Admiral Toyoda, though chief of a navy without a fleet, opposed unconditional surrender up to the war's ultimate disastrous end. He came relatively unscathed through this experience and died in September 1957, age seventy-two.

Lt. Gen. Kawabe, the last vice-chief of staff of the Imperial Army enjoyed a different fate. He too was well informed of Japan's dire situation. As seen above, Kawabe and others in the general staff were well informed about Japan's lack of war materials but would not confront realistically the consequences. His proposal in June 1945, along with the "Great Strategic Plan for the Decisive Battle on the Home Islands" (*hondo kessen ni kan suru sakusen taikô*) drawn up by the Army General Staff in January 1945 involved turning the entire Japanese population into special attack units. This "strategy" was but an extension and expansion of suicide tactics in grim circumstances based on forced devotion to a fiction—the national essence. It entailed exalting the imperial way and an unscrupulous disregard for human life typical of those at the top of the Imperial Japanese order, including the emperor. Later, as noted above, at the end of the war over 500 officers committed suicide after the Mikado announced capitulation, taking responsibility for defeat.⁵⁹ Lt. General Kawabe himself did not practice what he demanded from others—suicidal devotion to the national essence and emperor. He survived the war; was not charged as a war criminal; and lived to be almost seventy years old.

All three of these war leaders advocated fighting to the bitter end, regardless of the cost, as the war approached a disastrous conclusion. After the war none committed suicide. Only one, Umezu, was convicted of war crimes. Toyoda was charged and acquitted. Kawabe was not indicted. Suicide was for others. The criterion for "war crimes" and the resulting "guilt" seems to have been quite nebulous and remains so even today.

War guilt

None of the leaders of the Imperial Japanese state and nation felt guilty about the death and destruction they had caused, but some, including the Emperor, had misgivings about being held responsible for it. Tôjô Hideki shortly after the war made a statement that for him summed up why Japan went to war and the irrelevance of treating this as a crime. He made it in very unfavorable circumstances:

> Japan's going to war was unavoidable. It was never something we wanted. Therefore, prosecuting the war should not be treated as a crime [...]
>
> However if the victorious powers want to treat this as a crime, all responsibility lies with me and no one else [...]
>
> The emperor did everything possible to avoid the war. That it finally came to war and war was unavoidable was due to my recommendations. That responsibility, formal as well as practical, lies with me alone.⁶⁰

Tôjô made this statement to Hoshino Naoki (1892–1987) his one-time cabinet secretary while awaiting the Tokyo War Crimes Trial in Sugamo Prison. He too was intent on justifying the war and relieving the Emperor from any possible war responsibility. He knew his cause was lost and sought to shield the emperor and imperial institution. This is often pointed out, but that was not his sole concern. After being found guilty and condemned to death, Tôjô told his family, "there should be absolutely no apologies [*iiwake*]." What did this mean? The term "iiwake" can mean explanation or self-defense, excuse, justification, and apology for a sin or crime. And it could have meant all of these things:

Tôjô was determined not to bow before the enemy and admit to their charge of conducting an unjust war. He unwaveringly maintained that for Japan it was a war of self-defense [*ji'eisen*].[61]

During the Tokyo War Crimes Trials the testimony offered by Tôjô Hideki, and gladly accepted by US officials,[62] succeeded in exonerating the Shôwa Emperor of war guilt. The debate, however, about Hirohito's participation in political and military affairs during the Second World War—whether or not (at first) and to what extent (later)—still continues. It will animate authors for years to come. Now most historians acknowledge that the Emperor was deeply involved, like all nation-state leaders at that time. The task at hand is to delve into the proceedings then in order to clarify and understand them and him better.

For some there remain unresolved moral and juridical questions: was the Emperor a war criminal? After the war was over Allied leaders resurrected and gave new meaning to a concept that gained credence after the First World War—war responsibility. The Kellogg-Briand Pact of 1928 "outlawed" war for the first time in history. It was initially signed by fifteen nations including Japan.[63] The pact had no provisions for enforcing this idea, which rested on "the moral force of world opinion." As can be seen clearly from the political and military actions of all involved in the following conflicts, especially the beastly handling of prisoners of war; non-combatant men, women, and children; and the lack of concern for civilian victims during bombing raids, a "world opinion" that might influence statesmen and impartially call individual persons to account for their activities was virtually nonexistent.

Nevertheless, many still insist on posing this question. Generally I do not think that historians should render moral or judicial judgments. Many Allied leaders believed that Hirohito was a war criminal and should be indicted as such. He was not indicted for reasons of expedience: first to expedite surrender; later to insure a peaceful occupation and to rebuild Japan as a bulwark against the "communist threat" in the Far East. However, General Douglas MacArthur did not prevent Hirohito's indictment. Rather the US government put it indefinitely on hold. The issue of his war culpability was shunted aside.[64] Based on the information known to me I would not presume to condemn or exonerate the Shôwa Emperor. Instead a differentiated answer vis-à-vis the Emperor's "war crimes" from a historical point of view: according to the definitions then, with the information we have now, yes he was guilty as some would charge. But much of this information was not available immediately after the war and the charges were based on "international laws" applied inconsistently ex post facto. The "war crimes" definitions were formulated knowingly and naïvely in the military-political context of that time. Under the circumstances, questions of war crimes guilt then are now irrelevant. The same might be said about America's fire bombing of Tokyo and the devastation of Hiroshima and Nagasaki with atomic bombs.

A concluding interpretation

At war's end many military leaders insisted that Imperial Japan fight on long after all was obviously lost. This included disparate measures such as the kamikaze tactics that appear not to have contributed to victory or even improved surrender terms. Rather, they were partly responsible for Japan's ruinous defeat due to their galvanizing effect on the enemy and to the unconscionable expenditure—waste—of men and materials. Many ask why Japanese leaders and many followers pursued defeat in this way. No doubt Tôjô and Kawabe were not alone with their conviction that it was an unjust war—a war of self-defense forced on Japan. This was important. According to Shôji Junichirô, Konoe Fumimaro, long before the war or his three terms as prime minister in the late 1930s and early 1940s, thought that securing US acknowledgment of Imperial Japan's right to exist was a necessary but problematic issue.[65] More significant, it appears that the disastrous prolongation of the war was rooted in the Japanese's collective hubris, the fruits of unquestioning belief in a religious ideology.

However, modern "unquestioning belief in a religious ideology" was something imported from the West. The founders of Imperial Japan envisioned the imperial line and *kokutai* as the spiritual basis of their empire infusing the minds and hearts of the people to follow unquestioningly government authorities, just as early leaders saw the role of Christianity in most Western nations: Christian teachings made God and his "chosen folk" ultimate concerns. Analogous, in Imperial Japan the national essence inclusive emperor was the "ultimate concern" for Japanese rulers and ruled alike. In their respective contexts each legitimized the state authority of those who spoke in the name of the Christian God on the one hand, the *kokutai* and Japanese emperor on the other.

Shortly after the war Paul Tillich explained this phenomenon. "Our ultimate concern is that which determines our being or not-being." Of considerable importance is the relationship between preliminary and ultimate concerns—various concerns about our worldly existence versus God, being and non-being. In particular not a few people elevate a preliminary concern to ultimacy.

This he unequivocally condemns. "Idolatry is the elevation of a preliminary concern to ultimacy." Tillich also says, "Theology has no right and no obligation to prejudice a physical or historical, sociological or psychological, inquiry." However, his theology might help us to better understand these past events. Tillich maintained, "the best example [of the elevation of a preliminary concern to ultimacy] is the contemporary idolatry of religious nationalism."⁶⁶ When a nation-state and the idolatry underpinning it are so elevated then the continued existence of this construct has ultimate meaning for its leaders and the general public as well.

During the Imperial era many Japanese were not unconcerned about the suffering they caused abroad or the sacrifices demanded at home. But something else was more important: Japan's gods, existence, being and non-being were linked to the survival of their folk and state. For Tillich "being [...] does not designate existence in time and space [...] 'being' means the whole of human reality, the structure, the meaning, and the aim of existence." But those who constructed and later guided the quasi-religious nation Imperial Japan were not concerned about the whole of human reality, only with Japan and the "Japanese race." According to two of the most important religious-ideological texts in Imperial Japan, the *Imperial Rescript on Education* and *the Fundamentals of Our National Polity*, mentioned earlier, the Emperor, the land Japan, and the Japanese people are a single entity. In the words of a modern interpreter, "A divine oracle did not determine the national essence. The national essence is from the beginning unmoving, unshakeable, and the oracle only made it known." The national essence was fundamental to Japan's very existence.⁶⁷ The Japanese were concerned about its, their, being and non-being.

Why did the Japanese continue the war when defeat was inevitable? They fought on, even when by every rational criterion all was lost, hoping to fend off their individual and collective demise, non-being. That which had been constructed—the land of the gods—was swallowed whole by most leaders and followers. The deception and coercion described in the pages above were of great significance. In Imperial Japan national pretenses and state intimidation materialized out of preliminary concerns employed to save a "unique" ultimate concern—the national essence including the eternal imperial line—even if it ultimately was a fiction. Finally, obsessed with their own preliminary concerns—a vision shrouded by ideological convictions and factual deceptions—military leaders were unable to save their state, but the Emperor successfully saved the nation, including himself.

The Shôwa Emperor was only human, long denied, and this is what the records show. He did what was expected at that time, in Japan and elsewhere, as the leader of a nation at war. He attempted to lead—to influence politics and military affairs in ways he thought would best serve the emperor, the Imperial House, and the nation—in that order. As titular head of state, as seen above, though ill-informed he was not ignored or uninformed about war matters, but he could not unilaterally mandate political or military policies. Moreover, beyond particular operations and general policies he knew that if worse came to worse, defeat, he and possibly his house would be held responsible. Despite this obvious risk, he could not dictate policies. Following the end of the war he aided and abetted those, including many Americans, who for various reasons whitewashed the wartime Shôwa Emperor for presentation to his people and the world. In so doing he sought, successfully, to preserve his Imperial House.[68] However ignoble it may now seem, after losing the war the Shôwa Emperor did what any other leader of a nation defeated in war tries to do—escape retribution.

Afterthought

The Asia-Pacific War's end as regards Japan is somewhat of a paradox, from a non-Japanese viewpoint. In the West, various philosophical and historical writings imply notions of survival or extinction. "Nature always strives to preserve itself" (Cicero). Or, "Nothing is difficult for Nature, at all events when it rushes toward its own doom" (Seneca).[69] The two options are envisioned as either-or propositions. But after surrender the Japanese were able to do both. Although the military, read state, rushed to its own destruction, the Imperial House, read nation, saw to its own preservation.

Notes

Preface

1 H.W. von Doemming, *Was Will Japan*? [What does Japan Want?] (Jena: Eugen Diederichs Verlag, 1934), 9–10.
2 Ibid., 2–13.
3 Ernest H. Pickering, *Japan's Place in the Modern World* (London: George G. Harrap & Co. Ltd., 1936), 322.
4 Ibid., 13.
5 Peter Wetzler, *Hirohito and War. Imperial Tradition and Military Decision Making in Prewar Japan* (Honolulu: University of Hawai'i Press, 1998), 202.
6 Kurt Pätzold and Manfred Weißbecker, *Geschichte der NSDAP, 1920 – 1945* [History of the National Socialist Democratic Worker Party, 1920–1945] (Cologne: PapyRossa Verlags, 2009), 280–317.
7 Michael Bentley, "The Liberal Party, 1900 – 1939: Summit and Descent," in *A Companion to Early Twentieth-Century Britain*, ed. Chris Wrigley (Oxford: Blackwell Publishers, 2003), 23–37.
8 Kokushi Daijiten Henshû I'inkai (ed.), *Kokushi Daijiten* [Great Dictionary of National History], 17 vols. (Tokyo: Yoshikawa Kôbunkan, 1987), 8:802–3.
9 For national resources, see Sanbô Honbu Shozô [Army General Staff Proprietors] (ed.), *Haisen no Kiroku* [War Defeat Documents] (Tokyo: Hara Shobô, 1967), 259–77, 268–70. For a similar account of this Imperial Conference, see Itô Takashi (ed.), *Takagi Sôkichi, Nikki to Jôhô* [Takagi Sôkichi, Diary and Information], 2 vols. (Tokyo: Misuzu Shobô, 2000), 2:878–80. Takagi's summary is based on the opinion of retired Admiral Toyoda Teijirô, Munitions Minister, Imperial Conference Report (*Gozenkaigi Hôkoku*) excerpt. Takagi Sôkichi (1893–1979) was a rear admiral at the end of the war. Kido Kôichi, *Kido Kôichi Nikki* [Kido Kôichi Diary], 2 vols. (Tokyo: Tokyo Daigaku Shuppankai, 1966), 2:1208–9, has an evaluation of this Imperial Conference but lacks the details of these records.
10 Bôeichô Bôeikenkyûsho Senshishitsu [Defense Agency, Institute for Defense Studies, War History Office], *Daihon'ei Kaigunbu Rengôkantai* [Imperial Headquarters, Navy Department, Combined Fleet], vol. 7 (Tokyo: Asagumo Shimbunsha, 1976). For the report to the throne June 8, 1945, see pp. 344–57; for animating the population, see p. 345; statement by Chief of the Imperial Navy General Staff Admiral Toyoda Soemu, see pp. 347–8.

11 Sanbô Honbu Shozô, *Haisen no Kiroku* [War Defeat Documents], 275–6. Hatano Sumio, *Saishô Suzuki Kantarô no Ketsudan*. *"Seidan" to Sengo Japan* [Prime Minister Suzuki Kantarô's Clear-Cut Decision. "Imperial Decision" and Postwar Japan] (Tokyo: Iwanami Shoten, 2015), 173–80.
12 Kawabe Torashirô, "Seiyô Minzoku no Aseia Seifuku to sono Bunpataru Beikoku Aseia he no Shinshutsu ni Kan suru Gaisetsu" [Survey of the Subjugation of Asia by Western Nations and as a Part thereof America's Advance into Asia], Summer 1946 (manuscript copy in the National Institute for Defense Studies [NIDS], Military Archives, Tokyo), 1–4.
13 The most famous example is the "Nanjing Massacre." For a measured treatment, see Rana Mitter, *China's War with Japan, 1937–1945. The Struggle for Survival* (London: Allen Lane, 2013), 119–40. For a clear summary, see Edward J. Drea. *Japan's Imperial Army. Its Rise and Fall, 1853–1945* (Lawrence: University Press of Kansas, 2009), 259–61.
14 Terasaki Hidenari and Mariko Terasaki-Miller (eds.), *Shôwa Tennô Dokuhakuroku, Terasaki Hidenari Goyôkakari Nikki* [Shôwa Emperor Monologue, Imperial Household Liaison Officer Terasaki Hidenari Diary] (Tokyo: Bungei Shunjû, 1991), 115–17. Suzuki Tamon, *"Shûsen" no Seijishi, 1943–1945* [A Political History of "Ending the War," 1943–1945] (Tokyo: Tokyo University Press, 2011), 122–3, 145n52, citing different primary sources says the same about the Imperial Conference.
15 Some claim that the Imperial Army's proposal to sacrifice the Japanese population in a final battle on the main islands never got beyond a paper plan. See Yoshimi Masato, *Shûsenshi. Naze Ketsudan Dekinakatta no ka* [History of Ending the War. Why Could Not a Firm Decision be Made?] (Tokyo: NHK, 2013), 21. However, Lt. General Kawabe Torashirô, the army vice-chief of staff who represented the army at this Imperial Conference, and Admiral Toyoda Soemu Chief of the Imperial Navy General Staff made this proposal part of the policy discussions and decisions at the time. See Chapter 5 of this book.

Introduction

1 Emperor Hirohito claimed to emulate the British constitutional monarchy, a claim as seen below that he took seriously but used and abused willfully, likewise the long history of emperors reigning but not ruling in Japan. *Kôkû* (country) and *kuni* (state) are used interchangeably in Japanese, as they were before the mid-nineteenth century. Earlier they referred to what we now term "*han*," a political entity quite different from the modern nation-state. See Joshua A. Fogel, 'Introduction,' in *The Teleology of the Modern Nation-State. Japan and China*, ed. Joshua A. Fogel (Philadelphia: University of Pennsylvania Press, 2005), 1–7, esp. 2–3; and Luke

S. Roberts, "Cultivating Non-National Understandings in Local History," in *The Teleology of the Modern Nation-State*, ed. Joshua A. Fogel (Philadelphia: University of Pennsylvania Press, 2005), 161–73, esp. 168–71. For God, see Jason Ānanda Josephson. *The Invention of Religion in Japan* (Chicago: University of Chicago Press, 2012), esp. 9–12, 100–1. On Hirohito and constitutional monarchy, see Wetzler, *Hirohito and War*, 163–78, 185–6, 201–2.

2 Reinhart Koselleck, *Vom Sinn und Unsinn der Geschichte* [On the Sense and Nonsense of History] (Berlin: Suhrkamp, 2010), 24: "Klassen, Staaten, und Nationen wurden, wie ehedem Fürsten oder Heilige, gern als vorgegebene Leitinstanzen eingesetzt und hingenommen." Class (struggle) has been deleted because this had very little to do with developments in Imperial Japan. For a very good essay on early Japanese approaches to the West, see Hirakawa Sukehiro, "Japan's Turn to the West," trans. Bob Tadashi Wakabayashi, in *Modern Japanese Thought*, ed. Bob Tadashi Wakabayashi (Cambridge: Cambridge University Press, 1998), 30–97.For the definitions, see Sarah Foot, "The Historiography of the Anglo-Saxon 'nation-state'," in *Power and the Nation in European History*, eds. Len Scales and Oliver Zimmer (Cambridge: Cambridge University Press, 2005), 125–42, 131. Susan Reynolds, "The Idea of the Nation as a Political Community," in *Power and the Nation in European History*, eds. Len Scales and Oliver Zimmer (Cambridge: Cambridge University Press, 2005), 54–66, 54.

3 "Das Volk, das ist der Leib Gottes. Eine Nation verdient diesen Namen nur, so lange sie einen eigenen Gott hat und hartnäckig alle anderen von sich stößt …
Der Staat oder die organisirte Unmoralität…
inwendig: als Polizei, Strafrecht, Stände, Handel, Familie
auswendig: als Wille zur Macht, zum Kriege, zur Eroberung, zur Rache."
Friedrich Nietzsche, *Nachgelassene Fragmente 1887–1889* [Posthumous Fragments], in *Friedrich Nietzsche Sämtliche Werke. Kritische Studien Ausgabe in 15 Bände*, eds. Giorgio Colli and Mazzino Montinari (Munich: Deutscher Taschenbuch Verlag GmbH & Co. KG, 1967–77), 13, 151, 187. For a slightly different translation of the part on the state, see Walter Kaufmann (ed.), *Friedrich Nietzsche, The Will to Power*, trans. Walter Kaufmann and R.J. Hollingdale (New York: Vintage Books, 1968), 382.

4 For the definition, see Anzu Motohiko and Umeda Yoshihiko (eds.), *Shintô Jiten* [Shintô Dictionary] (Osaka: Hori Shoten, 1968), 316–19. For Kokutai in the nineteenth and early twentieth centuries, see Klaus Antoni, *Shintô & die Konzeption des japanischen Nationalwesens (kokutai)* [Shintô & the Concept of the Japanese National Essence *(kokutai)*] (Leiden: Brill, 1998), 166–71. For Shôtoku, see Ôyama Sei'ichi (ed.), *Nihon Shoki no Nazo to Shôtoku Taishi* [The Riddle of the Nihon Shoki and Crown Prince Shôtoku] (Tokyo: Heibonsha, 2011), 5–21, passim. Ôyama first presented the thesis that Shôtoku never existed in 1996. He claims

(7) that since then no one has presented evidence showing he did in fact exist. For Hozumi, see Walter A. Skya, *Japan's Holy War. The Ideology of Radical Shintô Ultranationalism* (Durham, NC: Duke University Press, 2009), 56.

5   *Shôwa Tennô Jitsuroku* [Actual Record of the Shôwa Emperor], abbreviated *STJR*. Imperial Household Agency (eds.), *Shôwa Tennô Jitsuroku*, 19 vols. (Tokyo: Tokyo Shoseki KK, 2015–19). The Imperial Household Agency put the record on a CD (60 vols.). I refer to the CD and the printed version: Kunaichô Copyright, *Shôwa Tennô Jitsuroku* ([Actual Record of the Shôwa Emperor] (Tokyo: Tokyo Shoseki KK, 2016), vols. 8 and 9. The pagination of the printed version is different from the CD. Since all information is presented in chronological order finding specific items is no problem. *Asahi Shimbun* (Newspaper) reported March 14, 2019, that there are some 5,000 errors in the published version of this text. But they are (supposedly) of no historical significance. Individual readers with a special interest in a particular topic may want to check the Imperial Household CD against the published version. Both are cited. The Imperial Household Agency plans to publish a list of corrections for each volume.

6   *Senshi Sôsho* [War History Series], Bôeichô Bôeikenkyûsho Senshishitsu [Defense Agency, Institute for Defense Studies, War History Office], 102 vols. (Tokyo: Asagumo Shuppansha, 1966–1980).

7   Bôeichô Bôeikenkyûsho Senshishitsu [Defense Agency, Institute for Defense Studies, War History Office], *Daihon'ei Rikugunbu* [Imperial Headquarters, Army Department] (Tokyo: Asagumo Shimbunsha, 1975), 10:74–8.

8   Drea, *Japan's Imperial Army*, passim. Emiko Ohnuki-Tierney, *Kamikaze, Cherry Blossoms, and Nationalism. The Militarization of Aesthetics in Japanese History* (Chicago: University of Chicago Press, 2002), passim. On the back cover Robert N. Bellah lauds the author for "rescuing" this historical, cultural memory.

9   Robert J.C. Butow, *Tojo and the Coming of the War* (Stanford, CA: Stanford University Press, 1961), 503–4.

10 Dômei Tsûshinsha Seikeibu [Dômei News Agency, Politics and Economics Department] (ed.), *Hisshô no Daidô* [The Road to Certain Victory], Tôjô Sôridaijin Gikai Enzetsu Tôben Shû [Prime Minister Tôjô Speeches and Rejoinders in Parliament] (Tokyo: Dômei Tsûshinsha, 1943), 177–80.

11 Antoni, *Shintô & die Konzeption*, 271. Wetzler, *Hirohito and War*, 149.

12 For this and the following, see Paul Tillich, *Systematic Theology*, vol. 1, *Reason and Revelation; Being and God* (Chicago: University of Chicago Press, 1951), 13–18.

Chapter 1

1   For an integrated treatment, see Butow, *Tojo and the Coming of the War*. For a brief introduction to Tôjô, see Wetzler, *Hirohito and War*, 61–81. There are a vast

number of secondary works, published and unpublished source materials pertinent to these events. Examining all of them is impossible. For brief evaluations of various sources, see Itô Takashi and Suetake Yoshiya (eds.), *Kin- Gendai Nihon Jinbutsu Shiryô Jôhô Jiten* [Dictionary of Modern and Contemporary Japanese Personnel Source Information], 4 vols. (Tokyo: Yoshikawa Kôbunkan, 2004–2011).

2   Bôeichô, *Daihon'ei Rikugunbu*, vol. 8, photo-repro at the beginning of the volume. *Gyokusai* means literally "smashed jewels."

3   See notes 5 and 6 in the Introduction.

4   See the various summaries and discussions in, *Asahi Shimbun* (*Asahi Newspaper*, International Edition), September 9, 2014 [in Japanese].

5   Hosaka Masayasu, *Shôwa Tennô Jitsuroku. Sono Omote to Ura. Taiheiyô Sensô no Jidai* ([Actual Record of the Shôwa Emperor. Above and Below the Surface. The Pacific War Era], 2 vols. (Tokyo: Mainichi Shimbunsha, 2015), 1:12–22. Hara Takeshi, *"Shôwa Tennô Jitsuroku" wo Yomu* [Reading the "Actual Record of the Shôwa Emperor"] (Tokyo: Iwanami Shinsho, 2015), 2–7.

6   STJR, CD 29, 102, November 5, 1941; Tokyo Shoseki, 8:534. See the Introduction, note 5 for more information. All translations are the author's unless otherwise indicated.

7   STJR, CD 29, 102–3, November 5, 1941; Tokyo Shoseki, 8:532–4.

8   STJR, CD 29, 126–8, December 1, 1941; Tokyo Shoseki, 8:562–5. Takeda Tomoki, "Tôjô Hideki—Shôwa no Higeki no Taikensha" [Tôjô Hideki—Embodiment of the Shôwa Tragedy], in *Shôwashi Kôgi, Gunjin-hen* [Lectures on Shôwa History, Military Personnel Volume], ed. Tsutsui Kiyotada (Tokyo: Chikuma Shinsho, 2018), 35–52, 39–40.

9   STJR, CD 29, 130, December 3, 1941; Tokyo Shoseki, 8:567.

10 STJR, CD 29, 138, December 8, 1941; Tokyo Shoseki, 8:577.

11 See for example, Wetzler, *Hirohito and War*, 35–8.

12 *Shôwa Jûrokunen Jôsô Kankei Shoruisetsu* [Materials Relating to Imperial Audiences in 1941, vol. 1, *September–December 1941*], "Daihon'ei Rikugunbu: Sammitsu Dai 438-go Dai 1" [Imperial Headquarters, Army Department: Secret Proceedings no. 438-1), MS, NIDS Military Archives. See Wetzler, *Hirohito and War*, 35 (translation), 234n10, 235n13.

13 *Senshi Sôsho*. See the beginning of vol. 102, *Riku, Kaigun Nenpyô* [Army Navy Chronology] for a table of the volumes and their titles and themes. For a short overview, see Edward J. Drea, *In the Service of the Emperor. Essays on the Imperial Japanese Army* (Lincoln: University of Nebraska Press, 1998), 272–3.

14 *Sanada Jôichirô Shôshô Nikki* [Major General Sanada Jôichirô Diary], 48, MS, NIDS Military Archives. (Compare to, Bôeichô, *Daihon'ei Rikugunbu*, 8:483–4.) The Diary extends from October 1939 to December 1945. During this time Sanada was, among others, Operations Section chief (*sakusenka kachô*), Operations Department chief (*sakusenbu buchô*), and Military Affairs Bureau chief (*gunmukyoku kyokuchô*).

These were the three most important posts in the general staff bureaucracy. This means of course that Sanada was privy to much very sensitive information and that he was not only a talented officer but also shared the views of, and enjoyed the confidence of, two very important war leaders, General Sugiyama Hajime, Army Minister and later chief of staff, and Prime Minister General Tôjô Hideki. (See Itô and Suetake, *Kin-Gendai Nihon Jinbutsu*, 1:194.)

"Nakazawa Gunreibu Dai'ichi Buchô Nôto" [Navy General Staff, 1st Department, Department Head Nakazawa Notes], included in his service diaries are "Sakusen Sankô" [Operations Information] and "Senkyô" [The War Situation], 589n31, and "Dairokujûichi Kôkû Sentai Sentô Shôhô" (61st Air Squadron Detailed Combat Report), 594n154, MS, NIDS Military Archives. See also Bôeichô, *Daihon'ei Kaigunbu*, 5:562–7.

15 Yamada Akira and Matsuno Seiya (ed. comp.), *Daihon'ei Rikugunbu Jôsô Kankei Shiryô* [The Imperial Headquarters Army Department Records Relating to Imperial Audiences] (Tokyo: Gendai Shiryô Shuppan, 2005). The term *tôsuibu*, supreme command, can refer to the *daihon'ei* and/or the general staff of the army and/or navy. The Daihon'ei, Imperial Headquarters, met in the imperial palace under the chairmanship of the emperor; the general staffs met in their respective offices under their chief of staff. The former was authorized according to an ordinance of November 17, 1937, to be formed only in times of war or when there was an "incident" (*jihen*). Previously it could only be formed in times of war. These records are copies of handwritten documents selected by Yamada and Matsuno to show the Shôwa Emperor was clearly involved in military planning and strategic decision-making (see p. 1). As seen in my commentary below, I find the records very useful but do not always agree with the editors' interpretations of them. For a brief description of the "imperial general headquarters," see Drea, *Japan's Imperial Army*, 192–3.

16 Yoshimi, *Shûsenshi*, 315–16. This organizational process is described based on Nakamura Takafusa, *Shôwashi* [Shôwa History], 2 vols. (Tokyo: Tôyô Keizai Shimbunsha, 2012), 1:473–6. Nakamura emphasizes that this decision-making process is different from the top-down systems in Germany, Great Britain, the USA, and USSR at the time.

17 Tsutsui Kiyotada, "Shôwa Rikugun no Habatsu Kôsô—Maegaki ni Tsutaete" [Factional Strife in the Shôwa Army—Prefatory Information], in *Shôwashi Kôgi, Gunjin-hen* [Lectures on Shôwa History, Military Personnel Volume], ed. Tsutsui Kiyotada (Tokyo: Chikuma Shinsho, 2018), 9–34, 24–5, 31–3.

18 Teshima Yasunobu, *Nihon Kaigun to Seiji* [The Japanese Navy and Politics] (Tokyo: Kodansha, 2015), 201–2.

19 Hattori Takushirô, *Daitôa Sensô Zenshi* [A Complete History of the Great East Asia War], 4 vols. (Tokyo: Masu Shobô, 1953; Repr. Hara Shobô, 1965), 560–79. For the

note on sources, see 1073–5. For the sources listed by Inaba Masao in an appendix including his commentaries, see 1074:

Kimitsu Sensô Nisshi [Secret War Journal], the so-called Secret Shôwa War Diary
Daihon'ei Seifu Renraku Kaigi Bangiroku [Imperial Headquarters – Government Liaison Conference Deliberations Record], the so-called Sugiyama Memo
Daihon'ei Seifu Renraku Kaigi Ketteiroku [Imperial Headquarters – Government Liaison Conference Decisions Record]
Gozen Kaigi Gijiroku [Imperial Conference Proceedings Record]
Dairikumei (Kaigun—Daikairei), the so-called Army (Navy) Orders of the Imperial Headquarters
Dairikushi (Kaigun—Daikaishi), Instructions by the Army (Navy) General Staffs
Jôsô Shorui [Imperial Audience Documents],
Sakusen Keikaku oyobi Daimei Hatsudô nado ni kan suru Jôsô [Operations Planning and Imperial Commands etc. related Imperial Audiences]
Kimitsu Sakusen Nisshi [Secret Operations Journal], mainly sent and received secret military cables.

20 Yanagisawa Ken, *Toyoda Soemu Jutsu. Saigo no Teikoku Kaigun* [Toyoda Soemu Narrator. End of the Imperial Navy] (Tokyo: Sekai no Nihonsha, 1950), 135–6; for Saipan, see 135–46.
21 Hattori, *Daitôa Sensô Zenshi*, 1075.
22 Hosaka Masayasu, *Shôwashi no Shinsô. 15 Sôten kara Yomitoku* [Shôwa History in Depth. Considered from the Point of View of 15 Issues] (Tokyo: Heibonsha, 2010), 134–6. John W. Dower, *Embracing Defeat. Japan in the Wake of World War II* (New York: W.W. Norton, 1999), 38, says "Several hundred individuals, most of them military officers committed suicide." An endnote puts the number at "527 army and navy men, plus a small number of civilians" (569n6).
23 For Toyoda at war's end, see Chapter 5.
24 Takayama Shinobu, *Futari no Sanbô, Hattori Takushirô to Tsuji Masanobu* [Two Staff Officers, Hattori Takushirô and Tsuji Masanobu] (Tokyo: Fuyô Shobô, 1999), 219–22.
25 For the plot, see *The Japan Times*, Tokyo, February 28, 2007.
26 Yamamoto Tomoyuki, *Nihon Rikugun Sensô Shûketsu Katei no Kenkyû* [Japanese Army Research on the Process of Terminating the War] (Tokyo: Fuyô Shobô, 2010), 236–52. For a short note in English on Hattori's career, see Butow, *Tojo and the Coming of the War*, 195n22.
27 Handô Kazutoshi and Hosaka Masayasu, *Shôwa Meishô to Gushô* [Great Leaders and Foolhardy Leaders of the Shôwa Era] (Tokyo: Bungei Shunjû, 2008), 174. Both nonfiction authors have been active for over fifty years researching and writing about Imperial Japan and the Second World War.
28 Ibid., 192–3, emphasis in the original. Hattori headed a group in the No. 1 Returning Veterans Bureau, chief of the Department for Factual Historical

Research. Later renamed an agency, all members were former Imperial Army officers. A clique under Hattori's leadership authored this history later published under his name.

29 Inoue Kiyoshi, *Tennôsei* [The Emperor System] (Tokyo: Tokyo Daigaku Shuppankai, 1958).

30 For Tôjô's fall and the war's end, see Inoue Kiyoshi, *Tennô no Sensô Sekinin* [The Emperor's War Responsibility] (Tokyo: Gendai Hyôronsha, 1975), 169–217.

31 Fujiwara Akira, *Tennôsei to Guntai* [The Emperor System and the Military] (Tokyo: Aoki Shoten, 1978), 123–4, quotation 124.

32 Delmer M. Brown, *Nationalism in Japan, an Introductory Historical Analysis* (Berkeley: University of California Press, 1955), 232.

33 Robert J.C. Butow, *Japan's Decision to Surrender* (Stanford: Stanford University Press, 1954), 176.

34 See also Project Development Office Tatsumi, *Kyôkasho to Shimbun de kuraberu Taiheiyô Sensô* [The Pacific War Compared in Textbooks and Newspapers] (Tokyo: Tatsumi Shuppan, 2015), 84–5.

35 Butow, *Japan's Decision to Surrender*, 11n11.

36 Suzuki Kantarô, *Suzuki Kantarô Jiden* [Suzuki Kantarô Autobiography] (Tokyo: Nihon Zusho Senta-, 1997), 304–5. This work consists of two parts. The first part covers Suzuki's life up until he was appointed president of the Privy Council August 10, 1944. It was dictated between February 1939 and August 1944, and published in April 1949 as *Suzuki Kantarô Jiden* (Autobiography of Suzuki Kantarô). The second part covers the end of the war. It is the record of an eight-hour interview published in August 1946 as *Shûsen no Hyôjô* (Circumstances at War's End). The Recollections at the very end, with the exception of the last section, are from an article, *Tennô-sama no Sain* (A Signal from the Emperor), published in 1962. The work, as it is here, was first published as the *Autobiography of Suzuki Kantarô* in 1968 by Jiji Tsûshinsha. See the explanatory notes at the beginning of the volume and on page 360 at the end. As with many autobiographies, Suzuki's presentation of himself and his role in the events at the end of the war is open to question. In the *Circumstances at War's End* he extols especially Emperor Hirohito's peace-loving nature. However, the final part on the war's end was published during the Allied Occupation and War Crimes Trials. The latter meant that Suzuki was careful not to say anything that might harm the situation of those in Sugamo Prison. Also, the text was vetted by US authorities and they made some changes. Resignedly, Suzuki let it be published though he was not entirely in agreement with the redacted text. Suzuki Tamon, "Suzuki Kantarô to Nihon no 'Shûsen'" [Suzuki Kantarô and "War's End" in Japan], in *"Nitchû Sensô" to ha Nan datta no ka – Fukuganteki Shiten* ["Japan – China War," What Was It? from Multiple Perspectives], eds. Huang Zijin, Liu Jianhui, and Tobe Ryôichi (Tokyo: Minerva Shobô, 2017), 257–86, here 280–1.

37 Nakazawa Tasuku Kankôkai [Nakazawa Tasuku Publication Group] (ed.), *Sakusen Buchô, Jinji Kyokuchô Kaigun Chûshô Nakazawa Tasuku* [Operations Department Head, Personnel Bureau Head, Navy Vice-Admiral Nakazawa Tasuku] (Tokyo: Seiraikyô, 1979), 142. Compiled long after the war, this is a very useful source. However, some of the information attributed to Nakazawa is very self-serving, both for the former vice-admiral himself and also the Imperial Navy General Staff. See the discussions on the approval of kamikaze tactics and convoy protection below.

38 Yamada Akira, *Shôwa Tennô no Sensô Shidô* [The Shôwa Emperor's War Leadership] (Tokyo: Shôwa Shuppan, 1990), 177. Yamada Akira, *Shôwa Tennô no Gunjishisô to Senryaku* [The Shôwa Emperor's Military Thought and Strategy] (Tokyo: Azekura Shobô, 2002), 283–4. For an American account and assessment, see Rear Admiral Edwin T. Layton, with Captain Roger Pineau and John Costello, *"And I Was There." Pearl Harbor and Midway—Breaking the Secrets* (Old Saybrook, CT: Konecky & Konecky, 1985), 484–7. Col. Matsutani Makoto initiated the Section 20 studies on losing the war advantageously and made reports to army chief of staff General Tôjô and his Vice-Chief General Ushiroku Jun around June 10, 1944. On July 3, he was suddenly transferred to a post in the China Expeditionary Army, which he had held two years earlier, 3rd Section Leader. But he returned to Tokyo in late November and at the end of the war was administrative secretary to Prime Minister Suzuki Kantarô. Yamada, *Shôwa Tennô no Gunjishisô to Senryaku*, 284. Toyama Misao (ed.) and Jôhô Yoshio (sup. ed.), *Rikukaigun Shôkan Jinji Sôran* [A Personnel Compendium of (High Ranking) Army and Navy Officers], 2 vols. (Tokyo: Fuyô Shobô, 1981), vol. 1, *Rikugunhen* [Army], 461.

39 Drea, *Service of the Emperor*, 196.

40 Drea, *Japan's Imperial Army*, 193–4. Contrary to Hosaka and Drea, a new book for public consumption, that is not well documented, maintains that the Emperor was for the most part correctly informed about war operations. Lying to the emperor made one liable to legal punishment and was therefore unlikely. Dainihonteikoku no nazo Kensho I'inkai [Great Imperial Japan Riddle Investigation Committee] (eds.), *Taiheiyô Sensô Tsûsetsu no Uso* [Commonly Accepted Lies About the Pacific War] (Tokyo: Saizusha, 2017), 104. This seems like a very naïve assessment. No senior army or navy flag officers were punished during the war for making less than candid reports to the Emperor.

41 Hosaka, *Shôwa Tennô Jitsuroku*, 1:156–9. I agree with Hosaka and Drea.

42 Sugiyama Gensui Denki Kankôkai [Field Marshal Sugiyama Biography Publication Group] (eds.), *Sugiyama Gensui Den* [Biography of Field Marshal Sugiyama] (Tokyo: Hara Shobô, 1969), 207

43 David C. Earhart, *Certain Victory. Images of World War II in the Japanese Media* (Armonk, NY: M.E. Sharpe, 2008), 70, 180, 398–401 428.

44 John W. Dower, *Cultures of War. Pearl Harbor/Hiroshima/9-11/Iraq* (New York: W.W. Norton/The New Press, 2010), 216.

45 See Chapter 5.
46 Drea, *Japan's Imperial Army*, 240. Drea cites, Haruko Taya Cook, "The Myth of the Saipan Suicides," *MHQ* 7, no. 3 (Spring 1995): 12–19.
47 Richard H. Minear, *Victor's Justice. The Tokyo War Crimes Trial* (Tokyo: Charles E. Tuttle, 1972), 202–3.
48 Satô Kenryô, *Daitôa Sensô Kaikoroku* [Greater East Asia War Memoirs] (Tokyo: Tokuma Shoten, 1966), 252–4, for the following. This work was compared with the original handwritten manuscript at the NIDS Military Archives and also *Daihon'ei Rikugunbu* (*Imperial Headquarters, Army Department*, vol. 8 in the War History Series. There are several significant differences between the texts and these will be noted where relevant.
49 "Daitôa Sensô Shidô – Dai 2 Sakusen Shidô 16.12.8–19.10" [Greater East Asia War Leadership – No. 2 Operations Leadership, December 8, 1941–October 1944]. By former Army Ministry, Military Affairs Department Head Satô Kenryô, 0409–0432, 0409, MS, NIDS Military Archives.
50 Satô, *Daitôa Sensô Kaikoroku*, 252–3.
51 "Daitôa Sensô Shidô," MS, 0412–13.
52 Satô, *Daitôa Sensô Kaikoroku*, 253.
53 STJR, CD 31, 112–131, June 26–August 4, 1943; Tokyo Shoseki, 9:130–52. For the Emperor's statement, see June 30, 1943, 4:00 p.m. notation. CD, 31, 114; Tokyo Shoseki, 9:132. This is one of many such imperial exhortations.
54 Nakao Yûji (ed.), *Shôwa Tennô Hatsugen Kiroku Shûsei* [Collected Records of Remarks by the Shôwa Emperor], 2 vols. (Tokyo: Fuyô Shobô Shuppan, 2003), 2:222–3. This is a good source: the remarks by the emperor are cited in such a manner that it is quite clear where they may be found. STJR, CD 31, 117–18, July 8, 1943; Tokyo Shoseki, 9:136, is less informative.
55 Suzuki, *"Shûsen" no Seijishi*, 24–30, 43. For a succinct statement summarizing Imperial Navy strategy, see Suzuki Kantarô, *Suzuki Kantarô Jiden*, 312.
56 Suzuki, *"Shûsen" no Seijishi*, 39–41.
57 Gunjishi Gakkai [Military History Society] (ed.), *Daihon'ei Rikugunbu Sensô Shidô Han, Kimitsu Sensô Nisshi* [Secret War Journal of the Imperial Headquarters, Army Dept. War Leadership Group], 2 vols. (Tokyo: Kinseisha, 1998), 2:671.
58 Ibid., 2:681. Bôeichô, *Daihon'ei Kaigunbu*, 7:324–5, 328–9. Bôeichô, *Daihon'ei Rikugunbu*, 10:75–6.
59 Yamada and Matsuno, *Daihon'ei Rikugunbu Jôsô Kankei Shiryô*, passim, for example.
60 Nakazawa Tasuku Publication Group, *Sakusen Buchô*, 92–3.
61 Gunjishi Gakkai [Military History Society] (ed.), *Daihon'ei Rikugunbu Sakusenbuchô Miyazaki Shûichi Chûshô Nisshi* [Imperial Headquarters Army Department Operations Department Chief Lt. General Miyazaki Shûichi Diary],

"Sakusen zenpan ni kan suru sôkatsuteki shoken – Nantaiheiyô hômen, sakusen no tokusei nami kyôkun" [Summary Remarks Relating to Operations in General – South Pacific Area Operations Peculiarities and Lessons Learned] (Tokyo: Kinseisha, 2003), xiii-xiv, 383–9 for the following.

62 Ibid., xiv.
63 Nakazawa Tasuku Publication Group, *Sakusen Buchô*, 200–2.
64 Teshima, *Nihon Kaigun to Seiji*, 202.
65 See for example Satô, *Daitôa Sensô Kaikoroku*, 254.
66 Nakazawa Tasuku Publication Group, *Sakusen Buchô*, 111.
67 Ibid., 109–11.
68 Ibid., 109–10 for the citation.
69 Ibid., 139.
70 Nakao, *Shôwa Tennô Hatsugen Kiroku Shûsei*, 2:273–82 for this and the following remarks by Emperor Hirohito.
71 STJR, CD 32, 89 and 90; Tokyo Shoseki, 9:367.
72 Nakao, *Shôwa Tennô Hatsugen Kiroku Shûsei*, 2:273, citing the recollections of Vice-Admiral Nakazawa Tasuku in Nakazawa, *Sakusen Buchô*, 141.
73 Nakao, *Shôwa Tennô Hatsugen Kiroku Shûsei*, 2:274, citing *Tatakau Tennô* (The Fighting Emperor; 1989) by Domon Shûhei, a former Imperial Army officer. Not included in STJR.
74 Nakao, *Shôwa Tennô Hatsugen Kiroku Shûsei*, 2:275, citing *Sanada Jôichirô Shôshô Nikki* (Major General Sanada Jôichirô Diary), MS, NIDS Military Archives. Not included in STJR.
75 Gunjishi Gakkai [Military History Society], *Daihon'ei Rikugunbu Sensô Shidô Han*, 2:542–50. Not included in STJR.
76 Ibid., 547.
77 Ibid., 542. Not included in STJR.
78 For this and the June 12 and 13 notations, see ibid., 542–3. Not in STJR.
79 Ibid., 545. In STJR, as noted above the emperor was informed of the landing, but if he was given any details they are not recorded.
80 Ibid.
81 Itô Takashi, Hirohashi Tadamitsu, and Katashima Norio (eds.), *Tôjô Naikaku Sôridaijin Kimitsu Kiroku. Tôjô Hideki Taishô Genkôroku* [Tôjô Cabinet Prime Minister's Secret Record. A Record of General Tôjô Hideki's Words and Deeds] (Tokyo: Tokyo Daigaku Shuppankai, 1990), 548; STJR, 32, 93, June 18, 1944; Tokyo Shoseki, 9:370. Nakao, *Shôwa Tennô Hatsugen Kiroku Shûsei*, 2:274.
82 Akamatsu Sadao, *Tôjô Hishokan Kimitsu Nisshi* [The Secret Diary of Tôjô's Secretary] (Tokyo: Bungei Shunjûsha, 1985), 150.
83 Takagi Sôkichi. *Takagi Sôkichi Nikki* [Takagi Sôkichi Diary] (Tokyo: Mainichi Shimbunsha, 1985), 235–7.

84 Diary notation June 17, referring to June 16, see ibid., 238–9. For the fear of a cabinet fall, see Takagi Sôkichi, *Shikan Taiheiyô Sensô* [A Personal View of the Pacific War] (Tokyo: Kôjinsha, 1999), 196.
85 Teshima, *Nihon Kaigun to Seiji*, 185–6.
86 Kido, *Kido Kôichi Nikki*, 2, 1111.
87 See notes 124, 125.
88 Gunjishi Gakkai [Military History Society], *Daihon'ei Rikugunbu Sensô Shidô Han*, 2:545.
89 Ibid., 547.
90 Ibid., 543, 545. One must bear in mind that this is an army record. Since the army and navy were not on good terms there are a number of critical comments about the navy included in it. For example, on June 5, an officer Horie, in the Army General Staff, noted "In general, within the Navy General Staff an awareness and sense of responsibility for [convoy] escorting and guarding are still lacking. Especially in the Combined Fleet it is so" (541). In considering the reliability of these sorts of comments one must also consider the source. Nakazawa Tasuku Publication Group, *Sakusen Buchô*, 129–34, has a very detailed account by then Rear Admiral Nakazawa of the extensive preparations for sending the troops to Saipan including protection of the transport ships.
91 Layton with Pineau and Costello, *"And I Was There,"* 484–5. This is confirmed in the earlier recollections of Vice-Admiral Nakazawa. See Nakazawa Tasuku Publication Group, *Sakusen Buchô*, 127–8.
92 For the events, see Bôeichô, *Daihon'ei Kaigunbu*, 4:130–40; for the postmortem investigations, see 142–5. See Layton with Pineau and Costello, *"And I Was There,"* 473–6, in which the US Navy's interception of these messages is detailed and the attack on Yamamoto authorized.
93 Bôeichô, *Daihon'ei Kaigunbu*, 4:146.
94 Sugiyama Gensui Denki Kankôkai, *Sugiyama Gensui Denki Kankôkai*, 206–7.
95 See STJR; Nakao, *Shôwa Tennô Hatsugen Kiroku Shûsei*.
96 Gunjishi Gakkai [Military History Society], *Daihon'ei Rikugunbu Sensô Shidô Han*, 2:547.
97 STJR, CD 32, 94, June 20, 1944; Tokyo Shoseki, 9:371.
98 See Bôeichô, *Daihon'ei Rikugunbu*, 8:482–3.
99 Suzuki, "Shûsen" no Seijishi, 23.
100 Gunjishi Gakkai [Military History Society], *Daihon'ei Rikugunbu Sensô Shidô Han*, 2:548. Not in STJR.
101 STJR, CD 32, 96, June 22, 1944; Tokyo Shoseki, 9:373.
102 Gunjishi Gakkai [Military History Society], *Daihon'ei Rikugunbu Sensô Shidô Han*, 2:548.
103 For a little known exotic example, see the comparison of the Shôwa Emperor with Emperor Godaigo of Kemmu Restoration (1333–6) fame in Senzaki Akinaka,

"Mishima Yukio to Amino Yoshihiko—Shôwa Tennô wo Meguru Setten" [Mishima Yukio and Amino Yoshihiko—Points of Conjunction With the Shôwa Emperor], in *Shôwa Tennô. "Senzen no Kunshu" to "Sengo no Shôchô" Futatsu no Kao* [The Shôwa Emperor. "Prewar Sovereign" and "Postwar Symbol," Two Faces], eds. Hashizume Daisaburô and Itô Takashi (Tokyo: Yôsensha, 2015), 180–5.

104 For example, see Edwin O. Reischauer, *Japan Past and Present*, 3rd Rev. edn. (Tokyo: Charles E. Tuttle, 1964), 215–16; and Hata Ikuhiko, *Hirohito: The Shôwa Emperor in War and Peace*, ed. Marius B. Jansen (Folkestone: Global Oriental, 2007), 48–51.

105 Suzuki Kantarô, *Suzuki Kantarô Jiden*, 334–5.

106 For Saipan, see Yamada, *Shôwa Tennô no Sensô Shidô*, 176–8; and Herbert P. Bix, *Hirohito and the Making of Modern Japan* (New York: HarperCollins, 2000), 476–7. For an extended critique of Bix's book and his "remarkable ability to penetrate into the heads of the emperor and his advisors," see George Akita, *Evaluating Evidence. A Positivist Approach to Reading Sources on Modern Japan* (Honolulu: University of Hawai'i Press, 2008), 141–60, citation 145.

107 For opposition to Tôjô and the fall of Saipan, see Stephen S. Large, *Emperor Hirohito and Shôwa Japan. A Political Biography* (London: Routledge, 1992), 116–20.

108 This is my personal impression after reading assorted parts of the STJR. Also see the summaries and discussions in *Asahi Shimbun*, September 9, 2014.

109 Matsuda Yoshifumi, "Jôhô Kanrisha toshite no Kido Kôichi Naidaijin" [Lord Keeper of the Privy Seal Kido Kôichi as Information Manager], *Nihon Rekishi*, no. 678 (November 2004): 75–90; for Saipan and the Emperor, see 80–1. Suzuki Tamon, "Tôjô Naikaku Sôjishoku no Kei'i ni tsuite no Saikentô" [A Reexamination of the Activities Surrounding the Resignation of the Tôjô Cabinet], *Nihon Rekishi*, no. 685 (June 2005): 69–84; for Saipan, see 73–4. See also in his book: Suzuki, *"Shûsen" no Seijishi*, 30–44.

110 Drea, *Japan's Imperial Army*, 253–7 and passim.

111 Suzuki, *"Shûsen" no Seijishi*, 9–10. For an overview, see Nihon Kin- Gendaishi Jiten Henshû I'inkai [the Japanese Dictionary of Modern and Contemporary History Editorial Committee] (eds.), *Nihon Kin- Gendaishi Jiten* [Japanese Dictionary of Modern and Contemporary History] (Tokyo: Tôyô Keizai Shinpôsha, 1978), for the army, see 263–4, 688–9; for the navy, see 85, 168.

112 Rivalry between various high political and military leaders in the modern wars of the twentieth century is well documented. During the War in the Pacific feuding among US Army and Navy commanders was of course not unknown, but it did not undermine the war effort as it did in Japan. See Mark Perry, *The Most Dangerous Man in America. The Making of Douglas MacArthur* (New York: Basic Books, 2014), 226–33, 275–84, and passim; Layton with Pineau and Costello, *"And I Was There,"* 487–8; and Frank E. Vandiver, "Foch and Eisenhower: Supreme Commanders," in *The Great World War 1914-45*, vol. 1, *Lightning*

Strikes Twice, eds. Peter Liddle, John Bourne, and Ian Whitehead (London: HarperCollins, 2000), 416–27.

113 Herbert P. Bix, "War Responsibility and Historical Memory: Hirohito's Apparition," section "Hirohito: Japan's Last Empowered Emperor," in *The Asian-Pacific Journal: Japan Focus* 6, no. 5. Archive May 6, 2008. As far as I know, vis-à-vis the Japanese emperor, substantive question = command is not a widely entertained assumption.

114 Bôeichô, *Daihon'ei Rikugunbu*, 5, 350–3. See Yamada Akira, "Daigensui Shôwa Tennô no 'Hatsugen' wo Yomu" [Reading the "Remarks" of the Supreme Commander Shôwa Emperor], in Hashizume and Itô, *Shôwa Tennô*, 192–8, here 194–5.

115 Yamada, *Shôwa Tennô no Gunjishisô to Senryaku*, 316–18.

116 Yamada Akira, "Daigensui Shôwa Tennô no 'Hatsugen' wo Yomu," 192–8. Yamada's point is that the Emperor actively commanded military forces during the war, not that he was deceived. He describes the deception but does not comment on its significance for active imperial command of imperial forces.

117 Yamada Akira, *Daigensui Shôwa Tennô* [The Supreme Commander Shôwa Emperor] (Tokyo: Shinnihon Shuppansha, 1994), 240–2.

118 For this and the below, see Bix, *Hirohito and the Making of Modern Japan*, 466–8.

119 See the above disagreement between Satô and Nakazawa.

120 Bôeichô, *Daihon'ei Rikugunbu*, 7, 158–9.

121 "Jôsô. Kongo no Sakusen ni kan suru Ken" [Report to the Throne. Concerning Operations Hereafter], September 15, 1943, Navy General Staff Chief Nagano Osami; Army General Staff Chief Sugiyama Hajime, in Yamada and Matsuno, *Daihon'ei Rikugunbu Jôsô Kankei Shiryô*, 384–96.

122 Ibid., esp. 393–6 and the editors comment, 19.

123 Yamada and Matsuno, *Daihon'ei Rikugunbu Jôsô Kankei Shiryô*, 2–10.

124 Handô Kazutoshi, Hosaka Masayasu, Mikuriya Takashi, and Isoda Michifumi, *"Shôwa Tennô Jitsuroku" no Nazo wo Toku* [Solving the Riddle of the Actual Record of the Shôwa Emperor] (Tokyo: Bungei Shunjû, 2015), 205–7. See also, Hosaka, *Shôwa Tennô Jitsuroku*, 1:156–60. The Chamberlain Ogura Kuraji Diary (*Ogura Kuraji Jijû Nikki*) reports that no enemy planes were shot down over the home islands. See "Ogura Kuraji Jijû Nikki" [Chamberlain Ogura Kuraji Diary], "Shôwa Tennô Senjishita no Nikugoe" ["The Actual Voice of the Wartime Shôwa Emperor"], in *Bungei Shunjû* 85, no. 5 (April 2007): 118–90, 160. Handô Kazutoshi provided the commentary for the Diary's publication and certainly knew of its contents. Handô makes no comment here, though he says later in the above work that the Emperor received falsified reports about the Doolittle raid. In his commentary accompanying the Ogura Diary, Handô wrote that the Diary does not note the losses at Midway and that the General Staff of the Navy lied to the Emperor about the losses there (162).

125 STJR, CD 30, 107, June 10, 1942; Tokyo Shoseki, 8:732–3; CD 30, 119, July 6, 1942; Tokyo Shoseki, 8:745–6. For the lost carriers in the Combined Fleet Reorganization Plan, see Handô et al., "Shôwa Tennô Jitsuroku," 204–5. In fact the United States lost one carrier and one destroyer, approximately 150 planes were downed, and 347 officers were killed. The Japanese lost four carriers, one cruiser, 322 planes were downed, and 2,500 officers and men were killed. Layton with Pineau and Costello, "And I Was There," 448. These statistics were not available then, but certainly the Imperial Navy General Staff was informed about their own carrier losses. Aircraft carriers were not simply expendable hardware.

126 Kido Kôichi Kenkyûkai [Kido Kôichi Research Group] (ed.), *Kido Kôichi Kankei Bunsho* [Documents Relating to Kido Kôichi] (Tokyo: Tokyo University Press, 1966), 128; Noriko Kawamura, *Emperor Hirohito and the Pacific War* (Seattle: University of Washington Press, 2015), 119. For the meaning and significance of "advance in a different direction" (*tenshin*), see Chapter 4.

127 Yamada, *Daigensui Shôwa Tennô*, 191, 275–6.

128 Hosaka, *Shôwa Tennô Jitsuroku*, 1:126–32, quotations 129 and 130. Hosaka comes to these conclusions by comparing the STJR with other sources, for example, here the Major General Sanada Jôichirô Diary.

129 Ibid., 1:133–4. Here Hosaka compares the STJR with the *Daihon'ei Happyô no Shinsôshi* [The True History of Imperial Headquarters Announcements] by Tominaga Kengo, formerly a lt. col. in the Communications Department of the Imperial Headquarters during the war.

130 Handô et al., "Shôwa Tennô Jitsuroku," 209–11. For the report to the throne *Shinpû Tokkôtai Osetsumei Shiryô* [Kamikaze Special Attack Unit Explanation to the Throne Documents], see Yamada, *Shôwa Tennô no Gunjishisô to Senryaku*, 305–6. See more in Chapter 2. Ohnuki-Tierney, *Kamikaze*, 161, indicates the first attack at Leyte was much more successful: 20.8 percent of the attackers hit a vessel.

131 Record of Answers to the Throne to Questions by the Emperor during Imperial Conferences (*gozenkaigi gijiroku*). See Tamura Yasuoki, "Senzen- Senchûki ni oite Shôwa Tennô ha tada Saika dake shite ita no ka?" [Did the Shôwa Emperor Merely Provide Sanctions before and during the War?], in Hashizume and Itô, *Shôwa Tennô*, 138–43; for the following, see 141–3.

132 Kido, *Kido Kôichi Nikki*, 2, 905–6, 928–30.

133 Tamura, 141–2.

134 Chatani Sei'ichi, "Tai Bei, Ei Kaisen. Sensô Kaihi kara Kaisen he Keisha suru" [Opening a War with the USA and Great Britain. From Avoiding War to Leaning toward Opening a War], in Hashizume and Itô, *Shôwa Tennô*, 54–9, here 54–5.

135 Tamura, "Senzen- Senchûki ni oite Shôwa Tennô," 141–2.

136 See note 12.

137 Fujiwara, *Tennôsei to Guntai*, 123–4.

138 Large, *Emperor Hirohito*, 117, citing Tolischus.
139 Ibid., 118.
140 Inoue, *Tennô no Sensô Sekinin*, 176–9.
141 STJR, CD 32, 26–8, February 19, 1944; Tokyo Shoseki, 9:293–4.
142 Suzuki, *"Shûsen" no Seijishi,"* 34.
143 "Nakazawa Gunreibu Daiichi Buchô Nôto," "Sakusen Sankô," Dai-san, no. 3: 109. For the edict as well as Capt. Fujii's doubts below see Suzuki, *"Shûsen" no Seijishi,"* 34–5.
144 Suzuki, *"Shûsen" no Seijishi,"* 37–8, 43–4.
145 Yamada, *Daigensui Shôwa Tennô*, 243–4.
146 Bôeichô, *Daihon'ei Kaigunbu*, 6, 6–7.
147 Yamada, *Shôwa Tennô no Sensô Shidô*, 177. He cites Bôeichô, *Daihon'ei Kaigunbu*, 6, 22. STJR, CD 32, 90–107; Tokyo Shoseki, 9:366–84, reports sporadically on the US invasion from June 15, to July 7, when the remaining Japanese troops made their last suicide assault. This final assault and the annihilation of all imperial forces are not reported. (The final assault was made on July 7; the announcement in Japan came on July 8.) This report to the throne as well as the reports about battles in the Philippine/Mariana Seas June 20 and 22 (96) from the chiefs of staff include extremely "optimistic" false information about Allied and Japanese losses, detailed above. The former are inflated and the latter greatly deflated. The Emperor's demand that the island be retaken and the ensuing planning and discussions are not included in STJR.
148 Gunjishi Gakkai [Military History Society], *Daihon'ei Rikugunbu Sensô Shidô Han*, 2, 550. For a complete rendition of the Army's view of the situation, see Bôeichô, *Daihon'ei Rikugunbu*, 8:483–4. Information based on two primary sources: *Sanada Jôichirô Shôshô Nikki* [Major General Sanada Jôichirô Diary] and *Jijûbukan Ogata Kenichi Taisa Nikki* [Army Aide-de-Camp Col. Ogata Kenichi Diary].
149 Nakao, *Shôwa Tennô Hatsugen Kiroku Shûsei*, 2:278–82 for the June 25, deliberations in detail, follow-up remarks on June 26, and this conclusion. Suzuki, *"Shûsen" no Seijishi,"* 70–2 comes to the same conclusion.
150 STJR, CD 32, 97–107, June 25–July 10, 1944; Tokyo Shoseki, 9:375–85.
151 See, for example, Yoshimi, *Shûsenshi*, 307–10. Kawamura, *Emperor Hirohito*, 176–7.
152 Itô Takashi, "Shôwashikenkyû no Kadai to Shôwa Tennô" [Shôwa History Research and the Shôwa Emperor], in Hashizume and Itô, *Shôwa Tennô*, 78–83, 82.

Chapter 2

1 Bôeichô, *Daihon'ei Kaigunbu*, 6:332.
2 Suzuki, *"Shûsen" no Seijishi*, 183. Yamada, *Shôwa Tennô no Gunjishisô to Senryaku*, 316–18.

3   Takagi Ichinosuke, Ozawa Masao, Atsumi Kaoru, and Kindaichi Haruhiko (eds.), *Heike Monogatari*, in *Nihon Koten Bungaku Taikei*, vols. 32 and 33 (Tokyo: Iwanami Shoten, 1959–60), 32, 83. The Heike Monogatari text now used by most is the "Kakuichi-bon" developed by the blind Buddhist monk Kakuichi Akashi (1299[?]–1371). A disciple recorded it as he dictated shortly before his death. For this translation see Helen Craig McCullough (trans. and intro.), *The Tale of the Heike* (Stanford: Stanford University Press, 1988), 23; see also "The 'Heike' as Literature," 456–75. For an account of the Heike as a tale of military lore, see Kenneth D. Butler, "The Textual Evolution of the *Heike Monogatari*," *Harvard Journal of Asiatic Studies* 26 (1966): 5–51. For "nikudan" and "gyokusai" below, see Earhart, *Certain Victory*, 380, 387.

4   See, for example, Shirakawa Yoshinori, *Guntai Kyôikurei* [Army Education Proclamation] (Tokyo: Heiyô Tosho KK, 1927). My copy includes copious notes by the reader who purchased it for 45 Sen. Wada Kamechi, *Rikugun Tamashii* [Soul of the Army] (Tokyo: Tôsuisha, 1942). Recommended by the ministries of the army and education, and the Japan Publishers Cultural Association. For the wartime media, see Earhart, *Certain Victory*, passim.

5   For an account of detailed preparations for these type of attacks, see Bôeichô, *Daihon'ei Kaigunbu*, 6:321–47. Here, 328, 347n14. The authors cite the original Imperial Navy No.1 Department "Wartime Organization Revision Report to the Throne" (*senji hensei kaitei ni kan suru jôbunsho*). For specific types of "weapons," their production, and volunteer recruitment, see p. 329.

6   Bôeichô, *Daihon'ei Rikugunbu*, 9:72–4, 73 for the reports to the Emperor on August 2 and 4. *Shôwa Tennô Jitsuroku* (Actual Record of the Shôwa Emperor) says that Army Minister Sugiyama Hajime had an audience with the Emperor on August 2, 1944, in which he mentioned a "method of attacking enemy ships using close quarters attack boats" but no specifics are recorded. In the record of the August 4, audience with Army Chief of Staff Umezu Yoshijirô an "elite sea-going unit" is mentioned. STJR, CD 32, 125–6, August 2 and 4, 1944; Tokyo Shoseki, 9:406–8. For the beginnings of the army suicide tactics, and the first army suicide attacks, see Kawabe Masakazu, *Nihon Rikugun Seishin Kyôikushi Kô* [An Interpretation of Japanese Army Spiritual Education History], 2 vols. (Tokyo: Hara Shobô, 1980), 2:119–127; for the May 1944 attacks, see 121; for "The Soldier's View of Life and Death," see 2:127–9; and for authorship and publishing, see 1:1–8, esp. 1–2, 7–8.

7   For Jô's plan, see Nomura Minoru (ed.), *Jijûbukan Jô Ei'ichirô Nikki* [Aide-de-Camp Jô Ei'ichirô Diary], *Kindai Nihon Shiryô Sensho* 4 [Anthology of Modern Japanese Historical Documents No.4] (Tokyo: Yamakawa Shuppansha, 1982), 290–2, c. June 28, 1943. In Jô's diary the plan is sandwiched between June 28 and 29, on separate undated sheets. These sheets were memos made by Jô, "On the Organization of a Special Air Corps" (*tokushu kôkûtai no hensei ni tsuite*) at

the earliest in June, at the latest in July 1944, according to Nomura Minoru. Nomura was the official in the War History Office who hand-copied the original on September 1, 1969. See "(Navy) Capt. Jô Ei'ichirô Memo: 'Tokushu Kôkûtai Hensei to Tokushu Kôgeki Kinôsei Yôkyû ni Kan suru Jô Ei'ichirô Memo'" [The Organization of a Special Air Corps' and Special Attack Plane Performance Requirements], memo, NIDS Military Archive. The memo was made on lined paper from the Imperial Household Ministry (*kunaishô*). The information in Bôeichô, *Daihon'ei Kaigunbu*, 6:322–4, derives from this copy. Jô's diary and this memo demonstrate his intensive continuing interest in this tactic. The information therein was circulated among selected naval officers, including Vice-Admiral Ônishi.

8   Nomura, *Jô Nikki*, 294. Cited in Bôeichô, *Daihon'ei Kaigunbu*, 6:323. Bôeichô Bôeikenkyûsho Senshishitsu [Defense Agency, Institute for Defense Studies, War History Office], *Kaigun Shôgô Sakusen (2) Fuiripin Oki Kaisen* [Navy Victory Offensive (2) Philippine Off-Shore Naval Battle] (Tokyo: Asagumo Shuppansha, 1972), 107. Jô's plan entailed using available warplanes and converted civilian aircraft. The special suicide glide plane with a bomb in the nose called "Ôka" was construed differently from those in Jô's proposal. For its design, construction and effectiveness, see Takashi Nishiyama, *Engineering War and Peace in Modern Japan, 1868-1964* (Baltimore: Johns Hopkins University Press, 2014), 73–83.

9   For his entry into the Naval War College, see Nomura, *Jô Nikki*, 282–3, 369.

10 The *Chiyoda* was originally commissioned as a seaplane tender in 1938. It was converted to a light carrier in late 1943. This was Jô's first command, which turned out tragically for him and everyone on board, over 1,400 men. For a detailed description of the attack on the *Chiyoda*, futile attempts to save her, and other ships in the group, see Bôeichô, *Kaigun Shôgô Sakusen (2)* 406–38; specifically for the *Chiyoda*, see 413–14, 421–2, 425–6, 434–8. Capt. Jô was promoted posthumously to rear admiral. There is nothing about his actions at this time in these descriptions. Officers and some enlisted men were promoted posthumously if they reportedly had died honorably.

11 Hiroyuki Agawa, *The Reluctant Admiral. Yamamoto and the Imperial Navy*, trans. John Bester (Tokyo: Kodansha International, 1979), 222–3. Ônishi Takijirô and Genda Minoru also drafted plans for the Pearl Harbor attack as experts in naval air operations.

12 Bôeichô, *Daihon'ei Kaigunbu*, 6:321–2. The source for the first meeting is the "Duty Diary of Rear Admiral Nakazawa Tasuku Navy General Staff 1st Dept. Chief" (*gunreibu daiichi buchô Nakazawa Tasuku Shôshô gyômu nisshi*). Obviously Nakazawa was informed of these developments, despite his later denials.

13 Bôeichô, *Daihon'ei Kaigunbu*, 6:324.

14 Bôeichô, *Kaigun Shôgô Sakusen (2)*, 107–8.
15 Ibid.
16 For this and the following, see Mori Shirô, *Tokkô to ha Nanika* [Special Attack, What Was It?] (Tokyo: Bungei Shunjû, 2006), 34–7.
17 Bôeichô, *Kaigun Shôgô Sakusen (2)*, 107–9. The text is reproduced on p. 108. In the original the opinions of competent persons are appended but not noted. The translation of *tai'atari* as "body ramming" follows Earhart, *Certain Victory*, 430-1.
18 Toyoda, "Saigo no Teikoku Kaigun" [End of the Imperial Navy], April 30, 1945, Seikai no Nihon Shakan, 613n61, quoted in Bôeichô, *Kaigun Shôgô Sakusen (2)*, 109.
19 Ibid., 114–5.
20 Mori, *Tokkô to ha Nanika*, 62–6. On September 10, 1944, Matsu'ura was attached to the Navy General Staff in Tokyo and served in a number of other staffs until the end of the war. He graduated in the 55th Naval Academy Class (1927) and the 38th Naval Staff College Class (entry 1940). He was promoted on November 1, 1943, to commander. He did not participate in a kamikaze attack or commit suicide after the end of the war (postwar interview).
21 For this and the following, see Nakazawa Tasuku Publication Group, *Sakusen Buchô*, 156–7; and Suzuki, *"Shûsen" no Seijishi*, 88.
22 Ryuji Nagatsuka, *I was a Kamikaze* (London: Abelard-Shuman Ltd., 1973; Repr. Stroud: Amberley Publishing, 2014), back cover. At the time of writing (mid-2019), there is a profusion of popular paperback books about kamikaze fliers and their fates in Japanese.
23 See for example, Inoguchi Rikihei and Nakajima Tadashi, *Shimpû Tokbetsu Kôgekitai* [Divine Wind Special Attack Unit] (Tokyo: Nihon Shuppan Kyôdô Kabushiki Kaisha, 1951). For a critic, see Ohnuki-Tierney, *Kamikaze*, 158–9.
24 Bôeichô Bôeikenkyûsho Senshishitsu [Defense Agency, Institute for Defense Studies, War History Office], *Okinawa, Taiwan, Iôshima Hômen Rikugun Kôkû Sakusen* [Okinawa, Taiwan, Iwo Jima Area Army Air Force Operations] (Tokyo: Asagumo Shuppansha, 1970), 305–6.
25 Ibid., 306–7.
26 See for example, "Sugawara Michiô Chûshô Kaisôroku" [Recollections of Lt. General Sugawara Michiô]; "Seishin Kyôiku yori Kan taru Kôkûhei Ichi Butaichô no Kaisô" [Recollections of the Commander of the 1st Army Air Unit Seen from the Perspective of Spiritual Education], esp. ch. 5 "Rekidai Taichô no Shidô Seishin" [Leadership Spirit of Successive Unit Commanders], ch. 6 "Gunjin Seishin no Shôchô" [Rise and Fall of the Soldiers Spirit]; and "Shiseikan" [View of Living and Dying], in "Dairoku Kôkûgun Shireikan de atta Sugawara Michiô Chûshô Kaisô" [Recollections of Lt. General Sugawara Michiô Commander of the 6th Army Air Force], MS, NIDS Military Archives, Tokyo.

27 "Kôkû Sôran ken Kyôdô Kôkûgun Shireikan, tsuide Dairoku Kôkûgun Shireikan de atta Sugawara Michiô Chûshô no Kaisô" [Recollections of Lt. General Sugawara Michiô, Air Force General Supervisor and Air Force Training Command Commanding Officer, then, 6th Army Air Force Commanding Officer]; and "Rikugunshô Gunmukyoku, Gunjika, Henseihanchô, nochi Daihon'ei Rikugunsanbô Matsuda Masao Chûsa no Kaisô" [Recollections of Lt. Col. Matsuda Masao, Army Ministry, Military Affairs Bureau, Military Section, Organization Group Leader, later Imperial Headquarters Army General Staff Member] both cited in Bôeichô, *Okinawa, Taiwan, Iôshima Hômen*, 306–7, 630, 631. Handô and Hosaka, *Shôwa Meishô to Gushô*, 246–7.

28 "Tokkô Sakusen no Shiki ni Ninji taru Gunshireikan toshite no Kaisô, tôji 6FA Shireikan Chûshô Sugawara Michiô" [Recollections of One Appointed as Commanding Officer of Special Attack Operations, then 6th Air Force Commanding Officer Lt. General Sugawara Michiô], *Shôwa 44, 8, 7 kijutsu* [August 7, 1969 description], esp. 62–105, MS, NIDS Military Archives, Tokyo. Handô relates that in 1961 he sought out Sugawara on his farm, but the former general refused to talk to him about the kamikaze attacks. Handô and Hosaka, *Shôwa Meishô to Gushô*, 248–9.

29 Hosaka Masayasu, *"Tokkô" to Nihonjin* ["Special Attacks" and the Japanese] (Tokyo: Kodansha, 2005), 181–6. For a slightly different opinion, see Tsuneo Watanabe (ed.-in-chief), *From Marco Polo Bridge to Pearl Harbor: Who was Responsible?*, ed. James E. Auer (Tokyo: Yomiuri Shimbun, 2006), 236–8.

30 Nakazawa Tasuku Publication Group, *Sakusen Buchô*, 157–8.

31 Hosaka, *"Tokkô" to Nihonjin*, 178–81.

32 Ibid., 185.

33 Bôeichô, *Daihon'ei Kaigunbu*, 6:321–2.

34 For this and the following, see Bôeichô, *Daihon'ei Rikugunbu*, 9:72–3.

35 Suzuki Kantarô, *Suzuki Kantarô Jiden*, 321–2, citation 321. For a description of this work, see Chapter 1, n36.

36 Bôeichô, *Daihon'ei Kaigunbu*, 6, 327–31. Based on "Tokushu Heiki Kinkyû Seibi Keikaku" [Special Weapons Emergency Preparations Plan]. See the Ministry of Health and Welfare Archives "Tokkô Shiryô Tsuzuri" [Special Attack Documents Collection], 347n15, no date, but the contents indicate it was written around July 10, 1944. An excerpt from this document may be seen on pp. 329–30, and for the "special capacity" conditions, see p. 329.

37 Bôeichô Bôeikenkyûsho Senshishitsu [Defense Agency, Institute for Defense Studies, War History Office], *Riku, Kaigun Nenpyô* [Army, Navy Chronology] (Tokyo: Asagumo Shuppansha, 1980), 357.

38 Bôeichô, *Daihon'ei Kaigunbu*, 6:327, 328–9, 330. Bôeichô, *Riku- Kaigun Nenpyô*, 356, says that 120 were planned but none were ever used.

39 Bôeichô, *Daihon'ei Kaigunbu*, 6:327, 329, 330. For the operations commentary, see Bôeichô, *Riku- Kaigun Nenpyô*, 330.

40 Bôeichô, *Daihon'ei Kaigunbu*, 6:327, 329, 330. For the operations commentary, see Bôeichô, *Riku- Kaigun Nenpyô*, 331.

41 Yamada, *Shôwa Tennô no Gunjishisô to Senryaku*, 304.

42 For this and the following, see ibid., 305–6. It appears that Yamada quotes this document in full. I doubt the veracity of the attack results because at this stage of the war the general staffs often embellished battle results reported to the Emperor. See Chapter 1.

43 Ibid., 306. The audience with Admiral Oikawa and the subsequent report to the throne about kamikaze tactics are not noted in Nakao, *Shôwa Tennô Hatsugen Kiroku Shûsei*. In STJR on October 26, "attack results of the divine wind special attack unit, Shikishima unit etc." is mentioned without going into detail. Likewise on October 28, the formation and attack results of "divine wind special attack units" are noted giving no details. STJR, CD 32, 182; Tokyo Shoseki, 9:471–3.

44 Hosaka, *Shôwa Tennô Jitsuroku*, 1:177–80; for the citations, see 180. Hosaka unfortunately does not say where these citations come from.

45 Nomura, *Jô Nikki*, 144.

46 Earhart, *Certain Victory*, 414–27, extensively describes the midget submarines, the men who manned them, the various attacks made, and portrayals of those involved in the attack on Pearl Harbor as posthumous war heroes. Included are many Japanese press photos from that time eulogizing those who died.

47 For this and the following, see Bôeichô Bôeikenkyûsho Senshishitsu [Defense Agency, Institute for Defense Studies, War History Office], *Hawai'i Sakusen* [Hawai'i Operations Strategy] (Tokyo: Asagumo Shuppansha, 1967), 160–5. For a sketch of this "torpedo," which looks like a two-man mini-submarine, see p. 163; for the citations, see p. 161. The information is based on postwar recollections by various Imperial Navy officers and engineers involved in the project. See 167nn39–51.

48 For the names, ranks, and a photo of those manning the mini-submarines, see Ibid., 249–50; for the attack and recovery plan, see pp. 287–90. For photos of the nine "Warrior Gods," see Earhart, *Certain Victory*, 415–16.

49 Nomura, *Jô Nikki*, Commentary, 4–5.

50 Ibid., 5.

51 Bix, *Hirohito and the Making of Modern Japan*, 450–1. Compare with Nomura, *Jô Nikki*, 4–6, 142–3; for relevant career information, see 366–74.

52 Bôeichô, *Daihon'ei Rikugunbu*, 9:73. Two sources are listed for this information: "Ogata Nisshi" [Ogata Diary], the Diary of Col. Ogata Ken'ichi, Aide-de-Camp (this diary is family private property not available to the public), and "Ôtsuka Fumirô Bibôroku" [Ôtsuka Fumirô Memorandum], cautionary notes made after various events, NIDS Military Archives, Tokyo. It is a poor copy of a handwritten

text, and for me as well as a Japanese expert in places it is impossible to decipher. August 1–5, 1944, are found in vol. 8, 2285–2312. My information about the Emperor depends on the above Bôeichô, *Daihon'ei Rikugunbu*, vol. 9.

53 Itô et al., *Tôjô Naikaku Sôridaijin Kimitsu Kiroku*, 552–3. Hosaka, *"Tokkô" to Nihonjin*, 187.
54 Itô et al., 535.
55 Butow (1961), 442.
56 Hosaka, *"Tokkô" to Nihonjin*, 189.
57 Naitô Susumu, *Nihon Rikugunkôkû Hiwa* [The Inside Story of the Japanese Army Air Corps], cited in ibid., 189–90.
58 Hosaka, *"Tokkô" to Nihonjin*, 190.
59 See Tôjô Hideki, *Kokumin Gige, Senjinkun* [Field Service Code, Explanation to the People], ed. Okayama Kendô (Tokyo: Kyôzaisha, March 30, 1941). Published for public use approximately two months after its issue within the army by the Army Minister at that time, Lt. Gen. Tôjô Hideki.
60 Kisaka Junichirô, *Shôwa no Rekishi* [Shôwa History], vol. 7, *Taiheiyô Sensô* [The Pacific War] (Tokyo: Shogakkan, 1982), 152–3. Drea, *Japan's Imperial Army*, 212–13. Mombushô [Ministry of Education] (eds.), *Kokutai no Hongi* [The Essential Principles of the National Polity] (Tokyo: Mombushô, 1937), May 1943, 13, cited in Ryusaku Tsunoda, Wm. Theodore de Bary, and Donald Keene (comp.), *Sources of the Japanese Tradition* (New York: Columbia University Press, 1958), 785–94, 787. Tsunoda's translation. For a translation of and brief commentary on the Imperial Rescript on Education, see 646–7. Also, see John Owen Gauntlett (trans.) and Robert King Hall (ed. and intro.), *Kokutai No Hongi. Cardinal Principles of the National Entity of Japan* (Cambridge MA, Harvard University Press, 1949). For the genesis of this work, see Shida Nobuyoshi, *Shôwa no Shôgen* [Shôwa Era Witness] (Tokyo: Shibundô, 1990), 27–38. In the 1930s Shida was an assistant in the National Spirit and Culture Research Institute (Kokumin Seishin Bunka Kenkyûjo), and under the direction of a commission of highly regarded scholars and Ministry of Education officials, the chief of the Thought Bureau, Itô Zenkichi, and its research section chief Ogawa Yoshiaki he drafted the *Kokutai no Hongi* text. Hasegawa Ryôichi, *Kôkokushikan to iu Mondai* [The Problem of Emperor-Centered Historiography] (Tokyo: Hakutakusha, 2008), 77. After the war he became a professor of Japanese language and literature.
61 Tôjô, *Senjinkun*, 9:81. For the samurai tradition, see, for example, 103–7, "Considering Life and Death."
62 Ibid., 24, 23, 13. Watanabe, *From Marco Polo Bridge*, 147, 248, has a slightly different translation of the first injunction.
63 Nakashiba Suezumi, *Kokumin Senjinkun* [Citizens Field Service Code] (Tokyo: Futami Shobô, 1943). In the library of the Showa-kan/National Showa Memorial

Museum, Kudanshita Tokyo are ten different publications from 1941 and 1943 on this topic. They range from a small pamphlet with no commentary other than a short introduction, to works such as Nakashiba's with the text and extensive clarifications of its meaning. See also, for example, Ôtsuki Shizuo, *"Senjinkun" Kyôiku no Sankô* [Education Information on the "Field Service Code"] (Tokyo: Nippon Heisho Shuppan Kabushiki Kaisha, 1941); and Kawabe Masakazu, *Nihon Rikugun Seishin Kyôikushi Kô*, 2:114–19.

64 See Wetzler, *Hirohito and War*, 70–4. On fighting to the death for lost causes, see Ivan Morris, *The Nobility of Failure: Tragic Heroes in the History of Japan* (New York: Secker & Warburg, 1975).

65 Nishio Kanji et al., *Atarashii Rekishi Kyôkasho* [A New History Textbook] (Tokyo: K.K. Fusô, 2001), 279. This is a highly controversial xenophobic textbook, but the verse accurately illustrates the "departing poem" written by most kamikaze fliers (some wrote letters) just prior to their missions. Deleted from the revised 2005 edition.

66 Personal conversations with the man whose name I have forgotten. He showed me a worn ID card with his picture on it indicating that while he probably was exaggerating, for which he was well known, he was basically telling the truth.

67 Klaus Scherer, *Kamikaze. Todesbefehl für Japans Jugend* ([Kamikaze. Death Orders for Japan's Youths] (Munich: iudicium, 2001), passim.See Earhart, *Certain Victory*, 409–59. See also Ohnuki-Tierney, *Kamikaze*, esp. 157–242, pt. 3, "The Making of Tokkôtai Pilots."

68 Scherer, *Kamikaze*, 76.

69 Ibid., 41.

70 Ibid., 77.

71 Ohnuki-Tierney, *Kamikaze*, 192–242.

72 Scherer, *Kamikaze*, 53–4.

73 Drea, *Service of the Emperor*, 75–90; Akamatsu, *Tôjô Hishokan Kimitsu Nisshi*, 215–18.

74 See, for example, Watanabe, *From Marco Polo Bridge*, 236–7. Hosaka, *"Tokkô" to Nihonjin*, 148–51. The radio broadcast is quoted by Hosaka (pp. 142–3) but not in the Watanabe source. Unfortunately Hosaka does not tell us when the broadcast took place.

75 Yamada, *Shôwa Tennô no Gunjishisô to Senryaku*, 316–7.

76 Sanbôhonbu [Army General Staff] (ed.), *Sugiyama Memo* [Sugiyama Memoranda], 2 vols. (Tokyo: Hara Shobô, 1967, Repr. 1989), 2:20. See also Kawamura, *Emperor Hirohito*, 119–20.

77 Suzuki, *"Shûsen" no Seijishi*, 123, 126.

78 See Wetzler, *Hirohito and War*, 56–9.

79 Nishiyama, *Engineering War and Peace*, 82, 220n114.

80 Watanabe, *From Marco Polo Bridge*, 237.
81 Ohnuki-Tierney, *Kamikaze*, 161–2.
82 Wilson D. Miscamble, *The Most Controversial Decision. Truman, the Atomic Bombs, and the Defeat of Japan* (Cambridge: Cambridge University Press, 2011), 46–7, 81–2. For the kamikazes, see Richard B. Frank, "Ketsu-Gô: Japanese Political and Military Strategy in 1945," in *The End of the Pacific War: Reappraisals*, ed. Tsuyoshi Hasegawa (Stanford, CA: Stanford University Press, 2007), 65–94, here 75, 82.
83 *Asahi Shimbun* (*Asahi Newspaper* International Edition), January 8, 2017: 16.
84 Satô Hiroô, "Shinkoku Shisô" [Divine Land Thought], in *Nihon Shisôshi Jiten* [Japanese Thought History Dictionary], eds. Ishida Ichirô and Ishige Tadashi (Tokyo: Tokyodo Shuppan, 2013), 108–9.
85 *Asahi Shimbun*, January 8, 2017: 16.
86 Tanaka Satoshi, "Takatori Masao. 'Kono Yo no Soto ni Tsukidasu Minzoku Shûkyô'" [Folk Religion Thrust Out of this World], in *Shintô no Seiritsu* [The Birth of Shintô] (Tokyo: Heibonsha Sensho, 1979), cited in Koyasu Nobukuni (ed.), *Nihon Shisôshi* [History of Japanese Thought] (Tokyo: Jinbun Shoin, 2011), 44–9n45.

Chapter 3

1 Butow, *Tojo and the Coming of the War*, 503–4. This work is still the most complete consideration of Tôjô in English by far, and it surpasses many Japanese studies. I do not agree with all of his interpretations, especially the mechanistic description of "puppet politics" in Japan at the time (see, for example, p. 308).
2 Takeda, "Tôjô Hideki—Shôwa no Higeki no Taikensha," 47–8. Kiyomizu Temple is in Kyoto. The terrace is some 13 meters (almost 43 feet) high.
3 Hosaka Masayasu, *Kaisen, Tôjô Hideki ga Naita* [Opening the War, Tôjô Hideki Wept] (Tokyo: Mainichi Shinbunsha, 2007), 120–1. *Japan Times*, July 23, 2018: "Tojo was convinced of victory before Japan attacked Pearl Harbor, newly unearthed memo shows."
4 Fujimoto Hiromichi, *Rikugun Saigo no Hi* [The Last Day of the Army] (Tokyo: Shinjinsha, December 1945), 23–6. Fujimoto describes the situation in Japan shortly before the end of the war. Although Tôjô was no longer active in politics or the army, Fujimoto is very critical of his dictatorial ways. I do not know who the author was, but he seems to have been quite well informed about government and military matters at that time. Of course, many other persons were very critical of Tôjô during his term of office as well as immediately before and after the end of the war. This is but one contemporary example. See Butow, *Tojo and the Coming of the War*, 468–9.
5 Hosaka, *Kaisen*, 173–4, 177–8. Hosaka calls the celebration "frivolous" rather than ebullient.

6   For this and the seating order below, see Akamatsu, *Tôjô Hishokan Kimitsu Nisshi*, 52–3. Akamatsu was one of the secretaries present at the celebration. Hosaka, *Kaisen*, 178–9.
7   Yuma Totani, *The Tokyo War Crimes Trial. The Pursuit of Justice in the Wake of World War II* (Cambridge, MA: Harvard University Press, 2008), 144–5.
8   Butow, *Tojo and the Coming of the War*, 503–4.
9   Gunjishi Gakkai [Military History Society] (eds.), *Daihon'ei Rikugunbu Sensô Shidô Han, Kimitsu Sensô Nisshi* [Secret War Journal of the Imperial Headquarters, Army Department War Leadership Group], 2 vols. (Tokyo: Kinseisha, 1998); Itô et al., *Tôjô Naikaku Sôridaijin Kimitsu Kiroku*; Nakao, *Shôwa Tennô Hatsugen Kiroku Shûsei*; *Senshi Sôsho*; Bôeichô Bôeikenkyûsho Senshishitsu. Others cited above.
10 STJR [*Shôwa Tennô Jitsuroku*].
11 Tôjô, *Kokumin Gige, Senjinkun*, see Chapter 2 for more on this work; Itô Shunichirô, *Tôjô Hideki Den, Shisei, Tetsu no Hito* [Tôjô Hideki Biography, Sincere, Man of Steel] (Tokyo: Tenyû Shobô, January 17, 1942; Repr. January 28, 1942); and Dômei Tsûshinsha Seikeibu, *Hisshô no Daidô*.
12 Tôjô, *Kokumin Gige, Senjinkun*, 28–9.
13 Itô, *Tôjô Hideki Den*, 1–3.
14 Ibid., 243.
15 Ibid., 49–50.
16 Ibid., 139–50.
17 Ibid., 153.
18 For an early rendition of this "defense," see Tokyo Saiban Kenkyûkai [Tokyo Trial Research Group] (ed.), *Tôjô Hideki Sensei Kyôjutsusho* [Tôjô Hideki Sworn Affidavit], *Tennô ni sekinin nashi, sekinin ha waga ni ari* [The Emperor Bears No Responsibility; the Responsibility Is Mine] (Tokyo: Yôyôsha, 1948). Front cover, 114. Later Tôjô's principal defense attorney published, Kiyose Ichirô, *Hiroku, Tokyo Saiban* [Secret Record, the Tokyo Trial] (Tokyo: Yomiuri Shimbunsha, 1966). He condemns the trial as unjust and unfair.
19 Hosaka Masayasu, *Tôjô Hideki to Tennô no Jidai* [Tôjô Hideki and the Era of the Emperor], 2 vols. (Tokyo: Gendai Jânarisumu, 1979), 1:13–16. One *koku* of rice was theoretically the amount of rice an adult male consumed in one year, approximately 180 liters. Leaving out the Tokugawa Shôgun, Great Lords (*daimyo*) and their families, during the Tokugawa era (1600–1868) samurai family stipends averaged approximately 35 *koku* of rice per year. Middle-ranking samurai received about 100 *koku* of rice per year. Otto Ladstätter and Sepp Linhart, *China und Japan: Die Kulturen Ostasiens* [China and Japan: The Cultures of East Asia] (Vienna: Carl Ueberreuter Verlag, 1983), 354.
20 Leonard A. Humphreys, *The Way of the Heavenly Sword. The Japanese Army in the 1920s* (Stanford, CA: Stanford University Press, 1995), 32–3, 39–40. For important dates in his career, see Jôhô Yoshio (ed.), *Tôjô Hideki* (Tokyo: Fuyô

Shobô, 1974), 757–60. See also, Butow, *Tojo and the Coming of the War*, 3–9. Wetzler, *Hirohito and War*, 61–3.

21 Itô, *Tôjô Hideki Den*, 20–4.

22 Ibid., 27.

23 Hirota Teruyuki, *Rikugun Shôkô no Kyôikushakaishi* [A Social-Educational History of the Army Officer] (Yokohama: Seori Shobô, 1997), 175–6. Drea, *Japan's Imperial Army*, 94.

24 Hirota, *Rikugun Shôkô no Kyôikushakaishi*, 175.

25 Ibid., 177.

26 Ibid., 178. Here Hirota does not refer to Tôjô personally. He is citing an early practice at the Tokyo Regional Army Preparatory School, which Tôjô attended.

27 The future Emperor Hirohito was educated in special schools organized for him. Therein he too received extensive education (indoctrination) in culture and history as propagated in Imperial Japan. See Wetzler, *Hirohito and War*, 82–138. For applied history and genuine history, see Hasegawa Ryôichi, *Kôkokushikan to iu Mondai*, 64–5. Statement made by Mikami Sanji (1865–1939).

28 Hirota, *Rikugun Shôkô no Kyôikushakaishi*, 187–8. Jimmu Tennô was the putative founder of the imperial Line, who in fact never existed.

29 Suzuki, "Suzuki Kantarô to Nihon no 'Shûsen,'" 257–86, esp. 276n5.

30 Hirota, *Rikugun Shôkô no Kyôikushakaishi*, 187.

31 Nakao, *Shôwa Tennô Hatsugen Kiroku Shûsei*, 2:104.

32 Itô et al., *Tôjô Naikaku Sôridaijin Kimitsu Kiroku*, 40–1, citation 40.

33 Totani, *Tokyo War Crimes Trial*, 97.

34 Roberta Wohlstetter, *Pearl Harbor. Warning and Decision* (Stanford, CA: Stanford University Press, 1962), 351–4, citation 353.

35 Kusunoki cited in Hirota, *Rikugun Shôkô no Kyôikushakaishi*, 188. The brief description is my own, based on a contemporary work: E. Papinot, *Historical and Geographical Dictionary of Japan* (Tokyo: Sansaisha, 1909). For biographies in school histories, see Hasegawa Ryôichi, *Kôkokushikan to iu Mondai*, 59.

36 Papinot, *Historical and Geographical Dictionary*, 333–4. See Morris, *Nobility of Failure*, 106–142. Wetzler, *Hirohito and War*, 69–74. See Kaizu Ichirô, "Kusunoki Masashige to Nihonjin: Kyôkasho ni miru Masashige-zô no hensen" [Kusunoki Masashige and the Japanese: The Changing Image of Masashige as Seen in School Textbooks], in *Kusunoki Masashige no subete* [All about Kusunoki Masashige], ed. Satô Kazuhiko (Tokyo: Shinjinbutsu Ôraisha, 1989), 175–204. See also Carol Gluck, *Japan's Modern Myths. Ideology in the Late Meiji Period* (Princeton, NJ: Princeton University Press, 1985), 225. Also, Watanabe Masakichi, *Jikken Nihon Shûshinsho Nyûmon. Kan ichi. Jinjô Shôgaku Seitoyô* [Trial Text for an Introduction to Japanese Ethics. Vol.1. For Students in Elementary School] (Tokyo: Kinkôdô Shoseki, 1895), chs. 18, 19, and the text in note 23.

37 Monbushô [Ministry of Education], *Jinjô Shôgakkô Shushinsho* [Ordinary Primary School Ethics Text] (Tokyo: Monbushô, 1940), 10–20, here 16.
38 Ibid., 20.
39 For "The Emperor as the Father," see Ohnuki-Tierney, *Kamikaze*, 77–9, citation 78. See Stefan Tanaka, *Japan's Orient. Rendering Pasts into History* (Berkeley: University of California Press, 1993), 132–3.
40 Morohashi Tetsuji, *Daikanwa Jiten* [Great Chinese-Japanese Dictionary], 13 vols. (Tokyo: Taishûkan Shoten, 1957),4:971–2.
41 Hirota, *Rikugun Shôkô no Kyôikushakaishi*, 187.
42 Rikugun Shikan Gakkô hen [Army Academy] (ed.), *Rikugun Shikan Gakkô Ichiran* [Army Academy Overview] (Heiji Zasshisha, 1904), 111, cited in ibid., 176.
43 Itô et al., *Tôjô Naikaku Sôridaijin Kimitsu Kiroku*, 15, 17, 31.
44 Tôjô Yûko, *Daitôasensô no Shinjitsu* [The Truth about the Greater East Asia War] (Tokyo: Wakku Co., 2005), 27–33.
45 Akamatsu, *Tôjô Hishokan Kimitsu Nisshi*, 150–1. For the complete statement, see Chapter 4. See also Itô et al., *Tôjô Naikaku Sôridaijin Kimitsu Kiroku*, 552–3. Also cited in Watanabe, *From Marco Polo Bridge*, 249.
46 Higashikuni Naruhiko, *Higashikuni Nikki* [Higashikuni Diary] (Tokyo: Tokuma Shoten, 1968), 93.
47 Humphreys, *Way of the Heavenly Sword*, 106. This military "thought" came from General Araki Sadao. See his *Kôgun no Hongi* [Basic Principles of the Imperial Army] issued in 1928.
48 Hata Ikuhiko, *Gendaishi no Sôten* [The Issues of Modern History] (Tokyo: Bungei Shunjû, 1998), 172–3. For an episode, see Yamauchi Takeo, "'Honorable Death' on Saipan," in *Japan at War. An Oral History*, eds. Haruko Taya Cook and Theodore F. Cook (New York: The New Press, 1992), 281–92. For descriptions with illustrations, see Earhart, *Certain Victory*, 375–408.
49 Itô et al., *Tôjô Naikaku Sôridaijin Kimitsu Kiroku*, 478–9. Akamatsu, *Tôjô Hishokan Kimitsu Nisshi*, 82.
50 Itô et al., *Tôjô Naikaku Sôridaijin Kimitsu Kiroku*, 504–5. Statement from mid-May 1943.
51 Ibid., 535–8.
52 Akamatsu, *Tôjô Hishokan Kimitsu Nisshi*, 87–8.
53 Ibid., 49.
54 See, for example, Watanabe, *From Marco Polo Bridge*, 113–16. The investigations into relative industrial capacities then, and this recent work, demonstrate the powers of deception of the nation-state.
55 Takeda, "Tôjô Hideki—Shôwa no Higeki no Taikensha," 38; Tsutsui, "Shôwa Rikugun no Habatsu Kôsô—Maegaki ni Tsutaete," 26–30. Tôjô was Kwantung Army chief of staff from March 1, 1937, to May 30, 1938.

56 Akamatsu, *Tôjô Hishokan Kimitsu Nisshi*, 59. Statement from the beginning of March 1942.
57 Itô et al., *Tôjô Naikaku Sôridaijin Kimitsu Kiroku*, 518–20.
58 Ôtani Keijirô, *Shôwa Kempeishi* [History of the Shôwa Military Police] (Tokyo: Misuzu Shobô, 1987), 442–3, 453–4. Wetzler, *Hirohito and War*, 74–5.
59 Itô et al., *Tôjô Naikaku Sôridaijin Kimitsu Kiroku*, 4.
60 Ibid., 41–2.
61 Takeda, "Tôjô Hideki—Shôwa no Higeki no Taikensha," 49–50. Leslie Russell Oates, *Populist Nationalism in Prewar Japan. A Biography of Nakano Seigo* (Sydney: George Allen & Unwin, 1985). Summarized in Wetzler, *Hirohito and War*, 76–8.
62 For the introduction above and plan below, see Itô et al., *Tôjô Naikaku Sôridaijin Kimitsu Kiroku*, 536–7.
63 See Totani, *Tokyo War Crimes Trial*, passim. This is a long-discussed problem well covered by Totani.
64 Found in the *Shĭji*, compilation completed c. 91 BC. "The Scribe's Record" or "Records of the Grand Historian" by Sima Qian. See Burton Watson, *Records of the Grand Historian of China. Translated from the Shih Chi of Ssu-Ma Ch'ien*, 2 vols. (New York: Columbia University Press, 1961), 1:90.
65 Ôoka Tadasuke became famous during his time as a magistrate (*bugyô*) in Edo for his fair and lenient decisions. Due to his good reputation he was similarly active in various domains (*kuni*) and toward the end of his life made the Lord (*daimyô*) of Mikawa-kuni, the eastern part of present-day Aichi Prefecture.
66 Itô et al., *Tôjô Naikaku Sôridaijin Kimitsu Kiroku*, 525–6. The numerous illusions to classical Chinese and Japanese works here and elsewhere lead me to speculate that the secretaries who recorded what Tôjô said embellished the record somewhat. See the *Kôjien* for my reference information.
67 Ibid., 526.
68 Ibid., 478.
69 Akamatsu, *Tôjô Hishokan Kimitsu Nisshi*, 72. For a brief description of the former, see H. Paul Varley, *Imperial Restoration in Medieval Japan* (New York: Columbia University Press, 1971), 26–8. For a brief description and translation of this code, see David J. Lu, *Japan: A Documentary* History, 2 vols. (Armonk, NY: M.E. Sharpe, 1997), 1:106–7, 109–116.
70 Ôyama, *Nihon Shoki*, 5–21. Michael I. Como, *Shôtoku, Ethnicity, Ritual, and Violence in the Japanese Buddhist Tradition* (Oxford: Oxford University Press, 2008), 4–8, 86, 164–5.
71 Itô et al., *Tôjô Naikaku Sôridaijin Kimitsu Kiroku*, 516.
72 Akamatsu, *Tôjô Hishokan Kimitsu Nisshi*, 14.
73 Maruyama Masao, *Zôhohan, Gendai Seiji no Shisô to Kôdô* [Modern Political Thought and Action, Revised Edition] (Tokyo: Miraisha, 1964), 20, cited in Hirota, *Rikugun Shôkô no Kyôikushakaishi*, 228.

74　Sawada Shigeru, *Sanbojichô Sawada Shigeru Kaisôroku* (Memoirs of Vice-Cheif of Staff Sawada Shigeru], ed. Morimatsu Toshio (Tokyo: Fuyô Shobô, 1982), 310. For the officer candidates, see Hirota, *Rikugun Shôkô no Kyôikushakaishi*, 228, quoting from a diary by Sugimatsu Tomoyuki, March 8, 1927. (Hirohito's enthronement ceremony had yet to take place.)

75　See, for example, John S. Brownlee (ed.), *History in the Service of the Japanese Nation* (Toronto: Joint Centre on Modern East Asia, 1983). Stefan Tanaka, *Japan's Orient*.

76　Saburô Ienaga, *Japan's Past, Japan's Future. One Historian's Odyssey*, trans. Richard H. Minear (Lanham, MD: Rowman & Littlefield Publishers, 2001), 81. Hasegawa Ryôichi, *Kôkokushikan to iu Mondai*, 28–30 and passim.

77　Tachibana Takashi. *Tennô to Tôdai* [The Emperor and Tokyo University], 2 vols. (Tokyo: Bungei Shunjû, 2005), 2:203–4. Hasegawa Ryôichi, *Kôkokushikan to iu Mondai*, 39.

78　"Ogura Kuraji Jij. Nikki," 173.

79　For Hiraizumi, see Hata, *Hirohito*, 62; for the plot, see 68–70.

80　Hasegawa Ryôichi, *Kôkokushikan to iu Mondai*, 56–7. See Sakamoto Tarô, Ienaga Saburô, Inoue Mitsusada, and Ôno Susumu (eds. and annotators), *Nihon Shoki* [Chronicles of Japan], in *Nihon Koten Bungaku Taikei* [Great Collection of Japanese Classical Literature], vols. 67, 68 (Tokyo: Iwanami Shoten, 1967 and 1965), 67:146–9. W.G. Aston (trans.), *Nihongi. Chronicles of Japan from the Earliest Times to A.D. 697* (London: George Allen & Unwin, 1896; Repr. 1956), 69–70. For Ise Shintô, see Mark Teeuwen, *Watarai Shintô: An Intellectual History of the Outer Shrine in Ise* (Leiden: Research School CNWS, 1996).

81　Kitabatake Chikafusa, *Jinnô Shôtôki* [Succession of the Divine Sovereigns], 1339–43, in *Nihon Koten Bungaku Taikei* [Great Collection of Japanese Classical Literature], vol. 87, eds. and annotators Iwasa Masashi, Tokieda Motoki, and Kidô Saizô (Tokyo: Iwanami Shoten, 1965), 41. H. Paul Varley (trans.), *A Chronicle of Gods and Sovereigns. Jinnô Shôtôki of Kitabatake Chikafusa* (New York: Columbia University Press, 1980), 49. Varley's translation.

82　Tachibana, *Tennô to Tôdai*, 2:211–12.

83　Ibid., 206. For another example of Hiraizumi's vision of the meaning of Kitabatake's work for Imperial Japan see a lecture published by the Navy Technical Research Institute: Hiraizumi Kiyoshi, *Jinnô Shôtôki ni tsuite* [On the Jinnô Shôtôki] (Tokyo: Kaigun Gijutsu Kenkyûjo, April 27, 1936).

84　Hiraizumi Kiyoshi, *Higeki Jûsô* [Tragic Traverse] (Tokyo: Kôgakukan Daigaku Shuppanbu, 1980), cited in Tachibana, *Tennô to Tôdai*, 2:213. Therein is a 1932 to 1940 chronology of reminiscences (lecture, 416–17). On the length of the sword, 2 *shaku* 5 *sun* = 75.75 cm, 29.82 in. Minamoto Sanetomo was the third and last Minamoto shogun. Assassinated at age twenty-seven, he was in his day better known for his learning and poetry than martial prowess. Delmer M. Brown and

Ichirô Ishida, *The Future and the Past. A Translation and Study of the Gukanshô, an Interpretive History of Japan Written in 1219* (Berkeley: University of California Press, 1979), 190-1.

85 Tachibana, *Tennô to Tôdai*, 2, 220-1. Hiraizumi, *Higeki Jûsô*, 417-18.
86 For an overview, see Tsutsui, "Shôwa Rikugun no Habatsu Kôsô—Maegaki ni Tsutaete," 9-34.
87 On the suppression of the army peace faction, see Yamamoto, *Nihon Rikugun Sensô Shûketsu Katei no Kenkyû*, 256.
88 Satô Eisaku, *Satô Eisaku Nikki* [Satô Eisaku Diary] (Tokyo: Asahi Shimbun, 1999). The diary covers only the postwar years from 1952 to 1975. Several very important years, 1955, and 1957 to 1960 are not included because someone borrowed the notes from these years and they disappeared (Introduction by Itô Takashi).
89 Totani, *Tokyo War Crimes Trial*, 39-40, 271n57.
90 Itô et al., *Tôjô Naikaku Sôridaijin Kimitsu Kiroku*, 526.
91 Totani, *Tokyo War Crimes Trial*, 97. Butow, *Tojo and the Coming of the War*, 218n59, 224. For an excerpt from Tôjô's affidavit, see Kiyose, *Hiroku*, 150-2.
92 Minear, *Victor's Justice*, 114-5n83, citing the original Trial Proceedings.
93 Thomas F.X. Noble, *Late Antiquity: Crisis and Transformation*, 2 vols. (Chantilly, VA: The Teaching Co., 2008), 1:260. Noble terms this "an old motto in Roman law."

Chapter 4

1 Butow, *Tojo and the Coming of the War*, 430.
2 For the Tôjô-Okada meeting, see Itô, *Takagi Sôkichi, Nikki to Jôhô*, 2:747-8; for Takagi's dislike of Tôjô, see 746-7. The meeting account is from the "Okada Taishô Tôjô Shushô Kaikenki" [Admiral Okada, Prime Minister Tôjô Meeting Record]. Shôji Junichirô, "Konoe Fumimaro. Amerika to iu 'Maboroshi' in Kaketa Seijika" [Konoe Fumimaro. A Politician in Pursuit of an Illusion of America], in *Shôwashi kôgi 3—ri- da- tôshite miru sensô he no michi* [Lectures on Shôwa History 3—Looking at the Road to War Through Leaders], ed. Tsutsui Kiyotada (Tokyo: Chikuma Shinsho, 2017), 183-202, 195-6.
3 Prince Higashikuni's diary, cited in Drea, *Service of the Emperor*, 193.
4 Butow, *Tojo and the Coming of the War*, 433n60.
5 Butow, *Japan's Decision to Surrender*, 26-8, esp. n58.
6 Bix, *Hirohito*, 476-8.
7 Ibid., 478.
8 For the following, see STJR, CD 32, 108-9, July 13, 1944; Tokyo Shoseki, 9:387-8. Of course Bix did not have this record at his disposal when he wrote his book. Here I am not interested in refuting Bix's work. Others, for example George Akita, ch. 1, n106, have already done this.

9   STJR, CD 32, 111, July 17, 1944; Tokyo Shoseki, 9:390–1.
10 Haruko Taya Cook, "The Myth of the Saipan Suicides," *MHQ*, 7, no. 3 (Spring 1995): 12–19, cited in Drea, *Japan's Imperial Army*, 240.
11 STJR, CD 32, 112, 114, 18 July 1944. Tokyo Shoseki, 9, 391–4.
12 Now it is generally acknowledged that the Japanese had primitive radar equipment as early as 1942. But up until the end of the war it was not functionally important. Nakahara Shigetoshi, *Kokuryoku naki Sensô Shidô* [Managing a War with No National Resources] (Tokyo: Hara Shobô, 1989), 208–9, maintains both the army and navy did extensive research on radar but in the end they failed completely to develop any useful equipment. Bôeichô Bôeikenkyûsho Senshishitsu Defense Agency, Institute for Defense Studies, War History Office], *Rikugun Kôkû no Gunbi to Gunyô. Shûsen Made* [Army Air Force Armament and Uses, to the End of the War] (Tokyo: Asagumo Shuppansha, 1976), 3:233, says the first squadron of army aircraft equipped with radar was formed in June 1944.
13 Watanabe, *From Marco Polo Bridge*, 173–4. Tsunoda Tadashige, *Waga Tôjô Hideki Ansatsu Keikaku* [Our Plan to Assassinate Tôjô Hideki] (Tokyo: Tokuma Shoten, 1985).
14 Suzuki, *"Shûsen" no Seijishi*, 72–80.
15 Itô, *Takagi Sôkichi, Nikki to Jôhô*, 2:751–2, my translation. A key pronoun, "that," is unclear. One might interpret it to mean that nothing can be done even in the event of an act of terror. Or, one might say it means with such a drastic event as terror with no plan or objective one has no choice but to do something. Professor Kawamura seems to be of the latter opinion, meaning Kido implies here he favored a cabinet change, even involving violence if necessary. I am of the former opinion, supported by a Japanese philologist. For this and the following, see Kawamura, *Emperor Hirohito*, 132.
16 Suzuki, *"Shûsen" no Seijishi*, 93.
17 Bôeichô, *Daihon'ei Rikugunbu*, 8:496–508. Many sources are quoted showing these discussions, including diaries by Konoe Fumimaro, Kido Kôichi, and Prince Higashikuni Naruhiko.
18 Suzuki, *"Shûsen" no Seijishi*, 77–8.
19 Ibid., 78–9. Suzuki, citing Tôjô's Chief Cabinet Secretary Hoshino Naoki, says that Kishi's support of those seeking to bring down the Tôjô Cabinet may well have been done with an eye to his own future after the war had been lost (95).
20 Kawamura, *Emperor Hirohito*, 123; for the war in China, see 75; for the beginning of the war with the US and her allies, see 112–16; for mid-1943, see 118–19.
21 Suzuki, *"Shûsen" no Seijishi*, 112, 117–18.
22 For a startling graphic presentation of Japan's poor situation, see Nakahara, *Kokuryoku naki Sensô Shidô*, 217, figures taken from this graph; for the comparison, see 218; for the comparative lack of resources and lack of interest in these matters, see 212–42.

23 Nakazawa Tasuku Publication Group, *Sakusen Buchô*, 5–10.
24 Suzuki Kantarô, *Suzuki Kantarô Jiden*, 309–12, esp. 309–10.
25 Watanabe, *From Marco Polo Bridge*, 113–16; 114 for the Okada citation. For a comparison of various war-relevant materials, see Table 4, "National Strength of Japan, U.S. in *c.* 1940."
26 Takasugi Yôhei, "Suzuki Tei'ichi—Seibirô wo Tsuita Gunjin" [Suzuki Tei'ichi—the Suit Wearing Soldier], in *Shôwashi Kôgi, Gunjin-hen* [Lectures on Shôwa History, Military Personnel Volume], ed. Tsutsui Kiyotada (Tokyo: Chikuma Shinsho, 2018), 87–104, 94–103.
27 "Ishii Akiho no Shuki" [Ishii Akiho Memoranda], in *Gunmu Kyokuchô Mutô Akira Kaisôroku* [Military Affairs Bureau Chief Mutô Akira Memoirs], eds. Mutô Akira and Jôhô Yoshio (Tokyo: Fuyô Shobô, 1981), 235–75, 262–4. *Mutô Kaisôroku*, 393. Yamada Akira and Kawamura Noriko both say he was a war advocate. Yamada, *Shôwa Tennô no Gunjishisô to Senryaku*, 165–6; Kawamura, *Emperor Hirohito*, 97. Takasugi Yôhei presents a differentiated evaluation. Takasugi Yôhei, "Mutô Akira—'Seijiteki Gunjin' no Jitsuzô" [Mutô Akira—the Real Character of a "Political Soldier"], in Tsutsui, *Shôwashi Kôgi, Gunjin-hen*, 105–22, 117–21.
28 Akamatsu, *Tôjô Hishokan Kimitsu Nisshi*, 150–1. "Ikki" normally refers to a fighter plane, but later in the text "special boats" are also specifically mentioned. See also Itô et al., *Tôjô Naikaku Sôridaijin Kimitsu Kiroku*, 552–3. Cited also in Watanabe, *From Marco Polo Bridge*, 249.
29 Akamatsu, *Tôjô Hishokan Kimitsu Nisshi*, 154–5. Itô et al., *Tôjô Naikaku Sôridaijin Kimitsu Kiroku*, 555, dated June 28.
30 Bôeichô, *Daihon'ei Kaigunbu*, 6:13–15.
31 Okabe Nagaakira, *Aru Jiju no Kaisôki—Gekidô Jidai no Shôwa Tennô* [Record of the Recollections of a Chamberlain—the Shôwa Emperor's Turbulent Times] (Tokyo: Asahi Sonorama, 1990), 147.
32 For this and the following, see Nakahara, *Kokuryoku naki Sensô Shidô*, 253–6.
33 Ibid., 218.
34 Bôeichô, *Kaigun Shôgô Sakusen (2)*, 109.
35 Nagatsuka, *I Was a Kamikaze*, 60.
36 For this and the following, see former Vice-Chief of the General Staff Kawabe Torashirô, "Ichigayadai kara Ichigayadai he," Shôwa 19.7.18–20.8.14 [From Ichigaya Heights to Ichigaya Heights, July 18, 1944–August 14, 1945], 7 vols., 5:324–325–1. On p. 1 of vol. 1 Kawabe dates the record of his recollections to 1954, and his Introduction in the first book below, deleted in the second, is dated end of July 1954. MS, NIDS Military Archives, Tokyo. The two books by Kawabe are based in part on this manuscript: (1) *Ichigayadai kara Ichigayadai he, Saigo no Sanbô Jichô no Kaisôroku* [From Ichigaya Heights to Ichigaya Heights, Recollections Record of the Last Vice-Chief of the Army General Staff] (Tokyo: Jiji Tsûshinsha, 1962).

(2) *Kawabe Torashirô Kaisôroku. Ichigayadai kara Ichigayadai he* [Recollections Record of Kawabe Torashirô. From Ichigaya Heights to Ichigaya Heights] (Tokyo: Mainichi Shimbunsha, 1979). The first book, published two years after Kawabe's death, is closer to the original manuscript. In the latter volume the original MS has been extensively edited and includes excerpts from his diary. Each book deletes different portions of the above manuscript. The morbid description of the lack of aviation gasoline and the consequences are included in both. See Kawabe (1962), 222–4, citation 223; Kawabe (1979), 133–4. Ichigayadai is in central Tokyo. It was the location of the Imperial Army General Staff and Ministry. It is now the location of the Japan Defense Ministry.

37 Suzuki, *"Shûsen" no Seijishi*, 44. See also, Watanabe, *From Marco Polo Bridge*, 113–16.
38 Suzuki, *"Shûsen" no Seijishi*, 20–2. He cites both the Sanbôhonbu, *Sugiyama Memo*, 2:470–1 and Bôeichô, *Daihon'ei Rikugunbu*, 7:207–8. In the former source Privy Council President Hara expressed concerns about cooperation between the army and navy during the conference (471–2).
39 Bôeichô, *Daihon'ei Kaigunbu*, 6:12–16, esp. 15–16.
40 For the Kobe–Nagoya convoy, see Komamiya Shinshichirô, *Senji Yusô Sendanshi* [History of Wartime Freight Ship Convoys] (Tokyo: Kyôdôsha, 1987), 164–5; for the May 25, disaster, see 178; for the Kobe–Yokosuka voyage, see 170; for April to June, see various entries 158–92. This history includes notations about specific convoys: departure port and destination, respective dates, names of freighters and navy war ships accompanying them, and brief commentaries on some but not all of the convoys. According to a short list of sources the work is based on numerous primary sources from the Defense Agency War History Office, Ministry of Health and Welfare, Japan Post Shipping Co., Osaka Merchant Marine Mitsui Marine Co., Shôwa Merchant Marine Co., etc. However, there are no footnotes indicating the source(s) of individual notations. No one at the NIDS, Military Archive could say in February 2016 how much aviation gasoline was in one can. Komamiya estimates that during the war approximately 2,400 freight and transport vessels amounting to some 8 million gross tons were lost (406–7). He says that this comes to 80.6 percent of the ships available in Japan. By comparison 24.5 percent of the buildings, 34.2 percent of her industrial machinery, and 20.5 percent of the household effects were destroyed. A later work confirms the inordinate loss of shipping (80.2 percent): Nakamura Takafusa and Miyazaki Masayasu, *Shiryô. Taiheiyô Sensô Higai Chôsa Hôkoku* [Historical Documents. Survey Report on Pacific War Damage] (Tokyo: Tokyo University Press, 1995), 310.
41 Bôeichô, *Daihon'ei Kaigunbu*, 6:119. Drea, *Japan's Imperial Army*, 229–30.
42 Dômei Tsûshinsha Seikeibu, *Hisshô no Daidô*, 177–80. There is no mention of this issue in STJR at this time. But many of the persons who regularly had audiences

with the Emperor, for example, Prime Minister Tôjô and Lord Keeper of the Privy Seal Kido, may have mentioned it to him without the topic being noted in this record. Also the chiefs of staff may have mentioned it in their daily reports to the throne, but one cannot know this definitely as the notations usually only say the Emperor received a report on the war situation in one or the other area.

43 STJR, CD 32, 38, March 3, 1944; Tokyo Shoseki, 9:306–7.
44 STJR, CD 32, 44–5, March 17, 1944; Tokyo Shoseki, 9:314–5. A side note of interest: Kishi Nobusuke, future postwar prime minister (1957–60) and grandfather of Prime Minister Abe Shinzô, had an audience with the Emperor on March 27, 1944, as minister of state and reported on the disposition of materials in 1944 (STJR, CD 32, 49). He served in the Tôjô Cabinet from October 18, 1941–July 22, 1944, first as minister of commerce and industry, then minister of state after it was abolished November 1, 1943. He left office with the fall of the cabinet and first served again in a cabinet from December 23, 1956, as foreign minister; later his cabinet succeeded the Ishibashi Cabinet on February 25, 1957. He was especially interested in abolishing Article Nine of the 1947 Constitution forbidding maintenance of military forces, like his grandson Abe.
45 STJR, CD 32, 51–2, 89, March 30, June 12, 1944; Tokyo Shoseki, 9:322, 365.
46 STJR, CD 32, 52, March 31, 1944; Tokyo Shoseki, 9:323. The number and types of ships are not noted.
47 Drea, *Japan's Imperial Army*, 230.
48 Bôeichô, *Daihon'ei Kaigunbu*, 6:126–7.
49 In Sanbô Honbu Shozô, *Haisen no Kiroku*, the table of contents shows that from mid-1944 there were an increasing number of conferences dealing with ship procurement and shipping problems. For details, see Yamada, *Daigensui Shôwa Tennô*, 274–5, 328–9.
50 Komamiya, *Senji Yusô Sendanshi*, 37, 25.
51 Ibid., 383–4. In Sanbô Honbu Shozô, *Haisen no Kiroku*, the table of contents shows that especially tank ships for transporting oil and gasoline were a problem.
52 Bôeichô, *Daihon'ei Kaigunbu*, 6:348–9.
53 Yamamoto Chikao, "Kokka Sôryokusen Zuen no Keikaku to Jisshi" [National Total War, War Games Planning and Actuation], in *Tsuisô Kaigunchûshô Nakazawa Tasuku* [Recollection about Vice-Admiral Nakazawa Tasuku], ed. Suikôkai [Navy Support Association] (Tokyo: Tsuisô Kaigunchûshô Nakazawa Tasuku Kankôkai, 1978), 96–7.
54 Bôeichô, *Daihon'ei Kaigunbu*, 6:350–3.
55 Watanabe, *From Marco Polo Bridge*, 115.
56 David C. Evans and Mark R. Peattie, *Kaigun. Strategy, Tactics, and Technology in the Imperial Japanese Navy, 1887–1941* (Annapolis, MD: Naval Institute Press, 1997), 434–5.
57 Dainihonteikoku no nazo Kensho I'inkai, *Taiheiyô Sensô Tsûsetsu no Uso*, 214–19.

58 The 1931 *Heibonsha Daihyakka Jiten*, cited in Kang Sang-jung. *Kang Sang-jung no Seijigaku Nyûmon* [Kang Sang-jung's Introduction to Political Science] (Tokyo: Shûeisha Shinsho, 2006), 15.
59 Watanabe, *From Marco Polo Bridge*, 113–16, citation 114.
60 Itô et al., *Tôjô Naikaku Sôridaijin Kimitsu Kiroku*, 514. As noted above, a closer look shows that the comparisons were of unlike personnel.
61 For the above four points and the following, see Nakazawa Tasuku Publication Group, *Sakusen Buchô*, 144–7.
62 For the submarine attack on June 19, see ibid., 146. On "out of range" tactics, see the editor's note, 147.
63 Mori, *Tokkô to ha Nanika*, 61–3.
64 Iguchi Takeo, *Demystifying Pearl Harbor. A New Perspective from Japan* [original Japanese title: *Kaisen Shinwa*), trans. David Noble (Tokyo: International House of Japan, 2010), 62.

Chapter 5

1 Dower, *Cultures of War*, 216.
2 Suzuki, *"Shûsen" no Seijishi*, 112.
3 Ibid., 4.
4 Kawamura, *Emperor Hirohito*, 123.
5 Ian Kershaw, *The End. Hitler's Germany 1944–45* (London: Allen Lane, 2011; Repr. Penguin Books, 2012), 55.
6 Earhart, *Certain Victory*, 461.
7 Kido Kôichi's diary and the Hirohito Monologue cited in Suzuki, *"Shûsen" no Seijishi*, 216. Kido, *Kido Kôichi Nikki*, 2:1221. Terasaki and Terasaki-Miller, *Shôwa Tennô Dokuhakuroku*, 129.
8 Yoshimi, *Shûsenshi*, 309–10, 319–21.
9 Suzuki Kantarô, *Suzuki Kantarô Jiden*, 313–14, 337–9. For a description of this work, see ch. 1, n36.
10 Suzuki, *"Shûsen" no Seijishi*, 186–7.
11 Miscamble, *Most Controversial Decision*, 96. For a summary and the citation, see Tsuyoshi Hasegawa (ed.), *The End of the Pacific War: Reappraisals* (Stanford, CA: Stanford University Press, 2007), 6–7. See esp. Frank, "Ketsu-Gô," 65–94.
12 Suzuki Tamon, "Emperor Hirohito's 'Sacred Decisions' and the Political Process of Japan's Surrender," in *Fifteen Lectures on Showa Japan. Road to the Pacific War in Recent Historiography*, ed. Tsutsui Kiyotada (Tokyo: Japan Publishing Industry Foundation for Culture, 2016), 257–75, 265–6. Butow, *Japan's Decision to Surrender*, 58–9, 77–8.

13 Suzuki, *"Shûsen" no Seijishi*, 152–3, 164, 172. Suzuki, "Emperor Hirohito's 'Sacred Decisions,'" 266–7, 271. Frank, "Ketsu-Gô," 88–9.
14 Hatano, *Saishô Suzuki Kantarô no Ketsudan*, 75, 226–9.
15 See also, Suzuki Kantarô, *Suzuki Kantarô Jiden*, 294–5.
16 For the domestic situation, see Itô, *Takagi Sôkichi, Nikki to Jôhô*, 2:927. For Anami's response on the atomic bombs, see Suzuki, *"Shûsen" no Seijishi*, 168. Anami was well informed of the destruction caused by the Hiroshima bomb (203–4, n82). Richard B. Frank, *Downfall. The End of the Imperial Japanese Empire* (New York: Random House, 1999; Repr. London: Penguin Books, 2001), 290.
17 Suzuki, *"Shûsen" no Seijishi*, 192n6. For the two imperial decisions and Kawabe's feelings about them, see 187. Hatano, *Saishô Suzuki Kantarô no Ketsudan*, 175–6. Kawamura, *Emperor Hirohito*, 177–8. See also Shôji Junichirô, "Umezu Yoshijirô—'Atoshimatsu' Jinryoku shita Rikugun Taishô" [Umezu Yoshijirô—the Army General Who Assiduously Dealt with "Repercussions"], in *Shôwashi Kôgi, Gunjin-hen* [Lectures on Shôwa History, Military Personnel Volume], ed. Tsutsui Kiyotada (Tokyo: Chikuma Shinsho, 2018), 53–70, 65.
18 Gerhard Krebs, "Prinz Mikasa, der Zweite Weltkrieg und der Shôwa Tennô" (Prince Mikasa, the Second World War and the Shôwa Emperor), in *OAG Notizen 01/2018* (Tokyo: Deutsche Gesellschaft für Natur- und Völkerkunde Ostasiens, 2018), 12–53, here 31–2. The magazine *Sekai* August 1951, cited in "Shûsen Goro no Anami-san" [Mr. Anami Around War's End], in *Nihon no Sentaku, Dai Niji Sekai Taisen Shûsen Shiroku* [Japan's Options: World War II, Historical Record of Ending the War], ed. Gaimushô [Foreign Ministry], 3 vols. (Tokyo: Yamanote Shobô, 1990–91), 3:894, 973. For the Kyûjô Incident in some detail, see Itô, *Takagi Sôkichi, Nikki to Jôhô*, 2:928–9. For Anami suicide interpretation, see Tsunoda Fusako, *Isshi, Taizai wo Shasu. Rikugun Daijin Anami Korechika* [One Death, Forgive (My) Great Transgressions. Army Minister Anami Korechika] (Tokyo: Shinchôsha, 1980), 244–5.
19 Suzuki, *"Shûsen" no Seijishi*, 182–3. For the conspiracy, see Bôeichô, *Daihon'ei Rikugunbu*, 10:497–9, 503–5. Text based mainly on the Lt. Col. Takeshita Masahiko Memoranda [*Takeshita Masahiko Chûsa Shuki*]. Col. Hayashi presented a slightly different account of the meetings with Arao. See Hayashi Saburô, *Taiheiyô Sensô Rikusen Gaishi* [General History of Land Warfare in the Pacific War] (Tokyo: Iwanami Shinsho, 1951), 290–1; for Umezu, Shôji (2018), see 65–6. (For a different rendition of the conspiracies in English, see Kawamura, *Emperor Hirohito*, 178–80.)
20 Brown, *Nationalism in Japan*, 240, says Anami "'prostrated himself in tears' before the emperor and appealed to him to change his decision," to surrender. In an extended account Grand Chamberlain Fujita Hisanori says that everyone, including the Emperor, was in tears. Fujita Hisanori, *Jijûchô no Kaisô* [The Grand Chamberlain's Recollections] (Tokyo: Chûkô Bunko, 1987), 118–47, here 142–3.

Oki Shûji, *Anami Korechika Den* [Biography of Anami Korechika] (Tokyo: Kodansha, 1970), 10. "Shûsen Goro no Anami-san," 3:972–81, here 978–9.

21 Hayashi, *Taiheiyô Sensô Rikusen Gaishi*, 290–2. Sakomizu Hisatsune, *Shûsen no Shinsô*, 61–3. For a slightly different version, see Sakomizu, *Dainihon Teikoku Saigo no Yon ka Getsu*, 252–3. For Tôgô's reflections, see Tôgô Shigenori, *Tôgô Shigenori Shuki. Jidai no Ichimen* [Tôgô Shigenori Memoirs. One Aspect of an Age] (Tokyo: Hara Shobô, 1989), 366. For postwar interviewees, see Frank, "Ketsu-Gô," 259n39.

22 Butow, *Japan's Decision to Surrender*, 199–220, esp. 199–200, 203–4, 212–13, 219–220. Gunjishi Gakkai, *Daihon'ei Rikugunbu Sensô Shidô Han*, 2:751–65. Butow cites a wide variety of persons who were involved in these events. The Gunjishi Gakkai's (Military History Society) narrative is based on an account by Lt. Col. Takeshita Masahiko.

23 For this and the following, see "Shôwa 20 nen, 4 gatsu – 20.8. aida. Rikugun Daijin, Rikugun Taishô Anami Korechika Memo" [Memo of Gen Anami, War Minister, April–August 1945], MS NIDS Military Archives, April 12, 1699; Typescript, 3. For a detailed description of these events by Yasui Tôji see Oki, *Anami Korechika Den*, 9–15. Oki cites descriptions of Anami by thirteen persons at the beginning of his book, pp. 9–51. One is this portrait presented by Yasui on August 14, 1959. Previously Army Minister Anami recommended Yasui to Prime Minister Suzuki for the Cabinet Minister post, p. 16. Yasui enjoyed a close relationship with Anami. They attended the military prep school in Hiroshima and the Army Academy at the same time.

24 For the August 11 telegram, see Hatano, *Saishô Suzuki Kantarô no Ketsudan*, 177–8. For the August 14 telegram, see Yamada, *Shôwa Tennô no Gunjishisô to Senryaku*, 334–6. Itô, *Takagi Sôkichi, Nikki to Jôhô*, 2:926, also says a confidential telegram was sent to various units about controlling the troops on August 11.

25 For Navy Minister Yonai commenting to Takagi, see Itô, *Takagi Sôkichi, Nikki to Jôhô*, 2:928. For responses from commanders in the field on August 11, see Hatano, *Saishô Suzuki Kantarô no Ketsudan*, 176–7; for August 14, see Tsunoda, *Isshi, Taizai wo Shasu*, 229. For the visits overseas by imperial family members, see (Lt. Gen.) Arisue Seizô, *Shûsen Hishi. Arisue Kikanchô no Shuki* [Secret History of Ending the War. Arisue Liaison Bureau Chief Memoirs] (Tokyo: Fuyô Shobô, 1976), 48.

26 For Anami's order in the Army Ministry, see Itô, *Takagi Sôkichi, Nikki to Jôhô*, 2:926–7. For the farewell visit, see Suzuki Kantarô, *Suzuki Kantarô Jiden*, 305–6. Sakomizu was in Suzuki's office when Anami paid this visit. His rendition of events some years later is slightly different but confirms the account in Suzuki's autobiography, minus cigars. Sakomizu, *Shûsen no Shinsô*, 61–2. For Anami's request, see STJR CD 34, 46, August 14, 1945, Tokyo Shoseki, 9:768; for August 14, see CD 34, 43–9, Tokyo Shoseki, 9:764–71; for the emperor's announcement, see

CD 34, 46-7, Tokyo Shoseki, 9:768-70. The poem in Japanese, "Isshi motte taizai wo shashi tatematsuru," is well known, see, for example, "Anami Korechika" in the Japanese version of the Encyclopaedia Britannica. For Col. Hayashi, see Tsunoda, *Isshi, Taizai wo Shasu*, 228-9.

27 Tôgô, *Tôgô Shigenori Shuki*, 345. For the consequences if Army Minister Anami had resigned his cabinet office, or had he been murdered, see Sakomizu, *Shûsen no Shinsô*, 62-3. For Anami's statement to Minister Yasui, see Oki, *Anami Korechika Den*, 14; for Wakamatsu and Shimomura, see 32 and 35 respectively. Itô, *Takagi Sôkichi, Nikki to Jôhô*, 2:926-7, on August 12, Yonai told Takagi that he was ready to change his position when convinced that this would be more favorable for saving the nation (*kuni*).

28 "Anami Korechika Memo," August 9, 1805-9; Typescript, 50-2.

29 Ibid., July 14, 23, 25, 1819, 1821; Typescript, 54. August 8, 1799; Typescript, 48. For Anami's perceived options, see August 9, 1807; Typescript, 51. For the surrender conditions, see August 10, 1809; Typescript, 52. See also Hayashi, *Taiheiyô Sensô Rikusen Gaishi*, 254-5, 289-90; Gaimushô, *Nihon no Sentaku*... 1:364-5. For a short concise chronological account of Japan's surrender see again, Suzuki, "Emperor Hirohito's 'Sacred Decisions,'" 257-75.

30 Hayashi, "Shûsen Goro no Anami-san," 3:978-9.

31 For the Emperor's statement, see Sakomizu, *Shûsen no Shinsô*, 31-2; for the meetings below on August 10 and 12, see Gaimushô, *Nihon no Sentaku*... 3:882-3. Bôeichô, *Daihon'ei Rikugunbu*, 10:504-5.

32 Suzuki, *"Shûsen" no Seijishi*, 186-9.

33 Suzuki, "Emperor Hirohito's 'Sacred Decisions,'" 266-7, 269-71.

34 For this and the complete Imperial Rescript of August 14, 1945, broadcast on the radio the following day, see Butow, *Japan's Decision to Surrender*, 248; for the "Instruments of Surrender" below, see 249-50. For a study of the formulation of the Emperor's announcement to the people see Chaen Yoshio, *Misshitsu no Shûsen Shôchoku* [Imperial Edict Terminating the War (drafted) Behind Closed Doors] (Tokyo: Yûshôdô Shuppan, 1989).

35 For discussions on the "Byrnes Note," see, for example, Kawamura, *Emperor Hirohito*, 151-84, 167-77. For "unconditional surrender" mitigated by a "tacit understanding about preserving the monarchy," see Kenneth J. Ruoff, *The People's Emperor. Democracy and the Japanese Monarchy, 1945-1995* (Cambridge, MA: Harvard University Asia Center, 2001), 4. Whether or not this was so, depends on one's perspective. Certainly Secretary of State James Byrnes wanted absolute unconditional surrender. But Secretary of War Henry Stimson, Admiral William Leahy, and Secretary of the Navy James Forrestal for practical reasons argued for allowing Hirohito to remain emperor. Truman decided with the latter three. Yuma, *Tokyo War Crimes Trial*, 46-7. Japanese officials including the Emperor interpreted the note expansively, partly to encourage hope of saving the Imperial House, partly

to mollify the hardliners against accepting the Potsdam Proclamation. Suzuki, "Emperor Hirohito's 'Sacred Decisions,'" 268–71.
36 Dower, *Embracing Defeat*, 44.
37 Hayashi, *Taiheiyô Sensô Rikusen Gaishi*, 291.
38 For this and the following, see Suzuki, *"Shûsen" no Seijishi*, 111–14.
39 Original opinion paper quoted in ibid., 111.
40 Ibid., 112.
41 Hattori Takushirô, "Daitôa Sensô Shidô ni kan suru Kaisô Kiroku, Shôwa 16–20 nen" [Record of Recollections of Directing the Greater East Asia War, 1941–45], 85–6, MS, NIDS Military Archives, Tokyo.
42 Suzuki, *"Shûsen" no Seijishi*, 113. Lt. General Miyazaki Shûichi, head of 1st Department, Army General Staff oversaw the preparations for the home island defense. He did not participate in a suicide mission or commit suicide after the war. He died in 1969 at age seventy-four.
43 Iguchi, *Demystifying Pearl Harbor*, 62–3. Iguchi's father was assigned to the Japanese Embassy in Washington, DC, when the attack on Pearl Harbor occurred. Later he too became a diplomat in the Japanese Foreign Ministry. His book is another contribution to the debate about war responsibility in Japan. He seeks to relieve the Foreign Ministry and Japanese Embassy in Washington, DC, arguing the army was really responsible for holding up the final communication indicating a break-off of diplomatic relations with the United States and war, not the Foreign Ministry.
44 Kawabe, "Seiyô Minzoku no Aseia Seifuku to sono Bunpataru Beikoku," 1–4.
45 The most famous example of which is the "Nanjing Massacre." For a measured treatment, see Mitter, *China's War with Japan*, 119–40. For a clear summary, see Drea, *Japan's Imperial Army*, 259–61.
46 Suzuki, *"Shûsen" no Seijishi*, 189–90. Kawamura, *Emperor Hirohito*, 178–9.
47 Hasegawa Ryôichi, *Kôkokushikan to iu Mondai*, 31–43. For the textbook lawsuits, see Ienaga, *Japan's Past, Japan's Future*, 151–87. For Murao's role in the lawsuit, see "in the internet," webliojisho (weblio dictionary), s.v. "Murao to ha." For Hiraizumi, see Chapter 3 in this book. For official standard school texts see Gluck, *Japan's Modern Myths*, 123–4, 147; for right thought, see Hasegawa Ryôichi, *Kôkokushikan to iu Mondai*, 72–3.
48 For the following, see Nakazawa Tasuku Publication Group, *Sakusen Buchô*, 203–10.
49 Sawada Shigeru, *Sanbojichô Sawada Shigeru Kaisôroku* [Vice-Chief of Staff Sawada Shigeru Memoirs], ed. Morimatsu Toshio (Tokyo: Fuyô Shobô, 1982), 307–10, esp. 308–9. Hasegawa Ryôichi, *Kôkokushikan to iu Mondai*, 53–4.
50 Samuel B. Griffith (trans. and intro.), *Sun Tzu, The Art of War* (Oxford: Oxford University Press, 1963), 84, Griffith's translation.
51 Sawada, *Sanbojichô Sawada Shigeru Kaisôroku*, 310–15, esp. 312–13.

52 Nakazawa Tasuku Publication Group, *Sakusen Buchô*, 183. A phrase from a Kagoshima folk tale in southern Japan. Nakazawa was born and raised in far-away Nagano.
53 See, for example, Sei Shônagon (966–1017/1025). Ivan Morris (trans. and ed.), *The Pillow Book of Sei Shônagon*, 2 vols. (New York: Columbia University Press, 1967).
54 Suzuki Kantarô, *Suzuki Kantarô Jiden*, 341–3. The autobiography has nothing to say about events between the army revolt on February 26–29, 1936, and April 1945 when Suzuki was appointed prime minister. Suzuki Kantarô as a military leader, confident of Emperor Hirohito, and prime minister at war's end, has been extensively treated by Japanese scholars (see the endnotes to Suzuki, "Suzuki Kantarô to Nihon no 'Shûsen,'" but this remains to be adequately presented in English).
55 Suzuki Kantarô, *Suzuki Kantarô Jiden*, 341–8; for one year of a defeated Japan, see 343–5. On Suzuki's passivity, see Suzuki, "Suzuki Kantarô to Nihon no 'Shûsen,'" 257–86, 274. For a critique of the last part of the autobiography entitled "Circumstances at War's End," see Suzuki, "Suzuki Kantarô to Nihon no 'Shûsen,'" 280–1.
56 Suzuki, *"Shûsen" no Seijishi*, 215–17.
57 Oki, *Anami Korechika Den*, 34–5. Related by Shimomura Hiroshi. Sakomizu, *Dainihon Teikoku Saigo no Yon ka Getsu*, 251, includes Foreign Minister Tôgô Shigenori and Navy Minister Yonai Mitsumasa as key persons in this process.
58 We know little about the last chiefs of staff, Admiral Toyoda Soemu and General Umezu Yoshijirô. Both are portrayed as disciplined officers proud of their callings who, unlike many of their contemporaries, eschewed meddling in politics. For Umezu, see Jôhô Yoshio (ed.), *Saigo no Sanbôchô, Umezu Yoshijirô* [The Last Army Chief of Staff, Umezu Yoshijirô] (Tokyo: Fuyô Shobô, 1976), here 26–31. Toyoda's work is a somewhat self-flattering memoir (see below) and the work about Umezu a panegyric rather than a critical historical biography. For the court findings below, see Yanagisawa, *Toyoda Soemu Jutsu*, 252–6. An oddity: Army Chief of Staff Umezu, Navy Chief of Staff Toyoda, Army Minister Anami (all at war's end), and Shigemitsu Mamoru (foreign minister for one month immediately after capitulation) were all born between 1882 and 1887 in Ôita Prefecture, northern Kyushu. Umezu and Shigemitsu signed the surrender documents on the USS *Missouri* September 2, 1945.
59 Hosaka, *Shôwashi no Shinsô*, 134. Hosaka postulates that some of the officers committed suicide as a flight from reality: defeat was for them an unfathomable void (*kûkyoku*). Of course not all influential officers took this route. Among others besides Kawabe, as noted in Chapters 1 and 2, for example, Col. Hattori Takushirô and several other high-ranking officers did not.
60 "Hoshino Naoki Shuki" [Hoshino Naoki Notes], in Jôhô, *Tôjô Hideki*, 667–71, here 670.

61 Satô Sanae, *Tôjô Hideki Fûin Sareta Shinjitsu* [Tôjô Hideki, the Sealed Truth] (Tokyo: Kodansha, 1995), 254.
62 John R. Pritchard and Sonia Magbanna Zaide (eds.), *The Tokyo War Crimes Trial* (Complete transcripts of the proceedings of the International Military Tribunal for the Far East) (New York: Garland, 1981), 15, 36779–36781. The original Trial Proceedings, cited in Minear, *Victor's Justice*, 114–5, n83.
63 For this and a discussion of the applicability of the Pact and related concepts, see Katô Norihiro, Hashizume Daisaburô, and Takeda Seiji, *Tennô no Sensô Sekinin* [Emperor (Hirohito's) War Responsibility] (Tokyo: Komichi Shobô, 2000), 30–4.
64 Yuma, *Tokyo War Crimes Trial*, 51–7, 217.
65 Shôji, "Konoe Fumimaro. Amerika to iu 'Maboroshi' in Kaketa Seijika," 187–9.
66 For this and the following, see Tillich, *Systematic Theology*, 13–18.
67 Hasegawa Ryôichi, *Kôkokushikan to iu Mondai*, 79; for the citation, see 69.
68 For another extended account of the war ending process in Japan, including the Emperor's role in it, by Prime Minister Suzuki's chief cabinet secretary, see Sakomizu, *Dainihon Teikoku Saigo no Yon ka Getsu*, esp. "Kôbô wo Kakeru Hachinichikan" [Risking Destiny for Eight Days], "Saigo no Gozen Kaigi" [The Last Imperial Conference], and "Tsui ni Jitsugen Shita Shûsen" [War's End Finally Realized], 183–290. For many years the actual role of the emperor in politics and military affairs, including ending the war, was simply deleted from histories written in the West. See, for example, Brown, *Nationalism in Japan*. See also W.G. Beasley, *The Modern History of Japan* (New York: Frederick A. Praeger, 1963). When discussed Hirohito was presented as depicted by Robert J.C. Butow (Chapter 1) and much later debunked by Yamada Akira.
69 Alexander Demandt, *Philosophie der Geschichte. Von der Antike zur Gegenwart* [The Philosophie of History. From the Ancient World to the Present] (Cologne: Böhlau Verlag, 2011), 321–34, here 321. Marcus Tullius Cicero (106–43 BC): "Omnis natura vult esse conservatrix sui." "Stets ist die Natur bemüht, sich selbst zu erhalten." Lucius Annaeus Seneca (4 BC–AD 65): "Nihil difficile naturae est, utique ubi in finem sui properat." "Nichts ist schwierig für die Natur, jedenfalls wenn sie ihrem Ende zueilt."

Bibliography

Reference works

Anzu Motohiko and Umeda Yoshihiko, eds. *Shintô Jiten* [Shintô Dictionary]. Osaka: Hori Shoten, 1968.

Itô Takashi and Suetake Yoshiya, eds. *Kin- Gendai Nihon Jinbutsu Shiryô Jôhô Jiten* [Dictionary of Modern and Contemporary Japanese Personal Source Information]. Tokyo: Yoshikawa Kôbunkan, 2004–2011. 4 vols.

Kokushi Daijiten [Great Dictionary of National History], ed. Kokushi Daijiten Henshû I'inkai [Great Dictionary of National History Editorial Committee]. Tokyo: Yoshikawa Kôbunkan, 1979–97. 17 vols.

Morohashi Tetsuji. *Daikanwa Jiten* [Great Chinese-Japanese Dictionary]. Tokyo: Taishûkan Shoten, 1957. 13 vols.

Nihon Kin- Gendaishi Jiten Henshû I'inkai, eds. *Nihon Kin- Gendaishi Jiten* [Japanese Dictionary of Modern and Contemporary History]. Tokyo: Tôyô Keizai Shinpôsha, 1978.

Papinot, E. *Historical and Geographical Dictionary of Japan*. Tokyo: Sansaisha, 1909.

Toyama Misao, ed. and Jôhô Yoshio, sup. ed. *Rikukaigun Shôkan Jinji Sôran* [A Personnel Compendium of (High Ranking) Army and Navy Officers]. Tokyo: Fuyô Shobô, 1981. 2 vols.

Primary sources

Akamatsu Sadao. *Tôjô Hishokan Kimitsu Nisshi* [The Secret Diary of Tôjô's Secretary]. Tokyo: Bungei Shunjûsha, 1985.

Arisue Seizô. *Shûsen Hishi. Arisue Kikanchô no Shuki* [Secret History of Ending the War. Arisue Liaison Bureau Chief Memoirs]. Tokyo: Fuyô Shobô, 1976.

Daihon'ei Rikugunbu Jôsô Kankei Shiryô [The Imperial Headquarters Army Department Records Relating to Imperial Audiences], ed. Comp. Yamada Akira and Matsuno Seiya. Tokyo: Gendai Shiryô Shuppan, 2005.

Daihon'ei Rikugunbu Sakusenbuchô Miyazaki Shûichi Chûshô Nisshi [Imperial Headquarters Army Department Operations Department Chief Lt. General Miyazaki Shûichi Diary], ed. Gunjishi Gakkai [Military History Society]. Tokyo: Kinseisha, 2003.

Daihon'ei Rikugunbu Sensô Shidô Han, Kimitsu Sensô Nisshi [Secret War Journal of the Imperial Headquarters, Army Dept. War Leadership Group], ed. Gunjishi Gakkai [Military History Society]. Tokyo: Kinseisha, 1998. 2 vols.

"Daitôa Sensô Shidô – Dai 2 Sakusen Shidô 16.12.8 – 19.10" [Greater East Asia War Leadership – No.2 Operations Leadership, December 8, 1941–October 1944]. Former Army Ministry, Military Affairs Department Head Satô Kenryô, 0409-0432, 0409. MS, NIDS Military Archives, Tokyo.

Doemming, H.W. von. *Was Will Japan?* [What does Japan Want?]. Jena: Eugen Diederichs Verlag, 1934.

Fujita Hisanori. *Jijûchô no Kaisô* [The Grand Chamberlain's Recollections]. Tokyo: Chûkô Bunko, 1987.

Haisen no Kiroku [War Defeat Documents], ed. Sanbô Honbu Shozô [Army General Staff Proprietors]. Tokyo: Hara Shobô, 1967.

Hattori Takushirô. "Daitôa Sensô Shidô ni kan suru Kaisô Kiroku, Shôwa 16 – 20 nen" [Record of Recollections of Directing the Greater East Asia War, 1941–45]. MS, NIDS Military Archives, Tokyo.

Hattori Takushirô. *Daitôa Sensô Zenshi* [A Complete History of the Great East Asia War]. 4 vols. Tokyo: Masu Shobô, 1953; Repr. Tokyo: Hara Shobô, 1965.

Hayashi Saburô Shuki. "Shûsen Goro no Anami-san" [Mr. Anami Around War's End], in "Hayashi Saburô Shuki" [Hayashi Saburô Memoirs], in *Nihon no Sentaku, Dai Niji Sekai Taisen Shûsen Shiroku* [Japan's Options: World War II, Historical Record of Ending the War], ed. Gaimushô [Foreign Ministry], 3:894, 972–89. Tokyo: Yamanote Shobô, 1991. 3 vols.

Heike Monogatari [Tale of Heike], in *Nihon Koten Bungaku Taikei* [Great Collection of Japanese Classical Literature], vols. 32, 33, eds. Takagi Ichinosuke, Ozawa Masao, Atsumi Kaoru, and Kindaichi Haruhiko. Tokyo: Iwanami Shoten, 1959–60.

Higashikuni Naruhiko. *Higashikuni Nikki* [Higashikuni Diary]. Tokyo: Tokuma Shoten, 1968.

Hiraizumi Kiyoshi. *Jinnô Shôtôki ni tsuite* [On the Jinnô Shôtôki]. Tokyo: Kaigun Gijutsu Kenkyûjo, April 27, 1936.

Hiraizumi Kiyoshi. *Higeki Jûsô* [Tragic Traverse]. Tokyo: Kôgakukan Daigaku Shuppanbu, 1980.

Hisshô no Daidô [The Road to Certain Victory]. *Tôjô Sôridaijin Gikai Enzetsu Tôben Shû* [Prime Minister Tôjô Speeches and Rejoinders in Parliament], ed. Dômei Tsûshinsha Seikeibu [Dômei News Agency, Politics and Economics Department]. Tokyo: Dômei Tsûshinsha, 1943.

"Hoshino Naoki Shuki" [Hoshino Naoki Notes], in *Tôjô Hideki*, ed. Jôhô Yoshio, 667–71. Tokyo: Fuyô Shobô, 1974.

"Ishii Akiho no Shuki" [Ishii Akiho Memoranda], in Mutô Akira, *Gunmu Kyokuchô Mutô Akira Kaisôroku* [Military Affairs Bureau Chief Mutô Akira Memoirs], ed. Jôhô Yoshio, 235–75. Tokyo: Fuyô Shobô, 1981.

Itô Shunichirô. *Tôjô Hideki Den, Shisei, Tetsu no Hito* [Tôjô Hideki Biography, Sincere, Man of Steel]. Tokyo: Tenyû Shobô, January 17, 1942; Repr. January 28, 1942.

Jijûbukan Jô Ei'ichirô Nikki [Aide-de-Camp Jô Ei'ichirô Diary], in *Kindai Nihon Shiryô Sensho* 4 [Anthology of Modern Japanese Historical Documents 4], ed. Nomura Minoru. Tokyo: Yamakawa Shuppansha, 1982.

"Jôsô. Kongo no Sakusen ni kan suru Ken" [Report to the Throne. Concerning Operations Hereafter], September 15, 1943, Navy General Staff Chief Nagano Osami; Army General Staff Chief Sugiyama Hajime, in *Daihon'ei Rikugunbu Jôsô Kankei Shiryô* [The Imperial Headquarters Army Department Records Relating to Imperial Audiences], eds. comp. Yamada Akira and Matsuno Seiya, 384–96. Tokyo: Gendai Shiryô Shuppan, 2005.

Kawabe Masakazu. *Nihon Rikugun Seishin Kyôikushi Kô* [An Interpretation of Japanese Army Spiritual Education History]. Tokyo: Hara Shobô, 1980. 2 vols.

Kawabe Torashirô "Seiyô Minzoku no Aseia Seifuku to sono Bunpataru Beikoku Aseia he no Shinshutsu ni Kan suru Gaisetsu" [Survey of the Subjugation of Asia by Western Nations and as a Part thereof America's Advance into Asia], Summer, 1946, MS, NIDS Military Archives, Tokyo.

Kawabe Torashirô. "Ichigayadai kara Ichigayadai he," Shôwa 19.7.18 – 20.8.14 [From Ichigaya Heights to Ichigaya Heights, July 18, 1944–August 14, 1945], vol. 5, 1954, MS, NIDS Military Archives, Tokyo. 7 vols.

Kawabe Torashirô. *Ichigayadai kara Ichigayadai he, Saigo no Sanbô Jichô no Kaisôroku* [From Ichigaya Heights to Ichigaya Heights, Recollections Record of the Last Vice-Chief of the Army General Staff]. Tokyo: Jiji Tsûshinsha, 1962.

Kawabe Torashirô. *Kawabe Torashirô Kaisôroku. Ichigayadai kara Ichigayadai he* [Recollections Record of Kawabe Torashirô. From Ichigaya Heights to Ichigaya Heights]. Tokyo: Mainichi Shimbunsha, 1979.

Kido Kôichi. *Kido Kôichi Nikki* [Kido Kôichi Diary]. Tokyo: Tokyo Daigaku Shuppankai, 1966. 2 vols.

Kido Kôichi Kankei Bunsho [Documents Relating to Kido Kôichi], ed. Kido Kôichi Kenkyûkai [Kido Kôichi Research Group]. Tokyo: Tokyo University Press, 1966.

Kitabatake Chikafusa. *Jinnô Shôtôki* [Succession of the Divine Sovereigns], 1339–43, in *Nihon Koten Bungaku Taikei* [Great Collection of Japanese Classical Literature], vol. 87, eds. annotators Iwasa Masashi, Tokieda Motoki, and Kidô Saizô. Tokyo: Iwanami Shoten, 1965.

Kokutai no Hongi [The Essential Principles of the National Polity], ed. Mombushô [Ministry of Education]. May 1943 edn. Tokyo: Mombushô, 1937.

Layton, Rear Admiral Edwin T. with Captain Roger Pineau and John Costello. *"And I Was There." Pearl Harbor and Midway—Breaking the Secrets*. Old Saybrook, CT: Konecky & Konecky, 1985.

Monbushô [Ministry of Education]. *Jinjô Shôgakkô Shushinsho* [Ordinary Primary School Ethics Text]. Tokyo: Monbushô, 1940.

Nakashiba Suezumi. *Kokumin Senjinkun* [Citizens Field Service Code]. Tokyo: Futami Shobô, 1943.

"Nakazawa Gunreibu Daiichi Buchô Nôto" [Navy General Staff, 1st Dept., Dept. Head Nakazawa Notes], including "Sakusen Sankô" [Operations Information] and

"Senkyô" [The War Situation]; "Dairokujûichi Kôkû Sentai Sentô Shôhô" [61st Air Squadron Detailed Combat Report], MS, NIDS Military Archives, Tokyo.

Nietzsche, Friedrich. *Nachgelassene Fragmente 1887-1889* [Posthumous Fragments], in *Friedrich Nietzsche Sämtliche Werke. Kritische Studien Ausgabe in 15 Bände* [Friedrich Nietzsche, the Complete Works. Critical Academic Edition in 15 Volumes], vol. 13, eds. Giorgio Colli and Mazzino Montinari Munich: Deutscher Taschenbuch Verlag GmbH & Co. KG, 1967-77.

Nihon no Sentaku, Dai Niji Sekai Taisen Shûsen Shiroku [Japan's Options: World War II, Historical Record of Ending the War], ed. Gaimushô [Foreign Ministry]. Tokyo: Yamanote Shobô, 1990-91, 3 vols.

Nihon Shoki [Chronicles of Japan], presented at court in 720, in *Nihon Koten Bungaku Taikei* [Great Collection of Japanese Classical Literature], vols. 67, and 68, eds. Annotators Sakamoto Tarô, Ienaga Saburô, Inoue Mitsusada, and Ôno Susumu. Tokyo: Iwanami Shoten, 1967, 1965.

"Ogura Kuraji Jijû Nikki" [Chamberlain Ogura Kuraji Diary], "Shôwa Tennô Senjishita no Nikugoe" [The Actual Voice of the Wartime Shôwa Emperor]. *Bungei Shunjû* 85, no. 5 (April 2007): 118-90.

Okabe Nagaakira. *Aru Jiju no Kaisôki—Gekidô Jidai no Shôwa Tennô* [Record of the Recollections of a Chamberlain—the Shôwa Emperor's Turbulent Times]. Tokyo: Asahi Sonorama, 1990.

"Ôtsuka Fumirô Bibôroku" [Ôtsuka Fumirô Memorandum], August 1-5, 1944, in 8:2285-2312, MS, NIDS Military Archives, Tokyo.

Ôtsuki Shizuo. "*Senjinkun*" *Kyôiku no Sankô* [Education Information on the "Field Service Code"]. Tokyo: Nippon Heisho Shuppan Kabushiki Kaisha, 1941.

Pickering, Ernest H. *Japan's Place in the Modern World*. London: George G. Harrap & Co. Ltd., 1936.

Pritchard, John R., and Sonia Magbanna Zaide eds. *The Tokyo War Crimes Trial* (Complete transcripts of the proceedings of the International Military Tribunal for the Far East). New York: Garland, 1981. 22 vols. + vols. 26-7.

Sakomizu Hisatsune. *Shûsen no Shinsô* [The True Facts About War's End]. Chiba-ken, Kashiwa-shi, Hikarigaoka no Dôtoku Kenkyûjo [Ethics Research Institute, Chiba Prefecture, Kashiwa City, Hikarigaoka], 1955.

Sakomizu Hisatsune. *Dainihon Teikoku Saigo no Yon ka Getsu* [The Last Four Months of Imperial Japan]. Tokyo: Oriento Shobô, 1973.

Sakusen Buchô, Jinji Kyokuchô Kaigun Chûshô Nakazawa Tasuku [Operations Department Head, Personnel Bureau Head, Navy Vice Admiral Nakazawa Tasuku], ed. Nakazawa Tasuku Kankôkai [Nakazawa Tasuku Publication Group]. Tokyo: Seiraikyô, 1979.

Sanada Jôichirô Shôshô Nikki [Major General Sanada Jôichirô Diary], October 1939 to December 1945, MS, NIDS Military Archives, Tokyo.

Satô Eisaku. *Satô Eisaku Nikki* [Satô Eisaku Diary]. Tokyo: Asahi Shimbun, 1999.

Satô Kenryô. *Daitôa Sensô Kaikoroku* [Greater East Asia War Memoirs]. Tokyo: Tokuma Shoten, 1966.

Sawada Shigeru. *Sanbojichô Sawada Shigeru Kaisôroku* [Vice-Chief of Staff Sawada Shigeru Memoirs], ed. Morimatsu Toshio. Tokyo: Fuyô Shobô, 1982.

Shirakawa Yoshinori. Guntai Kyôikurei [Army Education Proclamation]. Tokyo: Heiyô Tosho KK, 1927.

"Shôwa 20 nen, 4 gatsu – 20.8. aida. Rikugun Daijin, Rikugun Taishô Anami Korechika Memo" [Memo of Gen Anami, War Minister, April–August 1945), MS, NIDS Military Archives, Tokyo.

Shôwa Jûrokunen Jôsô Kankei Shoruisetsu [Materials Relating to Imperial Audiences in 1941, 1, September–December 1941]. "Daihon'ei Rikugunbu: Sammitsu Dai 438-go Dai 1" [Imperial Headquarters, Army Department: Secret Proceedings no. 438-1], MS, NIDS Military Archives, Tokyo.

Shôwa Tennô Dokuhakuroku, Terasaki Hidenari Goyôkakari Nikki [Shôwa Emperor Monologue, Imperial Household Liaison Officer Terasaki Hidenari Diary], eds. Terasaki Hidenari and Mariko Terasaki-Miller. Tokyo: Bungei Shunjû, 1991.

Shôwa Tennô Hatsugen Kiroku Shûsei [Collected Records of Remarks by the Shôwa Emperor], ed. Nakao Yûji. Tokyo: Fuyô Shobô Shuppan, 2003. 2 vols.

"Sugawara Michiô Chûshô Kaisôroku" [Recollections of Lt. General Sugawara Michiô]. "Seishin Kyôiku yori Kan taru Kôkûhei Ichi Butaichô no Kaisô" [Recollections of the Commander of the 1st Army Air Unit Seen from the Perspective of Spiritual Education], ch. 5 "Rekidai Taichô no Shidô Seishin" [Leadership Spirit of Successive Unit Commanders]; ch. 6 "Gunjin Seishin no Shôchô" [Rise and Fall of the Soldiers Spirit]; "Shiseikan" [View of Living and Dying], in "Dairoku Kôkûgun Shireikan de atta Sugawara Michiô Chûshô Kaisô" [Recollections of Lt. General Sugawara Michiô Commander of the 6th Army Air Force], MS, NIDS Military Archives, Tokyo.

Sugiyama Memo [Sugiyama Memoranda], ed. Sanbôhonbu [Army General Staff]. Tokyo: Hara Shobô, 1967; Repr. 1989. 2 vols.

Suzuki Kantarô. *Suzuki Kantarô Jiden* [Suzuki Kantarô Autobiography]. Tokyo: Jiji Tsûshinsha, 1968; Repr. Tokyo: Nihon Zusho Senta, 1997.

Tôgô Shigenori. *Tôgô Shigenori Shuki. Jidai no Ichimen* [Tôgô Shigenori Memoirs. One Aspect of an Age]. Tokyo: Hara Shobô, 1989.

Takagi Sôkichi. *Shikan Taiheiyô Sensô* [A Personal View of the Pacific War]. Tokyo: Kôjinsha, 1999.

Takagi Sôkichi. *Takagi Sôkichi Nikki* [Takagi Sôkichi Diary]. Tokyo: Mainichi Shimbunsha, 1985.

Takagi Sôkichi, Nikki to Jôhô [Takagi Sôkichi, Diary and Information], ed. Itô Takashi. Tokyo: Misuzu Shobô, 2000. 2 vols.

Tôjô Hideki. *Kokumin Gige, Senjinkun* [Field Service Code, Explanation to the People], ed. Okayama Kendô. Tokyo: Kyôzaisha, March 30, 1941.

Tôjô Hideki Sensei Kyôjutsusho [Tôjô Hideki Sworn Affidavit], ed. Tokyo Saiban Kenkyûkai [Tokyo Trial Research Group]. Tokyo: Yôyôsha, 1948.

Tôjô Naikaku Sôridaijin Kimitsu Kiroku. Tôjô Hideki Taishô Genkôroku [Tôjô Cabinet Prime Minister's Secret Record. A Record of General Tôjô Hideki's Words and Deeds], eds. Itô Takashi, Hirohashi Tadamitsu, and Katashima Norio. Tokyo: Tokyo Daigaku Shuppankai, 1990.

"Tokkô Sakusen no Shiki ni Ninji taru Gunshireikan toshite no Kaisô, tôji 6FA Shireikan Chûshô Sugawara Michiô" [Recollections of One Appointed as Commanding Officer of Special Attack Operations, then 6th Air Force Commanding Officer Lt. General Sugawara Michiô], Shôwa 44, 8, 7 kijutsu [August 7, 1969 description], MS, NIDS Military Archives, Tokyo.

Wada Kamechi. Rikugun Tamashii [Soul of the Army]. Tokyo: Tôsuisha, 1942.

Watanabe Masakichi. *Jikken Nihon Shûshinsho Nyûmon. Kan ichi. Jinjô Shôgaku Seitoyô* [Trial Text for an Introduction to Japanese Ethics, vol. 1, For Students in Elementary School]. Tokyo: Kinkôdô Shoseki, 1895.

Yamamoto Chikao, "Kokka Sôryokusen Zuen no Keikaku to Jisshi" [National Total War, War Games Planning and Actuation], in *Tsuisô Kaigunchûshô Nakazawa Tasuku* [Recollection about Vice-Admiral Nakazawa Tasuku], ed. Suikôkai [Navy Support Association]. Tokyo: Tsuisô Kaigunchûshô Nakazawa Tasuku Kankôkai, 1978.

Secondary sources

Agawa, Hiroyuki. *The Reluctant Admiral. Yamamoto and the Imperial Navy*, trans. John Bester. Tokyo: Kodansha International, 1979.

Akita, George. *Evaluating Evidence. A Positivist Approach to Reading Sources on Modern Japan*. Honolulu, HI: University of Hawai'i Press, 2008.

Antoni, Klaus. *Shintô & die Konzeption des japanischen Nationalwesens (kokutai)* [Shintô & the Concept of the Japanese National Essence (kokutai)]. Leiden: Brill, 1998.

Asahi Shimbun [Japanese language Asahi Newspaper International Edition], September 9, 2014: various pages; January 8, 2017: 16; March 14, 2019: 1.

Aston, W.G. trans. *Nihongi. Chronicles of Japan from the Earliest Times to A.D. 697*. London: George Allen & Unwin, 1896; Repr. 1956.

Beasley, W.G. *The Modern History of Japan*. New York: Frederick A. Praeger, 1963.

Bentley, Michael. "The Liberal Party, 1900 – 1939: Summit and Descent," in *A Companion to Early Twentieth-Century Britain*, ed. Chris Wrigley, 23–37. Oxford: Blackwell Publishers, 2003.

Bix, Herbert P. *Hirohito and the Making of Modern Japan*. New York: HarperCollins, 2000.

Bix, Herbert P. "War Responsibility and Historical Memory: Hirohito's Apparition," section "Hirohito: Japan's Last Empowered Emperor," in *The Asian-Pacific Journal: Japan Focus* 6, no. 5 (2008). Archive May 3, 2008.

Bôeichô Bôeikenkyûsho Senshishitsu [Defense Agency, Institute for Defense Studies, War History Office]. *Daihon'ei Kaigunbu Rengôkantai* [Imperial Headquarters, Navy Department, Combined Fleet], vols. 4–7. Tokyo: Asagumo Shimbunsha, 1970–76.

Bôeichô Bôeikenkyûsho Senshishitsu [Defense Agency, Institute for Defense Studies, War History Office]. *Daihon'ei Rikugunbu* [Imperial Headquarters, Army Department), vols. 5, 7–10. Tokyo: Asagumo Shimbunsha, 1973–75.

Bôeichô Bôeikenkyûsho Senshishitsu [Defense Agency, Institute for Defense Studies, War History Office]. *Hawai'i Sakusen* [Hawai'i Operations Strategy]. Tokyo: Asagumo Shuppansha, 1967.

Bôeichô Bôeikenkyûsho Senshishitsu [Defense Agency, Institute for Defense Studies, War History Office]. *Kaigun Shôgô Sakusen (2) Fuiripin Oki Kaisen* [Navy Victory Offensive (2) Philippine Off-Shore Naval Battle]. Tokyo: Asagumo Shuppansha, 1972.

Bôeichô Bôeikenkyûsho Senshishitsu [Defense Agency, Institute for Defense Studies, War History Office]. *Okinawa, Taiwan, Iôshima Hômen Rikugun Kôkû Sakusen* [Okinawa, Taiwan, Iwo Jima Area Army Air Force Operations]. Tokyo: Asagumo Shuppansha, 1970.

Bôeichô Bôeikenkyûsho Senshishitsu [Defense Agency, Institute for Defense Studies, War History Office]. *Rikugun Kôkû no Gunbi to Gunyô. Shûsen Made* [Army Air Force Armament and Uses, to the End of the War], vol. 3. Tokyo: Asagumo Shuppansha, 1976.

Bôeichô Bôeikenkyûsho Senshishitsu [Defense Agency, Institute for Defense Studies, War History Office]. *Riku, Kaigun Nenpyô* [Army Navy Chronology]. Tokyo: Asagumo Shimbunsha, 1980.

Brown, Delmer M. *Nationalism in Japan, an Introductory Historical Analysis*. Berkeley, CA: University of California Press, 1955.

Brown, Delmer M. and Ichirô Ishida. *The Future and the Past. A Translation and Study of the Gukanshô, an Interpretive History of Japan Written in 1219*. Berkeley, CA: University of California Press, 1979.

Brownlee, John S. ed. *History in the Service of the Japanese Nation*. Toronto: Joint Centre on Modern East Asia, 1983.

Butler, Kenneth D. "The Textual Evolution of the *Heike Monogatari*," *Harvard Journal of Asiatic Studies* 26 (1966): 5–51.

Butow, Robert J.C. *Japan's Decision to Surrender*. Stanford, CA: Stanford University Press, 1954.

Butow, Robert J.C. *Tojo and the Coming of the War*. Stanford, CA: Stanford University Press, 1961.

Chaen Yoshio. *Misshitsu no Shûsen Shôchoku* [Imperial Edict Terminating the War (drafted) Behind Closed Doors]. Tokyo: Yûshôdô Shuppan, 1989.

Chatani Sei'ichi, "Tai Bei, Ei Kaisen. Sensô Kaihi kara Kaisen he Keisha suru" [Opening a War with the USA and Great Britain. From Avoiding War to Leaning Toward Opening a War], in *Shôwa Tennô. "Senzen no Kunshu" to "Sengo no Shôchô" Futatsu no Kao* [The Shôwa Emperor. "Prewar Sovereign" and "Postwar Symbol," Two Faces], eds. Hashizume Daisaburô and Itô Takashi, 54–9. Tokyo: Yôsensha, 2015.

Como, Michael I. *Shôtoku, Ethnicity, Ritual, and Violence in the Japanese Buddhist Tradition*. Oxford: Oxford University Press, 2008.

Dainihonteikoku no nazo Kensho I'inkai [Great Imperial Japan Riddle Investigation Committee], eds. *Taiheiyô Sensô Tsûsetsu no Uso* [Commonly Accepted Lies About the Pacific War]. Tokyo: Saizusha, 2017.

Demandt, Alexander. *Philosophie der Geschichte. Von der Antike zur Gegenwart* [The Philosophie of History. From the Ancient World to the Present]. Cologne: Böhlau Verlag, 2011.

Dower, John W. *Embracing Defeat. Japan in the Wake of World War II*. New York: W.W. Norton, 1999.

Dower, John W. *Cultures of War. Pearl Harbor/Hiroshima/9-11/Iraq*. New York: W.W. Norton/The New Press, 2010.

Drea, Edward J. *In the Service of the Emperor. Essays on the Imperial Japanese Army*. Lincoln: University of Nebraska Press, 1998.

Drea, Edward J. *Japan's Imperial Army. Its Rise and Fall, 1853–1945*. Lawrence: University Press of Kansas, 2009.

Earhart, David C. *Certain Victory. Images of World War II in the Japanese Media*. Armonk, NY: M.E. Sharpe, 2008.

Evans, David C., and Mark R. Peattie. *Kaigun. Strategy, Tactics, and Technology in the Imperial Japanese Navy, 1887 – 1941*. Annapolis, MD: Naval Institute Press, 1997.

Fogel, Joshua A. "Introduction," in *The Teleology of the Modern Nation-State. Japan and China*, ed. Joshua A. Fogel, 1–7. Philadelphia: University of Pennsylvania Press, 2005.

Foot, Sarah, "The Historiography of the Anglo-Saxon 'nation-state,'" in *Power and the Nation in European History*, eds. Len Scales and Oliver Zimmer, 125–42. Cambridge: Cambridge University Press, 2005.

Frank, Richard B. *Downfall. The End of the Imperial Japanese Empire*. New York: Random House, 1999; Repr. London: Penguin Books, 2001.

Frank, Richard B. "Ketsu-Gô: Japanese Political and Military Strategy in 1945," in *The End of the Pacific War: Reappraisals*, ed. Tsuyoshi Hasegawa, 65–94. Stanford, CA: Stanford University Press, 2007.

Fujimoto Hiromichi, *Rikugun Saigo no Hi* [The Last Day of the Army]. Tokyo: Shinjinsha, 1945.

Fujiwara Akira. *Tennôsei to Guntai* [The Emperor System and the Military]. Tokyo: Aoki Shoten, 1978.

Gauntlett, John Owen trans. *Kokutai No Hongi. Cardinal Principles of the National Entity of Japan*, ed. and intro. Robert King Hall. Cambridge, MA: Harvard University Press, 1949.

Gluck, Carol. *Japan's Modern Myths. Ideology in the Late Meiji Period*. Princeton, NJ: Princeton University Press, 1985.

Griffith, Samuel B. trans., intro. *Sun Tzu, The Art of War*. Oxford: Oxford University Press, 1963.

Handô Kazutoshi and Hosaka Masayasu. *Shôwa Meishô to Gushô* [Great Leaders and Foolhardy Leaders of the Shôwa Era]. Tokyo: Bungei Shunjû, 2008.

Handô Kazutoshi, Hosaka Masayasu, Mikuriya Takashi, Isoda Michifumi. *"Shôwa Tennô Jitsuroku" no Nazo wo Toku* [Solving the Riddle of the Actual Record of the Shôwa Emperor]. Tokyo: Bungei Shunjû, 2015.

Hara Takeshi. *"Shôwa Tennô Jitsuroku" wo Yomu* [Reading the "Actual Record of the Shôwa Emperor"]. Tokyo: Iwanami Shinsho, 2015.

Hasegawa Ryôichi. *Kôkokushikan to iu Mondai* [The Problem of Emperor-Centered Historiography]. Tokyo: Hakutakusha, 2008.

Hasegawa, Tsuyoshi ed. *The End of the Pacific War: Reappraisals*. Stanford, CA: Stanford University Press, 2007.

Hata Ikuhiko. *Gendaishi no Sôten* [The Issues of Modern History]. Tokyo: Bungei Shunjû, 1998.

Hata, Ikuhiko. *Hirohito: The Shôwa Emperor in War and Peace*, ed. Marius B. Jansen. Folkestone: Global Oriental, 2007.

Hatano Sumio. *Saishô Suzuki Kantarô no Ketsudan. "Seidan" to Sengo Japan* [Prime Minister Suzuki Kantarô's Clear-Cut Decision. "Imperial Decision" and Postwar Japan]. Tokyo: Iwanami Shoten, 2015.

Hayashi Saburô. *Taiheiyô Sensô Rikusen Gaishi* [General History of Land Warfare in the Pacific War]. Tokyo: Iwanami Shinsho, 1951.

Hirakawa Sukehiro, "Japan's Turn to the West," trans. Wakabayashi, in *Modern Japanese Thought*, ed. Bob Tadashi Wakabayashi, 30–97. Cambridge: Cambridge University Press, 1998.

Hirota Teruyuki. *Rikugun Shôkô no Kyôikushakaishi*. [A Social-Educational History of the Army Officer]. Yokohama: Seori Shobô, 1997.

Hosaka Masayasu. *Tôjô Hideki to Tennô no Jidai* [Tôjô Hideki and the Era of the Emperor]. Tokyo: Gendai Jânarisumu, 1979. 2 vols.

Hosaka Masayasu. *"Tokkô" to Nihonjin* ["Special Attacks" and the Japanese]. Tokyo: Kodansha, 2005.

Hosaka Masayasu. *Kaisen, Tôjô Hideki ga Naita* [Opening the War, Tôjô Hideki Wept]. Tokyo: Mainichi Shinbunsha, 2007.

Hosaka Masayasu. *Shôwashi no Shinsô. 15 Sôten kara Yomitoku* [Shôwa History in Depth. Considered from the Point of View of 15 Issues]. Tokyo: Heibonsha, 2010.

Hosaka Masayasu. *Shôwa Tennô Jitsuroku. Sono Omote to Ura. Taiheiyô Sensô no Jidai* [Actual Record of the Shôwa Emperor. Above and Below the Surface. The Pacific War Era]. Tokyo: Mainichi Shimbunsha, 2015. 2 vols.

Humphreys, Leonard A. *The Way of the Heavenly Sword. The Japanese Army in the 1920's*. Stanford, CA: Stanford University Press, 1995.

Ienaga, Saburô. *Japan's Past, Japan's Future. One Historian's Odyssey*, trans. Richard H. Minear Lanham, MD: Rowman & Littlefield Publishers, 2001.

Iguchi, Takeo. *Demystifying Pearl Harbor. A New Perspective from Japan*, trans. David Noble. Tokyo: International House of Japan, 2010.

Inoguchi Rikihei, Nakajima Tadashi. *Shimpû Tokbetsu Kôgekitai* [Divine Wind Special Attack Unit]. Tokyo: Nihon Shuppan Kyôdô Kabushiki Kaisha, 1951.

Inoue Kiyoshi. *Tennôsei* [The Emperor System]. Tokyo: Tokyo Daigaku Shuppankai, 1958.

Inoue Kiyoshi. *Tennô no Sensô Sekinin* [The Emperor's War Responsibility]. Tokyo: Gendai Hyôronsha, 1975.

Itô Takashi. "Shôwashikenkyû no Kadai to Shôwa Tennô" [Shôwa History Research and the Shôwa Emperor], in *Shôwa Tennô. "Senzen no Kunshu" to "Sengo no Shôchô" Futatsu no Kao* [The Shôwa Emperor. "Prewar Sovereign" and "Postwar Symbol," Two Faces], eds. Hashizume Daisaburô and Itô Takashi, 78–83. Tokyo: Yôsensha, 2015.

Japan Times. "Tojo was convinced of victory before Japan attacked Pearl Harbor, newly unearthed memo shows," July 23, 2018.

Jôhô Yoshio ed. *Tôjô Hideki*. Tokyo: Fuyô Shobô, 1974.

Jôhô Yoshio ed. *Saigo no Sanbôchô, Umezu Yoshijirô* [The Last Army Chief of Staff, Umezu Yoshijirô]. Tokyo: Fuyô Shobô, 1976.

Josephson, Jason Ānanda. *The Invention of Religion in Japan*. Chicago, IL: University of Chicago Press, 2012.

Kaizu Ichirô. "Kusunoki Masashige to Nihonjin: Kyôkasho ni miru Masashige-zô no hensen" [Kusunoki Masashige and the Japanese: The Changing Image of Masashige as Seen in School Textbooks], in *Kusunoki Masashige no subete* [All about Kusunoki Masashige], ed. Satô Kazuhiko, 175–204. Tokyo: Shinjinbutsu Ôraisha, 1989.

Kang Sang-jung. *Kang Sang-jung no Seijigaku Nyûmon* [Kang Sang-jung's Introduction to Political Science]. Tokyo: Shûeisha Shinsho, 2006.

Katô Norihiro, Hashizume Daisaburô, and Takeda Seiji. *Tennô no Sensô Sekinin* [Emperor (Hirohito's) War Responsibility]. Tokyo: Komichi Shobô, 2000.

Kaufmann, Walter ed. *Friedrich Nietzsche, The Will to Power*, trans. Walter Kaufmann and R.J. Hollingdale. New York: Vintage Books, 1968.

Kawamura, Noriko. *Emperor Hirohito and the Pacific War*. Seattle: University of Washington Press, 2015.

Kershaw, Ian. *The End. Hitler's Germany 1944–45*. London: Allen Lane, 2011; Repr. Penguin Books 2012.

Kisaka Junichirô. *Shôwa no Rekishi* [Shôwa History], vol. 7, *Taiheiyô Sensô* [The Pacific War]. Tokyo: Shogakkan, 1982.

Kiyose Ichirô. *Hiroku, Tokyo Saiban* [Secret Record, the Tokyo Trial]. Tokyo: Yomiuri Shimbunsha, 1966.

Komamiya Shinshichirô. *Senji Yusô Sendanshi* [History of Wartime Freight Ship Convoys]. Tokyo: Kyôdôsha, 1987.

Koselleck, Reinhart. *Vom Sinn und Unsinn der Geschichte* [On the Sense and Nonsense of History]. Berlin: Suhrkamp, 2010.

Krebs, Gerhard. "Prinz Mikasa, der Zweite Weltkrieg und der Shôwa Tennô" [Prince Mikasa, the Second World War and the Shôwa Emperor], in *OAG Notizen 01/2018*, 12–53. Tokyo: Deutsche Gesellschaft für Natur- und Völkerkunde Ostasiens, 2018.

Ladstätter, Otto, and Sepp Linhart. *China und Japan: Die Kulturen Ostasiens* [China and Japan: The Cultures of East Asia]. Vienna: Carl Ueberreuter Verlag, 1983.

Large, Stephen S. *Emperor Hirohito and Shôwa Japan. A Political Biography*. London: Routledge, 1992.

Lu, David J. *Japan. A Documentary History*. Armonk, NY: M.E. Sharpe, 1997. 2 vols.

Matsuda Yoshifumi. "Jôhô Kanrisha toshite no Kido Kôichi Naidaijin" [Lord Keeper of the Privy Seal Kido Kôichi as Information Manager]. *Nihon Rekishi* 678 (November 2004): 75–90.

McCullough, Helen Craig trans. intro. *The Tale of the Heike*. Stanford, CA: Stanford University Press, 1988.

Minear, Richard H. *Victor's Justice. The Tokyo War Crimes Trial*. Princeton, NJ: Princeton University Press, 1971; Repr. Tokyo: Charles E. Tuttle, 1972.

Miscamble, Wilson D. *The Most Controversial Decision. Truman, the Atomic Bombs, and the Defeat of Japan*. Cambridge: Cambridge University Press, 2011.

Mitter, Rana. *China's War With Japan, 1937–1945. The Struggle for Survival*. London: Allen Lane, 2013.

Mori Shirô. *Tokkô to ha Nanika* [Special Attack, What Was it?]. Tokyo: Bungei Shunjû, 2006.

Morris, Ivan. *The Nobility of Failure. Tragic Heroes in the History of Japan*. New York: Secker & Warburg, 1975.

Morris, Ivan, trans. ed. *The Pillow Book of Sei Shônagon*. New York: Columbia University Press, 1967. 2 Vols.

Nakahara Shigetoshi. *Kokuryoku naki Sensô Shidô* [Managing a War With No National Resources]. Tokyo: Hara Shobô, 1989.

Nagatsuka, Ryuji. *I was a Kamikaze*. London: Abelard-Shuman Ltd., 1973; Repr. Stoud: Amberley Publishing, 2014.

Nakamura Takafusa. *Shôwashi* [Shôwa History]. Tokyo: Tôyô Keizai Shimbunsha, 2012. 2 vols.

Nakamura Takafusa, Miyazaki Masayasu. *Shiryô. Taiheiyô Sensô Higai Chôsa Hôkoku* [Historical Documents. Survey Report on Pacific War Damage]. Tokyo: Tokyo University Press, 1995.

Nishio Kanji + 13 contributors, *Atarashii Rekishi Kyôkasho* [A New History Textbook]. Tokyo: K.K. Fusô, 2001.

Nishiyama, Takashi. *Engineering War and Peace in Modern Japan, 1868–1964*. Baltimore, MD: Johns Hopkins University Press, 2014.

Noble, Thomas F.X. *Late Antiquity: Crisis and Transformation*. Chantilly, VA: The Teaching Co., 2008. 2 vols.

Oates, Leslie Russell. *Populist Nationalism in Prewar Japan. A Biography of Nakano Seigo*. Sydney: George Allen & Unwin, 1985.

Ohnuki-Tierney, Emiko. *Kamikaze, Cherry Blossoms, and Nationalism. The Militarization of Aesthetics in Japanese History*. Chicago, IL: University of Chicago Press, 2002.

Oki Shûji. *Anami Korechika Den* [Biography of Anami Korechika]. Tokyo: Kodansha, 1970.

Ôtani Keijirô. *Shôwa Kempeishi* [History of the Shôwa Military Police]. Tokyo: Misuzu Shobô, 1987.

Ôyama Sei'ichi ed., *Nihon Shoki no Nazo to Shôtoku Taishi* [The Riddle of the Nihon Shoki and Crown Prince Shôtoku]. Tokyo: Heibonsha, 2011.

Pätzold, Kurt, Manfred Weißbecker. *Geschichte der NSDAP, 1920 – 1945* [History of the National Socialist Democratic Worker Party, 1920–1945], 280–317. Cologne: PapyRossa Verlags, 2009.

Perry, Mark. *The Most Dangerous Man in America. The Making of Douglas MacArthur*. New York: Basic Books, 2014.

Project Development Office Tatsumi. *Kyôkasho to Shimbun de kuraberu Taiheiyô Sensô* [The Pacific War Compared in Textbooks and Newspapers]. Tokyo: Tatsumi Shuppan, 2015.

Reischauer, Edwin O. *Japan Past and Present*. 3rd rev. edn. Tokyo: Charles E. Tuttle, 1964.

Reynolds, Susan, "The Idea of the Nation as a Political Community," in *Power and the Nation in European History*, eds. Len Scales and Oliver Zimmer, 54–66. Cambridge: Cambridge University Press, 2005.

Roberts, Luke S. "Cultivating Non-National Understandings in Local History," in *The Teleology of the Modern Nation-State. Japan and China*, ed. Joshua A. Fogel, 161–73. Philadelphia: University of Pennsylvania Press, 2005.

Ruoff, Kenneth J. *The People's Emperor. Democracy and the Japanese Monarchy, 1945–1995*. Cambridge, MA: Harvard University Asia Center, 2001.

Satô Hiroô. "Shinkoku Shisô" [Divine Land Thought], in *Nihon Shisôshi Jiten* [Japanese Thought History Dictionary], eds. Ishida Ichirô and Ishige Tadashi, 108–9. Tokyo: Tokyodo Shuppan, 2013.

Satô Sanae. *Tôjô Hideki Fûin Sareta Shinjitsu* [Tôjô Hideki, the Sealed Truth]. Tokyo: Kodansha, 1995.

Scherer, Klaus. *Kamikaze. Todesbefehl für Japans Jugend* [Kamikaze. Death Orders for Japan's Youths]. Munich: iudicium, 2001.

Senshi Sôsho [War History Series]. Bôeichô Bôeikenkyûsho Senshishitsu [Defense Agency, Institute for Defense Studies, War History Office]. Tokyo: Asagumo Shuppansha, 1966–80. 102 vols.

Senzaki Akinaka. "Mishima Yukio to Amino Yoshihiko—Shôwa Tennô wo Meguru Setten" [Mishima Yukio and Amino Yoshihiko—Points of Conjunction With the Shôwa Emperor], in *Shôwa Tennô. "Senzen no Kunshu" to "Sengo no Shôchô" Futatsu no Kao* [The Shôwa Emperor. "Prewar Sovereign" and "Postwar Symbol," Two Faces], eds. Hashizume Daisaburô and Itô Takashi, 180–5. Tokyo: Yôsensha, 2015.

Shida Nobuyoshi. *Shôwa no Shôgen* [Shôwa Era Witness]. Tokyo: Shibundô, 1990.

Shôji Junichirô. "Konoe Fumimaro. Amerika to iu 'Maboroshi' in Kaketa Seijika" [Konoe Fumimaro. A Politician in Pursuit of an Illusion of America], in *Shôwashi kôgi 3—ri- da- tôshite miru sensô he no michi* [Lectures on Shôwa History 3— Looking at the Road to War through Leaders], ed. Tsutsui Kiyotada, 183–202. Tokyo: Chikuma Shinsho, 2017.

Shôji Junichirô. "Umezu Yoshijirô—'Atoshimatsu' Jinryoku shita Rikugun Taishô" [Umezu Yoshijirô—the Army General Who Assiduously Dealt with 'Repercussions'], in *Shôwashi Kôgi, Gunjin-hen* [Lectures on Shôwa History, Military Personnel Volume], ed. Tsutsui Kiyotada, 53–70. Tokyo: Chikuma Shinsho, 2018.

Shôwa Tennô Jitsuroku [Actual Record of the Shôwa Emperor], abbreviated STJR, eds. Imperial Household Agency. Tokyo: Tokyo Shoseki KK, 2015-19. 19 vols. The Imperial Household Agency put the Record on a CD, 60 vols. I refer to the CD and the printed version: Kunaichô Copyright. *Shôwa Tennô Jitsuroku* [Actual Record of the Shôwa Emperor], vols. 8, 9. Tokyo: Tokyo Shoseki KK, 2016.

Skya, Walter A. *Japan's Holy War. The Ideology of Radical Shintô Ultranationalism.* Durham, NC: Duke University Press, 2009.

Sugiyama Gensui Denki Kankôkai [Field Marshal Sugiyama Biography Publication Group], ed. *Sugiyama Gensui Den* [Biography of Field Marshal Sugiyama]. Tokyo: Hara Shobô, 1969.

Suzuki Tamon. *"Shûsen" no Seijishi, 1943–1945* [A Political History of "Ending the War," 1943-1945]. Tokyo: Tokyo University Press, 2011.

Suzuki Tamon. "Tôjô Naikaku Sôjishoku no Kei'i ni tsuite no Saikentô" [A Reexamination of the Activities Surrounding the Resignation of the Tôjô Cabinet]. *Nihon Rekishi* 685 (June 2005): 69–84.

Suzuki, Tamon. "Emperor Hirohito's 'Sacred Decisions' and the Political Process of Japan's Surrender," in *Fifteen Lectures on Showa Japan. Road to the Pacific War in Recent Historiography*, ed. Tsutsui, Kiyotada, 257–75. Tokyo: Japan Publishing Industry Foundation for Culture, 2016.

Suzuki Tamon. "Suzuki Kantarô to Nihon no 'Shûsen'" [Suzuki Kantarô and 'War's End' in Japan], in *"Nitchû Sensô" to ha Nan datta no ka - Fukuganteki Shiten* ["Japan - China War," What Was It? from Multiple Perspectives], eds. Huang Zijin, Liu Jianhui, and Tobe Ryôichi, 257–86. Tokyo: Minerva Shobô, 2017.

Tachibana Takashi. *Tennô to Tôdai* [The Emperor and Tokyo University]. Tokyo: Bungei Shunjû, 2005. 2 vols.

Takasugi Yôhei. "Suzuki Tei'ichi—Seibirô wo Tsuita Gunjin" [Suzuki Tei'ichi—the Suit Wearing Soldier], in *Shôwashi Kôgi, Gunjin-hen* [Lectures on Shôwa History, Military Personnel Volume], ed. Tsutsui Kiyotada, 87–104. Tokyo: Chikuma Shinsho, 2018.

Takasugi Yôhei. "Mutô Akira—'Seijiteki Gunjin' no Jitsuzô" [Mutô Akira—the Real Character of a 'Political Soldier'], in *Shôwashi Kôgi, Gunjin-hen* [Lectures on Shôwa History, Military Personnel Volume], ed. Tsutsui Kiyotada, 105–22. Tokyo: Chikuma Shinsho, 2018.

Takayama Shinobu. *Futari no Sanbô, Hattori Takushirô to Tsuji Masanobu* [Two Staff Officers, Hattori Takushirô and Tsuji Masanobu]. Tokyo: Fuyô Shobô, 1999.

Takeda Tomoki, "Tôjô Hideki—Shôwa no Higeki no Taikensha" [Tôjô Hideki—Embodiment of the Shôwa Tragedy], in *Shôwashi Kôgi, Gunjin-hen* [Lectures on Shôwa History, Military Personnel Volume], ed. Tsutsui Kiyotada, 35–52. Tokyo: Chikuma Shinsho, 2018.

Tamura Yasuoki. "Senzen- Senchûki ni oite Shôwa Tennô ha tada Saika dake shite ita no ka?" [Did the Shôwa Emperor Merely Provide Sanctions before and during the War?], in *Shôwa Tennô*. "Senzen no Kunshu" to "Sengo no Shôchô" Futatsu no Kao [The Shôwa Emperor. "Prewar Sovereign" and "Postwar Symbol," Two Faces], eds. Hashizume Daisaburô and Itô Takashi, 138–43. Tokyo: Yôsensha, 2015.

Tanaka Satoshi. "Takatori Masao. 'Kono Yo no Soto ni Tsukidasu Minzoku Shûkyô'" [Folk Religion Thrust Out of this World], in *Shintô no Seiritsu* [The Birth of Shintô]. Tokyo: Heibonsha Sensho, 1979, in *Nihon Shisôshi* [History of Japanese Thought], ed. Koyasu Nobukuni, 44–9. Tokyo: Jinbun Shoin, 2011.

Tanaka, Stefan. *Japan's Orient. Rendering Pasts into History.* Berkeley, CA: University of California Press, 1993.

Teeuwen, Mark. *Watarai Shintô: An Intellectual History of the Outer Shrine in Ise.* Leiden: Research School CNWS, 1996.

Teshima Yasunobu. *Nihon Kaigun to Seiji* [The Japanese Navy and Politics]. Tokyo: Kodansha, 2015.

Tillich, Paul. *Systematic Theology*, vol. 1, *Reason and Revelation; Being and God.* Chicago, IL: University of Chicago Press, 1951.

Tôjô Yûko. *Daitôasensô no Shinjitsu* [The Truth about the Greater East Asia War]. Tokyo: Wakku Co., 2005.

Totani, Yuma. *The Tokyo War Crimes Trial. The Pursuit of Justice in the Wake of World War II.* Cambridge, MA: Harvard University Press, 2008.

Tsunoda Fusako. *Isshi, Taizai wo Shasu. Rikugun Daijin Anami Korechika* [One Death, Forgive (My) Great Transgressions. Army Minister Anami Korechika]. Tokyo: Shinchôsha, 1980.

Tsunoda, Ryusaku, Wm. Theodore de Bary, Donald Keene, comp. *Sources of the Japanese Tradition.* New York: Columbia University Press, 1958.

Tsunoda Tadashige. *Waga Tôjô Hideki Ansatsu Keikaku* [Our Plan to Assassinate Tôjô Hideki]. Tokyo: Tokuma Shoten, 1985.

Tsutsui Kiyotada. "Shôwa Rikugun no Habatsu Kôsô—Maegaki ni Tsutaete" [Factional Strife in the Shôwa Army—Prefatory Information], in *Shôwashi Kôgi, Gunjin-hen* [Lectures on Shôwa History, Military Personnel Volume], ed. Tsutsui Kiyotada, 9–34. Tokyo: Chikuma Shinsho, 2018.

Vandiver, Frank E. "Foch and Eisenhower: Supreme Commanders," in *The Great World War 1914 – 45*, vol. 1, *Lightning Strikes Twice*, eds. Peter Liddle, John Bourne, and Ian Whitehead, 416–27. London: HarperCollins, 2000.

Varley, H. Paul. *Imperial Restoration in Medieval Japan*. New York: Columbia University Press, 1971.
Varley, H. Paul, trans. *A Chronicle of Gods and Sovereigns. Jinnô Shôtôki of Kitabatake Chikafusa*. New York: Columbia University Press, 1980.
Watanabe, Tsuneo, ed.-in-chief. *From Marco Polo Bridge to Pearl Harbor: Who was Responsible?*, ed. James E. Auer. Tokyo: Yomiuri Shimbun, 2006.
Watson, Burton. *Records of the Grand Historian of China. Translated from the Shih Chi of Ssu-Ma Ch'ien*. New York: Columbia University Press, 1961. 2 vols.
Wetzler, Peter. *Hirohito and War. Imperial Tradition and Military Decision Making in Prewar Japan*. Honolulu, HI: University of Hawai'i Press, 1998.
Wohlstetter, Roberta. *Pearl Harbor. Warning and Decision*. Stanford, CA: Stanford University Press, 1962.
Yamada Akira. *Shôwa Tennô no Sensô Shidô* [The Shôwa Emperor's War Leadership]. Tokyo: Shôwa Shuppan, 1990.
Yamada Akira. *Daigensui Shôwa Tennô* [The Supreme Commander Shôwa Emperor]. Tokyo: Shinnihon Shuppansha, 1994.
Yamada Akira. *Shôwa Tennô no Gunjishisô to Senryaku* [The Shôwa Emperor's Military Thought and Strategy]. Tokyo: Azekura Shobô, 2002.
Yamada Akira. "Daigensui Shôwa Tennô no 'Hatsugen' wo Yomu" [Reading the 'Remarks' of the Supreme Commander Shôwa Emperor], in *Shôwa Tennô. "Senzen no Kunshu" to "Sengo no Shôchô" Futatsu no Kao* [The Shôwa Emperor. "Prewar Sovereign" and "Postwar Symbol," Two Faces], eds. Hashizume Daisaburô and Itô Takashi, 192–8. Tokyo: Yôsensha, 2015.
Yamamoto Tomoyuki. *Nihon Rikugun Sensô Shûketsu Katei no Kenkyû* [Japanese Army Research on the Process of Terminating the War]. Tokyo: Fuyô Shobô, 2010.
Yamauchi, Takeo. "'Honorable Death' on Saipan," in *Japan at War. An Oral History*, Haruko Taya Cook and Theodore F. Cook, 281–92. New York: The New Press, 1992.
Yanagisawa Ken. *Toyoda Soemu Jutsu. Saigo no Teikoku Kaigun* [Toyoda Soemu Narrator. End of the Imperial Navy]. Tokyo: Sekai no Nihonsha, 1950.
Yoshimi Masato. *Shûsenshi. Naze Ketsudan Dekinakatta no ka* [History of Ending the War. Why Could Not a Firm Decision be Made?]. Tokyo: NHK, 2013.

Index

"absolute national defense perimeter" 13, 24-5, 30-1, 44-6, 50, 54-5, 137
"Actual Record of the Shôwa Emperor" (STJR) 9-14, 25-8, 31, 34, 37-41, 46, 48, 52, 56-7, 92, 125, 139-40
"A-go" operation 17, 32-6, 64, 144
aircraft allocations 52-3
aircraft losses 17, 22
aircraft production 137
Akamatsu Sadao 34-6, 91, 106-7, 133
Akita, George 41
American people, evaluations of: collective 130-1, 169; prominent individuals 33
Anami Korechika 7, 151-8, 172
Arao Okikatsu 153-4
Arima Masafumi 66-7
Arisue Seizô 16
Arisue Yadoru 34, 48-9
army-navy: combined command 26-9; lack of full co-operation between 5, 12, 17-18, 23-31, 35, 42-6, 53-4, 72, 124-9, 136-7, 140, 163, 170
Asahi (newspaper) 21-2, 37-8
Asaka, Prince 51, 148
Ashikaga Takauji 81, 101
Asia-Pacific War *see* Second World War
asianism xii
assassination plots 19, 118, 126-8, 154
atomic bombs 23-4, 150-2, 162, 176
Awahara Nobuhide 117

Battle of the Coral Sea 43-4
Battle of the Philippine Sea 17, 22-3, 45, 55, 64, 143
Battle of the Sea of Japan (1905) 32
Battle of Shijônawate (1348) 101
Bix, Herbert 34, 41-4, 76-7, 124-6
bomb-balloons 71-2
bombing raids on Japan 5, 23, 78-9, 148, 176
Brown, Delmer 21

B-29 bombers 5, 23, 78-9
Buddhism 87, 113
Butow, Robert J.C. 6, 21-2, 89, 91, 123-4, 154

cabinet resignations 156-7
Chiang Kai-shek 167
chiefs of staff and ministers combined into one person for each service 52-3, 126
Christianity 7, 176
Cicero 178
Cohen, Jerome B. 141-2
"Collected Records of Remarks by the Shôwa Emperor" 32, 36-7, 91
colonialism 100, 119
condolence money 139
Confucianism 102, 113
"continuing war" theory 161
control of the sea and air 169
culture, Japanese xii, 2

deception (and self-deception) by military leaders 149, 162-3
defeat, apprehensions about 83
"divine winds" 87-8, 135-6
Doemming, H.D. von xi-xii
"Doolittle Raids" (1942) 46
double standard of morality applied to Japan and the West xii
Dower, John 160
Drea, Edward 23, 42

Earhart, David C. 148
"early peace faction" in the army 119
education 102-3
elite groups 54
"emperor-centered" view of history 115, 164
emperors in Japan: role of 2-3, 8; supposed infallibility of 3; *see also* Hirohito
euphemisms used by the military 139-40

family relationships 102
Field Service Code 80-1, 85-6, 92-4, 105
filial conduct 101-3
food shortages 104
forced labor 91
foreign policy 16
Frank, Richard 151
Fuchida Mitsuo 144
Fujii Shigeru 53
Fujiwara Akira 20-1, 50-1, 55
Fujiwara Ginjirô 135
Fukudome Shigeru 167
Fushimi, Prince 70, 75, 123

Gaozu, Emperor 112
Genda Minoru 65, 70
Germany xii, 33, 105, 110, 142, 148, 166
Godaigo, Emperor 101
Gomurakami, Emperor 101
"Great Strategic Plan for the Decisive Battle on Home Islands" 160, 173
"Greater East Asia Co-Prosperity Sphere" xii
Guadalcanal 47, 139
gunbatsu 120
Gunjishi Gakkai 154

Halsey, William 33
Hamazono Shigeyoshi 83
Handô Kazutoshi 19, 46-7, 69, 74
Hara Takeshi 11
Hara Yoshimichi 12, 49, 137
"haragei" theory 153
Hasegawa, Tsuyoshi 150
Hasegawa Ryôichi 115
Hata, Ikuhiko 41
Hata Shunroku 159
Hatanaka Kenji 116
Hatano Sumio 151, 155
Hattori Hideo 87
Hattori Takushirô 16-20, 143, 161
Hawai'i 11-12, 166
Hayashi Saburô 153-4, 156, 158
Heibonsha Encyclopedia 142
Higashikuni, Prince 51, 105, 124, 129
Hiraizumi Kiyoshi 115-18, 153, 164
Hirohito, Emperor xii, xiv, 3, 5, 10-12, 121, 124-31, 134-40, 147-59, 171-8; authority of 46-57; involvement with kamikaze tactics 59-63, 67, 70, 73-4, 78-9, 85-8; knowledge of military matters and role in decision-making about them 9, 11-15, 18-28, 31-2, 38-50, 54-7; overall assessment of 177-8; relationship with Tôjô 89-91, 94, 97, 100, 104, 107, 109, 113-15, 121
Hiroshima 96, 150, 159, 176
Hitler, Adolf 120, 148
hohitsu 120, 165
Hôjô Yasutoki 113
"honorable death" practices 9, 55, 60, 72, 80-6, 105, 134, 157
Hosaka Masayasu 10-12, 19-22, 46-8, 69-70, 74, 91
Hoshino Naoki 174
Hosokawa Morisada 125
Hozumi Yatsuka 4
hubris xiv, 7, 176

idealists 108
ideologies, "marketing" of 8
Ienaga Saburô 115, 118, 164
Iguchi Takeo 145
Imperial Headquarters Army Department Records 14-16
Imperial Japanese priorities 172; influence on postwar politics 165
Imperial Order *649* 68
imperialism and imperial tradition xii, 114-15, 119
Inaba Masao 18
Inagaki Kiyoshi 76
"independence of supreme command", principle of 42
Inoue Kiyoshi 20, 51-4
Inoue Shigeyoshi 141
Inoue Tetsujirô 80
international laws 91, 175
Inukai Tsuyoshi 118
Irokawa Daikichi 118
Ishii Akiho 132
Ishiwara Kanji 108, 167
Itô Sei'ichi 63, 69, 145
Itô Takashi 57, 86
Iwakura Tomomi 170
Iwamoto Kaneji 75, 85

Jimmu, Emperor 4, 84, 98
jingoism 93
Jô Ei'ichirô 6, 62-4, 73, 76-8

Kamakura Shogunate 113
kamikaze tactics xiii, 4-6, 43, 47, 59-88, 105, 142-3, 160, 170, 176; beginning of 69-70; early plans for 62-4; Hirohito's involvement with 59-63, 67, 70, 73-4, 78-9, 85-8; irrationality of 72-3; number of deaths resulting from 86
Kawabe Masakazu 61-2, 81, 162-3
Kawabe Torashirô xiii, 136, 152, 162-3, 173-4, 176
Kawamura, Noriko 127-9, 148
Kellogg-Briand Pact (1928) 175
Kemmu Restoration (1333–36) 101
Kido Kôichi 16, 27, 31, 36, 47-52, 105, 124-9, 150
Kido Takayoshi 170
Kimura Heitarô 90
King, Ernest J. 22
Kishi Nobusuke 129, 137, 163-4
Kitabatake Chikafusa 116
Kodama Gentarô 170
Koizumi Junichirô 90
kokutai concept 3-4, 7, 113, 115-16, 153, 176
Komamiya Shinshichirô 140
Komura Jutarô 170
Konoe, Prince 35
Konoe Fumimaro 16, 51, 89, 115, 123-4, 131-2, 161, 176
Krebs, Gerhard 153
Kuroshima Kameto 63-4, 71, 85
Kusunoki Masashige 69, 81, 101-2
Kyûjô plot 153, 155

Large, Stephen 51-2, 55
law, Tôjô's understanding of 112-15
Laws of War 24
liberal politics xii
Lloyd George, David 110
Locke, Edwin Jr. 160
loyalty 100-5, 158

MacArthur, Douglas 33, 175
Manchurian Incidents (1928 and 1931) 155, 167, 169
Manchurian Network 164
Mao Zedong 120
Marshall, George 33
martial virtues *see* military spirit

Maruyama Masao 114
materials for war xiii-xiv, 4, 6-7, 71-2, 131-6, 141-3, 163, 166, 168, 170
Matsu'ura Gorô 66
Matsua Yoshifuma 41
Matsuzaka Hiromasa 151
Meckel, Jacob 95
Meiji Constitution 2, 28, 55, 98, 151, 165-6
Mikasa, Prince 153, 155
military spirit 60-2, 104
Minamoto Sanetomo 117
ministers of state 3
mini-submarines 75-6, 85, 161
Miscamble, Wilson D. 150
Mito School 4
Miyazaki Shûichi 29
modernity xii
Mongol invasions (1274 and 1281) 87, 169
moral history 54-5
moral values 97-104
Mori Shirô 64
Murao Jirô 164-5
Mutô Akira 130, 132-3

Nagano Osami 25, 46-9, 52, 63, 91, 137, 159
Nagasaki 150-1
Naitô Susumu 79
Nakahara Shigetoshi 134-5
Nakano Seigô 109, 119
Nakashiba Suezumi 81
Nakazawa Tasuku 22, 28-31, 39, 29-30, 65-70, 130-1, 139-45, 165-71
Napoleon 167
"nation", definition of 2
nation, Japanese: as distinct from state xiv, 1-3, 5, 9, 67, 158; preservation of 177-8
nation-state system 109, 116; building of 2
national consciousness 119
"national essence" of Japan 4, 7, 12, 23, 84-5, 89, 92, 95, 99, 105, 112-13, 119, 121, 133, 147-9, 152-5, 159-61, 172, 176-7
National Institute for Defense Studies (NIDS), Tokyo 14, 57
nationalism xi-xii, 21
nationalistic history 115-18
naval operations 16, 28-9, 141-3; *see also under* army-navy
Nazism xii, 148

Nietzsche, Friedrich 2
Nimitz, Chester William 33
Nishiyama Takashi 86
Nomura Minoru 77

Ogata Jô 84
Ogawa Kyôtarô 138
Ohnuki-Tierney, Emiko 67, 84, 86
Oikawa Koshirô 48, 69, 73-4, 141
Okabe Nagaakira 134
Okada Keisuke 35, 123-8
Okada Kikusaburô 131
Okinawa 85-6
"one big strike" doctrine 153-4
Ônishi Takijirô 5-6, 59, 62-70, 74-7, 85, 136
Ôoka Tadasuke 112
Ôyama Iwao 170
Ozawa Jisaburô 143-4

Pearl Harbor attack (1941) 11-14, 49, 63, 74-7, 85, 91, 168-9; criticisms of 65, 166
personality cults 92
Pickering, Ernest H. xi-xii
politics, Tôjô's approach to 107-9
Potsdam Proclamation 116, 149, 152-3, 156-9, 172
preparatory schools for training military officers 96-7, 103
prerogatives, imperial 56-7
protectio trahit subjectionem 121

racism xi-xii, 1
rape of Nanking 92
Reischauer, Edwin O. 41
religious nationalism 177
responsibility, soldiers' sense of 106
The Road to Certain Victory 92
Russo-Japan War (1904-5) 165, 169-70

Saipan 4, 7, 9-10, 13-45, 55-6, 59, 70, 125, 134-7, 147
"Saipan-ratio" 23
Sakamaki Kazuo 75-6
Sakomizu Hisatsune 154,158
samurai tradition 60, 80
Sanada Jôichirô 14, 39-40, 139
Satô Eisaku 119, 163-4
Satô Kenryô 24-6, 30, 44

Satô Sônosuke 80
Satsuma uprising (1877) 95
Sawada Shigeru 165-6, 171
school textbooks, accreditation of 164-5
sea transport 6-7, 133, 137-40
Second World War xii-xiv; inevitability of 12, 100, 132, 174; prolongation of 7, 121; reasons for Japan's defeat in xiii-xiv, 165-71
secret codes 37, 168
Secret War Journal of the Imperial HQ 32-3, 37-40
Secret War Records 91
seishinryoku (inner spiritual strength) 91
self-determination 2
self-sacrifice for emperor and nation 81-4
Seneca 178
Shida Nobuyoshu 164-5
Shigemitsu Mamoru 159
Shimada Shigetarô 28-9, 32, 35, 38, 52-5, 61-4, 70, 91, 123-6, 139
Shimazaki Tôson 80
Shimomura Hiroshi 157
Shintô 98, 116
Shôji Junichirô 176
Shôtoku, Crown Prince 4, 113
social harmony 113
Soviet Union (USSR) 23-4, 148-52, 162
"special attack" weapons 61, 64, 67-74, 82, 85-6, 120, 130, 135-6, 140-1
spiritual qualities 6, 97, 104
Stahmer, Heinrich Georg 133, 143
Stalin, Joseph 120
"state", definition of 2
state, church and *race* concepts in Japan xi
state, Japanese, as distinct from nation xiv, 1-3, 5, 9, 67, 158
students, mobilization of 110-11
STJR see "Actual Record of the Shôwa Emperor"
submarines, US 141
Succession of the Divine Sovereigns 116
Suetsugu Nobumasa 35
Sugawara Michiô 68-9
Sugiyama Hajime 20, 25-7, 30-1, 44, 47, 50-3, 91, 159
suicide attacks 5-6, 23, 48, 59-88, 133; as official policy 85-6; ordering of 67,

69, 84-5; Tôjô's involvement with 78-80
suicide boats 71, 78, 161
Sun Tzu 169
Supreme War Guidance Council 140
surrender by the Japanese 4-5, 24, 81, 105, 153-9, 164; unconditional 116, 129, 145, 147-50, 153-4, 157, 159
Suzuki Kantarô 22, 41, 72, 99, 131, 149, 151, 156-8, 172
Suzuki Tamon 27-8, 39, 41, 50-4, 127-9, 136-7, 147, 149-51, 161, 172
Suzuki Teï'ichi 131-2

Tachibana Takashi 115
Taira clan 69
Takagi Sôkichi 34-5, 66, 124, 127-8, 156
Takamatsu, Prince 51, 126
Takeshita Masahiko 116, 153, 164
Tale of Heike 69
Tamura Yasuoki 48-9
Tanaka Shinichi 49
Teshima Yasunobu 30
Thailand 100
thought war 93
Tillich, Paul 7, 176-7
Tôgô Heihachirô 32
Tôgô Shigenori 108-9, 150, 154-8
Tôjô Hidenori 94-5
Tôjô Hidetoshi 94
Tôjô Hideki xiv, 4-7, 12-13, 19-27, 32-5, 44, 50-5, 60, 63-4, 70, 78-84, 88-121, 123-30, 133, 137-9, 159, 174-6; approach taken to command 106-7; biography of 92-3, 95-6; overall assessment of 89-92, 120-1, 142-3; as a political leader 107-10; proximity to power 114-15; relationship with Hirohito 89-91, 94, 97, 100, 104, 107, 109, 113-15, 121; and suicide attacks 78-80
Tôjô Katsuko 90
Tolischus, Otto 51
Torisu Michiaki 164
Toyoda Soemu 17-18, 65-6, 158, 173-4
Truman, Harry S. 87, 160
Tsuneo Watanabe 86
Tsunoda Tomoshige 127

Umezu Yoshijirô 149, 154-5, 158-9, 172-4
United States xii-xiii, 5, 9, 12, 18, 72, 100, 119, 130, 134; Navy Operations Yearly Journal 38-40; Strategic Bombing Survey 160
Ushiroku Jun 78-9

"victors' justice" 90
"volunteering" for suicide missions 68, 82-6
V-1 flying bomb 33

Wakamatsu Tadakazu 157
war criminals and Tokyo War Crimes Trial 19-20, 24, 41, 90, 94, 100, 104-5, 112, 119-20, 132, 173-6
war culture 59-60
war guilt 174-6
"War History Series" 9-10, 13-14, 38, 54, 57, 63-4, 68, 91, 135
war industries 112; *see also* materials for war
War Logbook of the Army General Staff 91
war plans, lack of 167
war weariness xiii, 72
warfare xii; seen as a legitimate instrument of national policy 6, 89, 92
Watsuji Tetsurô 80
Who Was Responsible 86
wishful thinking by the military authorities 134

xenophobia 103

Yabe Teiji 127
Yamada Akira 28, 41-4, 47, 50-1, 54-5, 73-4, 85, 140, 155
Yamada Otozô 53
Yamada Yoshio 80
Yamagata Aritomo 167
Yamaguchi Kôsuke 164-5
Yamamoto Chikao 29
Yamamoto Gonnohyôe 168, 170
Yamamoto Isoroku 6, 37, 44, 63, 65, 75-7, 130-1
Yamamoto Sakae 77
Yamamoto Tomoyuki 12, 18
Yasuda Takeo 79

Yasui Tōji 155, 157
Yasukuni Shrine 90, 100
Yokuseikai association 107–9
Yonai Mitsumasa 22, 27, 35, 74, 126, 156–8

Yoshida Shigeru 12, 20
Yuzawa Michio 90

Zhang Zuolin 155